# The African Imagination in Music

# The African Imagination
# in Music

### KOFI AGAWU

OXFORD
UNIVERSITY PRESS

## OXFORD
UNIVERSITY PRESS

Oxford University Press is a department of the University of Oxford. It furthers
the University's objective of excellence in research, scholarship, and education
by publishing worldwide. Oxford is a registered trade mark of Oxford University
Press in the UK and certain other countries.

Published in the United States of America by Oxford University Press
198 Madison Avenue, New York, NY 10016, United States of America.

Library of Congress Cataloging-in-Publication Data
Agawu, V. Kofi (Victor Kofi), author.
The African imagination in music / by Kofi Agawu.
pages cm
Includes bibliographical references.
ISBN 978-0-19-026321-8 (pbk : alk. paper)—ISBN 978-0-19-026320-1 (cloth : alk. paper)
1. Music—Africa—History and criticism.   2. Music and globalization—Africa.   I. Title.
ML3760.A42 2015
780.967—dc23
2015024579

This volume is published with the generous support of the Manfred Bukofzer Endowment
of the American Musicological Society, funded in part by the National Endowment
for the Humanities and the Andrew W. Mellon Foundation.

*In memory of four friends and fellow workers*

*Willie Anku (1949–2010)*
*Robert Kwami (1954–2004)*
*Joshua Uzoigwe (1946–2005)*
*and*
*Kongo Zabana (1947–2014)*

# CONTENTS

# ACKNOWLEDGMENTS

A number of friends and colleagues shared information, offered advice, and encouraged me at various stages in the writing of this book. I'm grateful to each one of them: Jasper Addo, Eric Akrofi, Kwasi Ampene, Simha Arom, Daniel Avorgbedor, Daniel Biro, Scott Burnham, James Burns, William Chapman Nyaho, Mark Dingemanse, George Dor, Akin Euba, Serena Facci, Natalie Fernando, the late Nissio Fiagbedzi, Susanne Fürniss, Olakunle George, Christopher Hasty, Anri Herbst, Abiola Irele, Andrew Kaye, Ralf Kohler, David Locke, Patrick Mensah, Bode Omojola, Judith Opoku-Boateng, Sister Marie Agatha Ozah, Dominik Phyfferoen, Barak Schmool, Aissata Sidikou, Joseph Straus, and Polo Vallejo. My debts to workers in the field of African musicology are many, as will be obvious from my references and footnotes, but I would like to single out Meki Nzewi, whose influence on my thinking has been fundamental. Special thanks go to Kwabena Nketia, without whose pioneering work none of this would have been possible. I have also relied heavily on the research of Simha Arom and Gerhard Kubik. It was my privilege to hold the George Eastman professorship at Oxford University in 2012–2013, which freed up time for me to work on the book. Many thanks to my colleagues in the faculty of music at Oxford and to the master and fellows of Balliol College for their hospitality during that year. As always, I alone am responsible for what is written here.

**Photo credits**. The photographs in this book function either as direct illustrations of specific material resources being discussed in the text or—more usually—as broadly related images that might enhance the intertextual horizons of particular ideas. Of the 35 photographs, numbers 4.1, 4.2, 7.3 and 7.7 come from my own field work while 1.1, 2.4, 5.1 and 5.2 were supplied by Andrew Kaye. Polo Vallejo provided 2.1, 2.5, 2.6, 2.11, 4.3, 4.4 and Figure 2.1. Numbers 2.7, 2.8, 2.9, 7.1 and 7.2 were supplied by Natalie Fernando. Kwasi Ampene provided 1.2, 1.3, 1.4, 2.2, 2.3, 2.10, 4.5, 4.6, 7.4, 7.5, and 7.6. Divine

Gbagbo and Jasper Addo supplied 6.1 and 3.1 respectively. Figure 2.2 came from the J. H. Kwabena Nketia Archives at the Institute of African Studies, University of Ghana, Legon. My thanks to them for letting me include these previously unpublished images in this book.

## ABOUT THE COMPANION WEBSITE

www.oup.com/us/africanmusic

Username: Music4
Password: Book2497

Although most of the recorded material referred to in this book is available on commercial recordings, a few items may not be readily accessible to readers. Sixteen of these are included in a website created to accompany *The African Imagination in Music*. Each is signaled using the symbol 🜚 in the text. Thus, Web Example 1.1 🜚 identifies the first example in chapter 1 available on the website.

The African Imagination in Music

# Introduction

In its richness and diversity, African music remains one of the most vital repertories performed today. Its history reaches back into ancient times, its continued cultivation on the continent is as alive and human centered as it ever was, and its worldwide influence is deep, subtle, and profound. This book is designed to support exploration of some of the core features of African music. For the most part, emphasis is placed on the music itself rather than on external factors. Readers seeking chronologies and histories, or in-depth studies of individual genres, instruments, communities, and musicians, will find them in the many ethnographic studies and reference works that have been produced by ethnomusicologists, organologists, historians, and anthropologists since the early decades of the twentieth century. My task here is narrower: to supplement an acknowledgment of these resources with a discussion of musical creativity as manifest in a handful of repertory items. Aimed at the general reader rather than specialists, the book invites a scholarly dialogue with those who wish to deepen their understanding and appreciation of African music.

## "AFRICA"

Anyone who dares to talk about "Africa" is obliged to immediately acknowledge the size and diversity of the continent. Here are some sobering facts. Africa is the site of the earliest human population. Genetic variation among its people exceeds that of any other human group. Over one billion people live on the continent (as of 2015), making it the second-most populated. It is the second-largest continent by virtue of its thirty million square kilometers; indeed, you could fit all of the United States, China, Japan, India, most of Eastern Europe, Italy, France, Germany, Spain, and Portugal into its current space. With no fewer than 1,000 languages and perhaps as many as 2,500, Africa stands as the most polyglot continent on earth. Upward of 500 million Africans identify themselves as Christians and a comparable number as Muslims, two of the most influential organized religions in the world. A smaller number subscribe to the heterogeneous set of beliefs and practices consigned by our historical oppressors to the catch-all category "indigenous African religion."

All of this is by now conventional knowledge, the sort you can look up in any standard encyclopedia. But its overarching point is one that we are liable to forget, namely, that Africa is huge, diverse, and complex. The recurrent media focus on some of its failures and challenges (the AIDS epidemic, political insta-bility, the Ebola crisis, failed states, ethnic conflict, and genocide) may make us lose sight of the many contests in which Africa boasts a superior record. Musical life is one such contest, as I hope this book will affirm. One reason we some-times forget or suppress Africa's well-earned superlatives is that the pan-African vision that would gather our achievements and hold them up for constant view and inspiration, balancing them against the losses we have suffered, especially in the last two and a half centuries, is not necessarily the dominant one in con-temporary text making about Africa. Under epistemic regimes promulgated by anthropology, ethnology, and ethnomusicology, all of them made possible by European colonialism, Africa all too often spells difference and distance. It is reduced to tribes, ethnic groups, or nation states—configurations that proved manageable for the purposes of political administration and the production of certain kinds of knowledge in the nineteenth and twentieth centuries. The con-sequent scattering of the continent's many coherences delivers an unacceptably partial account of the potency of its collective expressive forms. The best way to study Africa is to rigorously maintain a sense of what V. Y. Mudimbe calls "the idea of Africa" without underestimating its internal complexity.[1]

## "AFRICAN MUSIC"

The phrase *African music* tends to suggest different things to different people. Some think immediately of the popular dance forms originating in urban Africa, others of the ancient songs and drums associated with traditional societies, and still others of new music composed for the concert hall. These are all legitimate forms of African music. The domain is so huge that some scholars prefer the phrase *African musics* (in the plural) to *African music* (in the singular). Further complications arise if we wish to distinguish between *African music* (implying music of African origins) and *music in Africa* (implying any and all repertories, irrespective of origin, that are performed on the continent).

1. V. Y. Mudimbe, *The Idea of Africa* (Bloomington: Indiana University Press, 1994).

While I do not believe that we stand to gain much from splitting hairs over definitions or from trying to delimit with surgical precision the domain of the rich and complex network of sounds and processes that we call "African music," I must nevertheless briefly explain my own usage. "African music" as used here refers to music conceived, created, and performed by African peoples. It includes vast repertories of precolonial origin, others of more recent vintage associated with the popular sphere, and still others produced in the mold of art-composed music. There is reason to believe that music was there in the beginning, alongside language; there is evidence that music has been a part of practically every community over the last 1,000-plus years of written history; and today, no one has any doubt that, as both a functional and an aesthetic phenomenon, music remains a vibrant force not only on the continent but also throughout the African diaspora.

(The idea of) African music both mirrors and inflects the collective profiles of its land, people, material and spiritual resources, and overall culture. African music displays a self-evident historical depth together with an astonishing diversity in its sound-producing objects, languages, ritual affiliations, styles, and aesthetic ideals. "Musicking" in Africa—borrowing Christopher Small's useful formulation[2]—is indexed by a variety of terms: we beat, shake, touch, and play; we say, recite, recollect, and sing; and we move, stir the body, look our way, and dance. In speaking of "African music," then, we do well to keep this expanded semantic horizon in mind.

We do well, too, to keep the *human* dimension in view. Music everywhere is a part of society, but because so many people on the continent live under the sign of a communal ethos, the musical forms they have produced over the years have collectively inscribed and at the same time interrogated sets of values in which a manifest plurality subtends a deep, internal singularity. The sense of connectedness is most apparent at what might be called a background level, and this aura is akin to the dynamics of bonding that one encounters, for example, in kinship systems. This fact alone enjoins us to listen beyond surfaces to the shared structures that prop up those surfaces.[3]

---

2. Christopher Small, *Musicking: The Meanings of Performing and Listening* (Middletown, CT: Wesleyan University Press, 1998).

3. The human centeredness of African music is widely acknowledged. Prominent articulations of this point may be found in John Blacking, *How Musical Is Man?* (Seattle: University of Washington Press, 1973) and throughout the writings of his student Meki Nzewi—see, for example, "Acquiring Knowledge of the Musical Arts in Traditional Society," in *Musical Arts in Africa: Theory, Practice and Education* (Pretoria: UNISA Press, 2003, 13–37). Typical is Nzewi's remark that "African music is feeling and communal therapy, a humanizing communion, a sharing in human-being-ness" (*African Music: Theoretical Content and Creative Continuum: The Culture-Exponent's Definitions* [Olderhausen: Institut für

## THE RECORDED LEGACY

From a cosmopolitan perspective, Africa's wealth and diversity in musical resources are most readily evident in the body of sound recordings produced since the early 1900s. In 1959, distinguished anthropologist and folklorist Alan Lomax pronounced Africa "the best-recorded continent musically speaking," by which he meant that by the mid- to late 1950s, more recordings had been made of its indigenous music than of the indigenous music of any other continent.[4] No figures accompanied that claim, but many would probably grant its intuitive rightness not least because Lomax's own quest to understand the social motivations for music making entailed extensive use of a wide variety of recordings from around the world. The significance of his remark has less to do with its empirical verifiability than with its indexical function: it compels attention to a rich set of resources distributed across various collections and archives both within and outside Africa.

Starting in the 1920s, Hugh Tracey (1903–1977) undertook a mammoth project "to discover, study and present in recorded form the original unaided genius of African musicians."[5] The result was a collection of "210 Long Playing Records of Music and Songs from Central, Eastern and Southern Africa," the largest such collection in the world. The two-volume catalog that accompanies *The Sound of Africa Series* (as Tracey called it) is a fascinating ethnographic document in its own right. It includes classifications of songs and instruments, scale measurements, and glossaries of "vernacular" words. It also contains notes identifying various performers, locations, and genres, and, perhaps most important, suggestive descriptions of a poetical and philosophical nature of what African musicians imagine in song. Although known to specialists, this remarkable resource has only recently come to the attention of a wider public, thanks to the creation of a website and the partial dissemination of the archive's contents in the form of compact discs as a complementary *The Music*

Didaktik populärer Musik, 1997], 23). For two among several discussions of the communal ethos, see Kofi Anyidoho, *Oral Poetics and Traditions of Verbal Art in Africa* (PhD diss., University of Texas at Austin, 1983), and Agawu, "The Communal Ethos in African Performance: Ritual, Narrative and Music Among the Northern Ewe," in *Approaches to African Musics*, ed. Enrique Cámara de Landa and Silvia Martínez García (Valladolid: Universidad de Valladolid, Centro Buendía, 2006), 181–200, available at http://www.sibetrans.com/trans/articulo/125/the-communal-ethos-in-african-performance-ritual-narrative-and-music-among-the-northern-ewe?lang=en.

4. Alan Lomax, "Folk Song Style," *American Anthropologist* 61 (1959): 952.

5. Hugh Tracey, *Catalogue: The Sound of Africa Series*, 2 vols. (Roodeport, South Africa: International Library of African Music, 1973).

*of Africa Series.* Surely the history of African music in recorded form is unimaginable without the Tracey materials.[6]

A notable resource is the Berlin Phonogram-Archiv, whose contents date back to the 1900s. Although only about a third of the archival holdings are from Africa, the collection is of importance to anyone who wishes to reconstruct the history of music in the twentieth century. Materials were assembled from various African countries, among them Angola, Cameroon, Egypt, Liberia, Mozambique, Libya, Ruanda, South Africa, Togo, Tunisia, and Uganda, and collectors include household names in African studies like Meinhof, Evans-Pritchard, Frobenius, Ankermann, Herskovits, Smend, Lachmann, Kubik, and Simon. The archive's first director was Hornbostel, a well-known figure in comparative musicology and also a distinguished Africanist.[7]

Another notable archive is the personal collection of veteran Austrian anthropologist and ethnomusicologist Gerhard Kubik (b. 1934), which contains close to thirty thousand items housed at the Phonogramarchiv in Vienna. Kubik boasts unmatched credentials as a fieldworker in Africa. He has worked in over eighteen countries and maintained a regimen of field research and active publication over the last five decades. His collection is testimony to this longevity and dedication. In addition to music and dance, there is a large quantity of speech or oral data. The material comes predominantly from eastern, central, and southern Africa. Although not as widely used as it might be, this valuable resource is poised to support decades of research into a variety of African expressive forms.

The Tracey, Berlin, and Kubik collections form only the tip of a giant iceberg. In Paris, London, Oxford, Mainz, and Tervuren, and elsewhere in Europe, libraries and museums house significant sets of recordings of African music.[8] On the African continent, the (sometimes precarious) archives of various national broadcasting corporations assembled since the early 1960s in

6. For two recent engagements with the recorded legacy of Tracey, see Noel Lobley, *The Social Biography of Ethnomusicological Field Recordings: Eliciting Responses to Hugh Tracey's* The Sound of Africa *Series* (DPhil thesis, University of Oxford, 2010), and Diane Janell Thram, *For Future Generations: Hugh Tracey and the International Library of African Music* (Grahamstown, South Africa: International Library of African Music, 2010). Also of interest is Paulette June Coetzee, "Performing Whiteness; Representing Otherness: Hugh Tracey and African Music" (PhD diss., Rhodes University, 2014).

7. Artur Simon, ed., *Das Berliner Phonogramm-Archiv 1900-2000: Sammlungen der traditionellen Musik der Welt* (Berlin: Verlag für Wissenschaft und Bildung, 2000).

8. These include the ethnomusicology department of the *Museé de l'homme* in Paris, the British Sound Archive in London, the African Music Archive in Mainz, and the Royal Museum for Central Africa in Tervuren.

Nigeria, Ghana, Kenya, Sierra Leone, the Democratic Republic of the Congo, and Uganda and elsewhere are filled with a great variety of recorded data, including samples of African popular music that emerged in the second half of the twentieth century. Finally, at universities and other institutions in the United States (in Los Angeles, Chicago, Bloomington, and Washington, DC), there are sizeable collections of African music on record—enough, indeed, to keep students of African music busy for several generations.[9] If we add to these the products of the many cassette and now CD, MP3, and DVD industries that are booming in various urban locations on the continent, not to mention the explosion on YouTube and other Internet sources, it becomes apparent that we are dealing with an extraordinary set of resources. Although the story of recorded African music remains to be told comprehensively, there is no room for doubting the depth and potency of this network of resources.[10]

No individual can be expected to be familiar with the entire recorded legacy of African music. I have therefore selected some one hundred recordings to serve as a kind of sonic backdrop to the ideas explored in this book (Figure I.1). Although a few items of popular and art music are included, the majority are of the so-called *traditional music*, which I regard as the backbone of Africa's musical thinking. Arranged in three parts, the list is made up of recordings that accompany books and monographs, free-standing field and commercial recordings spanning a variety of vocal and instrumental genres (these are arranged by country for the sake of convenience), and finally recordings conceived as collections with a thematic focus. The selections in Part 1 include continent-wide overviews (Herbst et al., Brandilly, Stone, Dauer), regional characterizations (Kubik, Stone, Charry, Muller, Djedje), music of individual ethnic groups or subgroups (Agawu, Fernando, Kisliuk, Omojola, Rouget), and, most commonly, music of individual genres (Ampene, Anku, Locke, Tang, Vallejo, Villepasteur, Waterman). Similar rubrics can be used to

---

9. The UCLA Ethnomusicology Archive, Los Angeles; the Center for Black Music Research, Columbia College, Chicago; the Archives of Traditional Music in Bloomington, Indiana; and the Smithsonian Institution in Washington, DC.

10. For the early phases of this history, see Alan P. Merriam, *African Music on LP: An Annotated Discography* (Evanston, IL: Northwestern University Press, 1970), and Ruth Stone and Frank J. Gillis, *African Music and Oral Data: A Catalog of Field Recordings, 1902-1975* (Bloomington: Indiana University Press, 1976). A valuable introduction to audio recordings of African music in the context of other world cultures may be found in Jennifer C. Post, *Ethnomusicology: A Research and Information Guide* (New York: Routledge, 2004), 124–136. Ethnomusicologists Sylvia Nannyonga-Tamusuza and Andrew N. Weintraub have recently written about one notable collection, Klaus Wachsmann's of Ugandan music. See their "The Audible Future: Reimagining the Role of Sound Archives and Sound Repatriation in Uganda," *Ethnomusicology* 56 (2012): 206–233.

Part 1: CDs accompanying books and monographs (1992–2012)

| Author/editor | Title |
|---|---|
| Agawu, K | *African Rhythm: A Northern Ewe Perspective* (Cambridge: Cambridge University Press, 1995) |
| Ampene, K. | *Female Song Tradition and the Akan of Ghana: The Creative Process in Nnwonkoro* (Aldershot, Hampshire, England: Ashgate, 2005) |
| Anku, W. | *Structural Set Analysis 1: Adowa* (Legon, Ghana: Soundstage Production, 1992) |
| Askew, K. | *Performing the Nation: Swahili music and Cultural Politics in Tanzania* (Chicago: The University of Chicago Press, 2002) |
| Brandilly, M. | *Introduction aux musiques Africaines* (Arles, Citel de la musique: Actes sud, 1997) |
| Burns, J. | *Female Voices from an Ewe Dance-Drumming Community. Our Music Has Become a Divine Spirit* (Farnham, England: Ashgate, 2009) |
| Charry, E. | *Mande Music: Traditional and Modern Music of the Maninka and Mandinka of Western Africa* (Chicago: University of Chicago Press, 2000) |
| Dauer, A., et. al. | *Musik in Afrika: mit 20 Beitragen zur Kenntnis traditioneller afrikanischen Musikkulturen* (Berlin: Museum für Völkerkunde, 1983) |
| Djedje, J. | *Fiddling in West Africa (1950s-1990s): the CD recording* (Los Angeles, CA: UCLA Ethnomusicology Publications, 2007). |
| Herbst, Anri, et. al., eds. | *Musical Arts in Africa: Theory, Practice and Education* (Pretoria: UNISA Press, 2003). |
| Kisliuk, M. | *Seize the Dance! BaAka Musical Life and the Ethnography of Performance* (Chicago: The University of Chicago Press, 1997). |
| Kubik, G. | *Theory of African Music, vol. 1* (Wilhelmshaven: F. Noetzel, 1994) |
| Kubik, G. | *Theory of African Music, vol. 2* (Chicago: The University of Chicago Press, 2010) |
| Locke, D. | *Drum Gahu: An Introduction to African Rhythm* (Tempe, AZ: White Cliffs Media, 1998) |
| Muller, C. | *Focus: Music of South Africa.* 2nd ed. (New York: Routledge, 2008) |

Figure I.1 One hundred recordings of African music.

## Part 1: CDs accompanying books and monographs (1992–2012)

| Author/editor | Title |
|---|---|
| Omojola, B. | *Yoruba Music in the Twentieth Century: Identity, Agency and Performance Practice* (Rochester, NY: University of Rochester Press, 2012) |
| Rouget, G. | *Un roi Africain et sa musique de cour: chants et danses du palais a Porto-Novo sous le règne de Gbèfa (1948-1976)* (Paris: CNRS Editions, 1996) |
| Stone, R., ed. | *Garland encyclopedia of World Music, vol. 1: Africa* (New York, Garland, 1998) |
| Stone, R. | *Music in West Africa: Experiencing Music, Expressing Culture* (New York: Oxford University Press, 2005) |
| Tang, P. | *Masters of the Sabar: Wolof Griot Percussionists of Senegal* (Philadelphia: Temple University Press, 2007) |
| Vallejo, P. | *Mbudi mbudi na mhanga: universe musical infantile de los Wagogo de Tanzania* (Madrid: Edicion del autor, 2004) |
| Vallejo, P. | *Patrimonio musical de los Wagogo (Tanzania): context y sistemática* (Madrid: Cyan, 2008) |
| Villepasteur, A. | *Ancient text messages of the Yoruba bàtá Drum: Cracking the Code* (Farnham, England: Ashgate, 2010) |
| Waterman, C. | *Jùjú: A Social History and Ethnography of an African Popular Music.* (Chicago: University of Chicago Press, 1990). |

## Part 2: Regional and ethnic musics (1973–2009)

| Country | Recording |
|---|---|
| Angola | *Mukanda na makisi: Circumcision School and Masks* (Berlin: Museum für Völkerkunde Berlin, 1981). |
| Benin | *Benin: Bariba and Somba Music* (Gentilly: Auvidis, 1994; orig. 1976) |
| Benin | *Yoruba Drums from Benin, West Africa* (Washington, DC: Smithsonian/Folkways, 1996) |
| Burkina Faso | *Lobi Country, Buur Xylophones* (Paris: OCORA Radio France, 2008) |
| Cameroon | *Nord Cameroun: Musique des Ouldémé: au rhythme des saisons* (Paris, France: Maison des Cultures du Monde, 2002) |

Figure I.1 (Continued)

## Part 2: Regional and ethnic musics (1973–2009)

| Country | Recording |
|---|---|
| Cameroon | *Flûtes des monts Mandara* (Paris, France: Maison des Cultures du Monde, 1999). |
| Cameroon | *Cameroon: Baka Pygmy Music* (Italy: EMI Italiana, 1977) |
| Central African Republic | *Africa: the Ba-Benzele Pygmies* (Cambridge: Rounder Records, 1998) |
| Central African Republic | *Central African Republic: Music of the Dendi, Nzakera, Banda Linda, Gbaya, Banda Dakpa, Ngbaka, Aka Pygmies* (France: Auvidis, 1989) |
| Central African Republic | *Musique Gbaya: Chants a Penser* (Paris: Ocora, 1992-95) |
| Central African Republic | *Centrafrique: anthologie de la musique des pygmies Aka* (France: Ocora, 1987) |
| Côte d'Ivoire | *Senoufo: Musiques es funerailles Fodonon* (France: Chant du monde, 1994) |
| Côte d'Ivoire | *Africa: The Dan* (Cambridge, MA: Rounder Records, 1998) |
| Côte d'Ivoire | *Côte d'Ivoire: Baule Vocal Music* (Ivrey-sur-Seine: Auvidis, 1993; orig. 1972) |
| Democratic Republic of the Congo | *Petites musiques du Zaire* (Paris: Buda musique, 1994) |
| Democratic Republic of the Congo | *Anthologie de la musique congolaise. 11 vols* (Belgium: Fonti musicali/Musée royal de l'afrique centrale, 2009) |
| Democratic Republic of the Congo | *Mafili [Zither]: Musiques des Baali de la forêt equitoriale* (Belgium: Colophon Records, 2005). |
| Democratic Republic of the Congo | *Sikiliza [Listen]: Rythmes et chants de la forêt de la savane [RDC]* ( Belgium: Colophon Records, 2005). |
| Gabon | *Musique des pygmées Bibayak: Chantres de l'épopée* (France: Ocora 1989). |
| Gambia | *Wolof Music of Senegal and Gambia* (New York: Smithsonian Folkways, 1998) |

Figure I.1 (Continued)

## Part 2: Regional and ethnic musics (1973–2009)

| Country | Recording |
| --- | --- |
| Ghana | *Master Drummers of Dagbon* (Cambridge, MA: Rounder Records, 2008) |
| Ghana | *Master Fiddlers of Dagbon* (UK: Continental Record Services, 2001) |
| Ghana | *Rhythms of Life, Songs of Wisdom: Akan Music from Ghana, West Africa* (Washington, DC: Smithsonian/Folkways, 1996) |
| Ghana | *Giants of Ghanaian Danceband Highlife, 1950's–1970's* (Tivoli, NY: Original Music, 1990) |
| Ghana | *Ghana: Rhythms of the People. Traditional Music and Dance of the Ewe, Dagbamba, Fante and Ga People* (Barre, VT: Multicultural Media, 2000) |
| Ghana | *Por Por: Honk Horn Music of Ghana: The La Drivers Union Por Por Group* (Washington, DC: Smithsonian/Folkways, 2007) |
| Ghana | *Music in Ghana: A Selection out of the Archives of African Music at the Institute of African Studies, University of Ghana, Legon* (Frankfurt: Popular African Music/African Music Archive, 1998). |
| Ghana | *Ewe Drumming from Ghana: The Soup which is Sweet Draws the Chairs Closer* (London: Topic Records, 2004) |
| Ghana | *Ghana: Music of the Northern Tribes* (New York: Lyrichord, 1993) |
| Ghana | *Yewe: Ritual Music and Dance of a Secret Society* (Morgantown: Azaguno, 2002) |
| Ghana | *Akom: The Art of Possession* (Portland, Oregon: Village Pulse, 1999) |
| Kenya and Tanzania | *The Rough Guide to Music of Kenya and Tanzania* (London: World Music Network, 1996) |
| Liberia | *Music of the Vai of Liberia* (Washington, D.C.: Smithsonian Folkways, 1998) |
| Madagascar | *Madagascar: Pays Bara* (France: Ocora, 1996) |
| Malawi | *From Lake Malawi to the Zambezi: Aspects of Music and Oral Literature in South-east Africa in the 1990s* (Frankfurt: Popular African Music, 1999). |
| Mali | *Jarabi: The Best of Toumani Diabate* (London: Hannibal UK, 2008) |

**Figure I.1.** (Continued)

**Part 2: Regional and ethnic musics (1973–2009)**

| Country | Recording |
| --- | --- |
| Mali | *An Bè Kelen (We are One): Griot Music from Mali* (Leiden: Pan Records, 1994) |
| Niger | *Anthologie de la musique du Niger* (Paris: Ocora, 1990) |
| Nigeria | *Heritage Drummers: Ajo Yio O (The Journey)*. Songs and music co-produced by Alani Ogunlade and Adebisi Adeleke ([Atlanta]: Cultural Promotions, 2006) |
| Nigeria | *Music from the Villages of Northeastern Nigeria* (Washington, DC: Smithsonian/Folkways, 2001) |
| Nigeria | *Yoruba Bata Drums: Elewe music and Dance* (Washington, DC: Smithsonian/Folkways, 1998) |
| Nigeria | *The Best of Fela Kuti* (Universal City, CA: MCA Records, 2000) |
| Nigeria | *Jùjú Music: King Sunny Adé and his African Beats* (New York, NY: Mango, 1982) |
| Rwanda | *Africa: Music from Rwanda* (Cambridge, MA: Rounder, 1999) |
| Sierra Leone | *Sierra Leone: Musiques traditionelles* (France: Ocora, 1992) |
| Tanzania | *Tanzanie: Chants Wagogo* ( Paris: Ocora, 2000). |
| Tanzania | *Tanzania: Music of the Farmer Composers of Sukumaland.* ([USA]: Multicultural Media, 2005). |
| Togo | *Togo: Music from West Africa* (Cambridge, MA: Rounder, 1992; orig. 1978). |
| Togo | *Togo: Orchestres et lithophones kabiyé* (Paris: Ocora, 2004) |
| Uganda | *Ouganda: Musique des Baganda* (Paris: Ocora, 2002) |
| Uganda | *Royal Court Music from Uganda: 1950 & 1952* (Utrecht, Netherlands: International Library of African Music, 1998) |
| Uganda | *Uganda: Village Ensembles of Busoga* (Geneva: AIMP & VDE-GALLO, 1997) |
| Uganda | *Evaristo Muyinda: Traditional Music of the Baganda as Formerly Played at the Court of the Kabaka* (Berlin: Ethnologisches Museum, 1991) |
| Uganda | *The King's Musicians: Royalist Music of Buganda, Uganda* (London: Topic Records, 2003). |
| Zambia | *Zambia: The Songs of Mukanda*. Music of the Secret Society of the Luvale People of Central Africa. ([USA]: Multicultural Media, 1997). |

**Figure I.1** (Continued)

**Part 3: Other collections**

| Artist/legend | Title |
|---|---|
| Various | *The Demonstration Collection of E. M. von Hornbostel and the Berlin Phonogramm-Archiv* (Washington, D.C.: Smithsonian Folkways, 2007) |
| Various | *Africa Dances* (Tivoli, NY: Original Music, 1973). |
| Various | *Jali Kunda: Griots of West Africa and Beyond* (Roslyn, NY: Ellipsis Arts, 1996) |
| Various | *The Music of Africa* (BBC/Horizon, RDC 4393, 1971) |
| Various | *The Rough Guide to West African Music* (London: World Music Network, 1995) |
| Mbuti pygmies | *Music of the Rainforest Pygmies Recorded by Colin Turnbull* (New York: Lyrichord, 1992) |
| Pierre-Laurent Aimard, pianist | *African Rhythms* (Germany: Teldec Classics, 2003) |
| Pierre Akendengué, arranger | *Lambarena* (New York, NY: Sony Classical, 1995) |
| Ladysmith Black Mamabazo | *Ladysmith. The Best of Ladysmith Black Mambazo* (Ho-Ho-kus, NJ.: Shanachie, 1992) |
| David Fanshawe, composer | *African Sanctus* (New York: Fanshawe Enterprises, 1994) |
| David Fanshawe, compiler | *Spirit of African Sanctus: The Original recordings by David Fanshawe* (Wotton-under-Edge, Glos., England: Saydisc, 1991) |
| Kronos Quartet | *Kronos Quartet: Pieces of* Africa (New York: Elektra Entertainment, 1992). |
| Lura | *Lura: Mbem di Fora [I've Come from Far Away].* New York: Times Square Records, 2007. |
| Various | *Putumayo Presents Africa.* 7 vols (New York: Putumayo World Music, 1999) |
| Osei Korankye and friends, performers | *Seperewa Kasa* (EU: Riverboat/World Music Network, 2008) |
| Nana Danso Abiam, conductor | *Pan African Orchestra Opus 1* (New York, NY: Real World, 1995) |

**Figure I.1** (Continued)

**Part 3: Other collections**

| Artist/legend | Title |
|---|---|
| W. Chapman Nyaho, pianist | *Senku: Piano Music by Composers of African Descent* (S.I: Musicians Showcase Recordings, 2003) |
| W. Chapman Nyaho, pianist | *Asa: Piano Music by Composers of African Descent* (Newtown, CT: MSR Classics, 2008) |
| Various | *Towards an African Pianism: An Anthology of Keyboard Music from Africa and the Diaspora.* 2 volumes (Pittsburgh: Department of Music, University of Pittsburgh, 2005). |
| Akin Euba, composer | *Chaka: An Opera in Two Chants.* City of Birmingham Touring Opera conducted by Simon Halsey (Point Richmond, CA: MRI Press, 1999). |
| Various | *Frozen Brass: Africa and Latin America* (The Netherlands: Pan Records, 1993) |

**Figure I.1** (Continued)

categorize those in Part 2, which covers a wide variety of regional and ethnic music arranged by country from Angola to Zambia. Those in Part 3 form a miscellaneous group. They include collections (such as the *Rough Guide* series), art music (as performed by Ghanaian-American pianist William Chapman Nyaho and by the Pan-African Orchestra), and material of purely historical interest (such as the Hornbostel demonstration collection).

Composing a selection such as this invariably arouses suspicion that qualitative measures have been applied, that the list represents some kind of "top one hundred" chart. No such lofty ambition motivated this exercise, only a practical need to lay bare the kinds of environments that have stimulated my own thinking and that, I believe, provide a formidable introduction to African sound worlds. I have preferred recordings that are readily available commercially or in public libraries to those locked away in specialized collections and archives. Keep in mind that for every song, lament, dance drumming or playsong included here, literally thousands of alternatives exist.

These recordings offer opportunities to explore different ways in which the African imagination has been exercised musically. Pay attention to instruments and their associated timbres, varieties of speech and song, and modes of rhythmic expression; notice the temporal feel, resultant forms, rhetoric, and succession of simultaneities. It is probably best to plunge in directly and without mediation, and listen to as many of the CDs as you can and in whatever order you choose. You will likely experience a range of emotions and reactions: you may be intrigued, surprised (pleasantly or otherwise), repulsed, or even puzzled. You will surely also find some of the offerings exhilarating, seductive, and even inspiring. Later, depending on what interests you have formed after a first pass through the list, you can search for the sorts of information that might enhance a second or third pass, including information about performers and performances, musical systems, and the purposes for which the music is made. It is hard to imagine an outcome from this initial exploration of a hundred CDs that will be anything less than edifying.[11]

While recordings allow us to experience a variety of sound worlds away from their performance sites, day-to-day observation sheds even more light on patterns of music making. Play, ritual, worship, and entertainment serve as pretexts for boys and girls and men and women to find pleasure, satisfaction, or meaning in singing and drumming, in beating bells and xylophones, in blowing horns and flutes, or in playing harps, fiddles, and lutes. There is no end to the number of styles and genres cultivated. Techniques of musical construction are equally varied, ranging from the use of melodic archetypes, rhythmic *topoi,* and rhythmic narratives to the coordination of multiple voices around a shared reference beat. And there is always dance to embody the music, to domesticate it in physical movement, and to unite participants along kinship, age, gender, mother-tongue, and occupational lines. Notable are the varieties of music that confront anyone who rides a taxi, bus, or lorry; visits dance halls on weekends; or attends weddings, outdoor ceremonies, church, modern-day funerals, festivals, political rallies, and football games.

## GROOVE AS ESSENCE

Despite the numerous variations in idiom, mode of performance, and social function, African music retains a level of procedural sameness based on certain broad organizational attitudes and propensities. It subtends a palpable essence

---

11. It would seem odd to have to make a case for listening to recordings in a book on music, but making such a case has become necessary because it is sometimes thought that African music is not music alone. While this is surely valid at a certain level of abstraction, we should point out that African music is never not music. And to the extent that music is made up of sequences of sounds (and silences), hearing those sounds (and silences) is critical to genuine appreciation. True, we listen at different levels of intensity depending on occasion or circumstance—we may listen closely, we may simply hear, or we may even overhear music. We may also don a variety of veils while listening. In all these modes, taking in sound through the ear is never dispensable. For an example of the rewards of close listening, see Achille Mbembe, "Variations on the Beautiful in the Congolese World of Sounds," *Politique africaine* 100 (2005): 69–91.

that indexes a deep-level expressive coherence. This view is often implicit (and sometimes explicit) in the writings of scholars, among them Lomax, Arom, Nketia, Brandilly, Schaeffner, and Nzewi. From this point of view, speaking of "African music" in the singular is no less defensible than speaking—with appropriate qualifiers—of "Russian music," "American music," or "European music." This larger perspective may be hidden from view whenever we confine our field of vision to individual ethnographic studies. If, however, we stand back and take a synoptic view, shared ways of proceeding become too compelling to be ignored.

Does African music have a specifiable essence? The answer is yes. While not necessarily reducible to a single formula, the essence of African music originates in a will to communal truth that is incorporative, generous, and inviting. It is highly disciplined in its temporal articulation and structured in such a way that it not only elicits but also demands participation—indeed, as John Miller Chernoff showed years ago, African music is in principle incomplete without the listener-dancer's participation. "The African orchestra," he wrote in 1979, "is not complete without a participant on the other side."[12] The outward sign of this nexus of belief and practice is a series of cycles, circles, grooves, and ostinatos upon which African music is based. Recurring patterns inscribe "different qualities of same-ness."[13] They function at a variety of structural levels and in several simultaneously unfolding dimensions, thereby guaranteeing the inner life of African music. As participants in the sonic worlds activated by grooves, we entrain with each other as a matter of necessity.[14]

Examples abound for those willing to embark on various sonic journeys. Start by listening—or better, dancing—to the drums, rattles, bells, and voices that combine in polyrhythmic alignment in the southern Ewe dance Agbadza, then follow that with an item from the Banda horn-orchestra repertory studied by Simha Arom, and you will be struck by overriding qualities of "ongoing-ness," perpetuity, and the difference-in-sameness of motion. Above all, you will encounter a compelling groove that resides at—but is not confined to—a deep level and threatens or disconcerts those who elect to be mere listeners rather than active participants. Listen, too, to the mesmerizing infinitude of Shona mbira music, with its cycles and circles, its looping of phrase beginnings and endings, and its potential for altering consciousness in those willing to let go. Start again with the word-borne music of Gambian and Malian griots and

12. John Miller Chernoff, *African Rhythm and African Sensibility: Aesthetics and Social Action in African Musical Idioms* (Chicago: University of Chicago Press, 1979), 50.

13. Nzewi, *African Music: Theoretical Content and Creative Continuum*, 44.

14. Ian Cross, "Music and Biocultural Evolution," in *The Cultural Study of Music: A Critical Introduction*, 2nd ed. (New York: Routledge, 2012), 21.

griottes, with its cool temporalities and unhurried accompaniment patterns that go over the same ground but at different ontological time points such that each repetition seems familiar and yet somehow different. Listen across the numerous *gonje* (one-stringed fiddle) repertories of West Africa, in which repeating melodic archetypes ground the in-the-moment composition of embellishments and variations; follow that with masenqo repertories in Ethiopia for a similar yet ultimately different exploration and exploitation of minimality; and take in the thirteen-minute track of Fela Anikulakpo Kuti's masterpiece, *Zombie*, for a similarly unpressured creation of musical time by means of harmonic trajectories that spiral and embody sameness even as they support the nonsameness of melodic narrative and (eventually) Fela's biting verbal critique.

Save some time for the numerous Pygmy repertories of Central Africa, monuments to ancient Africa that were erected as such by European scholars in the 1950s and 1960s. Pygmy music has fueled the imaginations—not always nobly— of jazz and pop musicians, as well as creators of "world music." Listening to the Aka, Baka, Mbuti, Babongo, Efé, or Twa, you will be caught up in an egalitarian play of vocal textures, in a dazzling display of individual utterance regulated by an underlying communality, and in a feeling for expression and even exclamation that says the same thing over and over again but never in the same way. You may well gain a dizzying sense of the essentially circular motion that grounds communal participation and affirms togetherness—the kind of oneness that comes only from repeated stepping, repeated moving, or repeated dancing together. Reserve a special place for children's repertories from Liberia, Sierra Leone, the Ivory Coast, Ghana, Togo, Uganda, Malawi, and Angola, where young minds compose exquisite nuggets of rhythm and melody in individual and memorable ways; check out ways of playing that combine cooperation with competition, and notice the exploration of sound and the sense of language against the backdrop of patterned grooves that guarantee the coherence of what the children do. Return to the balafon (xylophone) repertories in Burkina Faso, Mali, Niger, and Guinea, where tunes are embedded in other tunes and interlocked in yet other tunes, all played by different players but in such a way that the web of reciprocity is never compromised. Observe a similar ethical commitment among exponents of the Baganda and Chopi xylophone traditions, where numbers merely amplify sound and sonority but do not change the circles set in motion by melo-rhythmic motives.

If you're still up for more adventure, continue into the African diaspora and listen to Afro-Cuban bàtá music, including that which animates Santería ceremonies, and the Brazilian candomblé repertory; there, you will relive West African grooving but with new inflections of medium and message. Sample also the brass bands of Suriname and Jamaica, with their elemental successions and periodicities strongly reminiscent of Africa, even if distance, time, and experience have served to tweak the African heritage. All these repertories—and there are many, many more—are based on an indispensable foundation: an inviolate periodicity or groove regulates musical utterance and provides the condition of possibility upon which basic articulation and necessary departure, play, or improvisation take place. Groove and associated repetition are the ultimate guarantors of meaningfulness in musical performance.[15]

## DIFFERENCE?

Grooving in African music does not necessarily mark it as different from other world music. It would be lame if that was its purpose. Baule, Ewe, Vai, Tetela, Nkundo, and Igbo children, for example, devise cycles of tones and movements first and foremost for their own amusement, not to announce their difference from alien others (Indian, Chinese, or European). And they do so under the guidance of each community's aesthetic and ethical investments. Whether or not the techniques employed by them resemble those employed by others is not germane to their compositional thinking. Indeed, grooving is so basic to many forms of music making around the world that it is better regarded as an invariant element in musical creation.

The question of an African difference, however, is not so easily discarded. Some people hear difference but are unable to accurately specify its musical sources within the parameters of current analytic economies. Others insist on difference to satisfy a psychic or psychological, spiritual or ideological need (Africa *must* be different!). The most compelling intuition, however, stems from the view that if you juxtapose African music with other world music, the African difference is often immediately striking. We know, for example, that certain repertories of Bulgarian music are marked by complex

---

15. For discussions of groove, see Charles Keil and Steven Feld, *Music Grooves: Essays and Dialogues* (Chicago: University of Chicago Press, 1994), and Ingrid Monson, "Riffs, Repetition, and Theories of Globalization," *Ethnomusicology* 43 (1999): 31–65. Mark Abel has recently argued that groove is *not*, in fact, a quality of traditional African music; rather, it emerged in the context of postindustrial Western society at precisely the moment (early twentieth century) when long-standing and firmly established metrical practices were being interrogated in contemporaneous composition. The aggressive metrical presence promulgated by groove, according to Abel, is thus a reaction to a perceived metamusical threat at the dawn of musical modernism. (See Mark Abel, *Groove: An Aesthetic of Measured Time* [Leiden: Brill Academic Publishers, 2014].) Little concrete evidence is adduced from the varieties of African music (such as those listed in Figure I-1) to support Abel's position. It should be borne in mind that groove in African music is sedimented at varying levels. Some manifestations are subtle, nuanced, or barely perceptible, while others are firm, aggressive, or even in your face. To appreciate this and other overriding qualities claimed for African music, it pays to keep in mind that they are subject to differential degrees of salience.

rhythms. Since African music is thought to be rhythmically complex, we may assume a ready affinity between Bulgarian and African musics. And yet the Bulgarian approach, with its additive process and irregular meters, is never identical to the African sound. Similarly, although Balinese gamelan music shares a will to timbre-based exploration with xylophone ensembles from eastern and southern Africa, the two traditions remain distinct. The complex coordination that marks Georgian vocal polyphony may invite comparison with Pygmy polyphony, the polyphony of Wagogo children, or the polyphonic singing that is periodically manifest in Angolan *mukanda* (circumcision and initiation rituals), and yet these practices do not readily collapse into one another. Again, Steve Reich's *Clapping Music* (1972) uses a West African bell pattern, but its emerging groove departs soon enough from the African groove that inspired it. The environment of Reich's composition seems to deny the communality inscribed in the original African bell pattern.

Ultimately, any claim that qualities exist that set African music apart from other world music is more than an empirical claim; it is also an expression of desire, an article of faith, and a mark of pride (ethnic, nationalistic, or otherwise). Whether and how the analyses and descriptions offered in this book support the case for difference or nondifference is best left to readers to decide. It may be helpful, however, to introduce one more distinction to convey my own (ideological) leanings on the question of establishing the domain of African music. It is the distinction between something being *uniquely African* as opposed to it being *truly African*. (I am using the word *unique* in this context to mean singularity, something of which there is only one, not in the sense of excellence or having no equal.) Claims about African difference often seek support from things that are said to be uniquely African, things not found elsewhere. The bundle of qualities that might be brought as evidence ranges from the most concrete to the most elusive, from specific rhythmic patterns to less well-defined environments, auras, and spiritual ambiences. The burden for proponents of uniqueness is to show that what is found in African music is not found elsewhere. But this is a tall order. Moreover, it imposes an unnecessary burden by forcing critics to understate or undervalue much of what is shared with other music, and to emphasize that which has ostensibly not been seen or heard elsewhere. The imperative to establish an ultimate African difference is constricting. We're better off with less constricting alternatives.

That which is *truly African*, on the other hand, is always already desirable because it does not need to prove its difference; it only needs to act out its authenticity, to live out its status as sincere utterance. The truly African can be heard, sensed, or felt in the playing of nose flutes, xylophones, saxophones, harps, church organs, guitars, dùndúns, or side drums; it can be sung in Ekiti, Kpelle, French, Igbo, Portuguese, Xhosa, Siwu, Swahili, Twi, Lingala, Luo, or Wolof. It will not do, for example, to cite instances of antiphonal singing in the history of European Christian churches as evidence against call and response being *the* dominant formal principle in African music. Who says that its dominant formal principle should be found only in Africa? Who doubts the authenticity of its daily usage in thousands of verbal and musical acts across the continent? Without undervaluing historical or archaeological findings, one might nevertheless adopt the view that, when it comes to music, or indeed other cultural practices, acknowledging the dazzling displays of creativity through playing, dancing, and singing is far more significant than establishing ownership or origins of material resources and techniques. The burden of establishing uniqueness (or of denying nonuniqueness)—a burden, incidentally, that is often marked in the writings of non-African scholars—should be rejected. In its place we should *presume* authenticity as a matter of principle and go on to observe outcomes. The truth of a performance, for example, has little to do with the (foreign) origin of an instrument (like the piano) or musical technique (like the use of authentic cadences in major-mode compositions). Such truths are measured by the depth, subtlety, and authenticity or sincerity of utterance. I urge students, therefore, to train their sights on what is truly African as opposed to what is (thought to be) uniquely African.

## RATIONALE FOR ANOTHER INTRODUCTION

Several introductions have preceded this one. Notable among them is that of Cameroonian writer, composer, performer, and musicologist Francis Bebey, whose colorful primer, *African Music: A People's Art,* first published in French in 1969 and in an English translation six years later, is a mix of poetic reflection and enthusiastic appreciation, with emphasis on the ethical values that underpin African music. Another is J. H. Kwabena Nketia's *The Music of Africa* (1974), which has served to introduce a generation of students to the main aspects and qualities of African music. Then there is Monique Brandilly's concise *Introduction aux musiques Africaines,* published in 1997, a valuable orientation based on a slightly different African repertory from Nketia's. It is a pity that Brandilly's book remains untranslated, for its conciseness and judicious choice of illustrations are deserving of wide appreciation. Leonardo d'Amico and Andrew Kaye's reliable primer, *Musica dell'Africa Nera,* is the latest in the string of introductions. Published in 2004, it is the most explicitly historical of these introductions. Significant is its attention to popular music in the twentieth century, a repertory ignored by previous writers. Like Brandilly's book, it remains untranslated, however.[16]

I believe that there is room for a concise introduction with slightly different emphases. The Akpafu have a saying that "*Ɔwi gɔ ame apia ne, ɔira 'sama bra ne,*" which translates as "The time that you are in, its thing is what is done." This is their way of recognizing the pressures of contemporaneity; of observing and adapting to change, updating traditions so that their people are not left behind; and of doing things "according to today's open eyes," as is sometimes

---

16. Francis Bebey, *African Music: A People's Art,* trans. Josephine Bennett (New York: Lawrence Hill, 1975); J. H. Kwabena Nketia, *The Music of Africa* (New York: Norton, 1974); Monique Brandilly, *Introduction aux musiques Africaines* (Arles: Cité de la musique/Actes Sud, 1997); Leonardo d'Amico and Andrew Kaye, *Musica dell'Africa Nera: Civiltà subsahariane fra tradizione e modernità* (Palermo: L'epos, 2004). There is, of course, a vast literature on African music that cannot be adequately acknowledged here. A judicious guide to the field of Africanist ethnomusicology may be found in Christopher Waterman, "Africa," in *Ethnomusicology: Historical and Regional Studies,* ed. Helen Myers (London: Macmillan, 1992), 240–259. Nketia offers a historical perspective in "The Scholarly Study of African Music: A Historical Review," in *Africa: The Garland Encyclopedia of World Music,* ed. Ruth Stone (New York: Garland, 1997), 13–73. Among essential works, see Alan P. Merriam, *African Music in Perspective* (New York: Garland, 1982); Gerhard Kubik, *Theory of African Music,* vol. 1 (Wilhelmshaven: Florian Noetzel Verlag, 1994); Gerhard Kubik, *Theory of African Music,* vol. 2 (Chicago: University of Chicago Press, 2010); Anri Herbst et al., eds., *Musical Arts in Africa: Theory, Practice and Education* (Pretoria: UNISA Press, 2003); Ruth M. Stone, ed., *Africa: The Garland Encyclopedia of World Music,* vol. 1 (New York: Garland, 1998), together with its offshoot, *The Garland Handbook of African Music,* ed. Ruth M. Stone, 2nd ed. (New York: Routledge, 2008); *Musik in Afrika: mit 20 Beiträgen zur Kenntnis traditioneller afrikanischer Musikkulturen,* ed. A. M. Dauer et al. (Berlin: Staatliche Museen Preussischer Kulturbesitz, Museum für Völkerkunde, 1983); the collected Africa entries on individual countries in *The New Grove Dictionary of Music and Musicians,* ed. Stanley Sadie (London: Macmillan, 1980), and in its revised successor, *The New Grove Dictionary of Music and Musicians,* 2nd ed., ed. Stanley Sadie (London: Macmillan, 2001), together with its online version, *Grove Music Online*; Eric Charry's *Mande Music: Traditional and Modern Music of the Maninka and Mandinka of Western Africa* (Chicago: University of Chicago Press); Christine Lucia's edited collection, *The World of South African Music: A Reader* (Newcastle, England: Cambridge Scholars Press, 2005); and two major bibliographies: John Gray's *African Music: A Bibliographical Guide to the Traditional, Popular, Art, and Liturgical Musics of Sub-Saharan Africa* (Westport, CT: Greenwood Press, 1991), and Carol Lems-Dworkin's *African Music: A Pan-African Annotated Bibliography* (London: Hans Zell, 1991), both of which now require updating. For studies that incorporate critique, see Nzewi, *African Music: Theoretical Content and Creative Continuum,* and Agawu, *Representing African Music: Postcolonial Notes, Queries, Positions* (New York: Routledge, 2003). Jean Ngoya Kidula raises several pertinent issues about teaching African music in "Stereotypes, Myths, and Realities Regarding African Music in the African and American Academy," in *Teaching Africa: A Guide for the 21st-Century Classroom,* ed. Brandon D. Lundy and Solomon Negash (Bloomington: Indiana University Press, 2013), 140–155. Also of interest is Sylvia Nannyonga-Tamusuza, "What Is 'African Music'? Conceptualizations of 'African Music' in Bergen (Norway) and Uppsala (Sweden)," in *Ethnomusicology in East Africa: Perspectives from Uganda and Beyond,* ed. Sylvia Nanyonga-Tamusuza and T. Solomon (Kampala, Uganda: Fountain Publishers, 2012), 188–215.

said in the course of pouring libation. These beliefs have to be domesticated within particular scholarly practices, so one should not be under the impression that the translation of belief into action, of theory into practice, is a straightforward undertaking. Nevertheless, my understanding of the Akpafu injunction has inevitably influenced the approach taken here. While I address some more or less canonical topics (like music and society, or rhythm), I also include chapters on less frequently discussed dimensions (like melody or form). More significantly, only in an age that is friendly to analysis (such as ours) has it been possible to incorporate close readings of specific songs (as I do in chapter 5, on melody).[17] I have also depended on the recorded legacy to an extent that is largely without precedent in endeavors of this sort. The aim is to encourage exploration of a dazzling variety of sound environments representing "African music." It is my hope that this book will engender additional theoretical dialogue with colleagues in musicology and music theory, not just the usual suspects in African studies and ethnomusicology.

What, then, are the concerns of individual chapters? Chapter 1 describes the place of music in society. Music is shown to be a part of society rather than apart from it. Circles and cycles serve as archetypes in the organization of musical performances, and the chapter finishes with some speculation on the complicated relationship between musical structure and social structure, a relationship that is thought to be uncommonly close in Africa. Chapter 2 introduces sound-producing instruments (including the human voice) and their function and symbolism. I describe a selection of instruments and their sound ideals, urge closer attention to African-language designations for and ideas about musical instruments, and reject the Hornbostel-Sachs system of instrument classification. Chapter 3 explores several key aspects of the relationship between music

---

17. Although it is by no means the dominant or even privileged approach, analysis of African music has grown in significance in the last few decades. A random selection of writings that incorporate analysis would include Arom, *African Polyphony and Polyrhythm*; David Locke, "Africa/Ewe, Mande, Shona, BaAka," in *Worlds of Music: An Introduction to the Music of the World's People*, ed. Jeff Todd Titon, 5th rev. ed. (Belmont, CA: Schirmer Cengage Learning, 2009), 75–121; Martin Scherzinger, "Negotiating the Music-Theory/African Music Nexus: A Political Critique of Ethnomusicological Anti-Formalism and a Strategic Analysis of the Harmonic Patterning of the Shona Mbira Song *Nyamaropa*," *Perspectives of New Music* 39 (2001): 5–118; Nissio Fiagbedzi, *Form and Meaning in Ewe Song: A Critical Review* (Richmond, CA: Music Research Institute, 2009); Nzewi, "Analytical Procedure in African Music: Sounding Traditional Solo Aesthetic," in Nzewi, *A Contemporary Study of Musical Arts, Informed by African Indigenous Knowledge Systems*; vol. 4: *Illuminations, Reflections and Explorations* (Pretoria: Centre for Indigenous Instrumental African Music and Dance, 2007), 95–115; Nzewi, "Analytical Probing in African Musicology: Discerning Indigenous Epistemology," *Journal of the Association of Nigerian Musicologists* 6 (2012): 1–26; and Bode Omojola, *Yorùbá Music in the Twentieth Century: Identity, Agency, and Performance* (Rochester, NY: University of Rochester Press, 2012). See also the new journal, *Analytical Approaches to World Music* (2011–present), for a number of African offerings.

and natural language. I suggest that music and language are mutually constitutive and yet ultimately separate semiotic domains. I explore the interface between them as manifest in tone languages, talking drums, song (including the poetical imagination displayed in song texts), ideophones, metalanguage, and a certain linguistic sensibility in performance. The next four chapters tackle the core parameters of African music, starting with rhythm in chapter 4. I begin with broad schemes for understanding a variety of rhythmic expression and then turn attention to three aspects of the rhythmic imagination: the use of time-line patterns, polyrhythm, and the art of lead drumming. Chapter 5 deals with melody, a dimension said to be impoverished in African music. I reject this valuation and make a case for the richness of the African melodic imagination by examining a handful of melodies in detail. Chapter 6 is devoted to form, another undervalued parameter in African musical intellection. Beginning with the ubiquitous call and response, I include discussions of the variation impulse, paratactic forms, and, finally, moment form. There is an inevitable partiality to many African forms, and I suggest that alertness to their strategically fragmentary nature might be the key to appreciation. Chapter 7 deals with harmony, a form of simultaneous doing. I acknowledge a number of existing studies and competing nomenclatures and then describe a few of the common ways (many based on parallel movement) in which the harmonic imagination is exercised. European influences are acknowledged along with newer, emergent harmonies at the end of the chapter. Chapter 8, the final chapter, is devoted to questions of appropriation. After acknowledging the global impact of African music, I refer to specific appropriations of African music by specific composers of Western art music. The last word is given to composers of African art music because their acts of music-on-music exploration are likely to provide the most revealing commentary on the potentialities of African music.

Methodologically, I do not follow a single template throughout. Rather, drawing here and there from anthropology, ethnography, history, sociology, music theory, and ethnomusicology, and allowing myself to be guided by the nature of whatever phenomenon is being considered, I shift my stance depending on what I judge to be pertinent for a particular topic: description (chapters 1, 2, 3, and 7), close analysis (chapters 4, 5, and 6), critique (chapters 2 and 5), and overt advocacy (chapter 8). Such an eclectic approach may not be to everyone's taste, nor will my use of certain conventional rubrics. I am confident, however, that the core dimensions of African music can be adequately portrayed using everyday terms like *melody, form, harmony,* and *rhythm.* In titling this book *The African Imagination in Music,* I seek to acknowledge the existence of globally shared notions of "music" while at the same time delineating some characteristically African articulations of it. Indeed, the African difference is best highlighted under comparative regimes rather than in ethnographic segregation.

## WRITING/REPRESENTATION

To write about African music nowadays is almost by definition to write *against* a prior literature. While it is true that all texts are notionally burdened by their predecessor texts, the challenge for writers on African music is especially acute. From the sixteenth century on, writings on Africa generally and music in particular have been undertaken by European explorers, missionaries, amateurs, scholars, representatives of governments, members of scientific expeditions, anthropologists, ethnomusicologists, and even tourists. Some are fantastic imaginings fueled by prejudice, some are patronizing, some are meant to titillate a home audience looking to consume exotic products from faraway lands, and some represent a search for a European—or for that matter human—past from the contemporary practices of those of the human population who are said to have developed at the slowest pace. They include thoroughly narcissistic tracts by individuals who went to Africa to, as it were, find themselves. Some writings mirror the collective search by avant-garde composers for new approaches to musical organization outside the Western sphere, some seek to test various theories pertaining to the origins of music and the place of music in human society, and some are celebrations of repertories that sound familiar and yet are realized differently (including much in the realm of popular music). A number are technical studies of individual musical domains (like rhythm or polyphony) using analytic tools affiliated with European music.[18]

This literature is too large to characterize neatly without doing violence to it, but it is worth keeping its heterogeneous nature in mind. One result of this heterogeneity is a structural delay in the emergence of canons, both methodological and repertorial. Unlike our colleagues in African literature or film, for example, who seem to deploy a circumscribed body of reading technologies, and for whom acquaintance with *Things Fall Apart* or *Xala* can be taken for granted, music scholars do not seem to share the same body of canonical texts—texts that can be discussed and debated to centralize and sharpen the process of knowledge production. The closest we come to this is in the inclusion of Southern Ewe drumming or Shona mbira music in world music surveys, but neither of these repertories yet possesses a genuine canonical status that would require all participants in a training program to be acquainted

---

18. Critical reviews of writings on African music may be found in John McCall, "The Representation of African Music in Early Documents," in *The Garland Encyclopedia of World Music*. Vol. 1: *Africa*, ed. Ruth M. Stone (New York: Garland, 1998), 74–99; Simha Arom, *African Polyphony and Polyrhythm: Musical Structure and Methodology*, trans. Martin Thom, Barbara Tuckett, and Raymond Boyd (Cambridge: Cambridge University Press, 1991), 45–91; Carol Lems-Dworkin, *African Music: A Pan-African Annotated Bibliography*; and Agawu, *Representing African Music*.

with them. Similarly, one only needs to reflect for a moment on the contrasts among the approaches of a Rouget (painstaking description with due attention to language), an Arom (rigorous analysis and consideration of theoretical possibilities), an Nzewi (insightful analysis delivered passionately and always with an embattled tone), a Kubik (careful and thorough analysis without sparing mention of ethnographic status), and an Nketia (judicious formulations based on an awareness of the general and the particular, principle and exemplification) to appreciate the systemic plurality that rules in the field of African musicology. An open acknowledgment of this canonless terrain may help put things in perspective and engender more productive debate about how best to represent African music.

A related—if somewhat delicate—issue stems from the fact that a great deal of the institutionally prominent literature on African music has been produced by non-African scholars. In no other field of music study are culture bearers so painfully absent from the sites of knowledge production. Some readers may well balk at the presumed distinction between African and non-African voices, but this is probably one of those distinctions that is either grasped immediately or permanently out of reach. Although some have suggested that African scholars ignore the European legacy altogether and simply go by what Africans themselves have to say about their own music, not everyone feels inclined to take that exhortation literally, especially given its ramifications for the attainment of professional credibility in today's academy.

It is gratifying to observe the increasing diversification of the scholarly field. Since about 1980, more and more African (i.e., born-in-the-tradition) scholars have written about their own music. Scholars from Nigeria, Cameroon, Ghana, Kenya, Uganda, Tanzania, Zambia, the Democratic Republic of the Congo, South Africa, Togo, and Côte d'Ivoire (to mention only a handful) have made significant contributions to knowledge and, in the process, helped to diversify and complicate existing agendas and practices. A number of ironies attend this new development, however. For one thing, many African scholars write in metropolitan languages because those are the languages in which they first learned to write (not to speak) and because those are the only languages available for scholarly discourse. These scholars are also often trained in institutions modeled on those of Europe, so their work follows a certain scholarly protocol, although few of them would think the European protocol infallible or free of cultural biases. And their work is tilted in the direction of a European or American audience, unless it announces explicitly music educational goals. These factors hint at the internal diversification within African writing itself and suggest that the distinction between African and non-African scholars be handled with care. To deny it would be perverse; to misread it would be worse.

## READERSHIP

Many books on African music are written as if there were no readers in Africa. I reject such a stance. The readership I have in mind is not only the usual metropolitan one but also an African readership. I assume, for example, that students in Ghana and Nigeria, Uganda and the Democratic Republic of the Congo, the Côte d'Ivoire and Togo, Kenya and the Central African Republic, and South Africa and Senegal will, if they so choose, engage with some of the claims and formulations made here—agreeing with some, disagreeing with others, or simply being stimulated to offer their own perceptions based on knowledge of other traditions. Bringing an African readership to the center allows me to preempt the criticism that more contextual information should have been given (where are the photographs, maps, and first-level descriptions and translations of every last bit of text into English—the paraphernalia that allow us to continue to do Africa from scratch?) or that too much has been presumed. I ask, instead, that readers meet me partway. None of this is meant to excuse the book's shortcomings; it is simply meant to dramatize what I believe is a fundamental yet infrequently acknowledged difference in approach between those who write about African music as if their readers were "outsiders" looking in and those whose target readership includes continent-based Africans ("insiders") with a complicated relationship to the metropolis.

## HOW TO USE THIS BOOK

Finally, let me say a word about how one might use this book and what one might expect to get out of it. Music is an activity, a form of doing, a nexus of dynamic exertions. African music is best explored with this sense of doing in mind. The highest outcome from internalizing the portrait of African music offered in this book would be to compose and perform original musical works (written down on paper or carried in memories) in response to the routines, processes, and rationales described. Only a handful of people are skilled enough to do this, however. Nevertheless, the attempt to create new music as a way of registering an understanding of old (or other) music is in my view second to none in the hierarchy of creative engagements. A more likely group of readers will be looking to improve their understanding of African music and enhance their experiences as listeners. Even for this group, it bears reminding that African music is first and foremost a participatory art, and that incorporating actual (as opposed to merely imagined) music making is necessary for proper understanding.

In cultivating such a hands-on approach, readers might undertake four practical activities. (Some of these require additional bodies, so be prepared to collaborate with others where necessary.) First, speak words and sentences in indigenous African languages whenever possible. These could be greetings, oaths, ritual announcements, proverbs, or brief conversations. You could also recite poetry or read aloud from African-language texts, including translations of the Bible or popular written literature. Learning to produce these languages (including those that are not your own, as when a Yoruba speaker speaks Ewe, a Luo speaks Kpelle, or a Brazilian speaks Hausa) will stimulate an awareness of pitch and rhythm that will in turn deepen your appreciation not only of vocal music but also of instrumental music. Second, sing as often as possible. The repertoire might include children's songs and rhymes, popular songs and dirges, ritual or religious items, or even polyphonic songs. You may even be able to incorporate a little improvisation if you team up with one or two people who are familiar with the procedures associated with a specific genre. Third, clap, speak, and beat rhythms regularly to enhance familiarity with this domain. This could be done by rote, repeating patterns after a skilled practitioner, or along with a recording. So-called *time-line patterns,* for example, are good material for clapping. You might also assemble polyrhythmic textures through singing and clapping or foot stomping. Of course, polyrhythm is easier to enact if you work with others and each of you takes a distinct but complementary pattern. Any number of African dances could form the basis of this exercise. Repeating the rhythmic patterns many times is a necessary and valuable starting point; listening to the rest of the ensemble while producing your own pattern fosters a sense of musicianship. Fourth, dancing and movement are absolutely necessary if you are to correctly embody African rhythms. Since a significant portion of the repertory explored in this book is dance based, merely listening to the music will not convey all of its essential dimensions. Try out some simple dance steps, or join communal music-making events.

This fourfold routine, speak-sing-clap-dance, may be no more than an echo of the ambitions and philosophy of committed music educators. I'm pleased to acknowledge that work here, for it is all too easy for musicologists and ethnomusicologists to overlook some of the imperatives of pedagogy. Nevertheless, the pedagogical impulse is not the dominant motivation for this book. Rather, by selectively describing theory and practice, I hope to encourage direct and active engagement with African music as, among other things, an aesthetic phenomenon. I do so by sharing perceptions that might deepen appreciation, foster comparison, and altogether intensify respect and admiration for African creativity and intellection. Fascination with African music is of course long-standing; today, it is possible to supplement that fascination with a closer look at some of music's generative elements. This book is inspired by that possibility.

# 1

# Music and/in Society

Music making appears to be a universal phenomenon. Like natural language and religion, music as a system and practice seems to be essential to human existence. There are, to be sure, differences—some of them occasionally radical—among sound ideals, modes of performance, positions of musicians within society, relative densities of musical events in a given "soundscape," and values placed upon music making. But by and large, the presence of music, understood as organized sound with a (silent) choreographic supplement, is a defining feature of most human societies. Africa provides a particularly vivid illustration of the close and complex relationship between music and society.[1]

## NO WORD FOR MUSIC?

It may come as a surprise to learn that the word *music* does not occur in many indigenous African languages. Several writers have noted this absence and claimed a degree of significance for it. For example, surveying terminology associated with music and musicians among the Tiv of Eastern Nigeria in 1979, Charles Keil identified "biases" in Western conceptions of music and revealed absences in several African lexicons, leading him to re-evaluate not only "music" but also "musicology" and "ethnomusicology":

> The problem of our biases hit me rather forcefully when it became clear
> that a word corresponding to our term "music" could not be found in one
> African language after another—Tiv, Yoruba, Igbo, Efik, Birom, Hausa,

---

1. On the origins of music, see William Forde Thompson, *Music, Thought, and Feeling: Understanding the Psychology of Music* (New York: Oxford University Press, 2009), 19–41. The universality of music, language, and religion is a point made with particular conviction by John Blacking in *How Musical Is Man*? See also Ian Cross, "Music and Biocultural Evolution."

assorted Jarawa dialects, Idoma, Eggon, and a dozen other languages from the Nigeria-Cameroons area do not yield a word for "music" gracefully. It is easy to talk about song and dance, singers and drummers, blowing a flute, beating a bell, but the general terms "music" and "musician" require long and awkward circumlocutions that still fall short, usually for lack of abstraction, for example, "the voices of the tools of the dance," a way of bringing together instruments blown and beaten which when supplemented by "plus singing" almost adds up to "music." So what seems to us a very basic, useful, and rather concrete term is apparently a useless abstraction from a Tiv, Yoruba, perhaps even a pan-African or non-Western point of view. If it should turn out that West African cultures are typical and that the vast majority of the world's people do not bother with a word for "music," it's conceivable that we may eventually think it silly, ethnocentric, even pompous to be designating disciplines with names like "musicology" or "ethnomusicology." On the other hand, "music" may continue to define quite precisely the somewhat ambiguous range of patterned sound phenomena we are interested in exploring across all cultural borders. We may eventually coin a still more ambiguous term that includes both music and dance, something more elegant than "musico-choreographic," I hope, since song/dance/musical-accompaniment are virtually inseparable in many cultures.[2]

Christopher Waterman, who quotes a portion of this passage in an important reference article, adds that "Keil's list might be expanded to include Mandinka, Wolof, Serer, Bambara, Dogon, Dan, Kpelle, Twi, Ga, Ewe, Fulani, Bala-Basongye, Karimojong, Baganda, Shona, Venda, Zulu, Xhosa, various San languages and Chokwe."[3] Lester Monts says that "the Vai language has no generic term for the Western concept of music, though there are words for 'dance' (tɔmbɔ), 'song' (dɔŋ), and 'instrumental performance' (seŋ feŋ)."[4] According to Kubik, "there are no terms in [the languages] of eastern Angola whose semantic fields could be considered congruent with that of the Latin word *musica* and its derivatives in European languages." He finds this to be the case "in most Bantu languages."[5] And according to Maurice Djenda, *music*

2. Charles Keil, *Tiv Song: The Sociology of Art in a Classless Society* (Chicago: University of Chicago Press, 1979), 27.

3. Christopher Waterman, "Africa," 250.

4. Lester P. Monts, "Islam in Liberia," in Stone, Africa: *The Garland Encyclopedia of World Music*, 347.

5. Kubik, *Theory of African Music*, vol. 1, 330.

is "a term without an equivalent in most Central African languages."[6] From here on it would be a fairly predictable exercise to go down the list of numerous African languages and discover a similar pattern of absence. Waterman does not interrogate the presumed sameness in European-language usages of the equivalent of "music." Could it be that the meanings attached to "music" or its closest equivalent differ not only between the West and the non-West but also from language to language? Could it be, therefore, that the African difference is a matter of degree, if it is a difference at all? Keil thinks that the Western word *music* is probably "a useless abstraction" for African and non-Western people.

How significant is this absence? Seemingly provocative at first sight, further reflection suggests that the significance of the absence of the word *music* from indigenous languages may be ambiguous, a red herring perhaps. First, it is not an absence that has registered often in the writings of prominent African scholars. Perhaps Sowande, Bebey, Nketia, Euba, Vidal, Nzewi, Avorgbedor, Mapoma, Mukuna, Mensah, and others have not been struck by it; perhaps they think that communication is not threatened when the word *music* is used; perhaps they see similarly imperfect mappings of semantic fields between African languages; or perhaps they simply have a different set of priorities in writing about African music. Second, it may be that a self-evident distinction between music making and other modes of expression is presumed on ontological grounds. When I hear a man singing another's praises in exchange for cash, women mourning the dead in crying songs, drummers delivering coded messages on talking drums, or a group of hunters celebrating a big kill in songs and dances of bravery, heroism, and self-congratulation, I am immediately aware that these activities are linked in an immediate sense, that they represent the same sorts of escape from ordinary, lived time. They are forms of individual and group affirmation through singing and playing instruments within temporal spaces consecrated for no other purpose than to stage a departure from an ordinary realm into a marked one. I would not confuse music making with, say, eating, sleeping, or making love. What the absence of a word for "music" suggests is not that African conceptions are radically different from Western ones, or that there is a significant discontinuity between semantic fields, or even that abstractions are missing from African talk about music; rather, it suggests that the semantic range of the convenient, all-encompassing, indeed all-purpose term *music* is distributed differently in some (African) languages. Keil, in fact, notes that the word enshrines an ambiguity that may well ensure its continued usefulness.

6. Maurice Djenda and Michelle Kisliuk, "Central African Republic," in *Grove Music Online*, accessed June 27, 2013.

A sign of such an expanded semantic range is the relatively fluid and unstable set of referents for instrumental music as distinct from vocal music. No indigenous African language lacks a word for "language," a vital component of vocal music. Further, many African languages have words for "song." And although "song" carries a range of meanings, its basic function in denoting certain forms of vocalization is generally secure. Of course, allowance should be made for diversity in production: articulation may be syllabic or melismatic or take the form of vocalise; we may speak, sing, or hum a song; and the temporal framework could be strictly metrical, partially metrical, free, or declamatory. These varieties notwithstanding, "song" as a partial referent for "music" in Africa is at a gross level ontologically proximate to song in other world cultures.

The other half denoting instrumental music seems to resist translation to a greater extent, but even here the matter is largely one of degree. Ostensibly "pure" instrumental music (for tuned or at least tonally differentiated sets of drums, lamellophones, and wind instruments, for example) is sometimes conceptualized as "song," as possessing a verbal basis or a verbal motivation. According to Ruth Stone, Kpelle flutes and lutes are said to possess "voices" and are heard to "sing."[7] Their repertory may therefore be characterized as "songs." Some African instrumental music is likewise conceived as wordless songs, songs whose words are not nonexistent but have been relegated to a strong supplementary function. Klaus Wachsmann and Peter Cooke drew attention to such songs in the xylophone music of Uganda.[8] A genre of songs for reflection (*chants à penser*) was recorded by Vincent Dehoux from among the Gbaya in the Central African Republic. Its song-eliciting melodies played principally on the sanza allow individuals to construct bridges from the world of pure tone to the verbal world in which men call out to their loved ones, reflect upon misery and loneliness, and react to loss.[9]

The category "song" cannot, however, absorb all of African instrumental music. This task is left to the choreographic supplement or dance. Understood as patterned physical movement that is simultaneously a response to and a generator of music, dance assumes the role of a nexus or ultimate anchor. Again, no indigenous African language as far as we know lacks a word

---

7. Ruth Stone, *Music in West Africa: Experiencing Music, Experiencing Culture* (New York: Oxford University Press, 2005), 19.

8. Klaus Wachsmann and Peter Cooke, "Africa," in *The New Grove Dictionary of Music and Musicians* (London: Macmillan Publishers, 1980), vol. 1, 150.

9. CD, *Centrafrique: Musique Gbáyá:Chants à penser* (Paris: Ocora, 1995).

for "dance." In some, drumming and dancing are mutually implicated. Drumming can also bring on singing as an additional dimension, so that the domain of "dance" intersects with that of music making. We might say that between song and dance, the conceptual origins of instrumental music are well accounted for.

To say that African languages lack a term comparable to the English word *music* may, however, be helpful in fostering some self-awareness in the use of the all-purpose term. But to present the difference as categorical is to misconstrue the cross-cultural space that enabled this very observation. Moreover, the act of designating a species of expressive behavior as "music" represents a beginning, a first step in conceptual exploration, a point of departure; such an action does not describe a final state or outcome. The next step would be to see how this complex of actions and thoughts is expressed and critiqued within a given language to establish the patterns of prioritization enshrined in its conceptual schemes. In due course, webs of significance will be woven around the term, leading us to yet more nuanced understanding. We learn, for example, that among the Venda, the presence of an explicit meter is what separates "music" from nonmusic; that a "limited number" of Koranic scholars among the Hausa use the term *musika*; that among the Tswana of Botswana, "singing and dancing are regarded as virtually synonymous" (*gobina*); that the terms *mosoko* and *ngombi* in Sango have been introduced in the Central African Republic as equivalents for music; and that the Dan in Côte d'Ivoire lack a single term for music but have terms for dance song (*ta*), praise song (*zlöö*), and funeral laments (*gbo*).[10] These and other terms serve to orient us to cultural particulars within a broad regime of "music." "African music" is therefore neither incomprehensible nor obscure; rather, it packs in a number of contingencies that point to an expanded semantic field. "African music" is always already a provisional designation.

---

10. John Blacking, *Venda Children's Songs: A Study in Ethnomusicological Analysis* (Chicago: University of Chicago Press, 1995 [orig. 1967]), 17; David W. Ames and Anthony V. King, *A Glossary of Hausa Music and Its Social Contexts* (Evanston, IL: Northwestern University Press, 1971), ix; Felicia M. Mundell and John Brearley, "Botswana," in *Grove Music Online*; Maurice Djenda, "Central African Republic," in *Grove Music Online*; Hugo Zemp, "Cote d'Ivoire," in *Grove Music Online*. Dave Dargie supplies a list of words for "music" in various African languages in *Xhosa Music: Its Techniques and Instruments, with a Collection of Songs* (Cape Town: David Philip, 1988), 62. See also Kubik, "The Emics of African Rhythm," in *Cross Rhythms* 2, ed. Daniel Avorgbedor and Kwesi Yankah (Bloomington, IN: Trickster Press, 1985), 26–66; Kubik, *Theory of African Music*, vol. 1, 332–333; and Nzewi, *Musical Practice and Creativity: An African Traditional Perspective* (Bayeuth, Germany: Iwalewahaus, University of Bayreuth, 1991), for pertinent discussion of indigenous terminology and perspectives.

## HOW, THEN, DO AFRICANS TALK ABOUT "MUSIC"?

In navigating the semantic worlds linked to broadly comparable notions of "music," we encounter a colorful terrain in which explicit metalanguages and informal metaphors illuminate African thematizations of music as an expression of life. To acknowledge this vocabulary is to invite exploration of African ways of world making. One of the dangers of cross-cultural comparison is the temptation to reify terms and concepts that seem to mark difference. These initial differences or first impressions should be treated as beginnings, not endings. For example, for some speakers of American English, the Kpelle expression "a song going down the road" is immediately arresting because it differs from what they are used to—songs do not normally travel, much less travel down roads.[11] But the full significance of that translation can only emerge from a consideration of larger contexts of usage. Which roads, and what else travels down roads in this particular West African culture? These further acts of contextualization, which are in effect exercises in the philosophy of music, are sometimes missing from glossaries documenting African talk about music.[12]

With these caveats in mind, we can now proceed to a brief consideration of what some African languages say about music. Rather than quote from a variety of languages, however, I provide English-language equivalents of words and phrases that I believe have a wider currency beyond those languages. I recognize that translation is always already unequal, but perhaps this kind of strategic impoverishment will stimulate critical discussion beyond individual languages and bring insight.

Foremost among vocabulary items are names of instruments. Musical instruments acquire names from a variety of sources and motivations: from the functional role of an instrument within an ensemble ("the mother drum"), from the mode of enunciation ("the one who speaks"), from the material used in making the instrument ("the metal bell," "the gourd rattle," "the wooden shaker"), and as literal depictions of the kind of sound typically made by the instrument ("gbun-gbun," "dòndón," and other onomatopoeia). Equally significant are names of musical genres, including names for musical occasions: play songs, grinding songs, songs of insult, and songs of lamentation. Then there are terms that depict performance actions: "beat the inside of the voice," "put fire inside," "the song has caught my throat," and "the performance wears

11. Stone, "Commentary: The Value of Local Ideas in Understanding West African Rhythm," *Ethnomusicology* 30 (1986): 56.

12. But see Keil, *Tiv Song*, for a significant exception.

slowness." Related are terms for capturing music's expressive effect or affective character, announcing aesthetic assumptions and ethical motivations, or evaluating a performance: "it went inside deeply for me," "the song and dance agreed," "it was too much," and "she has a cooked tongue."

Finally, there are technical terms that are used routinely, albeit informally, by critics or analysts. Some are designations for parts of song, like "beginning" and "throwing away place" (for cadence). Others support a conceptual distinction between "deep structure" and "surface structure." Some convey processes of embellishment or variation: "change the voice," "turn it like this and like that," and "put salt inside." Then there are terms for musical parameters like pitch ("big voice" vs. "small voice"), melody ("the sounding of the voice"), harmony or polyphony ("first voice" vs. "second voice" or "the coagulation of voices"), tempo ("put fire inside"), timbre ("it is not smooth"), and dynamics ("let it be strong"). Another category that registers often, albeit indirectly, is form, the internal arrangement of parts in a composition. Especially prominent is the call-and-response procedure. "Call" may be rendered as "send the song," "remove the song," or "intone it," while "response" may be given by many terms, among them "catch the song," "love it," "agree to it," and "respond to it."

A concentration of usage in a particular location or community may occasionally elevate ad hoc terms to the status of a metalanguage. Crediting his grandmother, an Akan singer of *Ahenfodwom,* with the invention and regular usage of certain terms, Nketia distinguishes a call (*ɔfre*) from the response (*dzinsoɔ*) it elicits. The word *ntosuɔ* ("add on") denotes a layer above another layer, while *ntumu* means interruption. Finally, *mpaemu* refers to voice separation.[13] Similarly, Nzewi explains that the harmonic scheme in Igbo culture is "discussed in triadic terms of low, female voice (*nne olu*), high, male voice (*oke olu*), and the voice in-between (*agbalabo*)."[14] Neither Nketia nor Nzewi provides data on the extent of the sociocultural usage of this vocabulary, however.

At least three observations can be made about these terms and expressions. First, they are cultivated within very specific language communities. In this sense, their external appearances (or foreground features) have no necessary pan-African value; rather, it is the motivations that underpin individual terms (background features) that are widely shared. Second, they are often cultivated in specific institutions and performance contexts.

13. Nketia, *Akanfo nwom bi* [*Akan Songs*] (London: Oxford University Press, 1949).

14. Nzewi, *A Contemporary Study of Musical Arts*, vol. 4 (Pretoria: Centre for Indigenous Instrumental African Music and Dance [Ciimda], 2007), 100.

They come into being as needs arise. Where there is no need to designate a musical action verbally, no one invents a word for it. We should remember that most musical practices referred to in this book—and to which the previous words and phrases apply—are societies of primary orality. Effective performance, for example, need not be verbally mediated in such societies; models and instructions can be conveyed concisely in action, including movement or visual cues. There is thus a great deal that is conditional and contingent about these terms. Third, vocabularies change over time. The Ewe, for example, did not have a term for *conductor* before they came under Christian missionary influence in the 1840s. Since then, church choirs singing in an alien four-part harmonic texture (sopranos, altos, tenors, basses) with a designated conductor who faces the singers oppositionally have become a part of their tradition. Today, they refer to an *àtídalá*, "one who waves the stick." There will doubtless be further accretions in response to contemporary needs; old terms will be discarded and replaced by new ones. It is important to acknowledge this historically fluid process so that we are not tempted to essentialize the African musical mind on the basis of stand-out or exotic-sounding metaphors of limited circulation picked up in one location or another in the course of fieldwork.

A significant factor in the process of change is the invention of pedagogical terms for the purposes of cross-cultural teaching. The use of drum mnemonics, for example, has been widely reported as a traditional tool for teaching and transmission.[15] In more recent times, and especially as a result of increasing globalization of African music, new teaching methods have arisen. This development entails both losses and gains. Let me cite but one example of each. I once heard the popular clave rhythmic pattern ([3-3-4-2-4]) explained as a "five-beat pattern."[16] Students were encouraged to count 1-2-3-4-5 to help them render it. By "beat," the instructor was referring to the number of attack points or onsets, not the metrically constrained beats. The five onsets are not equal in duration; rather, they are distributed across *four* equidistant beats. Here, imperfect understanding of the concept of beat has led to usage that is potentially confusing. By contrast, the offbeat pattern played by the *kagan* drum in a dance like Agbadza is rendered as "the ups" by some English-speaking

---

15. See David Locke and Godwin K. Agbeli, "A Study of the Drum Language in Adzogbo," *African Music* 6, no. 1 (1981): 32–51, and Robert M. Kwami, "Towards a Comprehensive Catalogue of Eve Drum Mnemonics," *Journal of African Cultural Studies* 11, no. 1 (1998): 27–38.

16. The designation [3-3-4-2-4] is a durational matrix that represents a rhythmic pattern's interonset pattern. It serves as a convenient way of representing brief rhythmic patterns that recur in a great deal of African music.

performers of Ewe music, a rendition that effectively conveys its persistent off-beat metrical placement.[17]

Inscribed in African vocabularies for music are deep values associated with religious, ethical, and pedagogical beliefs. Some terms may betray haste, convenience, or arbitrariness in formulation, while others may emerge from careful consideration of technical accuracy. This is why we should treat them as suggestive points of departure for the exploration of particular conceptual worlds rather than critically proven items within a stable or explicit metalanguage. Some terms function as pawns in an elaborate game of improvisation; others enshrine speculation about actions that are not nameable in words. Some are figures of speech or metaphors, distant murmurs about things felt. In short, we should attempt to grasp the dynamic processes within which such semantic inventions take place by keeping an eye on the historical processes that produce the terms, always being alert to the time, place, and purpose of each invention.

Language begets language, and analyzing talk about music will invariably require additional perspectives from fields such as sociolinguistics, philosophy, and cultural studies. This is not the place for that more comprehensive study; the main point is to remind us of the vital place of language in talk and conceptualization of music. With this background in place, we can now turn to the main task of this chapter—to observe the role of music in society.

## OCCASIONS FOR MUSIC MAKING: WORK, RITUAL, AND ENTERTAINMENT

Contexts and occasions for music making in Africa are many, perhaps infinite. A summary claim like the following could be applied to any number of African communities:

The most common occasions for music-making . . . are name-giving celebrations, initiation rites, marriages, Christian, Islamic and animist religious rites and celebrations, funerals, post-funeral celebrations, agricultural and household work, harvest celebrations, and the praising of chiefs, elders and other important men and women.[18]

17. James Burns, "Rhythmic Archetypes in Instrumental Music from Africa and the Diaspora," *Music Theory Online* 16, no. 4 (2010), accessed February 1, 2011, http://mto. societymusictheory.org/issues/mto.10.16.4/mto.10.16.4.burns.html.

18. Wiggins and Rosellini, "Burkina Faso," *Grove Music Online*, accessed March 30, 2013.

Similarly, Rouget's summing up of the role of music in the Tadoid or Gbe languages of Benin, Togo, and Ghana may be generalized for other regions:

> Birth, marriage, death, seasonal rituals, collective work, district or village festivities, ancestor worship or ceremonies for the vodun, all provide an opportunity for music-making.[19]

An earlier discourse gave thematic emphasis to this abundance, and to the concomitant imbrication of "music" in "society." It was said that music accompanied the African from cradle to grave, that all known African societies had some form of organized music making, and that music was a necessary part of life, not a decorative part thereof. We were told that "music tends to be tied tightly to the socio-cultural events for which it is created; without the events, the music is not produced."[20] Each attribution originated in something observed about musical life. And yet, taken as generalizations, these claims seem exaggerated, incomplete, or misleading. As pointers to philosophies of music making in small, closed, often rural societies, however, they have some value. And so, as long as we are taking our bearings in this book from traditional music, we can rehabilitate some aspects of these claims.

A normative portrait of music making in Africa would identify three main sets of occasions: work (including manual and moral work), ritual, and entertainment.[21] Music associated with work includes work songs (by fishermen and manual laborers), music incorporated into the performance of domestic chores (like grinding and pounding songs), and music for community-wide activities like building bridges, weeding cemeteries, and clearing paths. It includes the

---

19. Rouget, "Benin," *Grove Music Online*, accessed March 30, 2013.

20. Alan P. Merriam, *African Music in Perspective*, 140.

21. Nketia's exposition of music's social and community roles (*The Music of Africa*, 21–50) remains unimproved, so I have drawn on it in what follows. Among other fine portraits of music's social moorings—where the "social" encompasses the extramusical, be it broadly cultural and historical or narrowly political—see Kelly Askew, *Performing the Nation: Swahili Music and Cultural Politics in Tanzania* (Chicago: University of Chicago Press, 2002); Frank Gunderson, *Sukuma Labor Songs From Western Tanzania: 'We Never Sleep, We Dream of Farming* (Leiden: Brill, 2010); and Chernoff, *A Drummer's Testament: Dagbamba Society and Culture in the Twentieth Century* (forthcoming; excerpts can be read at http://www.adrummerstestament.com/), which may be read profitably in conjunction with the film *Drums of Dagbon* (Princeton, NJ: Films for the Humanities, 2003 [orig. 1984]). For other vivid portrayals, see *Born Musicians: Traditional Music from the Gambia* (Princeton, NJ: Films for the Humanities, 2003 [orig. 1984]); *Growing Into Music in Mali and Guinea*, http://www.growingintomusic.co.uk/mali-and-guinea-music-of/films-of-growing-into-music.html; and the two-part documentary, *African Christianity Rising*, http://jamesault.com/.

songs, rhythms, and rhymes that street and market vendors use to attract cus-
tomers; music made by shepherds; and lullabies designed to soothe babies and
children. Work songs also include hymns that surgeons and their teams sing
before they operate on a patient, chants that are designed to inspire participants
in a sporting event, and the music that postal workers once made while canceling stamps (famously recorded by James Koetting at the University of Ghana
Post Office and prominently anthologized in a widely used textbook, *Worlds of
Music*).[22]

Music for moral work includes songs composed "against" individuals to
correct antisocial behavior through song. For example, "A real man does not
work two jobs," says one Northern Ewe song composed to humiliate a habitual
thief whose "second job" was stealing. The texts for such songs range from
mere allusion to graphic description of the offense. Singing may also accompany a procession through the village of a thief who has been caught stealing a goat or a chicken. The thief may be paraded carrying the stolen item
while others drum and sing to intensify his humiliation. Rhymes are sometimes created to tease adults who have violated an aspect of the moral code.
For example, because some farming communities frown on men having sex
with their wives in the bush, news that an individual has done just that may
elicit mocking songs or rhymes that culprits sometimes have a hard time living down. Work songs and work music as a whole bear a complex relationship
to work: the music may be generated by the activity (as when fisherman or
cloth weavers incorporate the rhythm of physical work directly into the music
they produce), the music may provide a contemplative backdrop but ignore the
activity's intrinsic rhythms, or music and work may unfold in the same time
and space but be unconnected organically.

A second occasion for music making is ritual. The birth of a male child
or of twins may occasion the performance of certain rites in and through
music. Circumcision rites may feature music making, while singing invariably
accompanies the celebration of puberty. Nketia cites examples of habitual bedwetting among the Ashanti eliciting singing from one's peers, and the loss of
a first tooth among the Fon being marked by song.[23] Town-purifying ceremonies and the onset of planting and harvesting seasons may be accompanied by
ritual music and dance. Especially elaborate is music making during funerals.
(We will return to this subject later in the chapter.) There are also rites for

---

22. See the compact disc set to accompany *Worlds of Music: An Introduction to the Music of
the World's Peoples*, ed. Jeff Todd Titon (New York: Schirmer, 1996), disc 1, track 13, "Postal
workers canceling stamps at the University of Ghana post office."

23. Nketia, *Music of Africa*, 36, 23.

healing the sick, as in the practice of dancing away one's disease among the Tumbuka of Northern Malawi.[24]

Festivals are big occasions for music making. Examples include the deer-hunting festival (Aboakyer) of the Effutu, the Osun festival of the Yoruba, the Iriji-Mmanwu spirit manifest festival of the Igbo, various yam and rice festivals, and festivals that mark a significant aspect of a community's past. A new chief may be installed amidst grand music making, while the reciting of histories of clans (as among the Dagomba) is equally a musical occasion. Various forms of music making occur on market days, as well as on colonially induced celebrations of Empire Day, May Day, Independence Day, Easter, and Christmas. Sundays in Christian communities are especially marked for (ritual) church music in the course of worship. Ritual music may be designed for specific rituals (and not performed otherwise) or may borrow from other sources. Music domesticated for a particular ritual does not necessarily reflect the ritual iconically, but is rather invested with contextually appropriate qualities.

A third and final category is music for entertainment, recreation, and play. Children's game songs are prominent in this category, as are after-hours performances by various professional and nonprofessional associations of hunters, warriors, farmers, and drivers. At various courts (that of King Glélé of Benin, the Asantehene of the Ashanti, the Oba of Lagos, and the Kabaka of Baganda), royal musicians often perform to reinforce the king's status, rehearse a historical record, or entertain the king and his guests. With the advent of popular music, venues like beach fronts, community centers, theaters, dance halls, and concert halls have become busy and important sites for music making. Entertainment music takes some of its cues from the nature of the entertainment (e.g., a heavy beat for certain forms of dancing by young people in large dance halls) and from the projections, indulgencies, and fantasies of individual musicians.

In sum, the combination of work, ritual, and entertainment serves as a framework for ordering the numerous occasions for music making in Africa. Each defines a network of activities, and all three may intersect in simple or complex ways. There is no necessary correlation between activity and musical trace; correlations have to be sought on an individual basis. Ultimately, music is made because people realize that outcomes on those occasions are likely to be impoverished if the opportunity (to make music) is forfeited.

The threefold division into work, ritual, and entertainment provides a synchronic account of music making. If we were positioned outside of these happenings and observed them from a distance, we would see work, ritual, and

---

24. Steven Friedson, *Dancing Prophets: Musical Experience in Tumbuka Healing* (Chicago: University of Chicago Press, 1996).

entertainment unfolding at the same time, albeit in different configurations within the community's spaces. This triangular dance is something of a conceptual and rhetorical conceit, however. While it can be readily imagined, it is not normally perceived as a totality by individuals. A less abstract way to think about music in society is to follow the linear unfolding of a network of musical events—the same events that we have just named—in the course of a normative life cycle.

## MUSIC ACROSS THE LIFE CYCLE

As material social practice, music making in Africa may be described along a number of axes and circular mappings ranging from the macrorhythms to the microrhythms of life, from complete life cycles marked by multiyear routines to yearly, seasonal, and eventually daily cycles. While the life cycle allows us to view the correlation between music making and major life events on a large scale, the daily cycle allows us to sketch more local correlations. "Macro" and "micro" are relative values, however. Communities observe the defining activities with different kinds of ceremony and different degrees of commitment. In assembling the following composite portrait, the reader should be under no illusion that designated events occur everywhere with the same degree of salience. The exception may be death, which more often than not elicits elaborate celebration, if not immediately then subsequently. Throughout Africa, one encounters death dances, funeral dirges, orations, crying songs, and lamentations. By temporarily removing the veil over allowable expression during the period of mourning, funeral celebrations become important channels for the expression of the deepest emotions brought on by the ending of life ("It is finished," the Akpafu say). Later in this chapter, I will offer a detailed discussion of music in the funeral celebration of one African community. But first I will describe the place of music within the life cycle.

A typical life cycle unfolds in roughly four contiguous stages: birth, puberty, marriage, and death. The sequence may be represented either as a linear succession or as a circular configuration, depending on whether the last stage is viewed as signifying an end, a new beginning, or both. Each stage comprises a network of events rather than a single event. Birth includes naming and outdooring ceremonies, as well as various initiation rituals affecting both child and new mother. The idea here is to acknowledge the miracle of birth, celebrate the mother's overcoming of this profound challenge (some Ewe congratulate a new mother for "escaping tragedy," for being "spared"), and welcome the young one as the passport to the future. Circumcision is also marked in certain societies. In Angola and Zambia, for example, young boys attend circumcision schools in preparation for the ritual, itself a sign of transition into young adulthood. Music making is a central activity within this institution.[25]

Puberty marks a moment of maturation; for girls, it begins with the onset of their menstrual cycle—an event some communities interpret as a sign that the young woman is fertile, has attained a level of physical maturity, and is thus ready for marriage. An iconic example is the so-called Dipo custom of the Krobo of Ghana, where girls who reach the age of puberty are taken in for a time, "prepared" through instruction in the performance of domestic duties and caring for self and family, and then offered to the community. The public display involves objectifying them, parading them in elegant but revealing costume to announce their readiness and availability for marriage and to attract the best possible suitors. Music making accompanies the Dipo procession through the town or village and in the course of various in-house rituals and prayers.[26]

Next in the life cycle is marriage, which also signifies a further level of maturity. It announces a willingness to take responsibility and may entail shifts in social location, expansion of the family unit, and reconfiguration of kinship ties. In pre-Christian Africa, marriage was not always a privileged moment within the life cycle (compared, say, to birth or especially death). Marriage (among the Dagomba, for instance) was sometimes prepared through a series of transactions between families, and music making often accompanied the movements of various entourages from the groom's house to the bride's, depending on the status of the individuals involved. The actual marriage ceremony, which often involved an exchange of material gifts and verbal transactions (commitments, queries, indirect insults, and self-congratulation), involved praise singing or the (musically constrained) reciting of genealogies. And music making often accompanied newlyweds to their dwelling place.

---

25. Kubik, "Mukanda—Boys' Initiation in Eastern Angola: Transference, Countertransference and Taboo Symbolism in an Age-Group Related Ritual Therapeutic Intervention," in *Weltkongress Psychotherapie. Mythos-Traum-Wirklichkeit. Ausgewählte Beiträge des 2. Weltkongresses für Psychotherapie*, ed. Alfred Pritz and Thomas Wenzel (Vienna: Facultas, 1999), 65–90; and Kenichi Tsukada, "Luvale Perceptions of Mukanda in Discourse and Music" (PhD diss., Queens University of Belfast, 1990).

26. In a 1963 publication, Hugo Huber offered a thorough description of dipo, or "initiation to womanhood and full tribal membership": *The Krobo: Traditional Social and Religious Life of a West African People* (St. Augustin: Anthropos Institute, 1963), 165–192. Although some of the material symbols used to perform the rites have changed in the five decades since Huber's book appeared, the basic framework and rationale remain unchanged. A measure of change in scholarly protocol may be observed by comparing Huber's 1963 study (of the Krobo) with a recent ethnography (of the Ewe) by Steven Friedson, *Remains of Ritual: Northern Gods in a Southern Land* (Chicago: University of Chicago Press, 2009).

Death ends one enactment of the life cycle, serving as a transition to the next world or, for those who believe in reincarnation, as the rebeginning of the life cycle. Those who believe that as some die they are replaced by others, or that specific ancestors return for second, third, or fourth lives, read the moment of death as simultaneously releasing an adjacent moment of rebirth, beginning the life cycle again. Death is by far the most important stage of the life cycle because it engenders reflection on the cycle as a whole; in that sense, it offers the most complete or synoptic view. This may explain, in part, why the kinds of musical behavior that death elicits are on the whole more elaborate, more intense, and more revealing of the soul of a given community than those of any other moment in the cycle. Preparation for burial, the burial itself, and the subsequent period of mourning all involve music in a series of events designed to help siblings, widows, relatives, and community members come to terms with the loss. Among the great funeral traditions of Africa, all of them invariably celebrated in and through music, are those of the Fon of Dahomey (studied by Herskovits), the Akan (studied by Nketia and Arhin), the Sukuma (studied by Hans Cory), the Igbo (studied by Meki Nzewi), and the Ewe (studied by James Burns).[27] The grandeur of these occasions varies according to the status of the deceased. I imagine that many of us retain memories of some of the funerals we have attended over the years. My own memories of two such occasions remain vivid. The death of the Asantehene Nana Opoku Ware in 1997, for example, was marked by vigorous music making, while the departure of Togbe Afede Assor, the Ewe paramount chief of Ho, was accompanied in August 2002 by an elaborate week-long celebration in music, dance, and ritual.

---

27. Melville Herskovits, *Dahomey*, vol. 1 (Evanston, IL: Northwestern University Press, 1967), 352–402; Nketia, *Funeral Dirges of the Akan People* (Achimota: Oxford University Press, 1955); Kwame Arhin, "The Economic Implications of Transformations in Akan Funeral Rites," *Africa: Journal of the International African Institute* 64, no. 3 (1994): 307–322; Hans Cory, *The Ntemi: The Traditional Rites in Connection With the Burial, Election, Enthronement and Magical Powers of a Sukuma Chief* (London: Macmillan, 1951); Nzewi, *Musical Sense and Musical Meaning: An Indigenous African Perception* (Amsterdam: Rozenberg Publishers, 2010), 64ff.; James Burns, *Female Voices from an Ewe Dance-Drumming Community: Our Music Has Become a Divine Spirit*, 105ff. Also of considerable interest is Gilbert Rouget, "La musique funéraire en Afrique noire: fonctions et formes," *Sonderdruck aus dem Bericht über den neuten internationalen Musikwissens-chaftlichen Kongress* II (1964): 143–155. Recent studies of African funerals are gathered together in *Funerals in Africa: Explorations of a Social Phenomenon*, ed. Michael Jindra and Joël Noret (New York: Berghahn Books, 2011). Funeral music is featured on dozens of recordings as well. See, for example, CD, *Sénoufo: Musiques es funerailles Fodonon* (1974), and CD, *Ceremonial Music from Northern Dahomey* (Phillips, 1974).

**Photo 1.1** Funeral, Tamale, Ghana.

**Photo 1.2** Adowa, Royal funeral, Kumase, Ghana.

**Photo 1.3** Fɔntɔmfrɔm, Royal funeral, Kumase, Ghana.

Given the rapid social changes that have taken place over the last half century or so, many institutional practices and associated modes of music making are being modified daily to reflect new social, economic, religious, or even aesthetic choices and realities. Some aspects of "tradition" are being abandoned, some are being transformed to yield newer traditions, and others are being replaced by modern ones. Of profound significance is the influence of the Christian church, the single most potent institution for eroding, diluting, and symbolically destroying many traditional African practices. The pouring of libation is replaced by "praying upward." Departed ancestors are no longer offered drinks with everyone's eyes open; we pray through Jesus Christ with our eyes shut. Christening and baptism now replace some naming rituals, so that the enactment of customary ways of naming (first-born son, first daughter, second child, child behind the twins, child at the end, and so on) and the deeply meaningful invocations that go with them are replaced by priest-led ceremonies in church. There was a time when a child would be ceremonially raised up to the skies (signifying the wish for him or her to have a similar elevation through life) or offered successive tastes of water and alcohol (the idea being that he or she would then grow up knowing the difference). Nowadays, an ordained minister may be on hand to say opening and closing prayers while a church choir, praise team, or singing band may be in attendance to provide choral music, complete with accompaniment on electronic instruments. Needless to say, conflicts some-times arise between traditional and modern impulses. Adherents of charismatic churches, for example, sometimes appropriate deep aspects of traditional cul-ture, which they then overlay with Christian language, doctrine, and practices. Intriguing cultural mixes result from such acts of appropriation and lead invari-ably to the emergence of new forms of expression.[28]

Funerals especially have been profoundly affected by Christian culture and beliefs. Older practices featuring all-night vigils marked by the singing of dirges, drumming, and dancing are now curtailed so that the Christians can sing their hymns and say their prayers until midnight. And the availability of various electric instruments and drum sets means that the rest of the night can be turned into a party of sorts, one that involves the playing of popular and neo-traditional music that keeps many young people happy.

Acknowledging these more recent influences should not lead us to the view that older traditions have simply been supplanted by newer practices. On the contrary, old and new coexist in a constellation, a kind of pluralistic cultural economy in which novel forms continue to emerge. In rural Africa, many older traditions remain as "authentic" as they ever were, even if the priest now wears a white glove, drinks imported Schnapps, or owns a cell phone. And in urban Africa, migrant groups sometimes import rural traditions from villages and proceed to intensify the markers of authenticity to counter the impact of the competing alien forms they encounter in urban spaces. The interface between tradition (a site for the display of an invented historical depth) and modernity (a complementary site for enacting and at the same time contesting various contemporary practices) is thus a key issue in contemporary African cultural criticism, one to which students of music stand poised to make a theoretical contribution. We will have occasion to revisit this in the course of this book.

## MUSIC IN FUNERAL TRADITIONS:
## AN AKPAFU EXAMPLE

Death occasions some of the most distinctive and deeply felt music making in Africa. The kinds of music, the density of musical events, and the periods of mourning vary with the status (commoner or royalty, wealthy or poor),

28. For a vivid example from 1999 of the conflict between tradition and modernity, see Tobias Robert Klein, "Fondling Breasts and Playing Guitar: Textual and Contextual Expressions of a Sociomusical Conflict in Accra," *Zeitschrift der Gesellschaft für Musiktheorie*, 2010, accessed September 9, 2015 http://www.gmth.de/zeitschrift/musiktheorie-musikwissenschaft/inhalt.aspx.

**Photo 1.4** "Tipre ne Amoakwa" Asantehemaa Ensemble, Kumase, Ghana.

gender, and age of the deceased and the cause of death ("good death" or "bad death," natural or accidental death). As an example of how the network of activities surrounding death and burial are permeated by music, I will describe the practices of one particular group, the Akpafu people of Ghana, using the ethnographic present of the mid-1980s.[29] Readers familiar with other African practices can compare them with the one offered here.

There are four main stages in the process of "taking a person and hiding him": announcing the death, bathing the corpse, laying the corpse in state for community viewing, and finally burying the corpse. Mourners' first task is to announce the death, and this they do by singing a specific dirge: "Who laid a mat for him so that he slept so deeply?" Performed by older, postmenopausal women, this dirge is an invariant element in the funeral scheme; it is sung only at this particular stage of mourning and at no other. If a prominent citizen dies, talking drums may be sounded to alert people to the fact that one of them has fallen. In the words of one of the dirges sung later, "[he] tripped and did not stand." News of the death goes out to various kin and kith both near and far.

The second stage is bathing the corpse. This is both a physical activity and a symbolic one: physical insofar as soap, sponge, and water are applied

---

29. This account is based on my article, "Music in the Funeral Traditions of the Akpafu," *Ethnomusicology* 32, no. 1 (1988): 75–105.

to the corpse by designated corpse bathers (usually older women), and symbolic because this act of cleansing is supposed to prepare the deceased for the
long journey ahead. Bathing is initiated by pouring libation to the ancestors.
Then several dirges are sung. The Akpafu deploy several event-specific dirges
while women bathe the corpse. One of them asks, "Who would dare to say that
s/he will never be bathed by the death sponge?"; another enjoins the wives of
the land to "bathe him for me." Elsewhere in the village, funeral drums are
beaten intermittently. Two favorite drum musics are "Otutuo" and "Opetresu,"
both reserved for people of status. Each features a polyrhythmic ensemble
of bells and drums repeating short patterns with an air of urgency. This is
drumming in the signal mode—no singing accompanies it and no decodable,
speech-based messages are beaten. We know only that something untoward
has happened.

At the third stage, the deceased is laid in state. Relatives, well wishers,
indeed the entire village (including children) file past the dead to pay their last
respects. This goes on for a good part of the evening and on through the night;
it coincides with the period of the most intense music making. At the heart
of these musical activities is the singing of dirges. The Akpafu dirge is pragmatically structured to serve as a vehicle for mourning, lamenting, and crying.
Typically, a dirge alternates spoken and sung sections, the whole accompanied
by wailing, ululation, spontaneous shouts and cries of pain, and exclamations
elicited by the particular death being mourned. Movement and dance sometimes accompany the performance of dirges, with the women pacing back and
forth, palms placed across the center of their scalps. Some of the dirges code
generalized responses to death or tragedy, while others mark specific moments
or events of the mourning period. During the all-night vigil, for example, there
is a midnight dirge ("We have touched Wɛnkɛ"), another that announces the
sighting of a "morning star," and a third that recognizes the cock's crowing.

The fourth stage is the actual burial, which is marked by an intensification of
expression. When all is said and done, one event-specific dirge, "Brɛbrɛgorɔ"
("Peace"), is sung. It tells the ancestors to forget everything that has been
uttered during this period of mourning: "We said it and said it, but we did not
(really) say it." This act of symbolic erasure is in fact a deconstructive move
designed to ensure that nothing uttered sincerely in the course of grieving
takes on grave consequences. If the ancestors were to respond to everything
said in the course of what is usually a difficult and emotionally charged period
of mourning, if they were to grant requests such as "Bring him back," "We
don't wish to be left behind," "I want to go with her," or "The river is full; let
us sail on a raft and go there," there would be obvious trouble. "Brɛbrɛgorɔ"
symbolically nullifies those aspects of mourners' verbal expression that might
affect them adversely in future. It is in effect a way of having their cake and

eating it too; that is, mourners say whatever they wish to say so that they can mourn deeply and without restraint, and then they cancel the undesirable consequences through one ritual song at the end.

Poetic expression in the Akpafu dirge is wide-ranging. It may convey individual sadness ("What have I done so as to be rendered naked?") and loss ("The crocodile has died leaving only the small fish" or "Mother who knows well how to cook is gone"), ask questions about how we mourn ("Who will I tell it to? I have no one"), and interrogate the meaning of life ("What have we come to this long world to come and take and eat?"). It may warn the living that their turn will come sooner than they think ("Get ready, death does not ask a person before it takes him"). Some dirges address the dead directly ("Why have you left me naked?," "Are you just lying there quietly [and not saying anything]?," "Who will look after me from now on?"), send messages to people on the other side of the river ("When you get there, we greet them"), and ascribe states of being to the dead ("Today it has cooled down for him"). Linguistic expression includes archaic words and expressions borrowed from neighboring groups who speak different languages. The dirge is especially rich in ideophones or picture words, words that intensify expression by depicting the sound of meaning.[30] Many texts are framed as questions to underline what is ultimately a philosophical thrust in the dirge. With its references to both the living and the dead, the material and spiritual worlds, the past and future, and the known and unknown, the Akpafu dirge provides a forum for enacting all manner of response to death.

Other music performed during the fourth phase of the funeral includes court music, sacred drums, and—especially nowadays—recreational music. If the deceased was a patron of the arts, the groups that he or she patronized will invariably be present to see him or her off. Sometimes groups from other villages with only the most tenuous connection to the deceased family will show up for the celebration. Occasionally, more than one group will perform at the same time.

It bears repeating that funerals are occasions not only for mourning but also for celebration. Even though the events are occasioned by death—a specific death—they splinter into myriad forms and resurrect a host of impulses, not all of which are a direct response to death. It is an interpretive mistake, therefore, to think of the funeral as an occasion on which sad songs are sung, on

30. For an excellent study of ideophones in Siwu, see Mark Dingemanse, "The Meaning and Use of Ideophones in Siwu" (PhD thesis, Max Plank Institute for Psycholinguistics, 2010), 51–76. Further information about the Akpafu, sound symbolism, and expressivity in African languages is available at Dingemanse's blog, "The Ideophone," accessed September 9, 2015, http://ideophone.org/.

which somber and restrained behavior is enacted. There surely are moments when a solemn demeanor is required, but there are also moments of vigorous and boisterous music making. Recreational drumming may alternate with crying songs, laments with the chants of warrior groups (*asafo*), and dirges with sacred drumming, the thought being that the authenticity of expression—the sincerity underlying weeping or shouting—is what ultimately matters.

After the burial, a specified period of mourning follows for the family of the bereaved. A widow, for example, may have her head shaven and go into confinement for forty days. After that, she will be released and married off to her oldest brother-in-law. The sharing of the property and debts of the deceased follows in the weeks after the burial. These postfunerary activities are not marked by official music making as such. In effect, they mark the transition from the period of ritual mourning to the old but at the same time new ordinary realm of existence.

The Akpafu funeral I have just described is the "traditional" one in the sense that it is a repository of practices and beliefs figured as being of ancient provenance. If you happen upon a funeral today, you will see and hear only some of what has been reported here, and some things will not be the same. This is the way of traditions in the modern world: variable rather than constant, precarious rather than fixed, always responding to contemporary challenges. During the first stage (announcing the death), for example, the availability of everything from motor transportation and a mailing system to telephones and even the Internet has altered the speed with which news of death is relayed. In the very old days, messengers walked to places to inform distantly placed relatives of the tragedy; nowadays, people in San Francisco, Melbourne, Paris, London, Mthatha, or Toronto will hear about the death within hours of it happening. Also, the availability of electric-powered refrigeration in mortuaries has significantly altered the traditional practice of burying the dead within a day or two so as not to risk the body decomposing. (This, however, remains the prescribed practice in Muslim communities.) For those without the means, the option of postponing the burial by paying extremely high mortuary fees is not available. Affluent families, by contrast, keep their dead in mortuaries for months as they make elaborate preparations for the funeral. There are no formal music-making activities to mark the period during which the corpse is kept in the mortuary, although this sometimes changes if the deceased was a figure of high status or a chief.

Music making, too, has been significantly altered in modern times. Christian services have sometimes replaced dirge-centered mourning, and not only hymns and anthems but also foreign-made films with voice-overs in the local language facilitate propagandizing on behalf of some evangelical Christian sect or other. Drum sets have replaced traditional drums in some locales, and the symbolic aspects of talking drumming, dirge singing, wailing, and crying songs have been replaced by a less differentiated and—dare I say—less nuanced cosmopolitan set of practices.

Institutions change, of course, and the African funeral continues to evolve. As long as there is life, there will be death, and life-loving Africans will continue to use occasions of death to affirm life. They will hold on to some musical practices while discarding others, and they will do this neither consistently nor thoroughly. These actions amount to a form of performance, and they point to the precariousness and fragility that underpin many structures in contemporary Africa.

## CATEGORIZING THE VARIETIES OF AFRICAN MUSIC: THE TRADITIONAL-POPULAR-ART GRID

I began this chapter with remarks on what is said (or not said) about music; I then described some of the contexts in which music is made. Two frameworks were introduced to enable us to think through the varieties of African music: a tripartite scheme encompassing work, ritual, and entertainment, and a scheme based on the life cycle. There is a third framework into which we can distribute the genres of music making as "traditional," "popular," and "art" music. Like earlier frameworks, this one, too, will need to be nuanced in application, but it will serve adequately to orient us to the origins and character of the principal genres of African music.[31]

Tradition has age and a mythical grounding on its side. For some people, it indexes the precolonial (i.e., African music before it was inflected or, as some would say, contaminated by other music). Traditional music is wedded to those things that traditional people do in the context of traditional life, and so it might include court music, ritual drumming at festivals and healing ceremonies, and funeral dirges. Some like to think of this music as authentic, as a symbol of true Africa, as old and ostensibly resistant to change in its essential aspects. This is because its sound environment contains some of the most distinctive traits associated with African music, including its polyphonic and rhythmic principles, linguistic and temporal structures, and manipulations of timbre.

Popular music belongs first and foremost to an urban sphere. Its origins go back to the early 1900s when, as a result of European presence in the coastal areas of West Africa, later spreading to other parts of the continent, new musical

---

31. A lucid and important early discussion, with emphasis on the "popular," may be found in Karin Barber, "Popular Arts in Africa," *African Studies Review* 30 (1987): 1–78. Also of interest is her introduction to *Readings in African Popular Culture* (Bloomington: Indiana University Press, 1997). See also my *Representing African Music*, xiv–xv and 15–20.

instruments, ideas, and imaginings became available.[32] A favorite instrument was the guitar, which was played by seamen and brought into view a new sound world. Although stringed instruments existed in traditional communities before that (fine examples include the Akan *seperewa,* the Mande Kora, and various Zande and Ugandan harp lutes), the guitar came with a different sort of harmonic baggage. Performance of certain kinds of popular music necessitated a new formality in dress and led to the wearing of suits and ties and evening dresses; high-life music was performed on these occasions for nonparticipating audiences.

Few people who live in an African city or town nowadays can escape the sound of African popular music, with its movement-eliciting beat. It is heard on radios; in clubs, cafes, dance halls, schools, and community centers; and on public transportation via taxis, lorries, and buses. Because it began as an overt synthesis of European (including American) and African musical elements, popular music tends to attract descriptions like hybrid, creole, syncretic, and mixed. Its sound is unmistakable: repetitions of brief harmonic progressions executed by a band leader (singer, guitarist, trumpeter) and his supporting cast, and catchy, memorable rhythms and sung melodies bearing a social message. Along with such popular arts as painting and literature, popular music has become a vital component of modern African living.[33]

"Traditional" and "popular" are generally larger categories than "art"— larger in terms of the numbers of producers and consumers. With art music, we enter a terrain that seems at first blush fully European derived; it comes with connotations of highness and elitism on the one hand and alienation and mimicry on the other. Art music, whose origins date back to the mid-nineteenth century, is music composed on paper by literate African musicians who have been exposed to a portion of the high-art tradition of Europe. Individual works bearing titles like sonata, symphony, cantata, and opera are claimed by individual composers and performed to listening audiences. Although the number of composers active in this tradition is relatively modest (compared to the thousands who "compose" traditional or popular music), the symbolic value of art music in postcolonial Africa is high.

Art music may be regarded as the equivalent of the tradition of African letters, a modern development made possible by colonial education and the

32. For an accessible guide to West African popular music, see John Collins, *West African Pop Roots* (Philadelphia: Temple University Press, 1992). The essays by Andrew L. Kaye, Cynthia Schmidt, Kazadi Wa Mukuna, Angela Impey, Christopher Waterman, and David Coplan in *Africa: The Garland Encyclopedia of World Music,* ed. Ruth M. Stone, offer valuable information and perspectives. On contemporary hip hop, see *Hip Hop Africa: New African Music in a Globalizing World,* ed. Eric Charry (Bloomington: Indiana University Press, 2012).

33. For an authoritative description of popular music's reach, see Kubik, "'Intra-African Streams: Super Areas of 20th c. Popular Music Styles," in Stone, *Africa: The Garland Encyclopedia of World Music,* 322.

circulation of European printed materials and their derived forms. The counterparts of composers like Ephraim Amu, Ayo Bankole, Bongani Ndodana-Breen, Halim El-Dabh, Akin Euba, Anthony Okelo, Fela Sowande, and Joshua Uzoigwe are the writers Chinua Achebe, Ayi Kwei Armah, Ngugi wa Thiongo, Wole Soyinka, and Chimamanda Adichie. But although many readers will surely have heard about or even read the works of these writers, few will know their affiliate composers. This is partly because the dissemination of art-music compositions has proven to be institutionally more demanding than the dissemination of literary works, partly because the works themselves are often in an unfamiliar musical language, and partly because the individualistic ethos that grounds art music stands in stark contrast to that which traditional and popular music are based on. African art music was initially ignored or greeted with skepticism and prejudice by critics, but its reception has improved in recent decades as more and more festivals devoted to art music have been organized in Europe, China, the Americas, and, of course, Africa itself.

What explanatory power might the traditional-popular-art grid hold? Its descriptive adequacy is signaled by the fact that practically all the major genres of African music can be accommodated within it. The three categories are not hard and fast, however; they will therefore need to be qualified in application. To show what insights the tripartition makes possible, it will be helpful to think critically through it under the guidance of six criteria that underpinned our earlier discussion of genres and occasions for music making: place in society; composers/producers and consumers; use of oral or written media; affiliation with precolonial, colonial, or postcolonial spheres; kinds of musical influence sedimented in them; and propensity for change. While some abstraction and provisional generalization is unavoidable in an undertaking like this, it is hoped that these internal comparisons will continue to fix and at the same time undermine the affiliations of various African genres.[34]

Traditional music is generally rural based, but increasing waves of rural to urban migration have ensured that it is cultivated in significant enclaves in and around urban spaces as well. Although popular and art music are born in urban environments, popular music travels in and out of the city, while art music is locked in the cosmopolitan sphere. Traditional music is communal, composers often doubling as performers; many traditional composers hold an anonymous status. Popular-music bands feature composer-performers, some of whom acquire star status; art-music composers are always named individuals to whom specific works are credited.

A great deal of traditional music is based on poetry and dance, and performance is usually open to people who share language, blood, or a belief system.

---

34. Barber, "Popular Arts in Africa."

It is in this sense ethnically bound, although the modern nation-state has facilitated interethnic contact through school, church-based cultural troupes, work, and forms of urban socialization. Art music is mostly written, popular music is occasionally written (more often sketchily rather than comprehensively), and traditional music is almost never written, operating within a dynamic oral/aural sphere. Traditional music has a lineage that reaches back to precolonial Africa, art music originated in the nineteenth century as a byproduct of the missionary encounter, and popular music is essentially a twentieth- and twenty-first-century phenomenon. Art and popular music are direct products of colonial contact with Europe. Traditional music has remained relatively stable, whereas popular music has been in a constant and relentless state of flux. Genres have their own internal histories and are subject to differently paced diachronic changes. For example, some sacred court music associated with institutions that prescribe the stability and authority of a self-consciously maintained tradition shows relatively little diachronic change (the various horn and drum ensembles cultivated at the court of the Asantehene are good examples[35]). By contrast, recreational music, whose creation is often stimulated by external, modern, or foreign influences, can seem to change rapidly. Innovations in popular music are often on the surface and readily identified, while those in traditional music are sometimes hidden or unfold over a longer period of time.

As for style, popular music is openly promiscuous, borrowing idioms from diverse sources, disguising them only slightly, and embracing the syncretic and the interstitial as positive values. Art music, too, shares the syncretism of popular music, but it intensifies the intentionality of such syncretism intellectually. Popular music often claims an immediate novelty, whereas traditional music wears an ancient look; art music is also mostly styled as new, but it has the option of cultivating an old sound by packaging tradition as new. Popular music also sometimes takes advantage of this mode of packaging. On the level of practice, traditional music remains the most widespread, essentially retaining its affiliation with rural Africa, as well as pockets of urban and semiurban Africa. Its dance and ritual roots have inhibited meaningful consumption in recorded form, while its use of indigenous languages has muted its potential cross-ethnic appeal. Some popular music, too, is ethnically confined, but a great deal of it is urbane or cosmopolitan in orientation, thanks not only to its derived harmonic and melodic idioms but also to its use of colonial languages (like English or French) or trans-regional languages that serve as lingua francas (Luba, Kiswahili, or Hausa).

35. See Joseph Kaminski, *Asante Ntahera Trumpets in Ghana: Culture, Tradition, and Sound Barrage* (Farnham, England: Ashgate, 2012), and Kwasi Ampene and Nana Kwadwo Nyantakyi III, *Engaging Modernity: Asante in the Twenty-First Century* (Ann Arbor, MI: University Lithoprinters, 2014).

The traditional-popular-art framework captures broad, normative tendencies within a complex and variegated set of musical practices. Ideally, the foregoing generalizations will serve as provocations, invitations to reflect upon the dynamics of production and consumption in specific contexts. We might ask, for example, whether there was any precolonial popular music of significant standing, or whether yesterday's popular music has not become today's traditional music. We may wonder whether and how traditional music will survive the current forces of globalization. What will become of traditional repertoires after their sponsoring social institutions have been dissolved? Can traditional music ever attain an international but nonorientalist status even while retaining its close affiliations with indigenous dance, belief, custom, and language, or does the path to cosmopolitanism necessarily entail a shedding of communalism? Can art music take root and eventually blossom on African soil, or is it doomed to foreign orientation?

The issues raised by the traditional-popular-art trichotomy will come up from time to time throughout the book. My aim in this preliminary discussion has been simply to recognize the affiliations of different kinds of material and to suggest generic homes for them as points of departure for a more nuanced discussion. I will now take up the connection between musical structure and social structure as another issue in the exploration of music's social affiliations.


## MUSICAL STRUCTURE AND SOCIAL STRUCTURE

To say that the musical-structure-versus-social-structure conjunction is a veritable *topos* of ethnomusicological research is not to exaggerate. Scholars like Alan Lomax, Alan Merriam, Steven Feld, and Marina Roseman, among others, have contributed to our understanding of its dynamics. The topic appears in the writings of a number of influential Africanists as well. Charles Keil's "ethnography of music in a classless society"—the subtitle of his book on Tiv song—explores the mutual imbrication of the social and the musical. John Chernoff is equally alert to social mediation. Speaking specifically of one of the canonical instrumental ensembles of West Africa, he writes:

> The Ewes sometimes think of their drums as a family. The bell is like the heartbeat which keeps things steady. Kagan is the baby brother; Kidi is the mother; Sogo is the elder brother; Kroboto and Totogi, when they are played, are the twin brothers; Atsimewu, the master drum, is the father, who, according to their tradition, is in charge of everything.[36]

36. Chernoff, *African Rhythm and African Sensibility*, 43.

Mapping ensemble structure onto a kinship unit in this way is not uncommon. In some traditions, it is the mother who is in charge, not the father. Meki Nzewi, for example, reminds us of the "mother drum" among the Igbo, the drum that organizes the rest of the ensemble. Like Chernoff, Nzewi is often led to the social residue in music. He explains cross-rhythm in terms of two moving objects nearing each other in space but avoiding collision at the last minute, and he likens this to the strategic withholding of the price of a bride to intensify desire. Within "the instrumental heterogeneity of a music ensemble in the Central African Republic," Vincent Dehoux identifies one of three xylophones as the "youngest child" (*kpembe*), while Maurice Djenda is said to have described one particular *mvet* (a popular Cameroonian instrument) as "polygamous."[37] Arom and Frédéric Voisin identify in Central Africa "various types of metaphoric designation of the slats of the xylophone." One slat "commands," another "responds," and a third "gives the song." Slats may assume roles such as "mother," "husband," "children," or "grandchildren."[38] Moya Aliya Malamusi writes similarly about the *ngorombe* (panpipe) music of a Mr. Sakha Bulaundi, a Mozambiquean refugee in Malawi in 1990:

> These pipes are often equated with people, as if they were part of a family. Thus among the panpipes there is a "father" and "mother," perhaps a "child," a "grandfather" and "grandmother." These names are given according to the pitch of the panpipe. The high sounding one given the name "child," a lower sounding one "mother," and the very low sounding pipe is called "old person" (*nkhalamba*).[39]

Finally, Nketia, in several writings, has shown a keen awareness of music's social role, including its evolving historical contexts; indeed, he once devoted an entire article to demonstrating "the juncture of the social and the musical."[40]

---

37. Nzewi, *African Music: Theoretical Content*, 36–39; cited in Maurice Djenda, "Central African Republic," *Grove Music Online*, accessed December 2012; Kubik, "African Tone Systems: A Reassessment," *Yearbook for Traditional Music* 17 (1985): 32.

38. Simha Arom and Frédéric Voisin, "Theory and Technology in African Music," in Stone, *The Garland Encyclopedia of World Music*. Vol. 1: *Africa*, 257.

39. Moya Aliya Malamusi, Jacket notes for the CD, *From Lake Malawi to the Zambezi: Aspects of Music and Oral Literature in South-east Africa in the 1990s* (Frankfurt: Popular African Music, 1999).

40. Originally published in *World of Music* 23, no. 2 (1981): 22–39, "The Juncture of the Social and the Musical: The Methodology of Cultural Analysis" is now reprinted in *Ethnomusicology and African Music: Collected Papers*. Vol. 1: *Modes of Inquiry and Interpretation* (Accra: Afram Publications, 2005), 71–92.

From a systematic point of view, we might ask what exactly the entities are in these diverse conceptualizations of function. First there is "music" and then "society"; then there is "musical structure" and "social structure"; finally there is "sound structure" and (again) "social structure." Although they carry slightly different connotations, the pairs of terms overlap, of course, and may even seem equivalent at a certain level of abstraction. In paradigmatic terms, "music," "musical structure," and "sound structure" are held to be equivalent, while "society" and "social structure" are also said to be equivalent. While the latter equivalence seems unproblematic, the former is not so straightforward. For some, sound and music are different entities for the simple reason that while all music is in principle made up of sounds, not all sounds qualify as music. The challenge of defining musical structure and social structure, therefore, arises less from the "society" end of things and more from the special nature of musical art.

Evaluating previous attempts to correlate musical structures with societal structures, Klaus Wachsmann and Peter Cooke, writing specifically about Africa in 1980, noted that "since the mid-20th century such ideas have become fashionable, tending to become dominant theory in the attempt to explain African musical structures." Then comes this warning: "in the absence of a music history they must remain mere conjecture."[41] Indeed, it appears that what we need are histories rather than *a* history to ground such explorations, and these will surely come with the accumulation of research data. In the meantime, we will continue to regard the fundamental claim that the sonic material of music—any music—embodies an "extramusical" supplement as at once suggestive but not always available for empirical verification.

There is one aspect of this equation for which no reasonable grounds for disputation exist, however—the materialist explanation. For example, given the material conditioning of life, work, and leisure, it is not surprising that natural or material resources present opportunities for constructing different kinds of instruments. People who live in forest areas and have access to trees often make drums out of tree trunks and drum heads from animal skin. Those who have access to bamboo make flutes or xylophones out of bamboo. And those who live where iron is plentiful often forge iron bells and castanets from this material. Felicia Mundell and John Brearley make much the same point about Botswana: "vegetation further restricts the construction of instruments to those types for which the new materials can be found locally, so that drums are generally found in forest areas, flutes where there are reeds and unaccompanied choral singing in open

41. Klaus Wachsmann and Peter Cooke, "Africa," 149.

grass plains."[42] These habits were especially evident in ancient, subsistence communities, and they are reminiscent of a time when interethnic trade and travel were relatively modest compared with today.

Mere availability of raw material does not mean, however, that the imagination to transform material into sound-producing objects is there as well. The motivation for music making, the choice of sound ideals, and the domestication and translation of social configurations into a sonic realm emerge from a complex set of circumstances and belief systems, some of them frankly mysterious. The vegetation surrounding the Akpafu, for example, includes bamboo and millet stalks, but the Akpafu have so far not invested in flutes or xylophones with bamboo slabs. There was a time when the Akpafu smelted iron, but they were more likely to forge implements such as hoes and cutlasses, which could be sold for profit, than to construct instruments like castanets and bells. A similar disconnect between material endowment and its appropriation for musical use is found in many communities. So while it is plausible that what a community has (whether through natural endowment or by acquisition) provides opportunities for instrument construction and therefore particular forms of music making, other priorities may intervene to render the connection unpredictable.

If the material level of the equation between musical and social structure is at the very least relatively plausible, what is one to make of the symbolic level? What kinds of symbolic or analogical transfer are possible? This is where things get somewhat complicated. Recall, for example, that aspect of Lomax's cantometrics project that sought predictive value for certain kinds of social arrangements in musical structure. Without reproducing all of his variables, categories, and modes of correlation, let us simply note the challenges involved in mapping one particular formal principle, the ubiquitous call-and-response procedure, on to a social configuration. Call and response features a leader and followers, big man and smaller men, individual and group. Thus, societies with strong hierarchic social organization (typically, a chief and his elders on one side, and common people on the other) might be expected to use the call-and-response principle, reproducing the chieftaincy arrangement in a performing ensemble so that the latter becomes a microcosm of the former. While there are indeed societies in which hierarchic political organization supports call and response in performance, not all manifestations of the principle involve pronounced hierarchies in society. Moreover, there are so many levels of cultural understanding of what it means to be a caller that we should be open to the possibility that there are other modes of transfer besides the iconic. A caller is not always the "boss" in an asymmetrical power relationship with his or her

---

42. Felicia Mundell and John Brearley, "Botswana."

subjects. Because the chorus serves as the foundation, because it elects and sends the caller, it has the power to undermine the caller if he or she fails to deliver. In this interpretation, the chorus, although a collective, has stronger claims to being "boss" than does the lead singer. The external contrast between one and many, which tempts students consumed by individualism into interpreting one as controller and many as controlled, may actually enshrine an inverted set of values.

Probably the most convincing enactment of the musical structure/social structure dialectic is in the embodiment of egalitarianism. The paradigmatic example is of various Pygmy groups in central Africa, whose brand of nonhierarchic polyphony is often said to mirror their nonhierarchic or egalitarian lifestyle. The frequent (though by no means absolute) absence of a strong call-and-response pattern, for instance, performs a leveling function. The Pygmy example is persuasive from an external or organizational point of view: just as many live without a chief and big men, so they organize their performing forces and the actual musical material to reflect a functional egalitarianism. But it is not clear to what extent this kind of gross mapping can produce insightful musical analysis. For one thing, hierarchies of various sorts are unavoidable when it comes to ordering tones and rhythms as music. Presumably, the pygmies' favorite pentatonic collection is chosen from a variety of options, the choice of melodic pitches is not random but based on a hierarchical conception of the source set, and the varying intensities produced in performance are intended to mirror priorities in expressive articulation. In short, while a sense of egalitarianism may be helpful in orienting us to macrolevel organization, the practical acts of composing and performing very quickly devolve into discriminatory, nonegalitarian practices.

It would be wise to keep an open mind about the nature of the connection with social structure. The alliance can be enacted positively (as when an aspect of social structure is reproduced directly in musical structure) or negatively (as when the two contradict each other). It is also possible that no generative relations are obtained between the two, or that the analytical units that would allow meaningful comparison are far too coarse to support any significant correlations. What we must *not* do is treat the isomorphism between musical structure and social structure as necessary or axiomatic beyond its most mundane sense.

Finally, it may just be that although African music has been burdened with contextual explanations for the better part of its history, it retains a measure of autonomy at an immanent level. Music exhibits the movements peculiar to its mode of proceeding. Thus, the modal consistency of a corpus of funeral dirges, the metrical stability of a dance, or the constancy of the melodic archetype that regulates a praise song may be "purely musical" processes that are "social" only in the most mundane sense. To uphold this level of autonomy is to uphold the distinctiveness of musical art. To deny this kind of autonomy is to endorse the sort of equivalence theory that would claim, for example, that poetry can be translated into music without any losses, music into painting, painting into architecture, and so on. But none of these expressive domains can substitute for another, however much their internal morphologies resemble each other. So, without disputing the possibility that music may be helpfully conceptualized as "social text," music itself is not ultimately reducible to anything but a musical text.

## CIRCULAR REPRESENTATION OF MUSIC AND/IN SOCIETY

The instinct to put it all together, to display the place of music in society in a single, synchronic state (i.e., as if constituent events were frozen in time and space, unfolding outside the sphere of history) has led a number of scholars to use circular diagrams. Creating such circles is a useful way of imposing conceptual order on the varieties of African music that circulate within individual communities. As a final framework for thinking about the relationship between music and society, I will now present four such diagrams along with independent remarks by Steven Feld. The circular representations were devised by Simha Arom, Suzanne Fürniss, Polo Vallejo, and Meki Nzewi for the Banda Linda, Aka, Gogo, and Igbo, respectively. All five scholars are united in shared concerns about the nature of a community's musical corpus and how to make sense of it conceptually, and their methods may prove suggestive for readers seeking a synoptic mode of representing music in society.

In his article "New Perspectives for the Description of Orally Transmitted Music," Arom aims to describe as fully as possible the *music* of an oral tradition (see Figure 1.1).[43] Although he recognizes the existence of both musical and "extramusical" data, he gives priority to the musical. Four concentric circles represent four different sorts of data. The first or innermost is the musical material itself, including the body of works and the elements that enable composition and performance. The second circle consists of "the material and conceptual tools which contribute to the validation of the data of the first circle." These include terms, names of instruments, and ways in which indigenous people talk specifically about their music. To the third circle belong "socio-cultural function(s) which integrate the musical corpus," as well as

43. Simha Arom, "New Perspectives for the Description of Orally Transmitted Music," *World of Music* 23 (1981): 57.

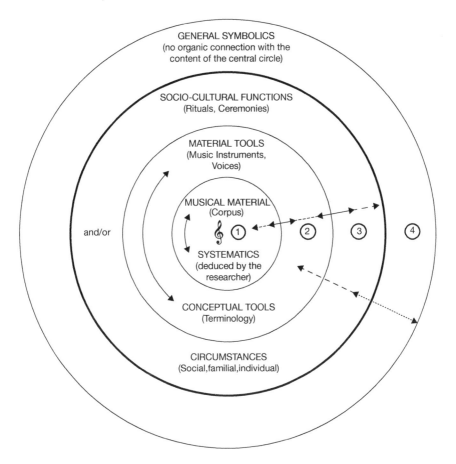

Figure 1.1 Simha Arom's circular diagram of music and discourse in an oral culture.

"circumstances" with which the music is associated. Rituals, ceremonies, and dances are examples of sociocultural functions, while social and kinship relations exemplify "circumstances." There is a fourth circle that plays a supplementary role. It includes "data belonging to the general symbolics," notably "myths of acquisition." Because there is no *organic* relation between such myths and the music itself, this circle is placed farthest from the core.

Music and its enabling structures are organized hierarchically. Circles are arranged according to the degree of organic relation they bear to the music. So when the Banda Linda, for example, tell stories about the origins of musical instruments, these are admitted only to the fourth circle, the one that is farthest from the center, because such stories offer little information about the musical repertory itself. Arom does not discount their affective value; he insists only on their conceptual distance from the musical material and its accompanying "systematics."

It is instructive to compare Arom's view in this 1981 article to Steven Feld's somewhat analogous attempt to capture "the social life of sounds" in a 1984 article, "Sound Structure as Social Structure."[44] Like Arom, Feld follows Jean Molino in conceiving of music as "a total social fact." This in turn leads him to postulate six broad areas of inquiry: competence, form, performance, environment, theory, and value and equity. Using a series of questions designed to stimulate further inquiry into each of these areas, Feld invites us to think through musical cultures in a broad way. His own data come from the Kaluli, whose culture is evidently rich in metatheoretical expression.

Feld's mode of inquiry forgoes two of the features that Arom insists on. The first is hierarchy, which does not enter into Feld's considerations here. This may be because the Kaluli, unlike the Banda Linda, are an egalitarian culture; it may also be because for Feld, the "six broad areas of inquiry into music as a total social fact" are equally valuable points of entry into the culture—because further prioritization is likely to distort, it is avoided. A second difference is that Feld is less drawn to the objectivity claimed by Arom's innermost circle. Very little is admitted as being of conceptual relevance unless it is in some way validated or at least valued by the Kaluli. In other words, Arom's second circle is indistinguishable from the first in Feld's view. The objectivity claimed by Arom in being able to define the corpus and deduce its "systematics" is thrown out the window by Feld; in his scheme, culture bearers are never excluded from any significant acts of theorizing.

The circular representation devised by Suzanne Fürniss to represent "the musical universe of the Aka" places a treble clef in the centermost position—surely the ultimate sign that this is a music-centered scheme (Figure 1.2).[45] Moving outward into the next circle, we encounter musical instruments ("tools of music making"), including voices and handclaps. Vernacular designations of various genres or repertories are shown in the next circle, but this "intermediate" circle has no independent existence from the last, outermost circle, which gives "the circumstance or function" of the performance of each repertoire. Aka culture is a song-based culture, and Fürniss's representation captures the essential vocality of culture's expression.

44. Steven Feld, "Sound Structure as Social Structure," *Ethnomusicology* 28, no. 3 (1984): 383–409.

45. Suzanne Furniss, "Aka Polyphony," in *Analytical Studies in World Music*, ed. Michael Tenzer (New York: Oxford University Press, 2006), 166.

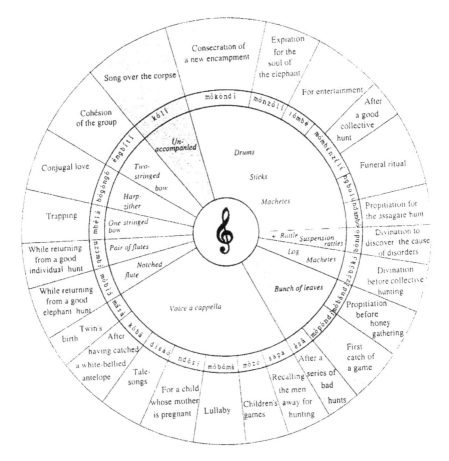

Figure 1.2  Suzanne Fürniss's circular diagram of the Aka musical universe.

Operating within the same intellectual lineage, Polo Vallejo has distributed the reality of the Gogo musical universe into a series of concentric circles with further refinements and emphases (Figure 1.3).[46] His core is now left blank—perhaps an even stronger indication of the transcendent status of the music itself?—and is enclosed by three circles. The first "specifies whether the repertory is associated with the voice or with instruments." The second gives generic names in the local language. And the third specifies the occasions on which the repertory is performed, everything from lullabies through songs to mark the first menstruation to those that bring rain. Like Fürniss's, Vallejo's

46. Polo Vallejo, *Patrimonio musical Wagogo: Contexto y sistematica* (Madrid: Fundación Sur, 2007), 109.

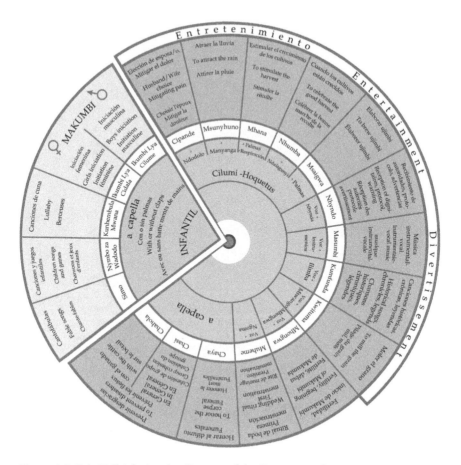

**Figure 1.3**  Polo Vallejo's circular diagram of the Gogo musical universe.

synopsis shows how the musical society as a whole (including its activating forces) is brought to life instrumentally.

A fourth example of circular representation comes from the work of Meki Nzewi (Figure 1.4).[47] Unlike those of Arom and his students, Nzewi's has a built-in diachronic element because its aim is to represent the form and content of an "event performance cycle" of Ese music. The diagram enables Nzewi to show all five segments of the performance (he calls them "compartments"), specifying what takes place in each segment ("nature of events"), the "musical characteristics" (character of accompaniment, tempo, and whether language is essential or not), and the indigenous nomenclature ("Ese music categories"). Again, things that are deemed essential are also found in the three earlier representations by Arom, Fürniss, and Vallejo: indigenous categories for music, musical features

47. Nzewi, *Musical Sense and Musical Meaning*, 187.

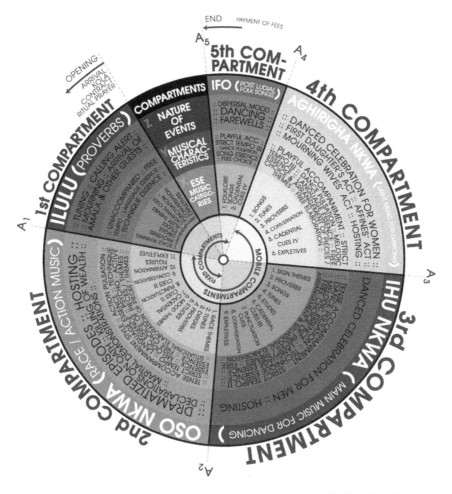

**Figure 1.4** Meki Nzewi's diagram of an "event performance cycle" of Ese (Igbo) music.

or systematics, and sociocultural functions. Nzewi does not say whether a qualitative change accompanies movement from the innermost to outermost circle; if it did, priority would seem to reside in "Ese music categories" and thus align Nzewi's ideology with Feld's. If no such prioritization was intended, we would still say that all four authors subscribe to more or less identical parameters as they seek to characterize the dynamics of music in society.

Not all circular representations imply internal closure. The kind of closure inscribed in synchronic framing often seems firmer than the necessarily provisional closure that marks daily music-making activities. Nevertheless, circles convey qualities of routine, repetition, and the "problematizing" of beginnings and endings, and this makes them suitable conveyors of the bases of African musical expression.

## CONCLUSION

In this chapter, we have explored the place of music in African society. I began by observing the absence of a word for music in African languages and then went on to outline some of what is said when Africans talk about "music." Next I described three main occasions for music making (work, ritual, and recreation), the role of music in a typical life cycle, and the place of music in one particular set of funeral traditions. I provided a simple tripartite scheme for categorizing all known genres of African music (traditional music, popular music, art music), and I finished with reflections on the relationship between sound structure and social structure, noting the importance of circular representation of musical societies.

Practically every survey of African music acknowledges the place of music in society. Although the preposition *in* sometimes competes with the conjunction *and*, the basic motivation is unchanged: to acknowledge the complex ways in which music and music making are shaped by—and in turn shape—a larger "social" process. When Klaus Wachsmann and Peter Cooke called for a history of African music to help us get a better handle on the musical structure/ social structure question, they were in effect urging us to be cautious about accepting the validity or relevance of theoretical ideas that have not been tried on African soil, corroborated by African experiences, or subjected to an African test. African students should be encouraged to evaluate particular theories according to whether they apply (or do not apply) in their communities, and to accept or reject them accordingly. Thus, every one of the notions that framed our discussion of music and society should be thought of through as many African contexts as possible: the absence of a word for music but the existence of discourse about music, the sheer presence of and presumed necessity for music making, the participatory and communal ethos inscribed in many forms, music's integration with sociocultural events, and the autonomy or relative autonomy of African music. In this chapter, I have sought to provide a background to coming discussion of the mechanics of musical organization.

# 2

# Musical Instruments

Africa's wealth in musical instruments is legendary. The primordial bow, now transformed into a modern concert instrument; innumerable varieties of drum; the balafon or xylophone; mbiras, castanets, bells, and rattles; harp lutes and one-stringed fiddles; bamboo flutes and elephant horns—all these exist alongside instruments of adoption such as guitars, trumpets, saxophones, harmoniums, and electronic keyboards. Sound-producing objects serve as outlets for individual and group expression. Just as occasions for music making are many and diverse, so the material means are abundant.

An inquiry into Africa's musical instruments is a multifaceted endeavor. At least four groups of questions might be posed. First are issues of manufacture. What are instruments made of? Are the materials naturally occurring, or are they synthetic and factory produced? What kinds of technology facilitate the construction of particular instruments? To what extent do changes in design inflect patterns of "consumption"? Second are historical issues. Where and how did a given instrument originate? What patterns of human migration, interethnic trade, political domination, and cultural exchange account for the current distribution of musical instruments? Third are questions pertaining to pedagogy, social function, and symbolism. How and by whom is an instrument learned? On what occasions is it played? Is it used in both secular and sacred contexts? Which aspects of a community's artistic conventions or spiritual beliefs are embodied in the physical design of instruments? Fourth and finally are issues of compositional process and musical aesthetics. What is the nature of the acoustic resource, the range of sounds available on a given instrument? Which sounds are admitted as music, and which are not? Do cultural insiders articulate a distinction between sound and music, or are all sounds potentially musical? How stable over time is a given sound ideal? How are available sounds recognized, understood, described, and evaluated? What and how does music communicate to knowledgeable listeners?

It would take not one but several volumes to answer these questions for the many societies of Sub-Saharan Africa. I raise them here not as yet another programmatic assertion of Africa's complexity but as suggestions for consideration in connection with specific regions and as a stimulus to research. Some answers may already be found in the great works of African organology produced in the twentieth century, among them books by scholars from Ankermann to Djedje.[1] There is, in fact, hardly a study of music in an African community that does not devote some attention, however fleetingly, to its musical instruments. To no small extent, then, answers to questions relating to origins, construction, performance techniques, and the use of African musical instruments, although packaged differently, are available in the literature. Some answers are implicit, while others are explicit, and many of them occur as part of self-contained studies of one African community or another, not necessarily as part of a continent-wide comparative study.

There is something of a paradox about this situation, however. In spite of the apparent abundance of information, the cumulative knowledge about instruments appears to raise just as many questions as it answers. What is most pointedly portrayed by this knowledge is the uncommonly precarious and delicate condition of many African soundscapes. The intended and the fortuitous, the planned and the accidental, and the improvised and the pre-composed exist side by side. As telltale signs of historical, material, and social processes, musical instruments reveal with unparalleled force the extent to which influences from the Middle East, Indonesia, Europe, and elsewhere are sedimented at the deepest, most "traditional" layers of African society. And because Africa's material resources are not always within her control, the story of musical instruments often betrays the power dynamics of external influences readily—more readily, perhaps, than narratives about creative procedures evident in rhythm, melody, and polyphony. In this as in other attempts to interpret contemporary African reality, then, an approach that is flexible and open to frequent improvisation will serve us far better than one that is cast in stone and overly confident about its ability to distinguish the "real" from the inauthentic.

How, then, might we approach a study of musical instruments? As with the place of music in society, musical instruments are best understood

1. See works by Bernhard Ankermann, Pervical Kirby, Klaus Wachsmann, Bertil Söderberg, Jos Gansemans, C. Da Cruz, Hugo Zemp, Olga Boone, Roger Blench, Jean-Sebastien Laurenty, Kwabena Nketia, Gerhard Kubik, Hugh Tracey, Gilbert Rouget, Paul Berliner, Eric Charry, Andre Schaeffner, Andy Kaye, Jackie Djedje, and several others in the bibliography.

within nested layers embodying different registers of social reality. At the deepest level are instruments associated with old Africa, instruments such as drums, iron bells, and musical bows that have endured for generations and have withstood changes in morphology, symbolism, and practical use without discarding their essences, and may therefore be said to possess great historical depth. A second layer consists of instruments that originated elsewhere (such as xylophones, one-stringed fiddles, and hourglass drums) but have acquired a permanence that has won them "traditional" status. Third is a layer comprising newer instruments, many of them imported from Europe and America during the last two hundred or so years, including organs; harmoniums and pianos; band instruments like saxophones, trumpets, and guitars; and even orchestral instruments like violins, cellos, and double basses. Although they are of manifestly foreign origins, some of them have gradually acquired local "accents" and will eventually stake unqualified claims to being considered African.

It is worth emphasizing that the musical traditions that sponsor these collective instrumental resources exist within the same timeframe—they are coeval. So, although thinking in terms of origins might assign the three layers respectively to distant, not-so-distant, and recent pasts, a synchronic account would draw attention to their mutual existence today. Such an account would also highlight several derivative instruments made in response to foreign models or as a result of the interaction between different groups. What we are witnessing in Africa today is a distinctive configuration in which old and new, traditional and modern, rural and urban, and local and foreign interact, inflect, and sometimes shed their identities, even as each layer retains a measure of provisional autonomy.

This chapter cannot hope to convey such a vast plurality in detail; what I propose to do, rather, is to rehearse a few ideas and perspectives that might stimulate further discussion. First, I will review a few "historical" sources of data on African musical instruments by quoting from a handful of early explorers. Second, I will supplement a brief critique of the hugely influential Hornbostel-Sach model with a variety of indigenous perspectives; although the latter have not yet been gathered into formal systems of classification, they convey some of what matters in African naming and discussion of African instruments. Third, I will highlight a handful of prominent traditional instruments or instrument classes, emphasizing the patterns of sound/music that they make both singly and in consort. It should be apparent that we are not working toward a single, grand statement about African musical instruments. What I hope will emerge are perceptions inspired by instruments and ways in which they resonate with trends in the larger discourse on African music.

## SOURCES OF DATA ON AFRICAN
## MUSICAL INSTRUMENTS

Data on African musical instruments comes in three principal forms. First and perhaps most important are verbal descriptions of musical instruments and contexts of performance. While the focus here is on written sources, the no-less-important oral sources will be acknowledged in subsequent discussion. Second are various iconic signs, including artworks, photographs, and diagrams. Third are recordings: audio recordings of sound instruments (which we have already referred to in the introduction); films and video recordings; and various Internet resources, including a sizeable number of YouTube clips featuring African instruments.

Descriptions of musical instruments are found in the journals, reports, and communications of various missionaries, explorers, and travelers. By way of illustration, and also to give the reader a flavor of these writings, I have chosen five passages, the first two from writings by Portuguese missionaries, the third from a Dutchman writing at the beginning of the eighteenth century, the fourth from a famous eighteenth-century Scottish explorer, and the fifth from an Englishman writing in the nineteenth century. While tone and expression may seem worlds removed from today's writing, there are surprisingly deep connections between the concerns of these earlier writers and their twentieth-century counterparts. We should pay particular attention not only to what is said but also how it is said, for the writings come from a period when Europe held an "imperial dominion" over Africa.[2] No observer, it seems, has been able to ignore the role of musical instruments in more general accounts of music making. While this may sound banal, it is possibly significant in alerting us to what is left out of such accounts. For example, while the physical features of instruments are often noted, the music itself or the aesthetic it engenders is treated more variably. In some cases, the "music" is not regarded as something to be described in an objective or detached way, but as something to be responded to subjectively.

Father Joao dos Santos, a Portuguese missionary and explorer, visited the Karanga people (a subgroup of present-day Shona in Zimbabwe and Mozambique) in 1586 and remarked, among other things, on their musical instruments. The following refers to the xylophone or *marimba* (the Karanga called it *ambira*), and I quote from Percival Kirby's *The Musical Instruments of the Native Races of South Africa*, one of the great works of African organology:

> Quiteve (the chief) makes use of another class of Kaffirs, great musicians and dancers, who have no other office than to sit in the last room of the

2. Cornell West, *Keeping Faith: Philosophy and Race in America* (New York: Routledge, 1993), 5.

king's palace, at the outer door and round his dwelling, playing many different musical instruments, and singing to them a great variety of songs and discourses in praise of the king, in very high and sonorous voices. The best and most musical of their instruments is called the *ambira*, which greatly resembles our organs; it is composed of long gourds, some very wide and some very narrow, held close together and arranged in order. The narrowest, which form the treble, are placed on the left, contrary to that of our organs, and after the treble come the other gourds with their different sounds of contralto, tenor, and bass, being eighteen gourds in all. Each gourd has a small opening at the side near the end, and at the bottom a small hole the size of a dollar, covered with a certain kind of spider's web, very fine, closely woven, and strong, which does not break. Upon all the mouths of these gourds, which are of the same size and placed in a row, keys of thin wood are suspended by cords so that each key is held in the air above the hollow of its gourd, not reaching the edges of the mouth. The instrument being thus constructed, the Kaffirs play upon the keys with sticks after the fashion of drum-sticks, at the points of which are buttons made of sinews soled into a light ball of the size of a nut, so that striking the notes with these two sticks, the blows resound in the mouths of the gourds, producing a sweet and rhythmical harmony, which can be heard as far as the sound of a good harpsichord. There are many of these instruments, and many musicians who play upon them very well.[3]

Dos Santos writes in detail about the contexts of royal music making, the routine of musicians, and the importance of praise singing (a widespread practice especially pronounced in the Sudanic belt and unfailingly present in royal circles). He describes the instrument and method of playing, sometimes employing a comparative framework. The sound of the xylophone, for example, carries "as far as the sound of a good harpsichord" (this in 1586, preceding the heyday of harpsichord usage in Europe), although Dos Santos may have underestimated the carrying power of the marimba. He recognizes the register-based and perhaps scalelike arrangement of the eighteen gourd resonators, which he likens to "the sounds of contralto, tenor and bass." The author does not eschew value or aesthetic judgments: the *ambira*, he reckons, is "the best and most musical of [the Karangas'] instruments"; the harmony is "sweet and rhythmical," and "many musicians ... play upon [the ambira] very well." In sum, this sixteenth-century account offers insight into the social function, morphology, acoustics, and aesthetics of an early form of the African xylophone.

3. Kirby, *The Musical Instruments of the Native Races of South Africa* (London: Oxford University Press, 1934), 47–48.

About the time of Father Dos Santos's visit to (what was then called) Eastern Ethiopia, Duarte Lopez, another Portuguese missionary who had lived for a decade in the Congo (present-day Democratic Republic of the Congo), published an account of his African sojourn that included observations on music making. The following was apparently written up by the Italian Filippo Pigafetta and is introduced and excerpted by Gary Tomlinson in the canonical text *Strunk's Source Readings in Music History*.[4] Mention is made of ceremonial drums of great carrying power (five to six miles, Lopez says) that accompany the king. Noting the absence of written records—time is measured "by the phases of the moon," while distance is reckoned "not in miles or any such units but in the days it takes a man . . . to get there"—Lopez embarks on a description of the physical properties of "certain strangely formed lutes":

> These are in the rounded part of the body and in the neck somewhat similar to ours, but the flat part, where we carve the rosette, is covered with a very thin skin, like a bladder, instead of wood. The strings are made from strong, polished hairs from the tail of an elephant or from certain threads from the wood of the palm tree. They extend from the bottom of the instrument to the end of the neck and are tied to pegs of various sizes affixed to the neck. From the pegs they hang very thin plates of iron and silver, of different sizes depending on the size of the whole instrument. These jingle in various ways, giving out an intermittent sound, as the strings are played and the pegs from which they hang vibrate. The players pluck the strings in good proportion with their fingers and without the sort of plectrum we use to play the harp.

Lopez continues with the manner of playing and the aesthetic impact of the music: "They play masterfully and produce a melody or noise (I know not which to call it) that delights their senses." Most interesting, perhaps, is his final observation about the use of this instrument as a speech surrogate, an observation that resonates well with the widespread practice associated with various instruments, among them flutes, xylophones, drums (preeminently), and harp lutes:

> Moreover—and it is a wondrous thing—with this instrument they signify the concepts in their minds and make them understood so clearly that almost anything they can put across in speaking they can also express by touching this instrument with their hands.

---

4. Leo Treitler, ed., *Strunk's Source Readings in Music History* (New York: Norton, 1998).

The idea that what can be spoken can also be played on an instrument slightly undercomplicates the dynamics of speech surrogacy, but Lopez is correct in identifying this as a common practice. He acknowledges other instruments, including "flutes and pipes" and "small drums," thus reminding us that although "talking drums" have for long constituted the dominant image of speech surrogacy in Africa, other instruments do talk as well.

A little over a century later, a Dutchman by the name of William Bosman published *A New and Accurate Description of the Coast of Guinea* (1704), which contains a section on musical instruments.[5] Dutiful rather than inspired, his description mentions horns, drums, and wind instruments. About horns, for example, he notes the material from which they are made, their weight, the manner of playing, and—significantly—their adornment, including the use of ritual blood. He also identifies a principle of motivic variation at work in the music:

> The chief [musical instruments] are the mentioned horns, made . . . of small Elephant's Teeth; though not so very small but some of them weigh betwixt twenty and thirty pounds, and others more: To adorn these they cut in them several images of men and beasts; and that so finely that it seems to be done litterally [*sic*] in obedience to the Second Commandment; . . . at the lower end of these horns is a piece of Rope coloured black with Hems or Sheep blood, and at the small end is a square Hole; at which by blowing they produce a sort of extravagant noise; which they reduce to a sort of tune and measure, and vary as they please.

Bosman is not reticent about expressing his reactions to the music: "Sometimes they blow upon these horns so well, that though it is not agreeable, yet it is not so horrid as to require a whole Bale of Cotton annually to stop one's ears, as Focquenbrog has it." He mentions ten sorts of drums, including some made from trees and covered on one end with sheepskin, some played with two long sticks or with hand and stick, and some played in ensemble with horns. He seems unwilling to hear anything but "noise" in some of these repertories. The sound of the drums "produce[s] a dismal and horrid noise," while the ensemble of horns and drums "afford[s] the most charming asse's musick that can be imagined." Although Bosman notices the iron bell playing what is nowadays referred to as the time line, he cannot stand its sound at all: "[it] makes a noise more detestable than the drums and horns together."

5. William Bosman, *A New and Accurate Description of the Coast of Guinea*, 2nd ed. (London: Printed for J. Knapton, 1721 [orig. 1704]).

A historical figure of note in the exploration (and attendant exploitation) of Africa is the Scotsman Mungo Park, whose travel narrative from 1799 includes an occasional description of musical instruments.[6] The following passage provides a flavor of Park's description. Its significance in this context includes the fact that it refers to Islamic-influenced Manding cultures. According to him, the principal instruments are

> —the *koonting*, a sort of guitar with three strings; —the *simbing*, a small harp, with seven strings; —the *balafon*, an instrument composed of twenty pieces of hard wood of different lengths, with the shells of gourds hung underneath, to increase the sound; —the *tangtang*, a drum open at the lower end; and lastly, the *tabala*, a large drum, commonly used to spread an alarm through the country. Besides these, they make use of small flutes, bowstrings, elephants' teeth, and bells; and at all their dances and concerts, *clapping of hands* appears to constitute a necessary part of the chorus.

Park goes on to mention the so-called singing men or *Jilli kea*. We know them as *Jali, jeliya,* or griots or griottes (also known by a number of regional names), wordsmiths who perform social roles as praise singers and guardians (reciters) of local histories. He also alludes to the crusading missions of Muslims ("Mohameddans"), which invariably include music. On the whole, the musical content of Park's *Travels in the Interior of Africa* is slight, but I mention it here because when he does refer to music it is mainly to material instruments. That such passing reference occurs in one of the best-known tales of discovery of Africa (in Park's case, the Niger River) is significant.

Finally, let us recall Thomas Bowdich's *Mission from Cape Coast Castle to Ashantee*, which was published in 1819 and includes an entire chapter (the tenth) on music, complete with transcriptions of various "airs" and a few pages on the music of "Gaboon" [*sic*].[7] The opening paragraph may serve as an illustration of his language and approach. With Bowdich, we are dealing not only with the external morphology of instruments but also with musical elements. Reference to intervals of thirds and fifths points to a degree of technical specification that is not reached by any of the authors previously quoted. (It is not surprising, then, that Bowdich's work makes an appearance at the beginning of Gerhard Kubik's magisterial account of multipart procedures in African

---

6. Mungo Park, *Travels in the Interior Districts of Africa* (Ware: Wordsworth, 2002 [orig. 1799]), 278.

7. Thomas Bowdich, *Mission from Cape Coast to Ashantee* (London: J. Murray, 1873 [orig. 1819]).

music, an aspect of music that is difficult to address without the use of technical terms.[8]) Bowdich also refers to one of the central genres of traditional music, funeral dirges, as well as to the technique of speech surrogacy on flutes. Interesting is the fact that the author seems a shade skeptical about the practice:

> Few of their instruments possess much power, but the combination of several frequently produces a surprising effect. The flute is made of a long hollow reed, and has not more three holes; the tone is low at all times, and when they play in concert they graduate them with such nicety as to produce the common chords. Several instances of thirds occur, especially in one of the annexed airs, played as a funeral dirge; nor is this extraordinary considering it is the most natural interval; the addition of fifths, at the same time, is rare. The natives declare they can converse by means of their flutes, and an old resident at Accra has assured me he has heard dialogues, and that every sentence was explained to him.

Bowdich follows this with detailed descriptions of the "*sanko*" (a generic term for a musical instrument, but one that is often applied to the Akan seperewa, a harp lute[9]), "horns made of elephant tusks" (known as mmensuoun[10]), a "rude violin" played by "Northerners such as Mosees, Mallowas, Bournas, the Oompoochwa" (known as *gonje* or by some other regional variant), and "drums, castanets, gong-gongs, flat sticks, rattles, and even old brass pans." Notable in Bowdich's account is a reference to the human voice, the first instrument so to speak, which other commentators often ignore or simply take for granted. About singing, he says that "almost all of [it] is 'recitative,'" which again points to declamatory patterns in free rhythm.

An inventory of names, modes of construction, playing techniques, social uses, and effects of African musical instruments as they show up in the five passages that we have just quoted (spanning the years 1586–1819) would confirm that the concerns of twentieth-century organologists are not radically different from those of the earlier writers.. Tracing these thematic continuities in detail would take us too far afield, however, but perhaps a brief mention of

8. Kubik, "Multipart Singing in Sub-Saharan Africa: Remote and Recent Histories Unravelled," in *Symposium on Ethnomusicology*, ed. A. Tracey (Grahamstown, South Africa: International Library of African Music, 1997), 85–97.

9. Johann Gottlieb Christaller, *Dictionary of the Ashante and Fante Language Called Tshi (Twi)* (Basel: Printed for the Basel Evangelical Missionary Society, 1933).

10. See Peter K. Sarpong, *The Ceremonial Horns of the Ashanti* (Accra: Sedco, 1990). For a comprehensive study of Asante horns, see Joseph Kaminski, *Asante Ntahera Trumpets in Ghana*.

some will illustrate the point. In Hornbostel and Sachs's well-known article about the world's musical instruments (1914), we are presented with a comprehensive classification system. (We will comment on its applicability to Africa later). Hornbostel's own ethnology of African sound instruments offers a scientific description (1933), Ankermann's 1901 treatise combines description with graphic illustration, and Kirby's musicological study (1934) includes sometimes detailed histories of instruments. Studies by Tracey (1948), Trowell and Wachsmann (1953), Laurenty (1960), Kubik (1982), Charry (1996), Wenger (1984), Jos Gansemans (1988), and Djedje (1999) collectively provide physical descriptions of musical instruments, tuning systems, methods of construction, and the nature of the music sound. Advanced students will doubtless be familiar with these sources, but the general reader may be surprised by the amount of attention given to instruments. For an example of how far we have come, the reader might consult Gerhard Kubik's excellent study of the origins, history, description (including indigenous designation), and diasporic afterlife of so-called lamellophones.[11]

While the core attributes of many "traditional" instruments in contemporary use are not significantly different from those found in the historical sources we have just mentioned, new materials and techniques have been adopted. Nylon strings, fishing nets, umbrella wires, cigarette cans, plastic containers, and bottle tops have firmly entered the construction industry. And on a scholarly level, modes of representation and measurement have benefited from larger advances in technology, so that it is possible, for example, to display in remarkable detail the acoustic makeup of individual sounds, as Cornelia Fales does in her studies of whispering Enanga from Burundi.[12] It is, however, not always the case that old instruments and old ways of representation are discarded; rather, newer ways are grafted onto traditional practices, making for a more complex layering.

Verbal descriptions are not the only sources of data; there are iconic representations as well. Diagrams of musical instruments, some sketched in the field by authors, others made later at home, function as important supplements to verbal description. For example, in Michael Praetorius's *Syntagma*

11. Kubik, "African and African American Lamellophones: History, Typology, Nomenclature, Performers, and Intracultural Concepts," in *Turn Up the Volume! A Celebration of African Music*, ed. Jacqueline Djedje (Los Angeles: UCLA Fowler Museum of Cultural History, 1999), 20–57.

12. Incorporated into a broader study of timbre in Fales, "The Paradox of Timbre," *Ethnomusicology* 46, no. 1 (2002): 56–95. See also Fales and Stephen McAdams, "The Fusion and Layering of Noise and Tone: Implications for Timbre in African Instruments," *Leonardo Music Journal* 4 (1994): 69–77.

*Musicum* (1620), there appears a drawing of a seven-string lute from Africa. Kubik suggests that it may have been brought to Europe by a German consul visiting Gabon.[13] Scottish artist Charles Davidson Bell produced a series of drawings depicting South African music makers in the nineteenth century (a few of these are reproduced in Kirby's book).[14] Bernhard Ankermann's treatise on African musical instruments is laced with no fewer than 170 drawings featuring all the major instrumental classes of Africa.[15] Walter Hirschberg assembled in 1969 a fascinating collection of "Early Historical Illustrations of West and Central African Music," which includes artists' impressions of instruments and scenes of music making, including dancing.[16] And in recent times, Willie Anku and Meki Nzewi have included drawings as illustrations of instruments, playing techniques, and compressed representations of musical societies.[17] Drawings, like verbal descriptions, are products of interpretation, traces of individual artistic imagination. Even though they exist in a different semiotic realm, drawings ostensibly resemble their objects; in that sense, they allow us more direct—less mediated—access to the thing itself. Compared to concept-burdened verbal description, they seem to take us to the thing itself.

When the technology for making photographs became available in the nineteenth century, drawing as a tool for organology went into partial decline. The ascendancy of photographs in turn meant that the interpretive layers entailed in rendering a given instrument as lines and shapes could be reduced, the thought being that photographs unveil a direct truth, not the mediated truth of diagrams and hand drawings. In truth, however, photography disguises some of the bases of choice without erasing the workings of an authorial hand.

13. Quoted in Kubik, *Theory of African Music*, vol. 1, 24.

14. Kirby, *The Musical Instruments of the Native Races of South Africa.*

15. Ankermann, *Die afrikanischen Musikinstrumente* (Berlin: Druck und Verlag von A. Haack, 1901).

16. Hirschberg, "Early Historical Illustrations of West and Central African Music," *African Music* 4, no. 3 (1969): 6–18.

17. Anku includes self-made illustrations in his PhD dissertation ("Procedures in African Drumming: A Study of Akan/Ewe Traditions and African Drumming in Pittsburgh" [PhD thesis, University of Pittsburgh, 1988]), in several pamphlets and articles (e.g., *Structural Set Analysis of African Music 1: Adowa* [Legon, Ghana: Soundstage Production, 2002]), and in a comprehensive study of African rhythm, *A Theory of African Music* (forthcoming). For a sampling of Nzewi's illustrations, some of them made in conjunction with German artist Doris Weller, see *Musical Sense and Musical Meaning* and *African Music: Theoretical Content and Creative Continuum.*

Works of African organology in the twentieth century have made effective use of photographs. Consider, again, a work like Kirby's *The Musical Instruments of the Native Races of Africa*, published in 1934. Its seventy-three plates include pertinent photographs of most of the instruments discussed in the book, thus making them indispensable. Included are ankle rattles, sticks, drums, bull roarers, whistles, flutes, bows, and lutes, each group designated by indigenous names. The effect is to aid the imagination by supplying forms and shapes that allow us quicker access to these aspects of African material culture. The valuable German-language *Musikgeschichte in Bildern* series, published between 1979 and 1989, includes four volumes on Africa, each of which makes ample use of photographs and illustrations.[18] Okwui Enwezor's pictorial history of the decades after World War II, *The Short Century: Independence and Liberation Movements in Africa, 1945–1994*, includes depictions of scenes of music making and associated dancing alongside sound-producing objects.[19] And the beautiful catalog *Turn Up the Volume! A Celebration of African Music*, edited by ethnomusicologist Jacqueline Djedje, contains some of the liveliest photographs of African musical instruments.[20] These are only a few of the available resources, but enough to indicate what is available.

With the advent of film technology, representing African musical instruments took a further step forward. Early efforts by Mantle Hood, Andrew Tracey, Kubik, Rouget, Rouch, and others have been supplemented by the productions of a professional like Gei Zantziger, whose documentation of musical life in Mozambique, Zimbabwe, and Southern Africa counts among the most vivid and imaginative.[21] Memorable, too, is the BBC series *Repercussions: A Celebration of African-American Music*, which includes episodes on the Gambian kora, the Dagomba *dùndún* and *luna*, and various modern instruments used by bands playing popular music. Another notable example is Taale Laafi Rosellini's film, *Great, Great, Great Grandparents'*

18. *Ostafrika*, ed. Kubik (Leipzig: VEB Deutscher Verlag fur Musik, 1982); *Westafrika*, ed. Kubik (Leipzig: VEB Deutscher Verlag fur Musik, 1989); *Nordafrika*, ed. Paul Collaer et al. (Leipzig: VEB Deutscher Verlag fur Musik, 1983); and *Zentralafrika*, ed. Jos Gansemans et al. (Leipzig: VEB Deutscher Verlag fur Musik, 1986).

19. Okwui Enwezor, ed., *The Short Century: Independence and Liberation Movements in Africa, 1945–1994* (Munich: Prestel, 2001).

20. Jacqueline Djedje, ed., *Turn Up the Volume! A Celebration of African Music* (Los Angeles: UCLA Fowler Museum of Cultural History, 1999).

21. See, among others, *Mbira: The Technique of the Mbira dza Vadzimu* (Zimbabwe) (1978), *The Chopi Timbila Dance* (Mozambique) (1980), and *A Spirit Here Today: A Scrapbook of Chopi Village Music* (Mozambique) (1994).

*Music* (1999), which conveys intergenerational investment in the playing of the balafon as a central feature of family life in a village in Burkina Faso.[22] On the whole, moving images, whether in film or posted on YouTube, allow even greater access to the ontology of musical instruments. By incorporating a temporal dimension that captures the actual production of sound, they bring us close to experiencing the imagined reality in instrumental performance.

Finally, we must acknowledge the thousands of audio recordings that have over the years brought the sound of African musical instruments to us in an immediate way. We remarked on this abundance in the introduction, citing Alan Lomax's remark that Africa in 1959 was already the "best-recorded continent." Since most readers are likely to have heard African music on recording, I will add here only that the thematic organization of individual recordings varies widely. It includes snapshots of musical life in villages or communities; representative musics of regions, countries, or ethnic groups; repertories of ensembles; samples of instrument families; and music belonging to single or multiple genres. Again, examples are many, so let us cite just two, one based on an older set of recordings, the other on a recent recording. The rereleases on compact disc of selected contents of the International Library of African Music (ILAM) are organized by instrument, with separate CDs devoted to guitars, drums, reeds, strings, flutes, and drums.[23] By the time listeners navigate their way through thirty-one tracks featuring drums, twenty-four featuring guitars, twenty-two featuring strings, twenty featuring reeds, and so on, they will have developed a pretty keen sense of the range of textures and timbres that each instrument family obtains. The other is a delightful recent recording of music from Ghana, titled *Por por honk music* and assembled by ethnomusicologist Steve Feld.[24] This features an unusual instrument, namely, the discarded squeeze-bulb horns normally mounted on lorries. It is heard here in consort with more traditional instruments (bells, rattles, drums, and voices). The performers are members of the La Drivers Union of Accra, Ghana, who traditionally perform at the funerals of their members, although by now the performance venues have been diversified. Although the selections feature entertainment music that draws on both local and imported dances and styles, the ambience is distinct—an enthralling musical dialogue stamped with the authority of tradition even as the expressive means push at its boundaries.

22. *Great, Great, Great Grandparents' Music* (Santa Cruz, CA: African Family Films, 1997).

23. International Library of African Music, CD reissues.

24. CD, *Por Por: Honk Horn Music of Ghana: The La Drivers Union Por Por Group* (Washington, DC: Smithsonian/Folkways, 2007). See also Feld, *Jazz Cosmopolitanism in Accra: Five Musical Years in Ghana* (Durham, NC: Duke University Press, 2012).

Passing invocations of "truth" in the previous discussion should not lead us to underestimate the interpretive control exercised in representations of instruments as material culture. As we have remarked, drawing, for example, relies on conventions of line, shade, and perspective; the artist makes decisions and implements choices. Painting offers choices in coloring and molding and in distance and depth of perspective, while the video camera's lenses typically move according to the photographer's plot, a plot that may lead him or her to focus on the sensational, the exotic, the marginal, or that which is merely "different." Even the making of audio recordings is based on choices that may have significant consequences. For example, because of the extensive use of repetition in African music, some makers of recordings have been led to offer only snippets of performances, the thought being that the music is all the same anyway. In so doing, African music is denied the kinds of cumulative form that derive from a structural use of repetition. Similarly, the prejudice that pitch is at best of secondary importance in African music has influenced some recording artists not to seek clear differentiation of pitch levels but to focus on the all-pervasive "percussive" quality of sound.[25]

## AGAINST THE HORNBOSTEL-SACHS SYSTEM OF CLASSIFICATION

The most influential system of classifying African musical instruments is that developed by Erich von Hornbostel and Curt Sachs and first published in Berlin on the eve of the first war in a journal called *Zeitschrift für Ethnologie*.[26] Entitled "Systematik der Musikinstrumente: Ein Versuch," this seminal article was subsequently translated into English by Anthony Baines and Klaus P. Wachsmann as "Classification of Musical Instruments" and published in a journal devoted to musical instruments, the *Galpin Society Journal*, in 1961. It seems that many more Africanists read the revised English version than the German original. By the 1960s, Hornbostel's contributions to the study of African music were well known, as were Sachs's comparative studies of musical instruments and rhythm. That the article drew considerable interest was therefore not surprising. It should be emphasized that "Classification of

25. See Wachsmann's discussion of these and related issues in "Music," *Journal of the Folklore Institute* 6 (1969): 164–191.

26. Erich M. von Hornbostel and Curt Sachs, "Systematik der Musikinstrumente: Ein Versuch," *Zeitschrift für Ethnologie* 4 (1914), trans. Anthony Baines and Klaus Wachsmann as "Classification of Musical Instruments," *Galpin Society Journal* 14 (1961): 3–29.

Musical Instruments" was written for a practical purpose: to enable museum curators to classify musical instruments from anywhere in the world. In other words, the classificatory system was not developed with Africa's specific needs in mind; rather, it had global or universal aspirations from the beginning.

In its broadest outline, the Hornbostel-Sachs system promulgates four main classes: *idiophones,* or self-sounding instruments; *membranophones,* or membrane instruments; *chordophones,* or string instruments; and *aerophones*, or wind instruments. Each class of instruments is subsequently subdivided. Rattles or "shaken idiophones" include suspension rattles, strung rattles, stick rattles, frame rattles, pendant rattles, sliding rattles, and vessel rattles. Chordophones are distinguished according to whether they have a resonator or not; whether they are lutes, lyres, zithers, or harps; and so on. And flutes, a subclass of aerophones, may or may not have finger holes, may be side-blown or end-blown, or may be constructed in multiples (panpipes) or singly. Hornbostel and Sachs sought a system of classification based on a logical principle of division. Thus, at the grossest level, "the physical characteristics of sound-production [constitute] the most important principle of division." At lower levels, criteria are more flexible, reflecting manner of playing, method of sound production, and external physical structure. And there are, of course, a number of hybrid instruments that do not fall neatly into their categories.

The Hornbostel-Sachs system is so prominent in Africanist ethnomusicology that it is easy to forget that it was developed not exclusively to depict African realities but to accommodate virtually all known musical instruments. The project is thus one of a piece with colonially inspired projects like comprehensive botanical classifications (a point made by Hornbostel and Sachs) and the classification of natural languages. Prominent African writers like Bebey, Nketia, Vidal, and Ekwueme adopted the Hornbostel-Sachs nomenclature; André Schaeffner elaborated upon it in his own organological work; Andrew Tracey used it to organize his discussion of instruments in Mozambique; and more recent writers like Brandilly, Djedje, Blench, and Fernando have continued to use it. Many students in English-speaking African universities are taught to describe their drums as "membranophones" and their bamboo flutes as "aerophones" instead of using indigenous names.

It is time for African musicologists to replace the Hornbostel-Sachs system with schemes that are more reflective of African realities. If, as Djenda writes, "Central African ethnic groups do not . . . categorize their musical instruments according to the criteria developed by Hornbostel and Sachs,"[27] one must wonder what sense there is in holding on to those criteria and the resultant system. As a totalizing scheme tied to the alien Dewey Decimal

27. Djenda, "Central African Republic."

Classification system in libraries, it seems inappropriately ambitious for our particular realities. Let us remember that in the actual reception of the system, it is the large picture—which is not in itself original to Hornbostel and Sachs—that has endured, not the rich details; in other words, instructors and students have for the most part accepted the fourfold large-scale classification but have not engaged to the same extent with its numerous subclasses. To reduce the scheme to its fourfold macrostructure, however, is to drain it of the very content that Hornbostel and Sachs labored to include in it. In any case, it was Belgian instrument curator Victor-Charles Mahillon (1841–1924) who in 1888 put forward the very scheme that we now associate with Hornbostel and Sachs. In a catalog reflecting the collection of (mainly) European instruments in the Brussels Conservatory of the time, Mahillon devised a fourfold classification of instruments: self-sounding instruments (instruments autophones), membrane instruments, stringed instruments, and wind instruments. At this level, the principal criterion was how sound was produced. He then proceeded to "lower" levels, subdividing each category to reflect the manner of playing. If Africanists, discouraged by the apparent lack of unified logic at the subclass level, wish only to retain the broad fourfold division, then credit must by rights go to Victor Mahillon before it is extended—if at all—to Hornbostel and Sachs.[28]

The more pertinent reason for rejecting the Hornbostel-Sachs system is that very little about it reflects indigenous African views about musical instruments. The system does not take account of how Africans (or other world indigenous peoples, for that matter), who after all are the original producers and users, conceptualize the physical and symbolic dimensions of their instruments. It is true that Hornbostel and Sachs sought to provide an objective, logical, and scientific system, a "systematic arrangement of musical instruments" that would aid musicologists, ethnomusicologists, and especially curators of collections and museum keepers. But insofar as systems of classification impose sets of associations on groups of objects, no system can be accorded a priori privilege.

It might be argued that the Hornbostel-Sachs system is convenient for containing the heterogeneity of African nomenclature. Just as the imposition of a colonial language on a nation can be said to provide a common language for communication across scores of languages, so the imposition of a colonial classification system might be said to facilitate comparison of different objects. And so—to continue the argument—if we want to have a degree of control over the scores of instrument types, we might as well adopt a scheme

28. Victor-Charles Mahillon, *Catalogue descriptif et analytique du Musée instrumental du Conservatoire Royal de Musique de Bruxelles*, 3 vols. (Ghent: A. Hoste, 1893–1922). Mahillon's scheme in turn had its antecedents in an ancient Indian classification system.

that allows us to group them. This would allow us to name and control the discourse about instruments. Objects would be placed inside boxes and described neatly according to explicit criteria.

We might counter that view by proposing that rather than avoiding or seeking to contain Africa's heterogeneity, it would be better to acknowledge it by entering patiently into the worlds signaled by local designation. And if those worlds inscribe a residual plurality, we should accept it rather than wish it away in the interest of so-called economy in classification. In what follows, I assemble a few indigenous ideas to convey the rich and complex possibilities for developing Africa-centered classification schemes. Of course, no one is obliged to accept Africa-centered schemes in place of the Hornbostel-Sachs system, but we should at least acknowledge the former's existence and potential.

## INDIGENOUS IDEAS ABOUT MUSICAL INSTRUMENTS

A list of names of musical instruments in the indigenous languages of Africa would fill several volumes: *bendere* for calabash drum in Burkina Faso; *zwilidzo* or "things that are made to cry" for musical instruments among the Venda; *ingoma* for a Burundi drum ensemble; *timbrh* for lamellaphone in Cameroon; *nyayaru* for one-stringed fiddle in Sierra Leone; *segbureh* for gourd rattle also in Sierra Leone; *atumpan* for a pair of talking drums among the Akan (also *tompani* among the Northern Ewe and *atungblan* among the Baule); *vu* for drum in Ewe; *fontonfrom* for large, cylindrical drums among the Akan; *mendzang* for gourd-resonated xylophone in Cameroon; *gankogui* for the bell in Ewe; *embulumbumba* for gourd-resonated bow in Angola—the list could go on. These names presumably reflect patterns of naming in the communities from which they emanate; therefore, a proper understanding of their significance will need to enter decisively into their respective cognitive worlds. In other words, insofar as the language used to describe musical instruments reflects the principles of conceptual worlding found in a given community, we should not fail to note the priorities enshrined in those cognitive universes.

It would already be something of an achievement if we all used African-language names for African instruments whenever possible. Learning to pronounce these names would encourage familiarity with the phonetic systems of other languages, open windows to other patterns of discourse within individual cultures, and counter the tendency to employ metropolitan categories over indigenous ones. It is true that there is an intimidating plurality to the African nomenclature, that some terms apply strictly to local contexts, and that cross-ethnic standardization has been slow. Kubik, for example, lists thirteen "common designations" for the mbira and sketches a complex history of usage of cognate terms like mbila, malimba, marimba, nsansi, kalimba, ilimba, likembe, kadongo, cisanzi, kanombyo, mucapata, mbo ngo, timbrh, and agidigbo in southern, central, eastern, and western Africa.[29] There are contexts in which using the all-purpose "lamellophone" is adequate, of course, but there are surely others in which an African-language designation would be more appropriate. To the extent that names signify qualities, the refusal to use African names for African objects deprives us of phenomenological insight. In some cases, the foreign name effectively redefines the object in question.

What is in a name? A number of names of instruments are onomatopoeia, that is, literal depictions of the characteristic sound made by the instrument. For example, among the Kpelle, *gbung-gbung* is the name of a cylindrical drum beaten with a stick; among the Vai, the same drum is called *gbemgbem*. There is a four-note xylophone in Cameroon by the name *ndum ndum ndum*. This pattern of naming is not surprising given that sound symbolism is pervasive in African languages. Some names are constructed according to a principle of reduplication and may be heard as a direct imitation of sounds native to—or characteristic of—the instrument in question. Reduplication enlivens the sonic and symbolic dimensions of many languages and is used to great rhetorical effect in riddles, word games, and folktale performances.

Some names refer to the material used in making instruments. For example, the Anlo Ewe *gankogui* is a metal bell (*ga* = metal, *kogui* = bell or sounding object), while the Northern Ewe *pamprovu* refers to a bamboo drum (*pampro* = bamboo, *vu* = drum). Certain drums are named after gods, deities, ancestors, or other ritual personages as befits their ascribed status. The Northern Ewe *Adabatram* is the name both of a greatly feared drum and of a god. Frequently names of instruments double as names of dances or genres. Finally, certain names are borrowed from other languages but modified in the new language. Thus, the Ewe *tompani*, used to designate a pair of talking drums, is clearly derived from the Akan drums of that name, *Atumpan*, just as *le week-end* or *das Computer* are accepted in French and German, respectively.

Some names depict musical function, as when instruments in an ensemble are referred to by the equivalents of leader, time marker, or filler. Constraints of modern pedagogy (some of it aimed at a cross-cultural clientele) have led some teachers to assign names to things that they did not previously name. In some cases, elaborate schemes have emerged to confer metaphorical names conveying function on the individual keys of an mbira, the slabs of a xylophone, or the holes on a flute. One sometimes finds a basic distinction between

---

29. Kubik, "African and African American Lamellophones."

big and small, as when a lower-pitched voice is referred to as "big" in contrast to a higher-pitched "small" voice, or when a "big drum" (like the Ewe *vugã*, which could also mean "important drum") is separated from a "small drum." "Big" in this context denotes both physical size and musical significance, the latter representing the patterns played and the player's role as the leader of the ensemble.

Modes of instrumental execution register frequently in indigenous discourse. According to Ruth Stone, the Kpelle and Gio of Liberia recognize two categories of instrument, those that are blown (Kpelle *fée*) and those that are struck (Kpelle *ygále*). Significant here are entangled meanings of different ways of playing or singing. Vocal music is a case in point. In Ewe, *Dzi ha* asks you to "sing the song," while *lé ha* means "catch the song," *xɔ ha* means "receive the song," and *lɔ ha* means "respond to the song"—all are ways of responding within a call-and-response framework. The phrase *Mi fo gbe me* ("beat the inside of the voice") is used to encourage singers to give a good account of themselves, to give it their all, to show what they are made of. Forms of behavior brought on by *Mi fo gbe me* may be louder singing, more nuanced enunciation, more deliberate articulation, greater ingenuity in the use of embellishments, or more imagination in the deployment of topical references. The verb *fo*, however, means beat and is more typically applied to the beating of drums. In Siwu, "touch it" (*pɛgu*) or "hit it" (*kpura*) are alternatives to the Ewe *fo* ("beat"). But it is not only voices or drums that are "beaten"; keyboard instruments (*sanko*) and stringed instruments may also be "beaten." Wind instruments, however, are blown (*ku kpẽ* in Ewe means "blow the horn"; mischievous children have been known to adapt this phrase to farting.)

Of particular interest are metaphorical projections onto ensembles, projections that often refer to some aspect of kinship or social order. The minimum ensemble is a pair, and a number of instrumental pairs are conceived as siblings (including twins), rivals (not in a competitive sense but in a complementary one), or, more commonly, male and female. Thus, the Akan *Atumpan* pair of talking drums is conceptualized as male and female, the male positioned on the left and possessed of a lower pitch. Interesting is the fact that although gender discrimination in pronouns is not available in Twi (nor for that matter in Ewe, Yoruba, Gã, Siwu, and many other languages), drums are distinguished as male or female. The "mother drum" in Igbo and Yoruba both delivers the most complex patterns and directs the affairs of the ensemble as a whole.

Ruth Stone cites several Kpelle instruments played in ensemble that, according to her, "reflect their social organization." For example, the mother *kono* or *kono-lee* is the largest and lowest-pitched instrument in an ensemble of slit idiophones, the others being "child" and "middle." Similarly, Meki Nzewi reminds us that in Igbo ukom and Yoruba ensembles, the lead drummer is the "mother drum" in part because of her strong creative and procreative capabilities.[30] Such metaphorical transfers have an immediate appeal because ensembles often behave like communities of instruments. At the same time, however, there is a certain makeshift quality to these transfers, and that should discourage us from drawing too many firm conclusions about this particular domestication of the social. Within each transfer, there is often a kink, misalignment, or missing particle, suggesting that ensembles are not formed as perfect mirrors of social units. In the Kpelle scheme reported by Ruth Stone, for example, "mother" and "child" frame the ensemble, but the third member is neutrally designated as "middle," a designation that foregoes kinship alliance for a purely ordinal or spatial dimension. Similarly, Chernoff's southern Ewe family allows the bell (an indispensable member of the ensemble) only the status of a heartbeat, this in contrast to other instruments given family-member status (father, mother, twin brothers, baby). Note also that the rattle, a regular member of the Agbekor ensemble, is excluded from this naming system.

In sum, metaphorical transfers between ensemble organization and social or kinship structure are tentative; no hard discovery principles have so far emerged in connection with such naming practices. We saw a similarly provisional pattern in the connection between musical structure and social structure at the end of chapter 1. Here, as in many areas of modern African expressivity, the spirit of naming is akin to a *commedia dell'arte*: makeshift, improvised, and spontaneous.

As for indigenous conceptions, no limits can finally be placed on the symbolic potential of African musical instrument names. Male-female dualities are reflected in other conceptual realms, notably the domain of religious symbolism, not just the musical. Drums, for example, hold a host of associations for various African communities: they are symbols of royal power (Burundi), they can be used to sound alarms or warn of war, they may be deployed in the summoning of subchiefs and clan heads, and they may be used to announce the end of a preharvest ban on drumming. Other instruments are similarly put to communicative use, be it in connection with religious rites, festivals, recreation, or invitations to courtship.

The gap between the worlds modeled in indigenous discourse and that of the Hornbostel-Sachs classification system seems huge, but is one system better than the other? The scientific concerns of Hornbostel-Sachs arose in response to specific social and institutional imperatives. It seems likely, then, that as more museums are built in Africa and curators seek effective and relevant schemes for classifying instruments, they will either turn to, modify, or

---

30. Nzewi, *Musical Sense and Musical Meaning*, 20.

adapt previous European efforts (including the Hornbostel-Sachs scheme) or develop fresh schemes based largely if not entirely on indigenous conceptualizations. Therefore, it is not simply a question of which is the better scheme—a question that is rather like comparing apples to oranges—but of recognizing the pressures and interests that have led to the development of this or that scheme. If the informal, heterogenous, but deeply suggestive metaphorical discourses of, say, the Kpelle, the Northern Ewe, the Hausa, and others seem so much richer than the dry, scientific decimal points of Hornbostel-Sachs, it should nevertheless be remembered that they issue from different descriptive economies and serve different purposes. African discourses are secure in their orientation to local usage; they are under no obligation to meet some transethnic standard. The European scheme seeks international, indeed global standing; as with all things colonial, it seeks to control.[31]

**Voice**. Pride of place among African musical instruments belongs to the voice. There is no known society in which a species of vocalization approximating song, broadly and flexibly conceived, is unknown. Many treatises on African musical instruments exclude the voice partly because it is not external to the body; it is not an object to be picked up, traded, multiplied, or displayed in a museum. The voice is part of the human body, inseparable from a given subjectivity; it is personal and may be identified with a complex combination of attributes. The African voice is the first instrument because it is the origin of sound as sound and of sound as language. It embodies a primal "cantological" impulse.[32]

Giving priority to the voice may help counter the once-pervasive view that drumming rather than singing is the most fundamental form of African musical expression. There is no denying the prominence and symbolic role of drums, but even within rich traditions associated with the Akan, Baule, Baganda, and Yoruba, the human voice is never far away. Could it be that difference-seeking outsiders are the ones who have drummed up the image of the drum (and the complexity of its attendant rhythms) as the African musical instrument par excellence? Might there be something exotic about the drum as a symbol of black Africa? We might recall that many African communities (including some Pygmy populations, or communities in Rwanda studied by Gansemans) do not invest in drumming at all. Perhaps the view persists

31. For a broader, non-Africa-centered critique of the Hornbostel-Sachs nomenclature, see Margaret Kartomi, "The Classification of Musical Instruments: Changing Trends in Research from the Nineteenth Century, with Special Reference to the 1990s," *Ethnomusicology* 45, no. 2 (2001): 283–314.

32. Gary Tomlinson, "Musicology, Anthropology, History," in *The Cultural Study of Music: A Critical Introduction*, 2nd ed. (New York: Routledge), 61.

because the drum would seem to trump voice in its peculiar materiality. That is, because it is an object, the drum can be bought, exchanged, stolen, and deposited in some (European) museum or other; it can be displayed more readily as a symbol of black Africa. By contrast, to display the voice as a living artifact, you would have to take the whole body, and although Europeans and Americans did indeed take whole African bodies to exhibit at fairs in Paris, Brussels, St. Louis, New York, and elsewhere from the 1880s on, the chief historical and economic interest was in the labor promised by muscle rather than vocal cords. Indeed, language and voice were among the first to be killed or suppressed by colonizers and slave traders because they appeared most threatening. African drumming, in any case, is so often bound up with meaningful utterance that its origin in speech, song, or voice, even when indirect, remains potent.

Singing may be a group or solo activity, but in both manifestations it is strongly marked as communal. The communal element is readily heard in the famous vocal polyphonies of various Central African Pygmy populations (the BaAka, the Aka, the Mbuti, and the Efe), where scores of individual singers typically contribute a part to a multipart texture. Here, metaphors of diversity in oneness, or oneness in diversity, or wholes whose parts are distinct yet mutually accommodating, reign. At the other extreme is solo singing, exemplified in the praise singing of numerous Jaliya or griots and griottes in Mande Africa; in the daily intoning of lullabies by mothers; in the intimate, self-delectative songs of the Gbaya; and in the epic singing of the Ubangi. Praise singing, for example, allows an individual to draw on actual or imagined historical events to construct a narrative in song directed at another individual in exchange for remuneration, pecuniary or otherwise. Although it is a solo activity—coordinating improvised praise phrases among several singers at once would be impractical, except in the free-wheeling shouting of appellations and heroic attributes of chiefs—praise singing nevertheless has an underlying communal impulse. Attentive listeners are often on hand to ensure that the historical record is correct, that memory lapses are fixed immediately, and that the actual showering of praise is made to appear as though it were coming from more than one individual. Lullabies, too, allow mothers to address their children, comfort themselves as they contemplate the challenges of life, or even cast insinuations on their enemies and rivals, including cowives within a polygamous community or neighbors perceived to be in competition. Again, although it is produced as a solo genre, the lullaby harbors a communal framework. And increasingly in modern times, solo singing (often self-accompanied on a kora, guitar, or harp lute), with its roots in traditional practices, is often mounted on stage by star singers with a group of backup singers.

Societies cultivate communal singing to varying extents—for some it is a daily, signature activity; for others it is an occasional feature of social life. It would be more accurate, therefore, to think of the profile of African society in terms of a mixture of generic practices. In the Republic of South Africa, for example, the powerful choral tradition epitomized in *isicathamiya* (an all-male singing tradition) is only one of several manifestations of voice; others include the singing of songs of resistance, traditional group singing, overtone singing among the Xhosa, and solo singing accompanied by the musical bow. The Wagogo of Tanzania cultivate several rich traditions of (often homophonic) multipart singing, sometimes enlivened by various iconic effects produced by clever use of voice registers. Some of these special effects are reserved for occasions rather than deployed routinely as part of daily life. Among the Northern Ewe of Matse, warrior (*asafo*) songs originating in encounters with the Akan in the nineteenth century are sung by all-male companies in a striking declamatory style. These "serious" and only occasionally performed genres exist alongside more routine work songs, farming songs, and recreational songs.

A wide range of sound ideals subtends the expressions of African voices, and although no single mode of vocal utterance is standard, a great deal of interest and admiration attaches to voices that remain attached to persons, languages, or ritual practices, not severed from them. Diversity in ideals is partly reflected in indigenous conceptions of "voice" and "singing" cited earlier. It appears that African-language verbs that translate the English words *say, recite, speak*, and *sing* often inhabit the same broad semantic field. In a call-and-response format, the "call" may be rendered as *lift, raise, begin, start, fetch*, or *send* (see Vai, Kpelle, and Northern Ewe, among other examples), while the response may use terms like *agree, receive, get*, or *catch*. Each metaphor has its own field of inspiration, engendering different sorts of traces on the quality of the sound produced.

Diversity is further reflected in range and mode of articulation. The compass, for example, of an individual song may accept the range of spoken language, confining the song's intervallic limits to a fourth, fifth, or sixth. This is especially true of children's rhymes and games involving word play, but it also may be heard in lullabies, folktale interludes, and children's game songs. There are, however, many instances in which the tessitura is extended upward to allow the singer more latitude for depth of expression. A vivid example, recorded by Hugo Zemp among the Dan in 1966, features a *zole* (described as "midwife and performer of excision operations") lamenting the loss of her husband in a dramatic declamatory style.[33] In absolute terms, the singer's range is about a tenth, but in the more subjective terms of vocal utterance, the range

33. Listen to "Solo Song of a Woman" on the CD, *Africa: The Dan*, track 3.

seems wide indeed, suggesting the following semiotic associations: exclamation and extreme expression of grief with higher registers, pausing or reposing with middle registers, and resignation and despair with low registers.

The use of registers often builds on what appear to be their natural functions. Where singing styles have been directly influenced by or modeled upon Arabic styles, a nasalized sound most often optimized in a mid- to upper register is cultivated. The sound ideal imagined and realized is precisely one of a strategic constriction of vocal cords. African song is not generally invested in especially low registers, but there are remarkable exceptions, such as the "whispering inanga" recorded by Cornelia Fales, with its somewhat eerie effects.[34]

Articulation in song is predominantly syllabic; that is, there is one note per syllable of text. This alignment preserves the temporal quality of spoken language and thus promotes ready comprehension of sung text. As we will see in the chapter on melody, however, language and music are often in tension in many vocal genres. While syllabic articulation is predominant, it is not exclusive. Melismatic expression occurs especially in declamatory styles with strong Arabic or Middle Eastern influence. Some Mande singing shows this influence, as do practices in Ethiopia, Somalia, Malagasy Republic, Chad, and elsewhere. In contemporary times, singers like Youssou N'Dour and Salif Keita cultivate high-register male styles strongly influenced by Arabic cantillation.

Modern styles of vocal production sometimes retain and vary those of tradition while also adopting or adapting foreign models. This is especially evident in the range of voice styles cultivated by singers of popular and art music. The guitar harmonies that accompany Sierra Leonean S. E. Rogie's deep-toned singing often impose a more diatonic or tempered regime on his singing, aligning his style with those of singers of global pop and protestant hymns. Jùjú musician King Sunny Ade, by contrast, often retains the tradition of Yoruba prosody and intonation, touching it up only in the direction of a pervasive modality that helps to authenticate his words and message. Lagbaja often straddles the divide between tradition and modernity in a strategically postmodern manner, juxtaposing vocal models in an eclectic vein. Ghanaian singer Osei Antwi is virtually a ventriloquist, taking over melodic styles of Western popular music and fitting them with Twi-language words, often in a strategically incongruous alignment that nevertheless has a wide appeal.

Singers of art music are equally eclectic in what they do. There are easy arrangements of folk songs that are sung with little elevation beyond the folk level—natural, sincere, un-self-conscious. Some imitate the bel canto style of Italian opera, complete with the (sometimes indiscriminate) use of vibrato and

---

34. Listen to track 3 ("Inanga chuchotee") of the CD accompanying *Africa: The Garland Encyclopedia of World Music*, ed. Stone.

a style of diction that sacrifices a proper articulation of words for an over-whelming privileging of voice and sonority. These and other styles are mag-nificently displayed in Akin Euba's opera, *Chaka* (1999), in which the stately bass voice of Chaka, the strangulated soprano voice of Noliwe, and the natural but assertive voices of the folk chorus intermingle in a dazzling display.[35]

Finally, the voice stands as the supreme bearer of emotion in African music. Listen to the crying songs (*avihawo*) of the Northern Ewe of Ghana and Togo, and you will hear singers exploring the range between speech and song, between spoken and sung language in a most affecting way. This range and flexibility in sonic and verbal articulation enables mourners to clear space for the unbridled registration of emotion engendered by death. Shouts, cries, sobs, and weeping, although in principle extramusical, are incorpo-rated into the intoning of mourning phrases, and performance is enlivened by modest movement, which could range from a gentle swaying from side to side through an agitated forward-backward walk to a vigorous bobbing of the head with palms placed in the center of the scalp. No other instru-ment allows performers to explore these vast spaces so authentically and to link the worlds of words and concepts with those of sound and sonority so felicitously. It is in this sense that the voice stands as the preeminent African musical instrument.

**Handclap**. Handclapping is such an integral part of music making in Africa that we are obliged to treat hands as sound-producing objects. Dale Olsen has suggested that we add "corpophones" to Hornbostel and Sachs's categories to take account of body parts as instruments.[36] The energy displayed in hand-clapping, the metrical and rhythmic reinforcement that they bring, and the variety of patterns that they engender all justify recognizing colliding palms as musical instruments.

Handclapping is close to being in the beginning, for it appears that the acquisition of spoken language, dance, and singing emerged in tandem with clapping. This early inducement to move and externalize a beat is often a key element in the musical socialization of African children.[37] Clapping provides a minimum accompaniment to singing, serving to transform lived time into musical time. Clapping and the coordinated slapping of other body parts are prominent in scores of game songs. They assume increasingly structural func-tions in adult dances.

35. CD, *Chaka: An Opera in Two Chants* (Richmond, CA: MRI Press, 1999).

36. Dale A. Olsen, "Note on Corpophone," *Society for Ethnomusicology Newsletter* 20, no. 4 (1980): 5.

37. Nzewi, *Musical Practice and Creativity*.

The diverse range of clap types is impressive. A clap may perform a simple metronomic function by reinforcing the gross beat. This function is often performed by community members who are participating at a minimum level in a group performance. There are clap patterns that reproduce time-line patterns and thus function as layers within a polyrhythmic matrix. Clap patterns can be vigorous and oppositional, serving to add spice to the rhythmic life; others are conformational, reinforcing a beat pattern that is either being articulated elsewhere in an ensemble or emerging from a confluence of other rhythms. It appears that clapping is never slow, never at a tempo below, say, quarter-note = 60. The reason for this may be practical. Clap patterns are often part of the music, not external, superfluous layers; they are definitional of structure rather than superstructural. Just as dance tempos are restricted on the slow end, so are musical tempos, including handclapping. If the dance is quick, its clap patterns are likely to be quick, too. It is precisely because of the motional constraint on hand movement that its corresponding tempos tend to be on the faster end.

African clap patterns are too many to illustrate concisely. Observing them in context can tell us interesting things about performing practice, rhythm, meter, and expectations regarding levels of participation. A good resource for exploring clap patterns is the multivolume *JVC-Smithsonian Folkways Video Anthology of Music and Dance of Africa*, which includes footage from eleven different countries: Egypt, Uganda, and Senegal (volume 1); The Gambia, Liberia, Ghana, and Nigeria (volume 2); and Kenya, Malawi, Botswana, and South Africa (volume 3). The vigorous clap patterns that accompany dances in Northern Ghana may be compared with the synchronized patterns of the San Bushmen and further contrasted with the beat-keeping motives of Vai children and adults.[38]

**Drum.** The instrument most readily associated in the popular imagination with Africa is the drum. So pervasive is the association that some are surprised to learn that some popular "African" drums are of foreign origins, that drumming may be as pervasive on other continents (as, for example, in South India) as it is in Africa, or that there are African communities that use drums sparingly or not at all. Still, drums occupy a privileged position in the economy of symbols that define Africa. Frequently associated with speech and dance, drums grace many a social occasion. High on the list are royal drums that signal the superior status of a king or a chief. The royal drums of the king of

---

38. *JVC-Smithsonian Folkways Video Anthology of Music and Dance of Africa* (Barre, VT: Multicultural Media, 1996).

Baganda, the drums kept by King Glélé of Benin, the drums that announce various chiefs in the Democratic Republic of the Congo, and the drums that display the splendor of the Asante empire—these are among the many royal drum entourages found in Africa. Drums may accompany processions of chiefs or be beaten to signal certain religious rites. A king may summon various clan leaders and subchiefs by having his chief drummer call them in drum language. In some places (say, among the Dagomba), drummers are custodians of the community's oral-historical records; accordingly, they are regarded as persons of high status.

At the lower end of social protocol is the use of drums for everyday recreational purposes. Where dancing is the predominant channel for community entertainment, drums, played singly or in groups, or in combination with other instruments, provide the backdrop. Drum rhythms are normally interpreted holistically rather than atomistically by dancers. Popular recreational dances, many of them built on drum rhythms, are often interpreted in this way, making spaces for the moderately skilled and the highly skilled. Some dances are of relatively recent provenance, and this may be reflected in the specific kinds of drums used, the movements preferred, or even the songs sung. In the space that separates royal drums from those used in popular and recreational music,

**Photo 2.1** Wagogo women with drums, Nzali, Tanzania.

**Photo 2.2** Drum carver James Acheampong, Kumase, Ghana.

**Photo 2.3** Kete drums, Kumasi, Ghana.

there exist other drums that aid ritual, enhance acts of mourning, facilitate worship, function as signals (of war, danger, imminent arrival, or whatever is deemed worthy of such signaling), or serve as instruments of communication.

The generic drum consists of a membrane (typically animal skin) stretched over the open end of a hollowed-out tree trunk or similarly shaped material, including a calabash, barrel, tin can, or woven column. This "Ur form" is subject to many variations of design, decoration, and functional use. Drums may be single or double headed. They come in a wide variety of sizes, ranging from tiny handheld drums (some playable by children) through sets of medium-sized drums (the tuned Ese drum rows of the Igbo are a case in point) to gigantic structures like the Enteboli of Uganda or Fontonfrom drums of the Ashanti. Drums may or may not be tuned; they may be played or scraped with sticks, hands, or some combination of stick and hand. Some drums are decorated (sometimes elaborately), while others are left in a relatively plain or natural state. Drums frequently have attachments that alter or augment the basic drum sound; this is done for a variety of reasons, some of them functional, others aesthetic, and still others symbolic. Some sacred drums are decked in material whose origins are often publicized as secret. For example, in some communities, human skulls may be attached to drums to symbolize a community's military prowess; in others, the drumhead itself may be made of human skin. Some drums are beaten not with sticks but with human bones.[39] Jingles attached to the drumhead or to some part of the body of the drum produce secondary rhythms that enhance the polyrhythmic effect.

Drums may be beaten solo or in groups. Certain sacred drums are beaten solo as befits their elevated status, and not just by any ordinary drummer but by a designated drummer, one who has been properly prepared according to the ritual or religious norms of the community in question. Some women's recreational groups may employ a male drummer to accompany their singing where women are not allowed to drum. Ensembles may contain the same drum type (dòndón ensembles in Dagomba, bàtá ensembles in Benin or Nigeria) or a mix of related and unrelated drums.

The kinds of musical material assigned to drums vary from community to community. A single dead beat, sounded intermittently, and accompanying a consecrated silence, may be used as a signal to call attention, to announce weighty news, or to induce contemplation. This forms the slow end of the tempo spectrum. The principle at work here is that the drum sound stages a departure from ordinary, lived time and takes us into musical, poetic, or ritual time. A drum may expose a simple rhythm as an accompaniment to singing

39. See Charles O. Aluede, "The Anthropomorphic Attributes of African Musical Instruments: History and Use in Esan, Nigeria," *Anthropologist* 8, no. 3 (2006): 157–160.

or produce a more complex rhythm to enhance the overall rhythmic texture. In some of the great genres featuring ensemble performance, a lead drum may create elaborate narratives of rhythms. Some of these narratives may signal sections of the dance to dancers and audiences, while others may embody virtuosity as a value in and of itself.

Although they are often referred to as percussion instruments, many African drums have a relational pitch dimension that endows them with a joint melodic and rhythmic function. Meki Nzewi coined the term *melorhythmic* to draw attention to these attributes and to remind us that African drums are not merely rhythm-producing machines.[40] Melody and rhythm in African drumming thoroughly inform each other as an alloy; they are separate only in concept, not in percept. Furthermore, listening for drum melodies may also heighten awareness of the timbral aspects of drum rhythms. An excellent example of the investment in timbre is the extensive set of mnemonics developed for certain traditions of drumming. The Southern Ewe, for example, have as many as seventeen names for different drum strokes.[41] While the existence of a rigid syntax of timbres is yet to be proven, there is evidence that composer-performers' choices are not arbitrary but follow preference rules beyond simply providing contrast.

Drums, then, serve as an important focus for inquiry not only into the nature of African instruments but also into larger questions such as the interface of language and music, the boundary between the musical and the "extramusical," and the limits of material and spiritual domains. For this reason, we need to look beyond the homogenizing and sensationalizing myths that have been related to the African drum and attend to its concrete and multiple cultural functions.

**One-stringed fiddle**. Known by a variety of regional names (*gonje* among the Dagbamba and Kusasi in Ghana and the Gurma in Burkina Faso, *goge* among the Hausa in Nigeria, *titi* to the Wolof in Guinea, *coucouma* to the Bilala in Niger, *ngali* or *takare* in Mozambique, *soko* to the Bwaa in Burkina Faso, *susaa* to the Mandinka in Gambia, and *nyayaru* to the Fula in Sierra Leone), the one-stringed fiddle occurs prominently in Sudanic West Africa (Senegal, Niger, Nigeria, Mali, Gambia, Cote d'Ivoire, Cameroon, and Burkina Faso), in parts of

40. Nzewi, "Melo-Rhythmic Essence and Hot Rhythm in Nigerian Folk Music," *Black Perspective in Music* 2, no. 1 (1974): 23–28.

41. See Robert Kwami, "Towards a Comprehensive Catalogue of Ewe Drum Mnemonics." On a possible syntax of mnemonics, see Wayne Slawson, "Features, Musical Operations, and Composition: A Derivation from Ewe Drum Music," in *African Musicology: Current Trends*, vol. 1, ed. Jacqueline Djedje and William Carter (Los Angeles: African Studies Center at UCLA and Cross Roads Press/African Studies Association, 1989), 307–319.

East Africa (Malawi, Tanzania, Ethiopia, Eritrea, and Somalia), in North Africa, and among populations with some Islamic or Arabic influence. The instrument has a long neck to accommodate the stretched string and sits on a calabash resonator with a hole (or two). It is played by rubbing or scraping the string with a bow made typically of horse hair. A portable instrument, the one-stringed fiddle indexes a tradition of solo performance, although there are ensembles of gonjes.[42] Thus, like the blues singer with a guitar or banjo, the fiddler can create "natural song" by singing and accompanying him- or herself. This type of song is most suitable for genres in which the spoken word is not sound alone—genres like praise, lamentation, satirical commentary, and even singing the news (as is reported in Ethiopia[43]). Lacking the pressures of ensemble performance, the imaginative gonje player is released to craft temporal structures that are flexibly ordered to enhance his messages—musical and verbal.

The music of the one-stringed fiddle reflects and celebrates the intrinsic minimality of the instrument's resources. Pitch is often pentatonic, and the musical procedure consists of repeating motives by means of a sawing, highly rhythmic action. When it accompanies song, the fiddle may or may not be temporally coordinated with the singing.

Probably the most important aesthetic and structural feature of the kinds of natural song accompanied by the one-stringed fiddle is a resultant heterophony, that is, rhythmically displaced melodic lines unfolding simultaneously. Adorno heard something similar in Mahler's orchestral song cycle *Das Lied von der Erde* and called it *unscharfe Unisono*, or blurred unison.[44] If we allow ourselves the liberty of a contrapuntal reading, we can hear parallels between "Western" and "African" usages of such indistinct unisons. Listen to the one-stringed fiddle recordings in the International Library of African Music collection, or those accompanying Jacqueline Djedje's magisterial study of the instrument and its repertory, and you will notice that although the fiddle means to play in unison with the voice, there is a perpetual "discrepancy" between its notes and those sung by the voice. Depending on the musical idiom, discrepancies may be more pronounced in the middle of phrases rather than at beginnings or endings. We might think of the gonje player as working with an expanded conception of sameness, as possessing a wider margin of

42. As heard, for example, on the CD, *Master Fiddlers of Dagbon* (Cambridge, MA: Rounder Records, 2001.

43. As heard on the LP, *The Music of Ethiopia 2: Cushites* (Kassel: Bärenreiter, 1970), track B4, "Masenqo Player, Singing the News."

44. Adorno, *Mahler: A Musical Physiognomy*, trans. Edmund Jephcott (Chicago: University of Chicago Press, 1992), 150.

tolerance for pitch disagreement. The discrepancies are strategic rather than accidental, however; the fiddler aims for such apparent slippage. Far from suggesting any sort of insensitivity to fine calibrations in pitch, this enactment of intended discrepancies (often below the semitone threshold) actually implies a rejection of certain thin or less tasty sound combinations. Moreover, the fact that the sequence of discrepancies is not systematic, the fact that song and string sounds are rhythmically coordinated by varying degrees of (non)discrepancy, suggests a fuller and richer awareness on the part of the fiddler than is typically conveyed by simply saying that he is operating within a different economy of pitch coordination.

The fiddle's repertory shows the instrument singing and talking, entertaining in song mode, and informing in speech mode. Like the voice and the drum, the one-stringed fiddle is able to travel the full gamut from spoken language to music. When singing accompanies the playing of the instrument, the beauty of the art rests in part on the variable ways in which the conceptual unison between the played and the sung is enacted. Mediating forces include the limited flexibility of the mode of articulation possible on the instrument, the performer's spontaneous pitch-matching skills, and the constraints imposed by prior tuning. Something of the same aesthetic tendency occurs in African genres in which instrumental timbres are inflected by buzzers, dampeners, and mufflers, as, for example, in mbira and xylophone performances. These are expressions of preference, not signs of unattained goals.

Photo 2.4  Gonje, Tamale Ghana.

**Bells and rattles**. Iron bells are among the most common and ancient of African musical instruments. Although they originated in the great iron cultures of the past,[45] they have by now spread across Africa and are used in cultures that never produced a metal strip. A practical advantage of the bell stems from its size, portability, and timbral stability. Although ensembles of bells may be found in Benin, Ghana, and Nigeria, among other places,[46] they are more typically incorporated into mixed ensembles where they are assigned specific musical roles.

Single-pronged bells are limited in their "talking ability," although their rhythmic potential and colors are often exploited. Double-pronged bells, by contrast, occasionally enable some conversing because they possess the minimum tonal differentiation that allows players to generate melorhythmic patterns. Bells can be played by children and adults, and by highly skilled and modestly skilled musicians. Variations in the design of bells are many: castanets, metal strips, boat-shaped bells, and metal sticks.

Probably the most iconic use of the bell is within West African drum ensembles. In the performance of popular Ghanaian dances like agbadza, agbekor, adowa, bawa, bɔbɔbɔ, gabada, and kpanlogo, among many others, the bell is typically entrusted with a signature rhythmic pattern that it repeats without variation for the duration of the dance composition. In the absence of actual bells made of metal, substitutes like sticks, cans, bottles, and blades of hoe may assume their musical function.

Rattles, too, come in a variety of shapes, sizes, and designs. Most common is a calabash or shell filled with seeds, stones, or sand to produce a buzzing sound. It may also be covered with beads. Like the gonje, mbira, and bell, the rattle is relatively small and portable. Rattles are for the most part accompanying instruments, often marking the beat or playing one of the simpler, unchanging rhythms within a polyrhythmic texture. In some recreational genres, large numbers of rattles may be used simultaneously to enhance the communal playing experience. Northern Ewe genres like gbolo and gabada may feature as many as forty rattle players. Women rattle performers are the norm.

Although relatively simple, rattles contribute vitally to the timbre and articulative resources of an ensemble. They may be shaken, stroked, palmed, or bounced off various body parts. Because they are typically constituted by tiny components in collision (seeds or beads), their sonic output is plural at the core. While players normally enact an agreed-upon beat or rhythm, the cumulative rattle effect reinforces this practical plurality. Any element of indistinctiveness that sets in is fully intended.

45. Jan Vansina, "The Bells of Kings," *Journal of African History* 10, no. 2 (1967): 187–197.

46. For an example from Eastern Nigeria, see Odyke Nzewi, "The Technology and Music of the Nigerian Igbo Ogene Anuka Bell Orchestra," *Leonardo Music Journal* 10 (2000): 25–31.

**Xylophones**. In its basic form, the xylophone consists of slabs of wood (or other material) of different sizes placed over a resonating chamber. This "keyboard" is played by striking the keys with sticks or mallets. The resonating chamber may be a dug pit or a set of calabashes. Keys are normally arranged in sequence from low to high, often reflecting the size of the slabs or resonating calabashes. Attached to the resonators are buzzers or other sound-inflecting material designed to enhance the primary sound by dulling its brightness, introducing a buzzing sound, or otherwise altering its timbre. Xylophones are common in East, Central, and Southern Africa and in pockets of West Africa. Among celebrated traditions are the timbilla orchestras of the Chopi in Mozambique, the akadinda and ama-dinda traditions of the Baganda in Uganda, the balafon traditions of Burkina Faso and Mali, and the gyil in Northern Ghana and the Côte d'Ivoire.

Xylophones are not usually regarded as exclusive instruments. They may be played on ritual occasions, as part of entertainment for royalty, for open-access community music making, and at funerals and circumcision parties. The spatial layout of the instrument allows it to be played by one or more players. Xylophones may be played singly or in ensemble.

The xylophone enables some of the greatest traditions of virtuoso performing in Africa. Fast, highly virtuosic and vigorous modes of articulation are heard in the playing of the Kouyate family from Guinea, of solo artists like Bernard Woma and Kakraba Lobi from Ghana, and of Neba Solo from Mali. Because of the will to virtuosity that it seems to foster, xylophone music may come off as autonomous or pure musical art. Like drums, xylophones sometimes speak; well-known songs with words may be used as the basis for improvisation on the instrument (e.g., "Ssemantima" tune studied by Peter Cooke[47]). There are, how-ever, periods in xylophone performances where songs and words as generative elements are superseded by the force of an intramusical improvisational impulse that highlights technique and agility and leaves the referential world behind.

Xylophones cultivate a native polyphony. As keys are struck and departed from, all of them within easy reach of the player, several melodies (and attendant harmo-nies) unfold simultaneously. Thus, as Kubik has often reminded us, the difference between real and apparent melodies, between what is played and what is heard, or between what is put in and what is emergent becomes significant in analysis.[48]

Of special significance is the experience of time promulgated by xylo-phone playing. The "frozen" pitch system or harmonic field—most usually pentatonic—engenders a feeling of harmonic succession rather than harmonic progression. In many genres, there are no large trajectories of periodicity by

---

47. Francis Katamba and Peter Cooke, "Ssematimba ne Kikwabanga: The Music and Poetry of a Ganda Historical Song," *World of Music* 29, no. 2 (1987): 349–368.

48. Kubik, "The Phenomenon of Inherent Rhythms in East and Central African Instrumental Music," *African Music* 3, no. 1 (1962): 33–42.

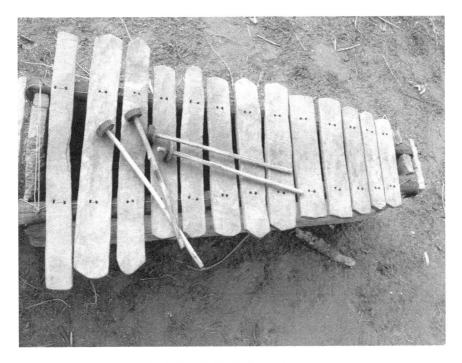

**Photo 2.5** Mkwajungoma (xylophone), Nzali, Tanzania.

which an earlier event can be said to have caused a later effect; rather, the temporal manner approximates the marking of time. Recoiling from the future and emphasizing presentness seems to be the desired goal. By compelling attention to the here and now, the xylophone aesthetic sets aside the stylized management of long-term desire that one so often encounters in European music of the common-practice era.

**Mbira**. Associated in the popular imagination with the Shona people of Zimbabwe, the mbira has attained a high level of prominence as both a national and an international instrument. Gerhard Kubik has researched the distribution of the instrument extensively, and he lists the following among countries where this lamellophone (his preferred standard term) is found: Angola, Cameroon, Central African Republic, Democratic Republic of the Congo, Malawi, Mozambique, Nigeria, Tanzania, Uganda, Zambia, and Zimbabwe. It is, in other words, more common in Eastern, Central, and especially Southern Africa than it is in West Africa.[49]

Morphologically, the mbira shares with the xylophone a graded series of sounding keys mounted on a sounding board and in some cases further amplified by being placed in a gourd or calabash. Keys are commonly made from

49. Kubik, "African and African American Lamellophone."

metal strips, but they could also be millet blades, bamboo pieces, pieces of wood, and umbrella parts. Various buzzers may be attached to the resonator to ensure a muffled sound. An mbira may have one or more manuals. A popular one, *mbira dzavadzimu*, has three—two on the left, one on the right. The method of playing is usually by plucking the keys by the thumbs and index fingers.

Given its size and modest sound, the mbira would appear to be an intimate instrument—designed for "chamber" rather than orchestral use, and well suited to individual or even private music making. It would join the one-stringed fiddle, the musical bow, and the kora in supporting performances of natural song and would be distinguished from "loud" ceremonial drums, horns, and bells. Mbiras are often played in ensemble, however, and what would seem to be an acoustic modesty is overridden by a higher symbolic legibility.

Like xylophone music, mbira music is engagingly and intensely repetitive, with a hypnotic, mesmerizing quality. Those familiar with minimalist music by Steve Reich, Lamonte Young, and John Adams will find an immediate resonance with the sound world created by mbira playing. A single mbira can give the illusion of an ensemble performance because of the intrinsic polyphonic layout of the instrument. Like the xylophone, mbira music often engenders a temporal experience oriented to the present. There is often something cyclic about this music, and the succession of notes may evoke a stream of endless melody. Its rhythms, unlike those associated with West African drum ensembles, sometimes blur their periodicity as they defer to pulse-based articulation. Mbiras can speak by imitating speech sounds, they make excellent accompanying instruments (superior, in this regard, to xylophones), and they can be used to cultivate the kinds of acoustical continuities that place music beyond the realm of decipherable language.

The singing that accompanies Shona mbira music is intimately wedded to the character of the instrumental sound, allowing practitioners to distinguish various voice types through mode of utterance (lyrical or declamatory) and registral segregation. The fullness of the vocal element in mbira performance suggests that when voice and instrument perform together, neither instrument "accompanies" the other; rather, the roles of lead and accompaniment are shared. This interlocking spirit lies at the heart of the competing groupings that many listeners discern in mbira music and may also explain why some participants in ceremonies involving spirit possession are transported by this idiom. As with certain xylophones, the entire range of the mbira is physically within easy reach of the player, and this allows an easy juxtaposition of low and high registers, which in turn mediates various melodic discontinuities and fosters new continuities.[50]

50. The standard work on Shona mbira music is Paul Berliner, *The Soul of Mbira* (Berkeley: University of California Press, 1978), which may be usefully read in conjunction with the CD, *Africa: Shona Mbira Music* ([Japan]: WEA International, 1977. See also

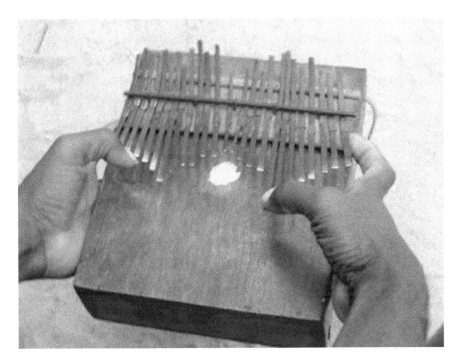

**Photo 2.6** Ilimba (lamellophone), Nzali, Tanzania.

**Flutes and horns**. Flutes and horns, core instruments in the African wind family, are found all over the continent. They are especially common in the Sudanic belt, where the savannah vegetation provides natural materials for transforming such things as millet blades into musical instruments. Flutes are relatively easy to play; they involve a direct production of sound by blowing while covering or uncovering holes to vary the pitch. The most pertinent variation in the design of the instrument is the number of holes it has—there may be as few as one or as many as eight. The instrument's timbre depends on several factors: the size of the resonating chamber, the nature of the mouthpiece, the material from which it is made, and the method of playing. Flutes may be played solo or in ensemble. Ensembles of multiple flutes known as panpipes are found in Eastern and South Africa.

Horns are made from wood, elephant tusks, antelope horns, or cow locks. Sometimes referred to as "whistles" (as among the Dan in the Cote d'Ivoire), they, too, may be played solo or in ensemble. Solo horns may serve as signaling

Scherzinger, "Negotiating the Music-Theory/African-Music Nexus," the didactic film *Mbira: The Technique of the Mbira dza Vadzimu* (Zimbabwe) (Devault, PA: Constant Springs, 1994), and the documentary, *Mbira dza Vadzimu: Dambatsoko, an Old Cult Center, With Mutchera and Ephat Mujuru* (University Park: Pennsylvania State University, 1978).

**Photo 2.7** Seven fógwòm flutes of the Mofou, Cameroon.

**Photo 2.8** Húrzozoŋ flute, Guiziga, Cameroon.

**Photo 2.9** Siili flutes of the Toupouri, Cameroon.

**Photo 2.10** Ntahera Ivory trumpets, Royal Funeral, Manhyia Palace, Ghana.

instruments (this practice is common in the Democratic Republic of the Congo), or they may be incorporated into ensembles of mixed instruments. Multiple horns may be formed into bands or orchestras. Three salient examples are the multiple horn ensembles cultivated at the palace of the Asantehene, the makondere horns from Uganda, and the horn orchestras of the Central African Republic.

The use of the mouth to blow air into a column brings the voice into close proximity with the flute. One of the most distinctive uses of the flute is in the playing of unmeasured music. The aesthetic may seem improvised, and it is often allied with the intonation of speech. It is not merely that some flutes function as speech surrogates but that certain flute idioms retain the spoken manner of speech. Flutes are also often played in ensemble. A fine example is the repertoire recorded by Natalie Fernando and Fabrice Marandola in the Mandara Mountains of Cameroon. Exclusive flute ensembles or mixed ensembles (with drums and voices) deliver musical textures consisting of brief motifs repeated in the manner of ostinato. Here, too, registral traversal is made easy by the nature of the instrument, freeing the performers to explore disjunct melodies that, in combination, reveal new lines of conjunction. This method is shared by horn ensembles, which may exploit the hocket technique whereby performers, mindful of a larger texture, nevertheless articulate only one of its parts, the thought being that as different performers articulate different parts, the ideal texture is realized. The resulting harmony is sometimes based on a preexisting song or model.

**Kora and seperewa**. Associated most readily with Mande cultures in West Africa, the kora is a privileged symbol of grounded domesticity and many-in-one-ness. Like the mbira, it indexes an intimate or private register of music making. The praise singer may accompany himself on the kora, a griot may be similarly supported, or the historian recounting the battles of his people may do so to a lute accompaniment. The sense of grounding comes from the instrument's function in marking or activating time and in taking a back seat as voice takes front seat. In such an avowed accompanimental role, the kora aesthetic is framed by melodic ideas that are often brief, provide contrast to the singer's lines, punctuate silences, or elaborate in tone what is being sung in song.

It is a sign of the kind of innovation associated with African creativity that what might have seemed an antivirtuosic traditional instrument, the kora, has become a channel for virtuosic display. An excellent example is the art of Malian kora player Toumani Diabate (b. 1965). Drawing on a vast array of local and cosmopolitan resources, Toumani Diabate has taken the kora to new heights of invention and virtuosity. Passing allusions to popular song, exclamatory scale passages often in descending motion, and a pulse-regulated mode of utterance typically ride on an ever-present groove, making for a delightful and fresh sound.[51]

---

51. For a sampling of Toumani Diabate's art, listen to his CD, *Jarabi: The Best of Toumani Diabate*.

**Photo 2.11**  Ipangwa (guitar), Nzali, Tanzania.

While the Akan harp or seperewa does not command the same degree of visibility on the international scene as does the Malian or Gambian kora, its potential is no less significant. Like other stringed instruments, the seperewa's essential morphology is a series of stretched strings attached to a curved stick stem. The popular method of playing is by plucking the strings. The instrument can be used to "sing," to accompany singing, or to relay messages by mimicking the patterns of speech. Osei Kwame Korankye, a gifted Ghanaian musician, composer, and performer, has developed an individual style in performing the seperewa. Blending traditional harmonies and melodies with others taken from a variety of modern sources, including those associated with popular music, and drawing on a vivid poetic imagination, Osei creates memorable structures in performance that are at once old and new. A bard in the old-fashioned sense, Osei sings and accompanies himself on the seperewa and does so with particular eloquence. Sometimes he incorporates literal imitations of speech on his instrument; more usually, he uses the seperewa to provide a chordal accompaniment to song or recitation.[52]

52. Osei Korankye's sound world may be sampled on the CD, *Seperewa Kasa*. His art and aesthetic are discussed by Tobias Klein, *Moderne Traditionen: Studien zur postkolonialen Musikgeschichte Ghanas* (Berlin: Peter Lang, 2008).

**Ensembles**. Most of the instruments described in the foregoing are playable either as solo instruments or in ensemble with other instruments. Ensembles consist of two kinds: those that are made up of the same instrument or family of instruments, and those that are assembled from a mixed group. Striking scenes of African music making featuring instruments of the same class include Pygmy encampments in polyphonic song, tuned Entenga drums from Uganda, tuned and graded ukom drums from the Igbo, giant xylophone orchestras of the Chopi, and eighteen-piece horn ensembles from the Central African Republic, to name only a handful. The Senegalese group shown in Figure 2.1 is made up of differently sized drums with complementary timbres. In general, the multiplication of sameness in ensemble music reinforces identity, solidarity, and collectivity and serves to project a community's symbolic power to those on the outside.

More common are ensembles in which instruments of different kinds and classes are brought together for the purpose of music making. Mixed groups meet an aesthetic need for contrast, contrariety, or variety in timbral, tonal, and rhythmic expression. In bringing together difference, mixed ensembles invite interpretation along social lines and encourage metaphors of complementation and hierarchy. Maurice Djenda writes: "The instrumental heterogeneity of a music ensemble [in the Central African Republic] will often (as among the Gbaya-Manza-Ngbaka) consist of three xylophones (bazanga: small xylophone; rgiringba: ancestors; kpembe: youngest child), a double-headed drum (bion) and small bells and rattles (ngala), in addition to hand-clapping."[53] And the Pan-African Orchestra (founded in 1988 by Nana Danso Abiam) comprises a variety of instruments, including drums, bells, rattles, xylophones, and bamboo flutes. Mixed ensembles may be found in many locations. We conclude our discussion of musical instruments by commenting on one of the canonical West African ensembles, the Anlo-Ewe agbadza dance ensemble (Figure 2.2).[54]

Sometimes referred to simply as drums (*vuawo*), drum (*vu*), or beaters of the drum (*vufolawo*), this ensemble typically consists of men's and women's voices (speaking and singing), handclaps, rattles, bells, a small drum, a medium-sized drum, and a lead drum.[55] It is in some ways a generic ensemble made up of a lead drummer (sometimes called a "master drummer") who takes charge of the performance, a group of instruments that play fixed patterns and may

53. Djenda, "Central African Republic," *Grove Music Online*, accessed May 25, 2015.

54. There are scores of mixed ensembles throughout Africa, although the function of each ensemble's components may differ from one location to the next.

55. This ensemble (or close relatives of it) is featured in numerous studies of Southern Ewe music, beginning with A. M. Jones and Seth Cudjoe in the 1950s, and extending to writings by, among others, Hewitt Pantaleoni, Alfred Ladzekpo, C. K. Ladzekpo, David Locke, Jeff Pressing, Zabana Kongo, James Burns, George Dor, and Paschale Young.

Figure 2.1 A Senegalese percussion ensemble.

Figure 2.2 Agbadza drum-dance ensemble.

be said to keep the time (bells, handclaps, and rattles), and a middle group comprising instruments whose patterns, though somewhat fixed, incorporate modest dialogue with the lead drummer, even though they are not granted the latter's improvisatory license. The resulting ensemble sound is timbrally distinct. The bell and rattles may play patterns that are very close or sometimes identical, but because these patterns are heard in distinct timbres and at different pitch levels, they come across as compound sounds rather than simple sounds. Similarly, the deep-toned master drum, although it may occasionally double up on one of the simpler rhythms (sometimes to ensure the security of the ensemble), retains its distinctiveness by virtue of the freer, occasionally word-affiliated, and generally more complex patterns that it exposes. The middle-pitched drums sometimes blend into each other or sometimes are absorbed into the thematic world of the two outer groups, but they remain ultimately distinct within the ensemble as a whole. There is, in short, unity in variety, allowing us to project a range of values onto this enduring texture: independence and autonomy on one hand, and dependence and cooperation on the other.

The music and dance associated with the Anlo-Ewe ensemble are by now quite well known. In Togo and Ghana, they continue to be cultivated in both rural and urban locations and by various folkloric, university, and community groups. In Europe and North America, individuals who have invested in these dances often teach them as part of world music classes or as ways of enriching curricula. Because the ensemble is well known, I will forego yet another description of its music for a brief consideration of one of its underlying values.[56]

In a suggestive study of the relationship between African and African American music, composer and scholar Olly Wilson proposed that the sound ideal that unites the two traditions of music making is rooted in heterogeneity rather than homogeneity.[57] The idea of a *heterogeneous sound ideal* has an immediate and intuitive appeal. It suggests, for example, that in forming ensembles, African and African American musicians prefer combinations in which individual instruments retain their distinct characters rather than blend into each other. Instruments do not usurp each other's timbres; rather, even if they encroach on each other's territories, they remain ultimately distinct. There is, therefore, a residual and irreducible plurality at the deepest

---

56. See George Dor, *West African Drumming and Dance in North American Universities: An Ethnomusicological Perspective* (Jackson, Mississippi: University of Mississippi Press, 2014).

57. Olly Wilson, "The Significance of the Relationship Between AfroAmerican Music and West African Music," *Black Perspective in Music* 2, no. 1 (1974): 3–22.

levels of the total ensemble sound. Wilson indeed cited the polyrhythmic tex-ture of agbadza as an example of the African approach and compared it with the ensemble used by James Brown in "Superbad" (voice, sax, trumpet, trom-bone, bass, and drums).

The opposing sound ideal—a homogenous ideal—is one in which instru-ments are combined precisely because their initial or outward differences (predominantly in timbre) can merge into one another to produce a single (or singular) rather than multiple result. Membership in some European orches-tras and choirs, for example, is premised on blending, not on the retention of individuality. Too distinct a string or brass sound might be seen as disrup-tive of the higher uniformity sought for that section of the ensemble, just as a strong soprano or bass who is unable to blend with others might be judged unsuitable for the performance of a mass by Josquin or Palestrina.

Wilson's theory finds immediate support in the kinds of material entrusted to each instrument (voices, bells, handclaps, and drums) within the ensemble. These may be seen in the snippet of transcription quoted in Example 2.1 and made by composer Steve Reich around 1971.[58] (A perfor-mance of agbadza may be heard at Web Example 2.1🌑). On the most imme-diate level, Reich's transcription captures the plurality that Olly Wilson was talking about. Each instrument (from top to bottom: gong, rattle, kagan, kidi, and sogo [master]) plays a different rhythm such that the resultant sound, although coordinated metrically, retains a timbral heterogeneity. This is another way of asserting polyrhythm, the simultaneous and repeated unfolding of more than one rhythm in a musical texture. Note, however, that the heterogeneity of timbre is held in check by the strictness of metri-cal coordination that is underreported by Reich. There are, first of all, a pulse and a beat, both of which inscribe a normalized pattern of movement for the dance. The bell and rattle patterns emerge in relation to this back-ground. In the same way, subsequent patterns are played with a firm sense of an underlying beat. Diversity in timbral layering, then, is mediated by an absolute nondiversity in temporal coordination. A heterogeneous ideal does not sanction a lackadaisical attitude to time; indeed, in that realm, there is only homogeneity.

The potency of the agbadza ensemble derives in part from its ability to foster an interplay between projections of sameness and difference. The collection of timbres enshrines an irreducible diversity, one that is mor-phologically resonant with social and kinship profiles. The collection of

58. Reich, *Writings on Music 1965–2000*, ed. Paul Hillier (Oxford: Oxford University Press, 2002), 62.

**Example 2.1** Steve Reich's transcription of *Agbadza*, an Ewe dance.

patterns promotes a complementary diversity in melorhythmic thinking, while the strict metrical coordination ensures a homogenous resultant often expressed by dancers. Some have claimed that the articulation of beginnings and endings is not crudely or obviously marked, but we surely know where "one" is if by that we mean knowing where the *felt beats* are (you just have to ask dancers about this). Few dancers require a secondary emphasis on "one." To deny that dancers possess this knowledge is to imply a level of freedom in musical organization that is worlds removed from what seasoned performers know.

A number of modern composers have exploited the heterogeneous sound ideal to good effect. The dazzling colors heard in performances by the Pan-African Orchestra result from a literal interpretation of "pan," whereby gonje, rattles, koras, bamboo flutes, bells, and varieties of drum are made to sound together. The result is at once a highlighting of different timbral properties and a demonstration of their deep-lying compatibilities once a metrical and harmonic framework has been imposed. In a similar vein, the orchestra for Akin Euba's opera *Chaka* includes various Western orchestral instruments such as the double bass, horns, and wind instruments, as well as Ashanti, Ewe, and Yoruba instruments, including *Atenteben* (bamboo flutes), *agogo* (double bell), rattle, and *dùndún* and *gúdúgúdú* drums. These instruments are used in various combinations to create a multistylistic ambience. The result, as in the case of the Pan-African Orchestra, is a managed heterogeneity that is traditional and modern at the same time. Even in a chamber work such as Joshua Uzoigwe's "Masquerade" for Ìyáàlù and piano, what might be called a timbral distance between the two instruments is exploited in an imaginative way. Trading speech-based motives and deploying percussionist articulation, neither instrument relinquishes its individuality at any point in the course of this engaging network of speech-song exchanges. In time, however, listeners are drawn into the sameness of their musical *intentions*, thus allowing a structural homogeneity to mediate the more surface timbral heterogeneity.

## CONCLUSION

Africa's wealth in musical instruments has led us down a variety of paths. As material and musical culture, instruments invite a variety of narratives. I began by acknowledging a handful of earlier writings about instruments, making the point that these writings adumbrate many of the major concerns of later twentieth-century writers. I then argued against the Hornbostel-Sachs taxonomic scheme— the dominant scheme for categorizing African musical instruments—suggesting that African-language designations and associations should lead the way in thinking about musical instruments. Finally, I described a small number of traditional instruments and occasionally commented on their creative potentials.

In closing, let us return briefly to the issue of nomenclature and its implications. As we have seen, musical instruments (excepting the voice for now) are first and foremost material objects; they are made of natural or synthetic materials, and they can be looked at, touched, beaten, stroked, carried, or carried away. The materiality of an instrument, however, may or may not have any bearing on its cultural significance. It may or may not feature in folk classifications of instruments. Materiality needs to be contextualized. Although it facilitates description and discussion, the material with which an instrument is made has no a priori significance.

Equally precarious is the significance accorded a given instrument within an indigenous taxonomy of instruments. Although taxonomies have been constructed for some groups[59] or incorporated into broader ethnographic studies, they are at present too few to support continent-wide generalization. Simply and obviously, African musical instruments are referred to according to a variety of criteria, including social use, size, musical function, material basis, nature of accompanying dance, sound, and shape. These and other criteria are significant in multiple ways. It seems unlikely, given the histories of change and borrowing among numerous African societies, that there can ever exist a single classificatory system of pan-African validity. Nomenclatures have emerged and will continue to emerge in particular circumstances at certain historical moments and for particular purposes. When Margaret Kartomi, drawing on studies by Hugo Zemp and Ruth Stone, seeks to establish a core human-centered conception of instruments in West Africa, a conception she says is categorically opposed to "Hellenic and Hellenistic views that musical instruments are inanimate objects,"[60] she slightly overstates her case. There

---

59. Among them, the Dan (by H. Zemp), the Kpelle (by R. Stone), the Vai (by L. Monts), the Hausa (by Ames and King), the Tiv (by Keil), and the Ankole (by van Thiel).

60. Margaret Kartomi, *On Concepts and Classification of Musical Instruments* (Chicago: University of Chicago Press, 1990), 241.

are many African peoples who refer to rattles, bells, flutes, horns, drums, and xylophones not as extensions of the human body but as objects with shapes that perform certain functions. And on the flip side, it is not unheard of for Euro-Americans to employ human-centered conceptions in referring to instruments by names that imply personification (jazz players give their horns names or equate the sound of the saxophone to the human voice, say). Acknowledging the contingency and heterogeneity of indigenous discourse, however, is not the same as refusing the invitation to develop indigenous classificatory systems; rather, it is a registration of the complexity of contemporary reality, a reality that has been shaped by, among other forces, intra-African influences and contact with other parts of the world. The stories told about the lives of African musical instruments sharpen our awareness of such complexity.

# 3

# Language and/in Music

In or near the beginning was the spoken word. Or so it appears throughout Africa. The word is meaning, magic, mystery, and sound. Its alliance with music is inescapable. Of the many properties of the spoken word, three are especially pertinent to music: pitch, rhythm, and timbre. Pitch registers the relative height of sounds; rhythm denotes their temporal extent, quality of association, and the ways in which they are differentially marked for attention; and timbre captures their grain, color, and character. Music will add to, modify, or even transform these properties. It will invest directly and abundantly in repetition, expand the possibilities for registral placement, and firm up the core continuity of language's sound. But music can never do without pitch, rhythm, or timbre. The sounding word is thus a kind of music, a proto-music perhaps—destined, in between, emergent. In this permanently transitional state, speech carries numerous potentialities for enacting the diverse behaviors we know as "music." Chief among such behaviors is singing. Like the spoken word, song lies at the heart of African musical expression and imagining. Without language, there would be no song; without song, African music would not exist. Language and music are thus tied, as if by an umbilical cord. No one who ignores its linguistic aspects can hope to reach a profound understanding of African music.

Specialists are divided on the number of languages that exist on the African continent. Some say that there are as few as eight hundred, not counting dialects, while others put the figure in the two thousand to three thousand range. By either reckoning, Africa emerges as the most polyglot continent on planet Earth. This endowment ought properly to be reason for celebration, given the exciting possibilities opened up for exploring and exploiting the many dimensions of syntax, sound, and sense. Only a small percentage of Africa's languages exist in written form, however. The most active register of use remains oral and aural. These are *living* languages in the most direct sense, and their oral milieu promotes certain habits while inhibiting others. For example, speakers

of some African languages are sharply alert to subtle calibrations in intonation, mood, attitude, and intention. This heightened aural awareness bespeaks
a "musical" sensibility. The absence of literacy, on the other hand, inhibits the
cultivation of certain informational and abstract registers of language. These
include usages that invest in symbolic rather than iconic modes of significa-
tion, those whose retrieval is not mediated by sound, and those that facilitate
complex presentational forms precisely because they eschew the intimacies
associated with face-to-face oral communication or interactive corroboration.
This does not imply any kind of deficiency, however, because all languages
are in principle equal to their essential tasks. Rather, it points to the potential
for domination within a global linguistic economy in which power accrues
to users of certain written languages because those languages have become
media for formal education, politics, trade, and intercultural communication.

## LANGUAGE AS FOUNDATION FOR MUSIC

Scholars who have studied African music *in Africa* frequently remark upon the
close connection between language (or speech or the spoken word) and music.
According to Cameroonian musician and writer Francis Bebey (1929–2001),
"It is scarcely an exaggeration to say that without African languages, African
music would not exist."[1] Klaus Wachsmann (1907–1984), who spent many
years in Uganda, declared that "there is hardly any music in Africa that is
not in some way rooted in speech." He was urging scholars to pay particular
attention to song texts and to remember that "drum beats" are taught and
understood through the mediation of language. Music either originates in or
is inflected at its foundations by language, Wachsmann seemed to say. Sung
song, for example, often derives from the spoken word.[2] Similarly, instrumental repertories such as xylophone music from Uganda, Mozambique,
or Burkina Faso frequently use preexisting song as the basis for paraphrase,
elaboration, and improvisation. John Miller Chernoff (b. 1947), who lived in
Ghana for some seven years, wrote in *African Rhythm and African Sensibility*
(1979) that "African music is derived from language."[3] He, too, must have been
struck by what Wachsmann saw in Uganda, namely, a seemingly ineradi-
cable linguistic supplement that mediates our experience of African music.
Although the American writer generously represents the spoken words of his

1. Bebey, *African Music*, 122.

2. Klaus P. Wachsmann, "Music," 187.

3. Chernoff, *African Rhythm and African Sensibility*, 75.

main collaborator, Alhaji Ibrahim Abdulai, in English translation throughout the book, he does not develop the abstract mechanics of the derivation of
music from language. Readers of his book nevertheless sense a linguistic aura
in the author's evocative description of aesthetics and social values among the
Ewe and especially the Dagbamba.

Introducing a "theory of African music," anthropologist, psychoanalyst,
and ethnomusicologist Gerhard Kubik (b. 1934), whose periods of fieldwork
in Africa span over fifty years, announced that African music is "closely connected with language, to an extent that it is hardly possible today to study
it without the necessary background in African languages." He went on to
recommend that students "link African music studies to the language map of
Africa."[4] By "language," Kubik means the system of natural languages, with
its plethora of sounding and signifying elements. Although his own analytical
practices seem weighted more toward instrumental rather than vocal genres
(he has a lot to say about harp and xylophone performance, for example), his
oeuvre as a whole includes studies of song (such as Yoruba *Àló* chantefables),
languages, and language about music. Indeed, no other writer on African
music has been a greater advocate of culturally specific information enshrined
in African languages.

Emphasis on language invariably goes hand in hand with emphasis on vocal
music. At the end of a chapter on musical instruments in a book introducing
African music to the general reader, Bebey wrote that "vocal music is truly the
essence of African musical art."[5] He singled out the human voice for special
celebration, reckoning on the basis of then-available recordings that in Africa
there are at least two pieces of vocal music for every piece of instrumental
music. Ghanaian ethnomusicologist Nissio Fiagbedzi (1931–2015) offers a resonant view: "Although to the outside observer drumming and dancing might
be regarded as central to Anlo music-making, to the traditional musician
songs constitute the primary focus of musical activity."[6] In an article devoted
to the procedures of improvisation published in a music education journal,
American ethnomusicologist and performer David Locke (b. 1949), who not
only studied Ewe and Dagomba music in Ghana but also has collaborated

---

4. Kubik, *Theory of African Music*, vol. 1, 9. Rosellini and Wiggins make a similar point
about Burkina Faso: "[There are] three general musical areas, the Voltaic, Mande and
Sahelian, which correspond fairly closely with the linguistic, ethnic and geographic divisions of the country" ("Burkina Faso," *Grove Music Online*, accessed July 20, 2013).

5. Bebey, *African Music*, 115.

6. Fiagbedzi, "The Music of the Anlo: Its Historical Background, Cultural Matrix and
Style" (PhD thesis, University of California Los Angeles, 1977), 10.

extensively with master musicians Abubakari Lunna, Gideon Alorwoyie, and Godwin Agbeli, drew attention to the overwhelming presence of vocal music as distinct from instrumental music: "Song is the heart of African music performance. Accompanied song is the most prevalent genre, and pure instrumental music is uncommon."[7] Echoing the voices of Wachsmann, Kubik, Fiagbedzi, and Bebey, Locke thus reinforced the high valuation of the language-into-music axiom.

Asserting the importance of language and the primacy of vocal music is one thing; investing heavily in African-language data through transcription, translation, and conceptual appropriation is another. Ruth M. Stone, who spent some of her childhood in Liberia, has written a number of in-depth studies of the musical culture of the Kpelle in which the centrality of the spoken word is displayed. Because language is a multifaceted phenomenon, it demands investigation of the temporal, rhythmic, and rhetorical aspects of performance. Stone's study of the Woi epic, for example, explores many dimensions of the sounding word, including movement, timing, and rhythm.[8] In his *Yoruba Drumming: The Dùndún Tradition*, published in Bayreuth in 1990, Nigerian scholar and composer Akin Euba (b. 1935) offers a comprehensive view of the mechanics of one of Africa's best-known speech surrogates.[9] The *dùndún* is a talking drum, and Euba, a native Yoruba speaker, probes intensely the musicolinguistic aspects of its performance tradition. Much is made of the relation between poetry and music, modes of signaling, textual composition, and the relationship between speech tones and melody. Euba also comments on the singing that accompanies *dùndún* performance, incorporating detailed analyses of four performances and emphasizing the place of the text and the sound of language. Recently, a fresh and forthright study of a related Yoruba instrument, the *bàtá*, was published by Australian scholar Amanda Villepastour (b. 1958). Reacting in part to the belief that the *bàtá* stammers rather than speaks, she has assembled an argument based on close collaboration with Yoruba master musicians to lay bare the encoding of speech and thus to contest the ostensible inarticulateness of the *bàtá*. Between transcriptions, recorded data, and close analysis, including comparative study of procedures associated with the *bàtá* and *dùndún*, Villepastour manages to keep alive the fascinating nature of

7. Locke, "Improvisation in West African Musics," *Music Educators' Journal* 66, no. 5 (1980): 128.

8. Stone, *Dried Millet Breaking: Time, Words and Song in the Woi Epic of the Kpelle* (Bloomington: Indiana University Press, 1988).

9. Euba, *Yoruba Drumming: The Dùndún Tradition* (Lagos: Elokoto Music Centre and Bayreuth African Studies Series, 1991).

the interconnection between the spoken word (language) and the drummed word (music).[10]

French scholar Gilbert Rouget (b. 1916), too, has produced some wonderfully detailed studies of African music in which dimensions of the spoken word are given due attention. Earlier studies of African prose forms and the behavior of speech tones in sung performances were supplemented in 1996 by a massive study of music, ritual, and symbolism at the court of King Gbèfa of Benin. Meticulous transcriptions of word and tone together with separate audio and video recordings facilitate serious inquiry into the musico-linguistic issues raised by this West African court repertory.[11] My own study of rhythmic expression among the Northern Ewe (1995) placed language at the center of several expressive modes ranging from gesture to dance. I drew attention to the mediative and generative capabilities of rhythm, explored the interaction between pitch and rhythm in spoken language, and described common ways in which language is molded in everyday song and verbal narratives.[12] And in a subsequent essay on African music as text, I explored the textual affinities of African music, including the linguisticity of instrumental music and the nature of metalanguages.[13] Finally, Ghanaian ethnomusicologist Kwasi Ampene's (b. 1965) book on a genre of Akan female songs known as *Nnwonkoro* is notable for the illumination it brings to this musico-verbal art.[14] A native Twi speaker, Ampene incorporates numerous transcriptions of the words and tones of *Nnwonkoro* texts. His explications refer to the subtlety and depth of language use by *Nnwonkoro* composer-performers. Of special significance are metaphor and allusive expression. More revealingly, Ampene, like Kubik and Nketia, seeks out native conceptualizations of various performance-related practices, effectively reconstructing a theory informed by the perspectives of born-in-the-tradition practitioners. Ampene includes detailed analyses of songs and song units, as well as suggestive information about aesthetic premises and methods of musico-textual composition.

10. Villepastour, *Ancient Text Messages of the Yoruba Bàtá Drum*. Also of considerable interest is the viewpoint of Nigerian musician and musicologist Bode Omojola in *Yoruba Music in the Twentieth Century*.

11. Gilbert Rouget, *Un roi africain et sa musique de cour: chants et danses du palais à Porto-Novo sous le règne de Gbéfa 1948-1976* (Paris: CNRS Editions, 1996). The transcriptions were made by Trân Quan Hai in collaboration with Rouget.

12. Agawu, *African Rhythm: A Northern Ewe Perspective*.

13. Agawu, "African Music as Text," in *Representing African Music*, 97–115.

14. Ampene, *Female Song Tradition and the Akan of Ghana*.

We can of course multiply the examples by citing research by Rycroft, Blacking, Christopher Waterman, Avorgbedor, Reed, Vallejo, Shelemay, Omojola, and numerous others, but what has been reported here should suffice as an indication of the importance that many scholars attach to language-music interconnections. It is not Africanists alone who have been struck by this; ethnomusicologists, musicologists, anthropologists, folklorists, linguists, music theorists, and cognitive scientists have contributed valuable research on the subject.[15] It is against this background that I offer the following remarks on selected aspects of the language-music connection in Africa. I do so in part to summarize some of what is known and in part to stimulate discussion. Six little topics seem to me to capture the essential dimensions of our subject: the relationship between speech tone and melody; talking drums; song (as an amalgamation of word and tone, as well as a site of poetic imagining); metalanguage; ideophones; and finally, the linguistic residue in performance sensibility. A fuller understanding of these topics will, I believe, enhance appreciation of African music.

## THE POETICS OF SOLO, DUET, AND ENSEMBLE PERFORMANCE

How might we characterize the content and expressive dimensions of sung language produced by one, two, or more singers? Let us begin with solo singing as heard daily in any number of genres across the continent.

An Mbenzele (Pygmy) mother sings a lullaby to soothe her child, cadencing periodically in accordance with the underlying tone system and phraseology, and using vocables to bring sound and sense into close alliance.[16] A Dan woman lamenting the death of her husband explores the interstices between singing and speaking to convey deep emotion and pain. Never losing the pentatonic archetype that constrains her singing, she will address the dead directly, incorporate vocables as a resting device from time to time, and extemporize references to all who are affected by the death, using a declamatory style of

15. Three excellent points of departure are Harold S. Powers, "Language Models and Music Analysis," *Ethnomusicology* 24 (1980): 1–60; Steven Feld and Aaron Fox, "Music and Language," *Annual Review of Anthropology* 23 (1994): 25–53; and Aniruddh D. Patel, *Music, Language, and the Brain* (New York: Oxford University Press, 2008). For a concise digest, see my chapter, "Music as Language," in *Music as Discourse: Semiotic Adventures in Romantic Music* (Oxford: Oxford University Press, 2009), 15–39.

16. CD, *Africa: The Ba-Benzélé Pygmies* (Cambridge, MA: Rounder, 1998), track 6, "Lullaby."

delivery.[17] An Ewe man from the village of Matse, Adjei Kɔmi, recounts the deeds of his people in song, mentioning names, tracing lineages and genealogies, and commenting selectively on historical achievement. Like his Dan relative, he intersperses songlike refrains in a manner that reinforces the musical basis of the genre.[18] Fabio, an Ubangi singer from the Democratic Republic of the Congo, unleashes a torrent of syllables as he narrates a set of mundane events in humorous style, accompanying himself on the *kundi* harp and activating the simplest of chordal accompaniments.[19] A griot from Guinea sings the praises of his patrons while injecting humor and critique into the performance. A griotte from Mali, Siramori Diabate (c. 1930–1989), sings of achievements by standout figures in her community as she gives praise to Sunjata Keita, founder of Mande society. This word-borne praise singing rests on an unobtrusive guitar accompaniment and intermittent finger snaps.[20]

Throughout Africa, the singing of stories as entertainment allows skilled performers to enact narratives that display some of language's phonetic qualities. A telling example can be heard on a 1985 recording in which two Leele men simultaneously collaborate and compete in the performance of the *mimbeenbee* story. Resonating open vowels, sustained notes in high registers, and variations in the pace of delivery allow the performers to craft a vivid narrative.[21] A Gambian kora player takes an ancient tune ("Alla l'aake") and spins a set of variations to support his performance of relatively recent history. The original tune had its own words, of course, so the set of variations being spun is never without a linguistic referent. The improvisatory impulse, however, leads him further and further away from the putative language source even as he "speaks" through the medium of musical notes. Mbombongo Nzoku, an Nkundo singer and pluriarc player from the Democratic Republic of the Congo, mourns a death in song by rehearsing the life, achievements, and failures of the deceased. His repertoire of devices is staggering: ululating,

17. CD, *Africa: The Dan* (Cambridge, MA: Rounder, 1998), track 3, "Solo song of a woman."

18. See CD accompanying Agawu, *African Rhythm*, tracks 14 and 15. For an uncannily similar mode of performance, this time from the Côte D'Ivoire, listen to track 6, "Singing at a Wrestling Match," on CD, *Africa: The Dan*.

19. CD, *Anthologie de la musique Congolaise*, vol. 10: *Musique de l'Ubangi* (Tervuren, Belgium: Fonti musicali/Musée royal de l'afrique centrale, 2009), track 18, "Ngai Ngbandi aya me o."

20. CD, *Siramori Diabate: Griot Music from Mali #3* (Leiden: Pan Records, 2002), track 1, "Sunjata fasa."

21. CD, *Anthologie de la musique Congolaise*, vol. 9: *Musique des Leele*, track 6, "Mimbeembee."

strumming a low-pitched note on his instrument, interspersing words with waiting melismas, responding verbally and nonverbally to his audience, deploying vowel-based exclamations, and utilizing repetitions for emphasis in the form of monosyllables (*yo yo yo yo*) lodged somewhere between speech and song.[22]

For whom does the solo singer sing? To whom is his or her utterance directed? While some traditional solo genres involve the transmission of information (as when a singer rehearses a genealogy or clan history), and although the presence of listening audiences sometimes influences the projection and direction of voice and song, the predominant orientation of solo singing is inward rather than outward. Whereas speaking in principle directs an utterance toward another in expectation of a response (unless you are a mad man talking to yourself), singing is primarily for oneself; only secondarily is it to or for another. It is true that the presence of audiences can affect a performance, inspire certain spontaneous forms of display, or elicit topical references. But the physical effort involved in intoning language correctly as song often nudges an utterance in the direction of self rather than other. Successful solo singers are those who reach audiences by singing primarily for themselves and only secondarily for those audiences. Musical acts thus rely on a degree of interiorization that exceeds that of verbal acts.

The move from solo to duet performance is a move toward greater rather than lesser interiorization. Participants in a duet, for example, are charged in the first instance with achieving unanimity or rapport, making music together, and realizing a synchronization that is at once planned and intermittently accidental. Success in duet performance owes less to a message communicated to audiences and more to the edification and satisfaction that come from observing two performers do their own thing.

This will to interiorization is spectacularly illustrated in the singing of lullabies by the Mbenzele, in the Akazehe greeting routines of Burundian women, and in the vocal games using two or more voices associated with Bibayak pygmies from Gabon. Significantly, these chamber textures are often associated with play, experimentation, and the lighter aspects of musical expression. Language as such takes a back seat in some genres, while the play element—which often privileges sound over semantic meaning—is pushed to the foreground. To play in music is to invest in repetition, and to embrace repetition is to emphasize sound over meaning, the phonological over the semantic. When pygmies use vocables, they set aside (or at least de-emphasize) the semantic

---

22. CD, *Anthologie de la musique Congolaise (RDC)*, vol. 11: *Musique des Nkundo*, track 11, "Chant de deuil avec longombe."

freight of language; in effect, the spoken word is reduced to its articulative function. The primary motivation for singing a duet, then, is to achieve a level of musical synchronicity and to celebrate such achievement. Rhythm, understood as a species of patterning regulated temporally, is of the utmost importance in achieving this purpose; words are sometimes incidental.

While the constraints on solo performance differ from those of duet performance, multiple-voice performances involve an intensification of duet circumstances, not a conceptual transformation. In keeping with a pervasive communal ethos, African performing practice is dominated by ensembles. These range in size from small (say, four to eight voices) through larger groups (of forty to sixty voices) to gigantic groups involving entire communities (three hundred or more voices). Asafo (warrior) singing in the Northern Ewe town of Matse sometimes features fifty or so men charged with singing heroic deeds to support troops headed for war (or so legend has it) or to celebrate the fortunes of those who returned with their lives intact from the war. Nonstratified pygmy populations throughout Central Africa engage similarly in deeply communal singing featuring scores of participants. In many of their repertories, lexical items are more of a means than an end; they include words or verbal phrases repeated over and over, eventually acquiring the character of signifiers without fixed signifieds. As a set of pitch and rhythmic sequences, music serves as an essential platform for collaboration. The sense of focus, the deep sense of mutual belonging, the feeling of unity in diversity—these are all achieved primarily at the musical level, and only secondarily at the linguistic level. Indeed, in polytextual genres, the music promotes the aura of singularity, while the text signifies multiplicity. When people in a North Borna village in the Democratic Republic of the Congo mourn the death of their chief's son, they adopt a melodic archetype (roughly, $E\flat 4$-D4-C4) as the vehicle, but they do not all sing the same words. While the archetype is heard from a distance as an emergent or summary shape, there is room for verbal and intonational divergence among individual participants.[23] Depth in bonding often comes from singing together rather than speaking together. The naturalness of speaking, together with an attendant communicative obligation, privileges a speaking-to regime in verbal genres, whereas the relative abnormality of singing directs energies inward, privileging a singing-with regime in musical genres.

The distinctions among solo, duet, and ensemble vocal performance noted here should be balanced against the deep-level communal ethos that underwrites much African music making. When our Dan woman enumerates the

23. CD, *Petites musique du Zaire*, track 12, "Lamentations."

qualities of her dead husband, or when singers of a crying song wonder how they are going to continue living without a departed father, they touch on issues that the rest of us have either experienced or can imagine and empathize with. In this sense, the singers are performing *with* us, not to us. Similarly, the intoning of warrior songs grips entire communities because the threat to their security and the resolve to defeat their enemies are not things they can afford to treat indifferently. In the traditional sphere, "performing with" often predominates over "performing to."

But what about audience reception? The audience for solo singing listens and empathizes with a singer, feeling his or her emotion and taking in his or her message. The audience for duets listens to and admires the chamber ensemble, identifying with the performers while also admiring their display of skill and poetry. The audience for a many-voiced ensemble is disposed to join in as soon as a suitable entry point can be found. "Many voices" often means "potentially all voices." In this sense, musical performance stands ready to envelop audiences, transforming them from passive to active participants. Such acts of transformation reflect shifting configurations in the enactment of a network of relationships affecting music and language.

## TONE AND TUNE

From a musician's point of view, the most immediate and at the same time far-reaching quality of many African languages is that of speech tone. As is well known, the overwhelming majority of African languages are tone languages, that is, languages in which differences in relative pitch trigger differences in lexical meaning. This fact is well established, and linguists and musicologists have explored its ramifications from their respective disciplinary viewpoints. While there is room for further exploration of speech tones as ordering, guiding, and constraining musical composition, my remarks here will focus on the fundamental constraints on musical understanding offered by tone.[24]

In a tone language, tone is said to be phonemic—that is, generative of meaning. (I use the abbreviations H for high, L for low, and M for mid to designate the relative tones of spoken language.) The word *kúkú* (HH) in Ewe means

24. For a valuable introduction to scholarly research on African languages, see *African Languages: An Introduction*, ed. Bernd Heine and Derek Nurse (Cambridge: Cambridge University Press, 2000). George N. Clements's chapter in that volume ("Phonology") includes a concise discussion of tone. See also David Odden, "Tone: African Languages," in *Handbook of Phonological Theory*, ed. John A. Goldsmith (Oxford: Blackwell, 1995), 444–475.

"hat," but the word *kùkú* (LH) means "death." In Gã, the difference between "Who roasted (it)?" and "Who farted?" turns on a single tone: *námɔ̀ shã̀?* (HLL) versus *námɔ̀ shã̂?* (HLM). These pitch differentials are typically accommodated within a fixed relational scheme based on approximations of highness and lowness. The number of tones varies from one language to the next: there are languages with two tones (Twi, Temne); three or four tones are common (Grebo, Yoruba, Ewe, Ibibio); some have five (Kporo, Dan); and Chori (Nigeria) has as many as six. For our purposes, it is immaterial how many tones there are in a given language as long as their relative heights are firmly imprinted in the speaker's or singer's mind. Tones may be level or terraced; some may glide or be rendered as upward or downward glissandi. The sequence of tones in a sentence may approximate a shape described as "downdrift" by linguists. According to this, the absolute distance between high and low tones decreases across the span of the utterance. In musical terms, we might say that if the interval between the lowest tone and its highest counterpart at the beginning of an utterance is, say, a minor seventh, that interval may decrease to, say, a perfect fourth by the close of the utterance. Some tones may be assimilated; others may function grammatically. While languages like Bambara, Ganda, Gbe, Twi, Hausa, and Mende have been studied in detail, there is a much longer list of unstudied African languages. One thing is certain, however: to live within the linguistic world (of tone) is to live within a *musical* or *proto-musical* world; to inhabit a tone language as sense and sound is to be acutely aware of relational pitch and—to a lesser extent—rhythm. From this vantage point, the gap between speaking and singing may sometimes be narrow or even nonexistent.

Not surprisingly, many scholars have seized on this quality of African languages to explain melodic behavior. The following claim is paradigmatic (i.e., for "Tswana," one may substitute any number of African languages): "Tswana is a tonal language, therefore the melodic line of a song is flexible, being largely controlled by the requirements of semantic tone."[25] We will have more to say about the melodic impetus in chapter 5, but our first concern here is with the nature of the connection between speech tones and melody—between "tone and tune" as it is affectionately called. This relationship has to be studied at many levels. [26]

25. Mundell and Breary, "Botswana," *Grove Music Online*, accessed March 30, 2013.

26. See earlier writers like Marius Schneider, Erich von Hornbostel, and A. M. Jones, or more recent writers like Paul Richards and Nissio Fiagbedzi. A summary of the literature up to the mid-1980s may be found in Agawu, "Tone and Tune: The Evidence for Northern Ewe Music," *Africa* 58 (1988): 127–146. A concise recent study with a broad range of reference is Murray Schellenberg, "Does Language Determine Music in Tone Languages?,"

A simple example may be helpful. Let us assume that the Northern Ewe dialect has three tones: low, mid, and high (L, M, and H). The word àɖàŋùtɔ´ (three syllables: à- + -ɖàŋù (diphtong) + -tɔ´), which means a "counselor" or "wise one," is pronounced as LLH. I would expect, therefore, that in a musical setting, the first two syllables would be on the same pitch, while the third would be on a higher pitch. For example, I might sing the word as E4-E4-A4, that is, as a rising perfect fourth, and this would be correct from a musical point of view. Note here that the rising fourth is iconic because the interval between these particular low and high tones is close to a perfect fourth in "normal" speaking voice. We can infer from this proto-musical situation that musical melody can be generated directly by speech tones. The process is one of firming up speech tones into musical tones. Indeed, we can think of any number of declamatory genres in which musical song (to invoke a redundancy to make a point) is little more than the consolidation of the intrinsic tonal qualities of speech.

But if music did no more than follow the imperatives of spoken language, if music only realized or made manifest that which had been handed to it by speech, it would not be interesting; indeed, it might even be seen as derivative and impoverished. Language crosses a systemic boundary and becomes music when it submits to a different regime, one in which the sonic material is given its full value or, indeed, an excess of value. Until it transcends its native value, language remains language, not (yet) music.[27]

The softening of boundaries is further possible because of the existence of another dimension of speech, namely, rhythm. We will have more to say about speech rhythm in the next chapter, but if we think of language for now as a confluence of quantity and stress, we can expose some of its intersections with music. Each syllable in language has a duration and a degree of markedness that must be expressed in music as well. So the baggage that a tone language brings into a musical setting is not just that of pitch but also of a more complex temporal dimension. We can easily verify the importance of rhythm by experimenting with different durations for syllables. In Ewe, Mε wɔ ayaa dɔ means "I have worked for the wind" (figuratively, "I have worked for nothing" because

*Ethnomusicology* 56 (2012): 266–278. See also the case study by Dafydd Gibbon, Firmin Ahoua, and Adjépolé Kouamé, "Modelling Song Relations: An Exploratory Study of Pitch Contours, Tones and Prosodic Domains in Anyi," *Proceedings of the International Congress of Phonetic Sciences* 17 (2011): 743–746.

27. Although the categorical distinction enshrined in this claim is theoretically necessary, we should not overlook those genres in which the boundary between language and music is porous; indeed, some traditional composers—such as the Southern Ewe legend Vinɔkɔ Akpalu—intentionally exploit the ambiguity between the spoken and the sung to great dramatic effect.

the wind has come and taken my work away); but by doubling the length of the vowel from *wɔ* to *wɔɔ*, the meaning of the sentence changes. *Mɛ wɔɔ ayaa dɔ* means "I habitually work for the wind." This "rhythmic" aspect of tone languages has been given far less attention than pitch partly because rhythm is a more elusive parameter; its ability to influence meaning (rather than expression or rhetoric) seems to be superstructural rather than essential. By contrast, rhythm in music holds an absolutely primary position. Obviously, then, the presence of a temporal, durational, or rhythmic dimension in language contributes to the blurring of boundaries whenever speech is activated as music.

An underlying constraint on musical composition is that whatever is prescribed within a given language for speech-borne melody has to be domesticated within the economy of music. Music itself is beholden to regimes of patterning made up of pitch, rhythm, and timbre, but the nature of the transformational processes will vary from language to language. In some cases, language travels only a short distance before becoming music; in others, the gap is much wider. For example, while the sequence of speech tones in a spoken line may be given as LMH, a melody that "sets" this text may assume different forms depending on the pitch system available in the particular culture. The placement of high, low, and mid tones will be rendered within bands or intervals of pitch activity, not as flat or discrete pitches. Anyone who tracks the manifestation of low, mid, and high through a given African-language song will quickly realize that lows, for example, taken by themselves, are not fixed pitch-wise but may span an interval. Similarly, "mid" and "high" span intervals.

Thus, the musical rendition of the word *àɖàŋ̀ùtɔ́* need not be a rising fourth; it could be a rising second, third, sixth, or even octave depending on the operative pitch system, the syntactical constraints on musical style, and the aesthetic goals. Just as the speech tones within an individual utterance are on some level controlled by the tonal system of the language, so musical utterances are on some level controlled by the musical system (like a pentatonic, hexatonic, or heptatonic collection). By placing the tonal constraints on speech within, say, an LMH system, we might infer that options for pitch variation are greater in music than they are in the systems governing tone languages. On the other hand, the subtle intonations of spoken language often display an expressive range that exceeds that of music based on fixed pitch.

Turning speech into song thus entails many negotiations. Imagine for a moment that you are composing a melody in a tone language. The overall shape of the melody could follow the contour of speech tones—this is a ready option, but not necessarily a requirement. If your melody takes on the exact shape prescribed by the speech tones, you have not added anything substantially new to that utterance except a certain iconic conformity within a musical system. You have, as it were, accepted the dictates of natural language. But in firming up pitches, in introducing fixed durations or perhaps an explicit accentual or metrical scheme, you will have introduced other considerations that do not necessarily originate in the sound of the spoken word. The speech tone constraint thus becomes only one of several song-making inputs. These constraints become significant and problematic at the same time.

Or suppose that you want your melody to begin somewhere near its highest pitch (a favorite device in traditional composition) and then descend gradually over the span of the utterance, perhaps replicating the downdrift contour. This would cause your LMH framework to take on different intervallic forms at the beginning and end of your composition. At the beginning, you may be working within a total interval size of, say, a major sixth, whereas by the end, you may allow yourself no more than a third. Thus, what was considered high (in speech tone terms) at the beginning may now approximate a mid level at the end.

The emerging consensus about the nature of the relationship between speech tone and melody is that while speech tones may influence melodic direction, they do not ultimately determine melodic contour.[28] This is both a logical and a pragmatic consensus. It is logical because it recognizes separate domains for music and language without denying their mutual interface. And it is pragmatic because it recognizes that acts of tonal imagination (as when a singer-composer activates language or words in song to express a sentiment, induce catharsis, or delight self and other) may take many forms; they may even transcend linguistic constraints if necessary.

Is communication ever threatened when speech tones and melody fail to align? If music and language are separate semiotic systems, operating by their own internal rules, and if the rules of language have no a priori validity in the domain of music (and vice versa), then the answer to the question is "no"— communication is not necessarily threatened when speech tones and melody go their separate ways. Whereas the distortion of speech tones in spoken speech directly affects meaning (at different levels and in different contexts), the distortion of speech tones in a musical context may have little or no effect. If song is not merely a reproduction of the natural music of language but an expression of something more—an expression, that is, of structural properties not available (or at least to the same extent) in spoken language (like strict meter)—then the spoken word together with its baggage will amount to no more than one of the elements that make up the expressive whole we know as song. In this way, language in song is always already inflected—alienated, marked, different, other. Lawrence Kramer once described the relationship between word and tone in

---

28. For example, Mundell and Brearley report that in Tswana, "the melodic line of a song is flexible, being largely controlled by the requirements of semantic tone" (*Grove Music Online*, accessed December 11, 2012).

song as "agonic,"[29] highlighting their nonidentity and the tension that attends their frequent cohabitation. Something of this enticing conflict lies at the base of African song and is readily heard in the interplay between tone and tune.[30]

## HOW DRUMS TALK

Another major manifestation of the close connection between language and music is the fascinating phenomenon of instruments "speaking," that is, reproducing patterns of speech in a nonspoken realm, thereby functioning as speech surrogates. Whistles, flutes, horns, xylophones, bells, harps, and one-stringed fiddles all have the capacity to speak, and examples of such speech have been recorded throughout Africa.[31] The talking instrument par excellence, however, is the drum. There is not one type of drum that talks; many drums indeed possess this capacity, and although natural language provides the condition of possibility for all forms of drum talk, the mechanics of the process vary. The Hausa dùndún and Dagomba dòndón drums speak within a wide palette of sounds, including several bending sounds. The Akan *atumpan*, the Baule *atungblan*, and the Northern Ewe *tompani* all speak through tonally differentiated pitches. Igbo *ukom* are tuned drums that enable players to mimic speech. The slit drums of the Igbo are also constructed on a binary pitch principle and can be used to communicate stylized text. Likewise, the slit drums of the Lokele in the Democratic Republic of the Congo have supported various forms of word-based communication. Central African drums played by the Banda Linda have the capacity to speak. And so on. When we say that a drum speaks, we are not speaking metaphorically; we do not merely mean that patterns of rhythm and sound played on a drum reach listeners as vaguely

---

29. Lawrence Kramer, *Music and Poetry: The Nineteenth Century and After* (Berkeley: University of California Press, 1984), 127.

30. In the future, we will need many more studies on the tone-tune question across scores of indigenous languages to improve our understanding of this issue. We will benefit especially from the testimonies of composers about how they negotiate this rich and fascinating precompositional constraint.

31. What Rosellini and Wiggins write about Burkina Faso is representative: "Most of the Voltaic and Mande languages are tonal so that messages and signals can be sounded on gourd, hourglass, conical and cylindrical drums. In many cases, especially with the xylophone, flutes and drums, music has a linguistic basis, so that even in the absence of singing or chanting, an underlying text is understood. Mossi musicians transmit the history of their empire, dating back to the 14th century, by the use of gourd, hourglass and cylindrical drums. This tradition may or may not be accompanied by a voice which translates the drum language" (*Grove Music Online*, accessed January 15 2014).

sensed utterance, as meaningful communication. We mean, rather, that talking drums manifest language directly in a nonlinguistic medium, that they expose recoverable speech. They quite literally *talk*.

How might we understand the various modes of drumming of which "talking" is the best known? Kwabena Nketia provided just such a framework in 1963, and it remains valuable today.[32] According to him, there are three distinct modes of drumming: the speech mode, the signal mode, and the dance mode. The speech mode, typically heard on talking drums, involves the direct reproduction of the pitches and rhythms of spoken language. It is an iconic mode, and the pattern of articulation is syllabic. In reproducing speech, the drum plays as many syllables as are required by the corresponding speech phrase. These patterns are sometimes interspersed with others, including waiting signals, attention-grabbing patterns, or other forms of punctuation. The signal mode also partakes in a limited way in speech, but unlike the speech mode, which is the rough equivalent of prose, the signal mode uses a diminished lexicon. Essentially, a phrase (often speech based) is repeated several times to signify fire, war, an emergency, the arrival of a stranger, or a mystery. While all three modes necessarily submit to a degree of repetition, the speech mode approximates a continuous narrative with sentences of different lengths, while the signal mode equalizes the lengths of the utterances. If the speech mode is isomorphic with ordinary language or prose, the signal mode is isomorphic with poetic language.

The dance mode in principle severs its connections with speech and underwrites the cultivation of purely musical rhythms. The many popular and memorable rhythmic patterns known as time lines (discussed in the next chapter) are in the dance mode—musically distinct, metrically constrained, often affiliated with movement, but not necessarily of linguistic origins. The dance mode is nominally tasked with providing a groove for community dancing, not with communicating a verbal message. Of course, rhythms are never affectless, which is why they can be adapted to various situations. But there is, in principle, a difference in character between drumming that does these three things: request that a man who has gone to the forest return to the village (speech mode), announce a danger (signal mode), and set up a groove for us to dance to (dance mode).

The progression from speech through signal to dance involves a gradual curtailing of the lexical universe. More lexical items are dispensed in the speech mode than in the signal mode, and more are dispensed in the signal mode than in the dance mode. It so happens, however, that the occasion for dance can sometimes feature speaking and signaling. A lead drummer may

32. Nketia, *Drumming in Akan Communities of Ghana* (Edinburgh: Thomas Nelson and Sons, 1963), 17–31.

**Photo 3.1** "Evu ʋuidina" (talking drums), Amedzofe, Ghana.

begin by speaking a poem on his drums; he may also employ specific signals in the course of a dance to instruct his dancers even while maintaining the groove. Dance emerges in this reading as the privileged mode insofar as it incorporates elements of the speech and signal modes as well, becoming in effect a repository of all three modes of drumming.[33]

The essential principle of talking drumming is the direct reproduction of the pitch and durational patterns of speech on the drum, and this is done without the benefit of vowels and consonants.[34] The process entails a direct transfer of patterns from a(n imagined) spoken realm to a(n executed) sounding realm. The transfer is mediated by a number of factors, including the timbre and tonal resources of the instrument, the tonal and durational structure of the language, and of course the skill and dexterity of the performer. Consider the example of the Akan Atumpan, a pair of differently pitched drums that have the capacity to mimic speech. The drummer can produce a minimum of two distinct tones (one low, the other higher) that are sufficient to render

33. For further discussion of signifying in instrumental music, see Agawu, *Representing African Music*, 112–114.

34. For a thorough discussion, see Simha Arom, "Language and Music in Fusion: The Drum Language of the Banda Linda (Central African Republic)," *TRANS* 11 (2007), accessed July 24, 2013, http://www.sibetrans.com/trans/a118/language-and-music-in-fusion-the-drum-language-of-the-banda-linda-central-african-republic.

spoken Twi, a two-tone language. Although each drum is further capable of producing other pitches, this basic binary attribute is enough to enable drummers to recite poetry, praise patrons, rehearse genealogies, narrate historical events, instruct or flirt with dancers, and offer philosophical ideas (often in the form of proverbs) for thoughtful listeners and dancers to reflect upon. This extraordinary resource, which has been exploited by the Akan (and other groups that practice analogous traditions) for generations, remains underappreciated when talking drumming is colloquially reduced to a vague, speech-like utterance enveloped in an overarching emotion rather than recognized for what it is, namely, a decodable utterance.

Drums are not voices, however; nor is drumming equivalent to singing. As beautiful as the abstract notion of talking drums is, its tokens attract other contingencies. The mechanics of capturing the sound and sense of speech on a drum bring other complications, often a deletion of parts of the linguistic universe. When I speak, I have at my disposal consonants and vowels, a range of pitches, and options for negotiating between them, including discrete jumps, glissandi, or slides, or any number of supplementary articulations. On a pair of Atumpan drums, however, I have far fewer options. I have a limited capability to sustain notes, I am pretty much limited to short-long or sound-silence sequences in my choice of rhythm, and without vowels and consonants I lack a crucial resource for certain kinds of articulation. If we imagine the process as a translation between two languages, we might say that the target language (in this case, the drummed language) is significantly diminished in comparison with the language of origin (the spoken language). For the Akan, the language of origin, spoken Twi, has a lexicon of several thousand words, while the target language (talking-drum language) has something like five hundred words.[35] This discrepancy is striking and instructive. It suggests immediately that drummers, no matter how versatile, simply cannot be as literally articulate when they drum as when they speak with their mouths. That is why talking drummers develop certain stylized ways of talking, why they employ certain disambiguating signals, why they repeat their patterns, and why their messages tend to be nominal, conventional, and subject to elaboration through an accumulation of synonymous attributes rather than through critical exegesis.[36]

35. Nketia, "Surrogate Languages of Africa," in *Current Trends in Linguistics: Linguistics in Sub-Saharan Africa*, ed. Thomas A. Sebeok (The Hague: Mouton, 1971), 711.

36. See Walter Ong, "African Talking Drums and Oral Noetics," in *Interfaces of the Word: Studies in the Evolution of Consciousness and Culture* (Ithaca, NY: Cornell University Press, 1977), 92–120.

Thanks to a significant number of recordings made since the early 1900s, we can sample the sound and character of talking drums (and other talking instruments) from different parts of Africa. Hugh Tracey's International Library of African Music (ILAM) collection includes a "drum message" from the Kanyok in the Democratic Republic of the Congo (Southern Belgian Congo). The instrument is a slit drum, and each phrase is first drummed and then spoken by mouth. The message apparently is a call to people to come and assemble.[37] Tracey also recorded three "drum signals" from among the Mangbele of Northern Congo. The first is a call to fight, the second a summons of the people by their chief, and the third an announcement of a death. These signals are more poetic than proselike, more repetitive and "musical" than the Kanyok drum message.[38] A third example from the Tracey collections is an illustrated lecture by a Rev. W. H. Ford on the topic, "Talking Drums of the Upper Congo," recorded in 1952.[39] Assisted by drummers Singili and Kobo with their wooden slit drums, Rev. Ford explains the underlying principles of talking drums. Much of this material seems to have come from John Carrington's excellent little book, *The Talking Drums of Africa* (1949), which, like Rev. Ford's lecture, is based entirely on the practices of the Lokele. Indeed, the Lokele are said to be famous for their drum messaging practice.[40]

We may also mention three later recordings from the output of Simha Arom that vividly illustrate the practice. The first, given the functional title "Drummed Message," comes from the Banda Linda of the Central African Republic. It is, according to Arom, "a message to a travelling village dweller, informing him that a child has just been born into his family and requesting him to return to the village."[41] This in situ recording, complete with the sounds of crickets, birds, and other night creatures, features a slit wooden drum common in Central and West Africa. It has the basic high-low polarity. The message itself is delivered in brief segments separated by patterns (some of them

37. CD, *Kanyok and Luba: Southern Belgian Congo, 1952 & 1957* (Utrecht: Sharp Wood Productions, and Grahamstown: International Library of African Music, 1998), track 1, "Drum message 1."

38. CD, *Music of Africa Series 29: Musical Instruments 3: Drums 1* (Grahamstown: International Library of African Music), track 9, "Three drum signals."

39. CD, *Forest Music: Northern Belgian Congo 1952* (Utrecht: Sharp Wood Productions, and Grahamstown: International Library of African Music, 2000), track 22, "Talking drums of the Upper Congo."

40. John Carrington, *Talking Drums of Africa* (London: Carey Kingsgate Press, 1949).

41. CD, *Central African Republic: Music of the Dendi, Nzakera, Banda Linda, Gbaya, Banda Dakpa, Ngbaka, Aka Pygmies* (France: Auvidis, 1989) (France: Auvidis-Unesco, 1983/1989), track 15, "Drummed message."

nonlexical) that reinforce a previous statement or serve as waiting signals to assist listeners in making sense of the message. These patterns of monotone intervention function as phatic signs, helping to underwrite the performance as a talking-drum performance. A second recording, also originating from the Banda Linda people, is a piece of recreational dance drumming in which a lead drummer "talks" as part of a polyrhythmic ensemble narrative. The drumming immediately elicits laughter and cheers from the audience, and Arom explains that this is because they understood directly the message being drummed (Web Example 3.1[●]).[42] A third recording, included in a recent multiauthored book, *Approaches to African Music*, offers a detailed study of a single but extended drum message from a semiological point of view.[43] Several of Arom's findings reinforce observations made by Walter Ong in his pioneering studies of orality and literacy about the art: redundancy in talking drumming, understanding of phrases rather than individual words, preponderance of conventional usages, and the "reproduction of the tonal pitches and ... rhythmic patterns of normal speech" as the basis of the drum language.[44]

It is significant that a number of recordings of talking drums are didactic in nature. An excellent example is the "Akan Talking Drum Text" recorded by ethnomusicologist Roger Vetter near Cape Coast, Ghana, in 1996. Here, a female speaker and male drummer perform a text honoring the King of Denkyira, one of the older kingdoms of Ghana. She speaks the text line by line while the drummer renders each line on the drum. In this way, one can appreciate the difference in character between the sonic world of spoken language and that of drum language. The text itself is in three parts: part 1 is a welcome to those present, part 2 is a praise song to the king of Denkyira, and part 3 is poetry honoring the Tano River. The third part is the most conventional; the lines are shorter and the mode of temporal succession closer to the poetic (or signal) mode than the speech mode evident in part 2. In sum, the larger rhythm of the text emerges as a juxtaposition of speech (part 1) and poetry (parts 2 and 3).[45]

Of particular interest are ways in which composers of modern idioms have incorporated talking drums into their art. To acknowledge this adaptation is to acknowledge departures from traditional practice. Let us mention just

---

42. Unpublished recording by Simha Arom.

43. See CD accompanying *Approaches to African Musics*, ed. Enrique Cámara de Landa and Martinez García (Valladolid: Universidad de Valladolid, 2006), tracks 1 ("Drum language") and 2 ("Drum language").

44. Walter Ong, "African Talking Drums and Oral Noetics," in *Interfaces of the Word*, 92–120.

45. CD, *Rhythms of Life, Songs of Wisdom: Akan Music from Ghana* (Washington, DC: Smithsonian Folkways, 1996), track 4, "Talking drum."

two examples: the use of talking drums in jùjú and the accretions to traditional drum language in the Southern Ewe dance *Agbadza*. King Sunny Ade's band from the early 1980s (as featured, for example, in his album *King Sunny Ade and His African Beats*, issued in 1992 by Island Records) includes guitars, voices, shakers, congas, bongos, keyboards, and—significantly for our purposes—"talking drums." These talking *dùndún* drums are featured at different moments in different songs and in different degrees of depth. In the song "Ja Funmi," for example, they function in three different but complementary ways: as part of the rhythm machine, as actual speech surrogates, and as simulators of speech. In their first function, *dùndún* drums simply reinforce the density and overall rhythmic texture of "Ja Funmi"; in this sense, although they are timbrally distinct, their patterns are complementary rather than oppositional to the patterns played by the other percussion instruments. In their second function, *dùndún* drums are called upon to "talk" or signify. The alternation of drummed and spoken text dramatizes their semantic and musical parallels while at the same time highlighting the timbral contrast. In a third function, *dùndún* drums execute rhythms and declamatory patterns that *sound like* speech but are not aligned with specific lexical items. Here, the drummers may be said to be drumming in the speech mode but they are not actually speaking—there is no recoverable verbal message. They are, as it were, affecting the manner of speech but not reproducing its substance. So, although Sunny Ade's musical thinking is on many levels shot through with language-inflected ideas, not all language-seeming patterns originate in meaningful utterances.[46] And in the realm of art music, a good example featuring talking-drum usage is Nigerian composer Joshua Uzoigwe's piano composition, "Masquerade," for Ìyáàlù and piano (mentioned in passing in chapter 2). This is a work of internal mimicry, whereby the two protagonists mirror each other in an extended and engaging motivic dialogue. By displaying original and copy, source and derivation, giver and receiver, Uzoigwe participates in that pervasive didacticism that one often encounters in talking-drum practices.

From a historical point of view, pretend talking drumming represents both a loss and a gain. The gain is a blurring of the boundary between the real and the simulated, thus increasing the resources available to an individual drummer. The loss stems from the fact that an increasing number of musicians can execute patterns on a talking instrument without knowing or understanding

---

46. Christopher Waterman, *Jùjú: A Social History and Ethnography* (Chicago: University of Chicago Press, 1990), 132–147. I. K. Dairo, dubbed the first *jùjú* superstar, is equally invested in the signifying power of dùndún drums. Listen, for example, to the explicit use of talking drums in the 1962 hit song "Salome." (The text is transcribed on pp. 105–107 of Waterman's book.)

the language from which the talking practice derives. Familiarity with intonational and rhythmic forms and shapes rather than associated semantic meanings drives this practice. The playing of patterns on a talking drum without talking is, however, not necessarily a modern development; it is not merely the product of forms of interethnic contact that have allowed the appropriation of other cultures' practices while at the same time introducing new opacities. The complication of an ostensibly transparent talking-drum practice has some precedent in history. In earlier times, and often as a result of migration and political domination, nonnative speakers of a language were sometimes called upon to drum in the language of their oppressors. There are many instances of this among the Northern Ewe, who came into contact with the Ashanti in the 1860s, and who subsequently inherited certain Ashanti court and ritual practices, including the use of talking drums. An adept Ewe *tompani* (the equivalent of Akan Atumpan) drummer from the town of Ho may render ancient patterns that are supposed to mean something in the Twi language, but he is not be able to express himself ordinarily in that language. While he can mimic the sound of spoken Twi on his drum, he cannot say anything that has not been said before. He is not able to create new utterances in the Twi language in the way that someone who is competent in a natural language can say new things based on an innate grammatical ability. He can only reproduce previously memorized phrases.

Another interesting new development is the practice of incorporating elements from contemporary repertories into traditional drum language. James Burns has described such a practice among the Southern Ewe performers of the popular dance *Agbadza*. Exploiting the tonal potential of their instruments, lead drummers are now able to render on drums snippets of various postcolonial musical forms: the Ghana National Anthem, melodies from gospel songs, and tunes of reggae music (like Bob Marley's "Kaya"). These contemporary accretions confer an endearing and sometimes humorous effect on the *vugbe* (drum language) of *Agbadza*. The traditional and the modern may thus be seen as engaged in dialogue. Sometimes their respective spheres are indistinguishable from each other; at other times, their tokens are presented in unintegrated configurations that might be described as postmodern.[47]

47. See James Burns, "The Beard Cannot Tell Stories to the Eyelash: Creative Transformation in an Ewe Funeral Dance-Drumming Tradition" (PhD dissertation, University of London, School of Oriental and African Studies, 2005). See also his "My Mother Has a Television, Does Yours? Transformation and Secularization in an Ewe Funeral Drum Tradition," *Oral Tradition* 20, no. 2 (2005): 300–319. Readers will surely have their favorite examples of talking drummers incorporating contemporary or foreign idioms. I once heard Yoruba dùndún virtuoso Bisi Adeleke render successively a Christmas carol, a gospel tune, and the ever-popular "Amazing Grace" on his instrument.

There are many instruments besides drums that have the capacity to "talk": stringed and wind instruments, bells, and xylophones. They all share the same basic principle of transposing the relational pitch and durational aspects of the spoken word into a different medium. One particularly interesting practice is the use of the speech mode in many flute repertories found across the continent, including in Uganda, Angola, Sierra Leone, Togo, and the Democratic Republic of the Congo. Because the sound of a flute is typically produced by the mouth—ignoring for now the way nose flutes are played—the proximity to voice and language is suggestive and may ultimately explain why flute performances can slide so effortlessly into speech mode from song mode and vice versa. Beautiful examples include four flute tunes recorded by Hugh Tracey in the Congo,[48] a mournful solo performed by the legendary Ugandan musician Evalisto Muyinda on an *endere* flute,[49] a haunting commentary in speech mode on a family of bamboo flutes played by the Asantehene's musicians in the course of a *kete* performance,[50] and a virtuoso display on a three-hole flute by a Fula schoolboy from Sierra Leone. Combining a quick traversal of registers, abundant motivic repetition, and occasional singing into the flute, the Fula boy is able to sustain an engaging nine-minute performance.[51] This and other solo flute performances possess a declamatory or free-rhythmic character that is strongly reminiscent of speech. And even though the specific verbal components of a given performance may be inaccessible to nonspeakers of the featured language, the morphology, contours, phraseology, and emerging forms still have a great deal to offer listeners.[52]

48. See CD, *On the Edge of the Ituri Forest: Northeastern Belgian Congo 1952* (Utrecht: Stichting Sharp Wood Productions, and Grahamstown, South Africa: International Library of African Music, 1998), track 12, "Four Flute Tunes"; for a transcription and close analysis, see Meki Nzewi's "Analytical Procedure in African Music."

49. CD, *Evaristo Muyinda: Traditional Music of the Baganda, as Formerly Played at the Court of the Kabaka of Buganda* (Leiden: PAN Records, 1991), track 5, "Omusango Gwabalere."

50. See the *JVC/Smithsonian Folkways Video Anthology of Music and Dance of Africa*, vol. 2 (JVC, 1996), clip 2–18.

51. See CD, *Sierra Leone: Musiques Traditionelles* (Paris: OCORA, 1992), track 3, "Solo De Flute Foula."

52. One of course ultimately needs to know the actual language in which the performer might be speaking to appreciate whether the flutist in question is saying something or merely pretending to be saying something. This is where an intra-African discourse may reap some benefits. Individual African musicians listening to music from other parts of the continent and in the process crossing ethnic lines are in a good position to offer insights that might enhance this kind of pan-African understanding.

## SONG

A universal mode of expression, song is a magnificent fusion of word and tone. Since the spoken word in many African languages bears an intrinsic tone, the moment of song is more properly imagined as an instance of doubling, a moment when word tone becomes music tone, when speech tone reaches its ultimate destination as living sound. No song is conceivable without language, and although the depth of influence (of language on music, or of music on language) differs from genre to genre, from group to group, and even from performance to performance, the word as an agglomeration of sound, sense, and meaning lies at the heart of African song.[53]

How might we characterize the broad affiliations between song and speech (oral text)? It should be conceded at the outset that although they exist in principle, the verbal origins of song are not always traceable directly. This is because some songs are made from pure rhythmic gesture, some are realizations of a (wordless) melodic shape, and some are translations of cultural archetypes. Origins aside, however, the production and reception of song invariably require a material vehicle and conceptual apparatus, and it is here that the spoken word becomes indispensable.

Songs typically convey a verbal message through repetition of key words or phrases. Linguistic freight is thus brought into a musical milieu. Communication is likely to be affected, however, when words as lexical items are modified in transmission. In some songs, words function primarily as vehicles for articulation, material means to a larger expressive end. In such contexts, sound and meaning are less important than the possibilities for consonant and vowel articulation, tonal and timbral differentiation, and rhythmic intensification. Semantic freight is then dispensable because the word as sound is notionally complete, requiring no supplement.

The most common mode of articulation in African song is syllabic (one note per syllable) as opposed to melismatic (several notes to a single syllable). There are, to be sure, melodies influenced by Middle Eastern or Arabic song styles in which wordless melismata occur with some frequency. The modern singing styles of Youssou Ndour and Salif Keita, for example, feature such highlighting of voice and sound. The dominant structural tendency, however, is away from florid vocalise toward separated, perhaps even percussive articulation. The syllabic mode endows song with a musical or repetition-filled aura; it is a

---

53. See also Gilbert Rouget, "African Traditional Non-Prose Forms: Reciting, Declaiming, Singing and Strophic Structure," in *Proceedings of a Conference on African Languages and Literatures, Northwestern University*, ed. Jack Berry et al. (Unpublished Typescript 1966), 45–58.

way of "beating the inside of the voice" (as the Ewe would say) to underline its vocalic quality.

What is the relative importance of the word as sound and sense across different genres? We may presume a range from little or no word dependency at one extreme to word indispensability at the other. In some children's game songs, vocables or song words enable articulation and contribute a timbral dimension, but they convey little or no semantic meaning. Game songs sometimes sacrifice the declamatory realism of speech for a metrical realism to enhance their memorability. Toward the middle of the continuum are instances of humming ("singing in the throat," as the Ewe say) that also seem to banish the word. But because what is hummed is either a known song or part of a song, its verbal meaning is never completely detached. Humming suppresses the immediate signifying function of words but relies nevertheless on sedimented (verbal) meanings. Humming often registers intense emotion, a declaration that "It is too much," where "too much" indexes excess, the crossing of an expressive boundary. Humming engenders a temporary departure from the ordinary world of words and their meanings to an interior world of wordless song. Even in this other world, however, one still catches a glimpse of semantic meaning on the horizon. The extra space that opens up when a performer takes to humming is a rich site for reflection, introspection, and speculation.

At the other end of the continuum are those genres that are not imaginable without word-borne information. The singing of epics in Mali, Niger, Gambia, and Senegal, for example, involves the declamation of volumes of text. The word is central to this genre. In execution, singers sometimes follow the natural contours of speech; others rely on musical archetypes (often in the form of gradually descending melodic lines) to "musicalize" narration. At no point, however, is verbal meaning dispensed with entirely, even when extralinguistic devices are deployed to enhance the performance. Praise singing among the Bambara, the Songhay-Zerma, the Yoruba, and the Shona similarly relies on word-borne information to construct genealogies, perform clan histories, or rehearse particular (historical) achievements. Sung genres they may be, but they depend crucially on listeners being able to recover information and messages.[54]

What kinds of worlds do carvers of song imagine and conjure up? In a word: no world is beyond the imaginative reach of African singer-poets. Any and all subjects may be chosen for terse or elaborate formulation as long as performers observe the relevant protocols for public speaking. Subjects may

---

54. An early study of the documentary value of song texts is Gilbert Rouget, "Court Songs and Traditional History in the Ancient Kingdoms of Port-Novo and Abomey," in *Essays on Music and History in Africa*, ed. Klaus Wachsmann (Evanston, IL: Northwestern University Press, 1971), 27–64. The bibliography for this topic is immense, however.

be ordinary or mundane, mystical or esoteric. In some communities, song is a privileged medium that allows the encoding of sentiments that are not normally permitted in ordinary speech. Indeed, at some carnival festivals, singing an insult, an insinuation, or a damaging secret rather than speaking it often protects performers from normal sanctioning.

A good way to imagine song worlds is simply to recall what people do daily, weekly, or seasonally and to consider the kinds of reflection that such activities might engender. The list is potentially infinite. There are counting songs that enumerate people, things, and places. Children's game songs may teach the rhythms of language, parts of the anatomy, and ethics and values. Metaphorical encapsulations of family values (e.g., the five fingers are a family—they need one another) are common. Songs may feature riddling (including tone riddling), profane language, and teasing one's peers. Circumcision rites (such as *Mukanda* in Angola) acknowledge passage from boyhood into adulthood and invite celebration of bravery alongside the learning of customs and manners. Puberty songs may likewise celebrate adulthood, express pride, portray beauty, and give advice about why one should marry well.

Lullabies offer palatable words and rhythms to soothe children. Mothersingers may fantasize about the future ("grow up and make a big farm from which we can all eat") or release tension by lamenting their plight as cowives or insulting their rivals. Word-borne genres cultivated by adults encourage the exercise of memory, the acquisition of sound knowledge of historical events, and the ability to perform histories in engaging and far-from-nonpartisan ways. In musico-dramatic genres like storytelling, narrators learn to link word to tone in diverse configurations, taking care to exploit sound symbolism and the intrinsic musicality of language when opportunities present themselves. The worlds conjured up in such narrations are sometimes framed as acts of strategic deception, the thought being that license to deceive liberates the narrator from the constraints of realism. In a Southern Ewe genre like *halo* (songs of insult, proverb songs), the immunity provided by musical intoning releases the imaginative poet to devise the most painful, often historically plausible insults against his or her opponents.[55]

---

55. For a fine study of literary expression in *haló*, see Daniel K. Avorgbedor, "'It's a Great Song!' *Haló* Performance as Literary Production," *Research in African Literatures* 32 (2001): 17–43. For other studies featuring critique of hegemonic discourses mediated through song, see, among others, Frank Gunderson, *Sukuma Labor Songs from Western Tanzania*; Brent Edwards, "The Sound of Anti-Colonialism," in *Audible Empire: Music, Global Politics, Critique*, ed. Ronald Radano and Tejumola Olaniyan (Durham, NC: Duke University Press, 2016; and Tejunmola Olaniyan, *Arrest the Music! Fela and His Rebel Art and Politics* (Bloomington: Indiana University Press, 2004).

Modern living has similarly stimulated poetic expression in song in a rich variety of ways.[56] When Pentecostal churches sing "No Jesus No Life," they are in the first instance appropriating a famous Bob Marley song, "No Woman No Cry." At the same time, they are opening the door to a wide intertextual field in which reggae, the African diaspora, Ethiopia, fundamentalist Christian evangelism, and the ultimately untenable separation between sacred and secular realms are placed in circulation. In other song contexts, witches, poverty, night life, road accidents, and doing good serve as subjects for reflection. Relationships between men and women, deceit, two-timing, and jealousy have inspired a number of song texts. Cosmopolitan influences are evident, too. James Brown's mannerisms, the rhythms of American urban rappers, and the antics of gospel singers, televangelists, and motivational speakers have all left traces on poetic expression in Nairobi, Enugu, Johannesburg, Lagos, Accra, and Kampala. Rapping in indigenous African languages is no longer a rarity. In some instances, such practices can be traced to the syllabic mode of traditional singing. Rapping transforms—sometimes destroys—some of a language's natural rhythms by imposing a rigid beat regime where there might have been a more fluid one.

Song has facilitated critique at various levels of social discourse. The expression of contrary opinions, views, and sentiments critical of a ruler, a hegemonic force, an enduring convention, or a common understanding may signify differently when mediated by song. Whereas speech signifies directly, and is therefore accorded the notional benefit of realism, song is always already beholden to a different ontology, one that typically invites interpretation as "other"—as play, or as distinct from speech. It is this additional ontological layer that gives song its privileged status, serving on the one hand as a protective shield while, on the other hand, sanctioning an aggressive realism through the heightened mode of intoning an idea, sentiment, or message. Again, the number of African examples is massive, ranging from the labor songs of the Sukuma in Tanzania to the exposition of political corruption and retarded cultural practices by Fela.[57]

Death elicits probably the most profound expression from African singerpoets. The subject may be engaged directly by crafting poignant expressions of sorrow, grief, sadness, or even anger at the (premature) departure of a loved one, or indirectly by folding thematizations of death into broad reflections on aspects of living. In general, constructional devices for songs associated with death are not categorically separate from those associated with poetic reflections on life experiences. Because the poetic imagination stimulated by death is vast and perhaps boundless, and because we have already described (albeit

---

56. See Karin Barber, *The Anthropology of Texts, Persons and Publics: Oral and Written Culture in Africa and Beyond* (Cambridge: Cambridge University Press, 2007).

57. Gunderson, *Sukuma Labor Songs*; Olaniyan, *Arrest the Music!*

briefly) music in one funeral tradition (see chapter 1), we can pass over this part of the discussion quickly. There is, indeed, a vast scholarly literature on poetic imagining in African song, ranging from funeral dirges and laments through popular entertainment songs and epics to ritual and work-related repertories. A factor to be considered is that, at the level of constructional device, the register of death is not brought to life any differently from registers of play and ritual. The same poetic devices are used for contrasting thematizations.

We give the last word on poetic imagining in song to contemporary Ghanaian hiplife singer Omanhene Pozoh. His 1999 song "Medɔfo adaada me" ("My lover has deceived me") displays the imagined world in a vivid way. The point here is not typicality, however, for it is almost impossible to erect any one song text as typifying a genre or repertory. The idea, rather, is to hear echoes of this particular songsmith's strategies in numerous other compositions that will be familiar to readers. The text in its entirety is given in Figure 3.1.

---

**Intro**. (Pozoh, Awurama Badu)
Old school, new school, ayɛ dɛ
*Old school, new school, it is sweet*

**Chorus 2x** (Awurama Badu)
Medɔfo adaada me aa
*My lover has deceived me aa*

Ɔdɔ adaada me oo
*My sweetheart has deceived me oo*

Medɔfo agya me awerehoɔ
*My lover has left me with a lot of sorrow*

Agyegye me akɔku me
*Provoked me and dragged me to my own doom*

**Raps** (Pozoh)
Mennhunuu bi da, mentee bi da, mennhyiaa bi da
*I have not seen anything like this before, nor heard of anything like it,*
    *nor run into anything like this.*

Obi na ɛkaaɛ a, nka medɔ Nyame sɛ Pozoh membelieve da
*If someone had said it, I swear to God that I, Pozoh, would never have*
    *believed it*

Wo ho ayɛ me nwanwa
*You've profoundly shocked me*

---

**Figure 3.1** Text of hiplife song "Medɔfo adaada me" ("My lover has deceived me") by Omanhene Pozoh.

Wose wohyiaa me foforɔ no
*You say that when you first met me*

Na wose wo Nyame ara ne me
*You said that I was your everything*

Ɛnɛ madane bonsam a wogyina abɔnten rebisa me sɛ hwan ne me
*Today I have become your devil, and you're there standing on the street*
   *asking me who I am*

Me ne me, ɔmanhene, me buroni, bebe
*I am still me, the king himself, my precious one, baby*

Ɛnnyɛ saa, awerehoɔ beku me
*Otherwise the sorrow would kill me*

Woabɛfa me kokoɔ so begya me subunu ani
*You took me from a safe place and left me stranded in the middle of the river*

Ɛde adeɛ bɛwɔ m'ani
*And poked me in the eye*

Ɛnnyɛ m'ani a
*It's not my usual self*

Ɔdɔ nti magyaagyae me ho
*Because of love I let down my guard*

Ama wode ntoma aye me fitaà
*You used cloth to deceive me*

Me tiri mu fitaa
*My thoughts about you are genuine*

Mede makoma ama wo sɛ gye na kita
*I entrusted my heart to your keep*

Mede me werɛ ahyɛ wo mu sɛ Yesu ne Peter
*I put my faith in you in the manner of Jesus and Peter*

Nso akokɔ ammɔn mmiɛnsa
*But the cock did not crow three times*

Woayi me ama, Nyame ama
*You betrayed me*

Na mekaa sɛ wodɔ me
*I thought you loved me*

Ɔdaadaafoɔ, sɛɛ daadaa bi na woadaadaa me
*Deceiver, not knowing you were lying to me all along*

Figure 3.1 (Continued)

**Chorus 2x** (Awurama Badu)

Medɔfo adaada me aa
*My lover has deceived me aa*

Ɔdɔ adaada me oo
*My sweetheart has deceived me oo*

Medɔfo agya me awerehoɔ
*My lover has left me with a lot of sorrow*

Agyegye me akɔku me
*Provoked me and dragged me to my own doom*

(Awurama Badu)

Adeɛ a mehunuuiɛ ara ne sɛ
*What I have noticed is that*

Medɔfo yi, n'ani ntɔ m'anim, n'ani ntɔ m'anim
*This darling of mine, he doesn't look me in the eye*

Ohu me a na ne bu afu
*When he sees me, he gets angry*

Ɔse metiri nnyɛ nti
*He says I am not a lucky one*

Efiri sɛ waware ne akyɛ
*Because he has been married to me for a long time*

Nanso wayɛ ayɛ ayɛ ayɛ
*Yet he had struggled and struggled*

Wannya sika a ɛda hɔ nti
*He has not struck it rich*

Sɛ ennɛ sɛ ne Nyame aboa ama ne nsa aka kakra a
*Now that God has put a little money in his hands*

Ɔse menkɔ
*He says I should leave*

Efiri sɛ ebia na nea ne nsa aka yi mpo, me ti bɔne nti na asan afiri ne nsa
*Because he might lose the little he has through my bad luck*

A woahu wiase yi, ɔdɔfo agya me awerehoɔ
*You see how the world is, my loved one has left me with sorrow*

Hɛɛ! Wiase yi mu ɔdɔfo agya me adwendwene
*In this world my lover has left me with troubled thoughts*

Agyegye me akɔku me
*Provoked me and dragged me to my own doom*

Figure 3.1 (Continued)

**Background**
*Don't cry! Don't cry!*

**Raps** (Pozoh)
Anokwa, saa na ewiase tee?
*Truly, is that how the world really is?*

Me ne no adi bankye ampesie saa
*She and I ate cassava ampesi for years*

Ɛnɛ a wayɛ yie anya sika a yɛde tɔ take-away
*Today he is doing well and has money to buy take-away*

Nti ɔse menkɔ away, abalaway, miniway, nɛkɛgbɛ, this way,
    ɔdɔ hyɛ akonwa no ase
*So he says I should go away, abalaway, which way, this way, this way,
    love has taken second seat*

Wagya no Kingsway
*He has abandoned it at Kingsway*

Ɔdɔ, wonnkae? Wonni bi na me na metɔ ma wodi, ma wonom, ma wohyɛ
*Sweetheart, don't you remember? When you did not have, I was the one who
    put food and drink on the table, and clothes on your back.*

ɛtɔ dabi koraa a me wia m'awofoɔ de ma wo efise mepɛsɛ biribiara ɛbɛhia wo
*Sometimes I would even steal things from my parents for you because I hated
    to see you want for anything*

"I love you like harmattan pawpaw"
*"I love you like harmattan pawpaw"*

"You are the apple of my eye"
*"You are the apple of my eye"*

Sɛ ne nyinaa yɛ Kwaku Ananse story
*I did not know they were all Kwaku Ananse fairy tales*

**Chorus 2x** (Awurama Badu)
Medɔfo adaada me aa
*My lover has deceived me aa*

Ɔdɔ adaada me oo
*My sweetheart has deceived me oo*

Medɔfo agya me awerehoɔ
*My lover has left me with a lot of sorrow*

Agyegye me akɔku me
*Provoked me and dragged me to my own doom*

Figure 3.1 (Continued)

**Raps** (Pozo)

'Had I known is always at last'
*'Had I known is always at last'*

Baby last! Menim sɛ sei nawobɛyɛ me a
*Baby last. If I had known that this was how you were going to treat me*

Nka metenaa me baabi twɛnn last bus
*I would have stayed put somewhere and waited for the last bus*

Ɛtenaa me baabi ɛdwene me ho
*Stayed put somewhere and minded my own business*

Wo ama manu me ho
*You have filled me with regret*

Sɛ wohyɛɛ me bɔ sɛ wo ne me bɛtena afebɔɔ
*You promised to be with me forever*

Nso woadi me hwambɔ ama mayɛ mmɔbɔ
*You've toyed with me and left me a pitiful mess*

Te sɛ asɔredan mu akura
*Like a church mouse*

Yɛkaa sɛ wobɛgya me asi nkwanta abɔ m'anim benkuta
*People said you would abandon me at some crossroads and leave me in disgrace*

Nso mammfa annyɛ asɛm
*But those warnings fell on deaf ears*

Ɔbaa Ataa, nti wo werɛ afi?
*Ɔbaa Ataa, so have you forgotten?*

ɛkaa me ne wo mmienu wɔ dan mu a
*If you and I were left alone inside a room*

Nkɔmmɔ a yɛbɔ, bɔɔl a yɛbɔ, goal a yɛhyɛ, ɛne ɛbɔ a mese yɛhyɛ
*The conversations we have, the ball we play, the goals we score, and the promises we made to each other*

Bebe, ah, mese 'Alomo'
*Baby, ah, I say 'Alomo'*

Figure 3.1 (Continued)

How is the song made? Pozoh literally grafts his message onto an old tune, "Medɔfo adaada me" ("My lover has deceived me") by female highlife singer Awura Ama Badu. Hers is "old school"; his is new. The performance begins with Badu's singable old-style melody. Pozoh then enters with a segment of rapping. She returns with some more singing, he with more rapping. She returns once more, and Pozoh finally rounds things off. The undisguised yoking of old to new is part of an aesthetic of appropriation frequently used by hiplife singers. This is of course part of a modern aesthetic in which copying, mimicking, and sampling give rise to simulacra at different levels. Pozoh announces at the outset that this kind of thing (play, performance) is "sweet." It allows for the construction of a particular lineage while at the same time heightening the difference between then and now. Old-school highlife is made from simple, memorable tunes whose refrains we can all join in. The new school is a world of verbal virtuosity in which syllables accumulate at a fast rate, rhythms are articulated with a kind of digital sharpness, rhymes of varying degrees of persuasion are spat out, and expressive styles are invoked from both the low and high ends of the class spectrum.

Song is song in part because, from the beginning of a performance to its ending, a period has been consecrated for play by the singer. Language is an important agent of such play, but the deeper condition of possibility is the beat or rhythm. Performers, listeners, and dancers (both real and imagined) are united in their dedication to preserving this interval. Indeed, we might say that it is precisely this temporal constraint that guarantees the ontology of song.

Pozoh uses a rich descriptive language. His characterization of this lover who has deceived him will be familiar to culturally attuned listeners. Contrasting past and present in the broken relationship, he reaches into the memory bank to retrieve memorable exchanges and transactions between the two lovers. He also reflects more broadly and philosophically on human foibles and deception. The singer's intertextual horizon encompasses biblical allusions, wise sayings, proverbs, American pop culture, and common sense. The result is a richly textured world to which listeners are invited to plug in their own values and experiences. The goal of the performance is not to deliver information as such (song, after all, is a singularly inefficient conduit of hard information) but to conjure up an imagined world rooted in rhythm and animated by a network of vocalizations for communal participation. Language and music entail each other in this business, but music always has priority when the two come together because it already implicates language.

If we had to single out a potent and widely used poetic technique for African song, it would be one based on parallelisms, oppositions, dualities, and binaries. It would also incorporate striking analogies and similes, as well as poignant and suggestive metaphors. Pozoh's 1999 song incorporates several of these devices, a sign not only of the rootedness of poetic imagining among hiplife artists but also of the interpenetration of the spheres of tradition and modernity. The ongoing contrasting of past and present buttresses the binary feel and enhances the crafting of a message of betrayal. "When you did not have anything, I provided for you. You and I ate cassava *ampesi*, but now you're eating take-away [a class-based contrast of cuisine]." The rhyme scheme, too, features complementation and opposition. Some rhymes work well, while others seem forced. For example, the rhyming of "Peter" (the disciple of Jesus) and "kita" ("hold" in Twi) is strained. Such moments of incongruity draw attention to the spinning wheel, the manufactured groove that underwrites this hiplife song and produces both felicitous and nonfelicitous rhymes and metaphors.

Pozoh's strategic use of different languages foregrounds his cosmopolitanism. The principal languages are Twi and English, but these are supplemented by American and British idioms. He also alludes to secular and sacred motives and firmly separates a desired past filled with domestic bliss from a hellish present. Alliterations reinforce the domain of sheer sound: "I've never *seen* such a thing, never *heard* such a thing, would never have *believed* such a thing." This sequence is delivered with a rhetorical crescendo underpinned by an element of regularity, a refrain perhaps. Finally, Pozoh's metaphors invoke the contemporary and modern city life: "take-away" (fast food), "Kingsway" (a famous shop), and "harmattan pawpaw" (especially precious because it is hard won, having reached fruition despite the adverse dry weather).

Omanhene Pozoh is one among scores of young hiplife and hip-hop artists who have been busy constructing texts to comment on and express various visions of life. The prerequisites for such creativity include high doses of poetic imagining. Although the temporal unit for Pozoh's delivery makes these collective repertories seem modern, the actual exercise of such a poetic imagination is of ancient origins.[58]

---

58. For a sophisticated study of hiplife in Ghana, see Jesse Weaver Shipley, *Living the Hiplife, Celebrity and Entrepreneurship in Ghanaian Popular Music* (Durham, NC: Duke University Press, 2013), and the companion film, *Living the Hiplife* (New York: World Newsreel, 2007). A valuable collection, broad in geocultural reference and giving due attention to language, is *Hip Hop in Africa*, ed. Eric Charry. Spoken-word-dominated genres lie formally in the domain of literary studies and so tend to get more attention from literary scholars than from ethnomusicologists. See, for example, Aissata Sidikou, *Recreating Words, Reshaping Worlds: The Verbal Art of Women from Niger, Mali and Senegal* (Trenton, NJ: Africa World Press, 2001), and Thomas Hale and Aissata G. Sidikou, *Women's Songs from West Africa* (Bloomington: Indiana University Press, 2014).

## METALANGUAGE

A metalanguage is a language about another language. If I say, "A bachelor is an unmarried man," I have used the same language in which the word *bachelor* occurs (English) to explain its meaning. Explanations of this sort are common in natural language, but is there a comparable phenomenon in musical language? Can a musical "sentence" be used to explain a musical "word"? Can African music perform metalinguistic acts? In a strict sense, a musical metalanguage that resides solely in the sphere of music and exhibits exclusively musical properties cannot exist outside the supplementary role of thought and language. To explain anything at all, we must fall back on the individuation of language, as semioticians taught us long ago.[59] Speakers of Luo, Shona, Yoruba, or Hausa can explain the word *bachelor* in their spoken languages, but there appears to be no comparable explanatory dimension for the (musical) language of Luo dirge singing, Shona lamentation, Yoruba praise singing, or Hausa epic performance.

Why does the issue of metalanguage arise in connection with the subject of this chapter? There are two main reasons. The first is that music behaves in certain ways that attract the designation *metamusical*, the presumed equivalent of metalanguage. Just as a metalanguage is a language about language, so *metamusical* denotes music about music. Second, the close connection between language and music suggests that the "linguistic" side of music may exhibit metalinguistic features. The first of these reasons is readily illustrated. If I sing a phrase one way, and then sing an embellished version immediately following it, my listener will immediately understand that I have sung two equivalent phrases of music. On a certain level of abstraction, both phrases "mean" the same thing despite divergences in their surface structures and in what they connote. I have therefore indulged in metamusical behavior by "explaining" the earlier phrase (varied repetitions tempt us to compare, and comparisons typically broach an exegetical or explanatory dimension), letting you hear the potential it harbors. While my primary aim as a singer is not necessarily to indulge in acts of criticism or pedagogy, the means that I employ involve me in such acts.

Given the preponderance of variation processes in African music, and given the many alternative renditions that are heard at different hierarchical levels of structure in any number of performances, we may conclude that there is a built-in explanatory dimension in African music, be it song based on archetypes or instrumental music based on recognizable figurae.

59. Émile Benveniste, "The Semiology of Language," in *Semiotics: An Introductory Reader,* ed. Robert E. Innis (London: Hutchinson, 1986), 228–246.

The repetition of an utterance *says* something about its previous occurrence, shows it in a different light, invites an intertextual hearing, and gestures toward a shared deep structure. But is this kind of "explanation" equivalent to saying that "A bachelor is an unmarried man"? Here we encounter a special difficulty in trying to imagine a musical metalanguage. Whereas the vocabulary for a given natural language may be gathered in a dictionary, enabling us to look up individual words and their meanings and associations, musical lexicons are less amenable to standardization and so are not so common. And when they are assembled, they tend to codify connotative values rather than translations as in a verbal dictionary. If music is a language, its metalanguage is not music but language. While the kinds of variation acts I've just mentioned occur as a normal part of "musicking" in Africa (they may also be regarded as the ultimate signs of iconism in African expression insofar as they privilege likeness), explanation as such is not their primary goal. To talk about or explain what is going on in Fela's "Lady," Ladysmith's "Pauline," or the funeral dirges of Nkundo, Avatime, and Fon women, we have to leave the realm of song and enter that of language. Actions that we had earlier imagined as constituting explanations are conceptually possible only through a concept-based language. Your realizing that the second phrase of my song is a variant of the first is an analytical insight made possible by your possession of concepts of resemblance and variance. Without concepts, we cannot concretize insight. African music cannot be its own metalanguage, its own "interpreting system"; rather, language serves in the first instance as the interpreting system of music.[60]

We must therefore look to verbal language to tell us what goes on in music. The cultivation of such metalanguages does not appear to have been of pressing concern to African musicians in traditional societies. In primary oral cultures, where music making is essentially an oral/aural activity, talk about music emanates from practical or utilitarian concerns. It may be directed toward the naming of genres, instruments, and performers or toward eliciting immediate performance actions, rather than toward abstract reflection on music's properties, effects, and enabling constructs and processes. Music is something to be made, first and foremost, not something to be talked about. Music is a doing, not a regarding. World cultures that cultivate extensive talk about music (including some in Western Europe) often do so within institutions or cultivated traditions. In written cultures, such talk often takes the form of intellectual capital packaged as tracts, treatises, and manuals. In oral cultures, such material is lodged in the memories of individuals.

---

60. Benveniste, "The Semiology of Language," 235. For a brief elaboration of this claim, see Agawu, *Music as Discourse*, 28–29.

As we saw in chapter 1, instances of verbal language used to talk about music have been gathered since the 1960s by a number of ethnographers in an attempt to codify indigenous priorities in the conceptualization of music. The modest glossaries of music-speak reconstructed by ethnographers point to the existence of informal discourses featuring names of genres, timbral qualities, and especially action words associated with performance. One of the best known of these is David Ames and Anthony King's *Glossary of Hausa Music and Its Social Contexts*, which includes indigenous names for musical instruments, terms for professional performers, terms for patrons and occasions for music making, and, perhaps most interestingly, terms associated with performance. Included are terms associated with dance, vocal music (subdivided into song, proclamation, acclamation, and ululation), instrumental music, and general performance features. Similar modes of linguistic denomination are found in other glossaries, including those by van Thiel (for the Ankole), Lester Monts (for the Vai), Charles Keil (for the Tiv), Joshua Uzoigwe (for the Igbo), and Misonu Amu (for the Ewe). So, although verbal talk about music has not been cultivated extensively in African communities, these works show what might be possible. And if we designate the body of terms contained in these works as *metalanguage* (a language about another language), then we can begin to glimpse an African musical metalanguage, that is, a vibrant conceptual field in which genres, instruments, modes of striking and blowing, and the spontaneous composition of everything from melodic embellishments through timbral flourishes to the in-the-moment choice of deep and affecting words are shown to lie at the heart of thinker-performers' art and to matter to their hearers. These metalanguages are available only through the crossing of semiotic boundaries between language and music.

## IDEOPHONES

Another manifestation of the close connection between language and music is the preponderance of ideophones in African languages. Although they are primarily linguistic phenomena, ideophones are of interest to music scholars because they open up a musical dimension by foregrounding certain sonic properties of language. Mark Dingemanse defines ideophones as "marked words that vividly depict sensory perception."[61] Each of the key words in his definition is immediately resonant with music: "marked" registers in the

---

61. Mark Dingemanse, "The Meaning and Use of Ideophones in Siwu," 27.

accentual dimension; "word" is analogous to the elementary signifying units of music; "depict" indexes an active portrayal that is totally in sync with music's enduring use of repetition and presentness; "sensory" suggests the spread of an ideophone's materiality across several domains, making ideophones multiply significant; and "perception" invokes the category most basic to the reception of music. Ideophones may be said to do musical work—or *potentially* musical work—in the realm of spoken language. If, as we noted at the beginning of this chapter, the spoken word already carries a musical charge, then ideophones are endowed with a heightened musical quality.

Writing specifically about Siwu, a Central Volta language, Dingemanse offers a description of ideophones that highlights "musical" elements like length, reduplication, repetition, accentuation, and expressive salience:

> Ideophones are conspicuous words. They stand out from other words in several ways: they are longer on average than nouns and verbs; they have deviant word structures (featuring for example long vowels as in sɔdzɔlɔɔ "oblong," or disyllabic reduplicated roots as in *sinisini* "smooth"); they are often only loosely integrated in the utterance, if at all; in actual use, they are often emphasized; and finally, they easily undergo expressive prosodic alteration—or example, in the above exchange, the final vowel of sɔdzɔlɔɔ is greatly lengthened and *sinisini* is repeated several times. The effect of all this is that ideophones are quite unlike ordinary words that do their work without attracting much attention themselves; instead, ideophones literally jump out as words that attract attention *qua* words, as speech heard in a special way. Set apart from the surrounding linguistic material, they draw us into the scene and invoke images of "being there." The term *Lautmahlerei* (sound painting), current in early-twentieth-century German writings on ideophones, provides a useful way of understanding this process: like paintings, ideophones invite the listener to savor them as depictions.[62]

The implicit music-in-language condition is rampant in a variety of genres, including narratives, riddles, folktales, funeral dirges, and greetings. In some folktale performances, for example, where the narrator's task is to bring a familiar story to life, ideophones are often drawn upon to heighten the sound sense of language. They may be used alongside onomatopoeia, reduplication, and other sound-symbolic devices. They help to intensify and vivify the expression; they add spice to the content.

62. Dingemanse, "Ideophones and the Aesthetics of Everyday Language in a West-African Society," *Senses and Society* 6, no. 1 (2011): 78–79.

If speech tones confer a continuous musical presence on spoken language, ideophones approximate rhetorical devices because of their intermittent rather than continuous usage. Their task is to intensify the expression by musicalizing speech. Speech tones are structural—they are not optional for speakers since they embody the vary basis of meaning; ideophones, by contrast, take on a superstructural quality since they are discretionary devices available to seasoned speakers. Speech tones and ideophones further facilitate certain forms of border crossing. Just as language's pitch and durational dimensions are transferred into a nonspoken realm in the practices associated with speech surrogacy (such as that of talking drums), so ideophones light up the iconic dimension in the conceptual progression from spoken language to music.

## A "LINGUISTIC" RESIDUE IN PERFORMANCE SENSIBILITY?

A final feature that suggests a close connection between music and language is also the most elusive of the ones discussed in this chapter: the prospect for a "linguistic" residue sedimented in African performance. By "linguistic," I mean the many attachments of language. Francis Bebey once attributed the special quality of African music to its close connection to language, and although he did not go on to say that speakers of African languages are usually more adept at performing African traditional music than nonspeakers, it is reasonable, I think, to make such an inference:

> The importance of language in African music . . . is what chiefly distinguishes it from the other art forms. No other art is quite so specifically African. Any talented sculptor could reproduce a Negro mask or statuette, but music is quite another matter; it entails the use of instruments that are made specifically in order to express a chosen language in musical terms. It is scarcely an exaggeration to say that without African languages, African music would not exist.[63]

Bebey's emphases are not meant to be exclusionary; non-African performers and listeners can and do enjoy varieties of African music without knowing African languages. But if the linguistic sediment is never convincingly eliminated from the list of essential properties of African music, then it is hard to see how its unavailability—or notional bracketing—can support an authoritative

---

63. Bebey, *African Music*, 122.

performance. Nor is it clear how one could deny that a hearing deprived of this linguistic residue has a significant deficit.

Some anecdotal evidence may be relevant here. We have probably all heard people play or sing who don't seem to—as we say—"have it." We sense that although they have gone through the motions, there is something missing. That something might be a feeling or sensibility, an aura or affect, an attitude or even a personality. The singing or playing feels mechanical or uninspired; it doesn't swing, and it feels labored, as if the performer was stiff, leaden, unnatural, or simply trying too hard. Some have used the word *unmusical* to describe such playing, but in our politically correct age, we know better than to claim that the distinction between a musical and an unmusical performance is categorical. Skeptics demand empirical support for such claims. Still, social disincentives to the making of such judgments say nothing about what motivates them in the first place. They often proceed from instinct or from a subjective stance and may be arrived at quickly or instantly; they are in fact regularly provoked by any number of performances. Critics are sometimes at a loss as to how to specify their reactions in verbal language. Is it possible—paradoxically—that such reactions converge on a broadly linguistic base? Does the critic sense a lack of understanding of the musical "language" on the part of the performer or a failure to grasp the essence of a genre, an essence that includes—but is not limited to—the natural language of the community to which the particular genre belongs?

Watching African drumming performances both on the continent and especially in the diaspora, I am sometimes led to the view that the missing element is precisely this "linguistic" residue. This far-from-dispensable supplement is often taken for granted by culture bearers. Lead drummers in Guinea, Côte d'Ivoire, Zimbabwe, Uganda, Nigeria, and Togo typically possess a combination of skills spanning music, language, and spirituality. The more African drumming has gone global in recent years, the more it has been "spoken" by nonnative speakers, and the more obvious it has become that its linguistic and spiritual dimensions do not always travel with it; drumming is redefined in terms of the mechanics of its rhythms rather than the poetry of its utterance. To drum Yoruba, Ewe, or Igbo drums properly, however, it is helpful to be able to speak Yoruba, Ewe, or Igbo, or at least to be able to re-create the sensibilities associated with those languages. Drummers who do not know the spoken language from which the musical drumming originates sometimes lack this sensibility.

This lack is significant, but it is not always damaging. It is especially evident in genres that depend fundamentally on the sound and sensibility of the parallel spoken language for articulate rendition. Not all genres are this way, of course, but a good many are, especially those in which an instrument "talks" either literally or metaphorically. Some drummers, for example, may acquire the required supplementary knowledge (manner, style, feeling) from competence in a related African language. Thus, an Ewe drummer drumming an Ashanti dance or a Luo drummer drumming an Igbo dance can achieve results comparable to those of native-speaker drummers. But the further a drummer's spoken-language background is from the language of the drumming, the more likely it is that he or she will impose an alien sensibility on the performance.

This claim is perhaps least contentious in connection with vocal music. African women with seasoned tongues who sing and improvise and who render feeling in culturally appropriate ways invariably possess a huge linguistic (and cultural) supplement that is brought to bear on each performance. It is notable that many forms of African vocal music are infrequently attempted by non-Africans. For example, the singing of epics, dirges, laments, and praises is far less popular among American and European performers of African music than the playing of mbiras or jembe drums. It is not accidental that the best exponents of Ewe drumming, for example, are born-in-the-tradition performers who possess the relevant cultural supplements, of which language is key. And it is not for nothing that the Ewe distinguish levels of understanding, separating those who grasp nuanced, deep-level meanings from those whose understanding is confined to the literal surface: "Amedzró sè gbè, mésè àdágáná o" means "The foreigner understands a language, but he or she does not understand the proverbs."

It is not ultimately possible to prove this point. I offer it here as a viewpoint that might engender productive discussion, not as a proven position. Certainly one can cite hundreds of African-language-speaking lead performers as prima facie evidence of the linking of musicianship to spoken-language competence, but one might also mention the scores of musicians who have attained some fluency in the performance of certain African idioms without knowing the languages from which the music originates. And at a time when border crossing has become a sign to be welcomed and celebrated, a claim for language competence as a prerequisite for, say, lead-drummer status is likely to seem out of date or even dismissed as obstructionist, elitist, separatist, or essentialist. I bring it up, however, not to reclaim African music for African musicians, nor to discourage the many non-African-language-speaking fans of African music from pursuing their interest, but simply to emphasize the rich and unique resources enshrined in African languages. Embracing spoken language as part of an authentic and comprehensive engagement with African music stands to augment the richness of the performing and listening experience.

## CONCLUSION

Language is key to defining human essence, and it is a deep tragedy that, despite noteworthy attempts in the years following independence to extend the domains of usage of indigenous languages in countries like Tanzania, Nigeria, and Ghana, the enduring colonial assault on Africa distracted policymakers from retaining that priority, from maximizing efforts to explore the many registers of indigenous language, especially those pertaining to reading and writing. African worlds of poetry, philosophy, and music are not ultimately accessible without knowledge of African languages. Indeed, no genuine African renaissance is likely to take place until we retrieve those aspects of spirituality, language, and music that European colonialism swept aside or otherwise mutilated.

The importance of language for music cannot be overemphasized. In this chapter, we have confined discussion to a handful of issues: the pressures that speech tones exert on the composing of melody, how drums talk, song as a fusion of word and tone, prospects for a musical metalanguage, the incidence of ideophones, and finally, what I have called a "linguistic" residue in performance sensibility. Ideally, each of these topics would form the point of departure for a much larger investigation, one that would eventually explore both resonances and dissonances among them. For that investigation, the specialized literature (especially that produced by linguists) will be indispensable. Navigating this body of work across myriad African languages is surely a daunting prospect, but we may well emerge reassured not only that the word was there in or near the beginning but also that it is always with us.

# 4

# The Rhythmic Imagination

## THE IDEA OF "AFRICAN RHYTHM"

More ink has been spilled on rhythm than on any other topic in African music studies. An entangled parameter embodying the temporal and accentual dimensions of music, rhythm is said to be the heart and soul of African music. Often associated with dance, rhythmic patterns are elaborated in ingenious and sophisticated ways not matched by any world music. Rhythm may well manifest the continent's most distinctive modes of rhetoric and expression.

Literally hundreds of statements from both popular and scholarly writings affirm this idea. Early European travelers to Africa, members of learned societies and scientific expeditions, missionaries, anthropologists, African nationalists, and ethnomusicologists have all remarked on the strengths and peculiarities of African rhythmic shapes. "Everywhere from the North to the South," writes Monique Brandilly about Chad, "a common feature is the presence of many drums and a wealth of rhythmic musics that are most often bound to dance."[1] Hornbostel came across a passage in which "the lower part is syncopated past our comprehension."[2] According to Gunther Schuller, "in respect to rhythm, African music is unquestionably the world's most complex music."[3] Ensemble textures are often characterized as polyrhythmic, while metrical order remains a subject of controversy. Some feel and hear regularities approximating the common meters of Western music (such as 4/4 and 12/8); others deny the existence of meter altogether, judge time signatures to be inconstant and elusive, or say that meter is irreducibly multiple. In a recent book on Ewe rituals published in 2009,

1. M. Brandilly, "Chad," *Grove Music Online*, accessed April 1, 2013.

2. Hornbostel, "African Negro Music," 52.

3. Gunther Schuller, *Early Jazz: Its Roots and Musical Development* (New York: Oxford University Press, 1986 [orig. 1968]), 10.

for example, American ethnomusicologist Steven Friedson denies that there is a "one" in African rhythmic practice; he hears a "suspended feeling" in Ewe drumming and claims that players rely not on the intellect but on "bodily knowledge" (as if there could ever be "bodily knowledge" that was not also mediated by the intellect). The essence for him is ambiguity.[4] And as if furthering Friedson's cause, David Locke, who hitherto had been on the side of those who found order, precision, and regularity in African rhythm, now prefers to speak of "simultaneous multidimensionality" to capture the complexity that he feels is being lost in some of the corrective structuralist-analytical accounts of the 1990s to 2000s.[5]

What motivates these diverse and often opposing views, and where might the truth lie? We would have our hands full trying to unpack them all here. Some see African music as the site of indescribable, incredible, or incomprehensible happenings. For them, rhythms are magical and indexical of spiritual or other-worldly realms. African rhythms are thought to defy notation—any notation—and are ultimately different from, if not superior to, those of Western music. Others (and I include myself in this group), although no less enchanted by African rhythm, conclude that the complexity of African rhythm is a *rational complexity*; that there is indeed a "one"; that there are on- and off-beats, meter, and periodicity; and that the multiplicity of inference that some vocal outsiders claim to hear is not a free, anything-goes affair but ordered arrangements of beats that allow dancers to embody sounds. The difference between African and Western rhythm, I would argue, is not categorical, not indicative of a radically different way of being in the world. The difference is largely a matter of emphasis and idiomatic preference. The truth is that no device or procedure found in African music is unheard of in Western music, especially if we consider the musical practices of Medieval Europe. This makes Africa's rhythmic endowments all the more remarkable.

The most reliable characterizations of African rhythm are likely to come from individuals who work across different world repertoires and thus bring a comparative perspective—sometimes explicit, other times implicit—to bear on their studies of African repertoires. Rhythm, after all, is basic to most music, so the perspective of a musician who already "speaks" one rhythmic language is likely to illuminate his or her speaking of another. (I am using the word *speaking* to denote a full engagement.) A survey of the literature suggests that the most penetrating studies have come from scholars who have proceeded

4. Friedson, *Remains of Ritual: Northern Gods in a Southern Land*, 144.

5. Locke, "The Metric Matrix: Simultaneous Multidimensionality in African Music," *Analytical Approaches to World Music* 1, no. 1 (2011.

comparatively, who come to African music with a genuine understanding of another musical culture. I am thinking of figures like André Schaeffner, Rose Brandel, Mieczslaw Kolinski, Nketia, Euba, Rouget, and A. M. Jones from an earlier generation, and Meki Nzewi, David Locke, Marcos Branda-Lacerda, Zabana Kongo, Simha Arom, James Burns, David Temperley, Rainer Polak, Godfried Toussaint, Chris Stover, and Willie Anku from a more recent one. Schaeffner's example may be held up as a model. In the mid-1950s, he said that "perhaps . . . rhythm in African music is more persuasive and more subtle than in any other music."[6] The telling qualification signaled by the word *perhaps* aside, we note that Schaeffner had studied African music both on the continent (through various field expeditions) and in Europe, notably in Paris; he was involved in the 1930 exhibition of world cultures and served as an adviser to the organizers about African musical styles; he wrote a great deal about African music, especially its instruments; above all, perhaps, he knew his own "native" music well, having studied with Stravinsky, Boulanger, and others, and having expressed that understanding through the composition of significant works. He was thus in a position to think across cultures and to bring a comparative perspective to bear on a topic that desperately needs a broad perspective. By engaging African music variously as collector, analyst, and composer, Schaeffner stood poised to illuminate its structures.[7]

How, then, might we frame an introduction to the study of African rhythm? The subject is vast, of course, so we need once more to be selective. I begin with a comment on musical time and then outline two frameworks for contextualizing rhythms (one from Curt Sachs and the other from my own work on Northern Ewe music). Then, referring mainly to the preeminent drumming ensemble of West African music, I describe three prominent features of African rhythm: time lines, polyrhythm, and the lead drummer's rhythmic narratives. I close by suggesting a generative approach to rhythmic organization as one that captures African intellection into rhythm most felicitously. The idea throughout is to orient the reader to the foundations of African rhythm and to advocate frameworks of understanding that affirm its rational basis.

6. Schaeffner, Jacket notes for *African Music from French Colonies*, ed. Alan Lomax, *The Columbia World History of Primitive Music*, vol. 2. (New York: Columbia Records, 1955–1956).

7. Tamara Levitz draws admirably on Schaeffner's wisdom to develop her argument about the representation of the Dogon. See her "The Aestheticization of Ethnicity: Imagining the Dogon at the Musée du quai Branly," *Musical Quarterly* 89 (2006): 600–642. Similar adaptations of Schaeffner for music-analytic purposes will, I believe, enhance Anglophone Africanist ethnomusicology's theoretical project.

## TIME

A path to understanding African rhythm that once seemed promising was to begin with time rather than rhythm and then to see how or whether African conceptions of time were translated into the sonic realm. Alan Merriam went this route, combing the ethnographies of various anthropologists for information about time reckoning. Predictably, while the West was credited with linear time, African societies like the Tiv, Nuer, Kaguru, BaKongo, and Basongye were said to reckon time differently:

> Time-reckoning is thought to be nonlinear; instead, it can be reversed, discontinuous, a "sliding scale," circular, or spiral. Time-reckoning is carried on in terms of referral to natural phenomena or, most particularly, social activity. Time is not reckoned as distance, it is not epochal, and it is not measured with special apparatus.[8]

In his search for the units of time, Merriam further claimed that "the smallest period in African time-reckoning is the division of the day."

The reified structures that studies of time had produced were of limited utility to understanding music making. Agricultural communities, for example, were said to subscribe to a circular (or spiral) as opposed to a linear view of time; the intensely cyclical element in dance drumming was then traced back to this sense of time. But the transfer was always already problematic, for while there is indeed a circular or cyclical element in dance drumming, there is at the same time a strongly linear or goal-oriented element as well. The two logically entail one another. The narratives of some lead drummers, for example, have a strongly linear trajectory. Moreover, the apparent absence of words indicating small units of time in African languages is neither accurate (Ewe refer to seconds as *aɖabafofo*) nor significant, for surely not every aspect of music making is designated in verbal language. Finally, what is one to make of the contrast between an ostensibly casual African sense of time—dictated by sun and shadows ("African time," which euphemistically denotes perpetual lateness)—and the amazing precision in timing that one finds, say, in xylophone ensemble performances? The time of music is its own time. Musical time is not—or not necessarily—a microcosm of ordinary time; it is not a domestication or translation of some other temporal realm. Indeed, it is a sobering thought that not a single enduring insight into musical structure has come from reflections on lived time in relation to music.[9]

---

8. Merriam, "Concepts of Time Reckoning," in *African Music in Perspective*, 457.

9. Prominent works on African music that take time into account are Ruth Stone, *Dried Millet Breaking*, and Kubik, *Theory of African Music* vol. 2. The latter includes a listing of a variety of African-language words for time.

## RHYTHMS OF SPEECH VERSUS RHYTHMS
## OF THE BODY

A good framework for distributing the reality of rhythmic processes is to distinguish between rhythms of speech and rhythms of the body.[10] All rhythms notionally originate in one of these two realms. The rhythms of speech are the durational, accentual, and periodic patterns produced in the course of speaking. In ordinary, day-to-day speech in numerous African languages, syllabic durations alternate between long and short, accentual patterns emerge from phenomenal stress associated with either timbre or tonal change, and periodicity is sensed in the asymmetrical succession of segments of performed speech, be it a greeting, the swearing of an oath, a town crier's announcement, the pouring of libation, a minister's sermon, a radio announcer's interview, the chief's linguist's admonition, or a medicine man's incantations. The rhythms of speech are the rhythms of language in motion—individual words and their succession, sentences and paragraphs, conversation and interrogation. Language itself may be manifest as ordinary speech or poetic speech. Whereas ordinary speech typically displays variability in sentence length, certain kinds of poetic speech incorporate regularity in one domain or another. Except in special circumstances, ordinary speech is not normally confined metrically.

The rhythms of the body are dance rhythms. They are profiled in thousands of dances performed daily across the African continent: *baakisimba* (Uganda), *kpanlogo* (Ghana), *mganda* (Zambia), *bikutsi* (Cameroon), *gele* (Togo), *sindimba* (Tanzania), *atilogwu* (Nigeria), *soukous* (Democratic Republic of the Congo), *makossa* (Cameroon), *luhya* (Kenya), and *azonto* (Ghana), among many others. These rhythms are nurtured by repetition; they enable, motivate, or simply accompany movement. Harold Powers acknowledges their widespread distribution and generative function: "Repetitive rhythms rooted in bodily movements whether of work or of play, lie behind much of the world's instrumental music."[11] A palpable beat normally guides movement, and this in turn contributes a metrical feel. Whereas rhythms of the body are modes of communal expression, rhythms of speech are modes of individual expression. Whenever speech takes on a mode of communality, it submits to regulation; it is molded into poetry. The rhythms of dance, then, are closer to music than to speech because their purpose is to carve time in response to movement. While rhythms of the body have the capacity to communicate messages, their primary purpose is to make play possible.

10. Curt Sachs, *Rhythm and Tempo: A Study in Music History* (1953); elaborated by Harold S. Powers, "Rhythm," in *The New Harvard Dictionary of Music*, ed. Don M. Randel (Cambridge, MA: Harvard University Press,1986).

11. Powers, "Rhythm," in *The New Harvard Dictionary*, 704.

Distinguishing the rhythms of speech from those of the body allows us to present their conjunction as a basic syntactical unit in African performance. Many dance genres have an external form made up of two contrasting sections: free leading to strict; slow followed by fast; or in terms of the dichotomy we are developing here, speech yielding to song. A declamatory section featuring the rhythms of speech typically initiates proceedings. This portion of the performance is valued for its contemplative or philosophical import. Proverbs, deep thoughts, and enigmas put performers (and listeners) in mind of those things that lie beyond, powers that exceed their own; this is a way of underlining the seriousness or solemnity of the occasion. Only after this acknowledgment has been made does the performance proceed to a second main section, one in which rhythms of the body are expressed in physical movement. Dancing may involve pairs of performers, small groups, or sometimes larger groups. Individual dances may foreground different parts of the anatomy. *Gabada,* for example, emphasizes rapid foot movement; baakisimba makes much of the midriff and buttocks, as does bamayaa; and agbadza highlights the upper torso, adowa the hands, and egwu-amala the hands and feet. What is emphasized naturally reflects the aesthetic premises of the community in question. Invariably, however, an underlying constraint in the form of a regular beat or cycle played by the musicians makes the work of dance not only possible but also enjoyable for participants.

The distinction between speech and body rhythms may be further aligned with the dichotomy between free and strict rhythm. Rhythms of speech are "free" in the sense that they are not metrically constrained; their patterns of repetition are more elusive, residing on a more abstract level. Rhythms of the body are "strict" because, with the intervention of dance, a beat requirement is put in place and a cyclic or periodic constraint follows naturally. An analogous set of qualities is enshrined in the well-known musicological distinction between recitative and aria in opera, as well as that between the "speech mode" and "song mode" in instrumental music.[12] Recitative is free or ametrical, while aria is strict or metrical. The temporal feel of recitative promotes efficiency in the communication of verbal messages, while the intramusical focus of aria obscures, undermines, or otherwise transforms its verbal-communicative functions. Because it is speechlike, recitative foregrounds a semantic dimension; because it is songlike, aria begins to diminish that dimension and replace it with elements of play, redundant elements whose function is to make movement or contemplation possible. Finally, the speech dimensions of recitative facilitate the articulation of a future sense—a narrative that traverses two

12. For a brief discussion, see Agawu, *Music as Discourse*, 98–102.

moments separated in time. The song element in aria traps us in the present and dispenses with the past except as memory or afterthought.

Numerous ethnographic recordings allow us to experience the contrast between rhythms of speech and those of the body. Performance of the popular Akan funeral dance, Adowa, normally begins with drum narration filled with verbal messages. This is meant to induce contemplation on the part of participants and listeners. Only after the lead drummer has thus "spoken" does the rest of the ensemble join in to activate the full instrumental texture and initiate the dancing. In the Northern Ewe dance Gabada, a cantor or two will typically begin with declamatory singing, often with drum commentary in speech mode. After presenting these deep messages (e.g., "I was bitten by a snail"), the cantor signals the rest of the ensemble to begin the dance proper, at which point bells, rattles, chorus, and dancers join in the stricter portion of the dance.

## REPRESENTING THE DOMAIN OF RHYTHMIC EXPRESSION

Another framework for conceptualizing different forms of rhythmic expression is shown in Figure 4.1. Originally devised to explain the rhythmic practices of a cluster of Ghanaian communities, its explanatory potential may well extend to other groups. The idea behind this representation is to recognize a broad domain of rhythmic expression and to seek its internal order based on either the generation of one element by another or the existence of analogous structures among elements.[13]

The model originates in gesture and terminates in stylized gesture or dance. In between, it encompasses the principal forms of rhythmic expression. First comes gesture, an external manifestation of a more fundamental communicative urge, here postulated as the primordial rhythmic event. (Right-pointing arrows in Figure 4.1 describe generative processes.) Gesture generates the spoken word in the sense that it releases speech from a prior nonverbal but concept-based state. While the aura of language underlies both gesture and the spoken word, gesture is rhythmic but silent, whereas the spoken word is rhythmic *and* manifest in sound. Two of the spoken word's fundamental attributes, speech tone and rhythm, will directly generate song or vocal music. Song is marked by a number of distinctions, the

13. Agawu, *African Rhythm: A Northern Ewe Perspective*, 27–30 and 180–185. Sachs's distinction between rhythms of speech and rhythms of the body discussed earlier is incorporated into Figure 4.1 and the ensuing discussion.

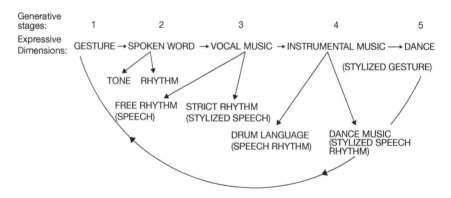

**Figure 4.1** A framework for conceptualizing the domain of rhythmic expression.

most important being the just-noted difference between free rhythm and strict rhythm. "Free" or declamatory rhythm is unmetered, anchored to the periodicities of speech; its segments are of variable length and succeed each other asymmetrically. Strict rhythm is metrical rhythm, constrained by an explicit cycle of beats throughout. The cycles of strict rhythm are structural; their rhetorical representation varies according to genre and performer interest. Free and strict rhythm may be further aligned with the spoken word: free rhythm in song is ordinary speaking, whereas strict rhythm is a stylized or regulated speaking.

Vocal music, in turn, generates instrumental music in the sense of motivating it materially. Dance drumming, for example, takes over the musical qualities of song while incorporating sung songs as an additional layer. The practice of talking drums resembles recitativelike free-rhythmic singing, even though it is more directly generated by the previous element in the model, the spoken word. Finally, stylized gesture emerges in response to both instrumental and vocal music. Dancing is an outcome, a necessary outcome of the singing of songs and the drumming of drums. In short, an initial gesture representing a communicative need is transformed over the course of the model into a stylized gesture representing a response to speech and song. And with this arrival at a form of stylized gesture, we have come full circle.

The generative process outlined in Figure 4.1 is something of a simplification; our description has hinted at porous boundaries, noncontiguous affiliations, and putative left-pointing arrows. A model such as this is meant to provide only a general orientation and to encourage refinement at more local, analytical levels. The main claim to consider here is that the different forms of rhythmic expression found in a given community are related, some more closely than others. The rhythms of speech, for example, are related to those of song, instrumental music, and dance; retaining this broader horizon enhances our understanding of the individual domains.

Photo 4.1 Pouring libation, Matse, Ghana.

## FREE AND STRICT RHYTHMS IN SONG

Just as performed speech comes in both free and strict forms, so song displays a similar contrast as it firms up the musical core that was only latent in spoken language. We have already mentioned the alternation between a declamatory introduction and a stricter dance drumming as a favorite syntactical unit in African performance. Within this natural conjunction of unmeasured and measured values, singers explore a range of temporalities and deliver a variety of messages. In declamatory singing, the "dry" enunciations of ordinary language are replaced by the more sonorous enunciations of song. And further along the continuum, the emergence of a clear meter and strict rhythm represents a further distancing of the expression from ordinary language. Song inherits many of the rhythmic qualities of speech, but in developing a new ontology, it sustains some of these qualities, introduces others (notably the rhythms of tonal movement), and erases or "problematizes" still others.

In part because rhythm is a resultant or emergent quality, it appears in numerous contexts throughout this book. We will postpone analytical discussion of song for now and simply invite readers to savor different kinds of temporal environment for different kinds of song. Figure 4.2 assembles examples of five such environments grouped into self-explanatory categories: unaccompanied and accompanied singing in free or unmeasured rhythms, unaccompanied or accompanied singing in strict or measured rhythms, and singing that progresses from free to strict rhythm.

| Rhythmic manner | Recorded examples |
| --- | --- |
| Free rhythm (unaccompanied) | 1. "Solo Song of a Woman" (CD, *Anthology of World Music: The Dan*, track 3) <br> 2. "Vai Call to Prayer" (CD, *Garland Encyclopedia of World Music: Africa*, track 4) <br> 3. "Miyehe" (CD, *Anthologie Congolaise*, vol. 9, track 13) <br> 4. "Nbu" (CD, *Africa: The Ba-Benzélé Pygmies*, track 3) ) <br> 5. "Lullaby" (CD, *Central African Republic*, track 2). <br> 6. "Choeurs des Peuls Wodabe" (CD, Brandilly, *Introduction aux musiques africaines*, track 3) <br> 7. "Lamentations" (CD, *Petites musiques du Zaire*, track 12) <br> 8. "Halanao" (CD, *Madagascar: Pays Bara*, track 17) <br> 9. "Funeral Lament" (CD, *Benin/Bariba and Somba Music*, track 10) <br> 10. "Funeral Laments" (CD, *Senufo*, track 1) |
| Free rhythm (accompanied) | 1. "Lambango" (CD, *Worlds of Music*, CD 2, track 3) <br> 2. "Kalefa Ba," (CD, Brandilly, *Introduction aux musiques africaines*, track 19) <br> 3. "Song for Grinding Millet" (CD, *Benin: Beriba and Somba*, track 8) <br> 4. Adjei komi's Song (CD, Agawu, *African Rhythm*, track 14) <br> 5. "Singing at a Wrestling Match" (CD, *Africa: The Dan*, track 6) <br> 6. "Ndenda Njofiri Joni" (CD, *Other Musics from Zimbabwe*, track 5) <br> 7. "Djebola" (CD, *Anthologie de la musique congolaise*, vol. 11, *Musique des Nkundo*, track 6, 0:00–4:56) |
| Strict rhythm (unaccompanied) | 1. "Song to Carry the Corpse" (CD, *Benin: Bariba and Somba Music*, track 11) <br> 2. "Akasisi Kannuma" (CD, *Musiques des Baganda*, track 11) <br> 3. "Miawoe zo" (CD, *Togo: Music from West Africa*, track 1) |

Figure 4.2 Temporal environments for different kinds of song: free versus strict.

| Rhythmic manner | Recorded examples |
|---|---|
|  | 4. "Little Girls' Sung Games" (CD, *Baule vocal Music*, track 7) |
|  | 5. "War chant" (CD, *Central African Republic*, track 9) |
| Strict rhythm (accompanied) | 1. "Mitoe ne Ayehawo" (CD, *Togo: Music from West Africa*, track 16) |
|  | 2. "Ggw'olidde Nsangi" (CD, *Musiques des Baganda*, track 9) |
|  | 3. "Counting Song," (CD, *Central African Republic*, track 4) |
|  | 4. "Adjame le wo Tawo" (CD, *Togo: Music from West Africa*, track 4) |
|  | 5. "Song to encourage African youth" (CD, *Fiddling in West Africa [1950s–1990s]*, vol. 2, track 4) |
|  | 6. "Nhemamusasa" (CD, *Africa: Shona Mbira Music*, track 1) |
|  | 7. "Kaniko Koye" (CD, *Guinea: Kpelle Music*, track 1) |
| Free-followed-by-strict rhythm | 1. "Adidi Magbe Torkor" (CD, *Agbadza* perf. by Gideon Alorwoyie and his group, CD 2, track 1) |
|  | 2. "Abeε mode" (CD, *Female Song Tradition and the Akan of Ghana*, track 4) |
|  | 3. "Dinaba, Myth of the Origins" (CD, *Benin: Bariba and Somba Music*, track 7) |
|  | 4. Mpre Adowa" (CD, *Ghana* [ICAMD], track 9) |
|  | 5. "Nnwonkoro" (CD, Ashanti Music Ghana, track 9) |

**Figure 4.2** (Continued)

## SPEECH MODE, SIGNAL MODE, AND DANCE MODES OF DRUMMING

The opposition between the rhythms of speech and those of the body is reflected in another fundamental distinction that captures the kinds of rhythm produced in the course of different modes of drumming: speech mode, signal mode, and dance mode.[14] The speech mode is affiliated with rhythms of speech, the signal mode with stylized speech, and the dance mode with rhythms of the body.

Drumming in the speech mode means beating out the relative durations and relational pitch elements of spoken speech on a drum. The semiotic mode of transfer is iconic; it entails resemblance and firstness. The primary obligation of drumming in the dance mode is to provide a rhythmic groove to which dancers can move their bodies. Often this means producing well-formed rhythms within an explicit metrical structure. The semiotic mode is symbolic and partly indexical—symbolic because the relationship between a dance rhythm and the dance is conventional, and indexical because within this convention, the rhythmic pattern literally elicits dance in response.

14. Nketia, *Drumming and Dancing in the Akan Communities of Ghana*, 17–31. For a comment, see Agawu, *Representing African Music*, 112–114.

Speech and dance modes come together in those genres that begin in declamatory style and continue in a stricter dance style. Just as some genres juxtapose unmeasured and measured singing, so certain dance-drumming genres exploit the distinction between an initial speech mode of drumming and a subsequent (and main) dance mode. The lead drummer of an Akan Adowa ensemble, for example, may begin a performance by saying things in speech mode on his Atumpan drums. These may be proverbs, poetic lines, wise sayings, or deep thoughts, each of which has a recoverable semantic content and philosophical significance. The drummer might announce, for instance, that "Before it rains, the wind blows"; that "The river crosses the path, the path crosses the river; which is the elder?"; or "A visitor is not a sibling" (the implication being that if we need to sacrifice a human being, the visitor is fair game!). These drum messages are heard and processed by audiences and performers alike. In cases in which drumming accompanies declamatory singing, drum messages may amplify what is sung or introduce a counternarrative.

Figure 4.3 assembles a few recorded examples of the three modes of drumming from various regions in Africa. Once again, it is impossible to be comprehensive

| Rhythmic mode | Recorded example |
|---|---|
| Speech mode | 1. CD, *Ancient Messages*, tracks 2-11 (Villepasteur).<br>2. CD, *Yoruba Music in the Twentieth Century*, tracks 1-4 (Omojola)<br>3. CD, *Rhythms of Life, Songs of Wisdom*, track 4 ("Talking Drum") ((Vetter)<br>4. CD, *Central African Republic*, track 15 ("Drummed message") (Arom) |
| Signal mode | 1. CD, *Drums 1* (ILAM), track 9 "Three drum signals" ([Democratic Republic of Congo. Mangbele (Northern Congo).<br>  i) a call to fight,<br>  ii) the chief summons his people;<br>  iii) to announce a death.] (H. Tracey)<br>2. CD, *On the Edge of the Ituri Forest* (ILAM), track 8 ("Four drum signals") (H. Tracey)<br>3. CD, Anthologie de la musique congolaise, vol. 6, (Musique des Kwese), track 1, "Mondo" (J. Gansemans) |
| Dance mode | 1. CD, *Ghana: Music of the People* tracks 2 ('Agbadza'), 3 ('Gadzo'), 6 (Boboobo'), 8 ('Bamaaya') and 12 ('Kpanlogo') (Paschale Younge).<br>2. CD, *Village ensembles of Busoga*, track 2 ("Mboine Kirabu") ((Peter Cooke),<br>3. (CD, *Uganda: Musique des Baganda*, track 10 ("Musique de tambour pour la danse Nnankasa") (Jean-Jacques Nattiez) |

Figure 4.3 Recorded examples of the three principal modes of drumming.

given the vastness of the continent. Those new to the phenomenon are in for a treat, however; those already familiar with it may well smile in recognition of practices rooted in ventriloquism. We normally speak with our mouths, so if we find ourselves speaking with drums, flutes, harps, or xylophones, we know that something is up. The staging of talking drumming suggests a deep level of pretense, play, and whimsy.

## THE PHILOSOPHY AND PRACTICE OF ENSEMBLE PERFORMANCE

What forms does the rhythmic imagination take in ensemble performance? There is, of course, no single dance-drumming ensemble that is prevalent throughout Africa, but the *idea* of an ensemble delivering a highly coordinated musical message refracted through a set of contrasting timbres is pretty standard.

Ensembles differ in size and type. They may range in size from small, "chamber" groups of three, four, or five musicians to a massive group of fifty or sixty instrumentalists and singers (famously in Chopi xylophone playing or in Senegalese Sabar drumming). In type, they may feature instruments of the same class (like the Chopi xylophone orchestras, Senegalese jembes, Yoruba bàtá ensemble, Yoruba dùndún ensembles, Dagomba dòndón) or they may feature a mixture of instruments (bells, rattles, drums). Whether the ensemble is homogenous or heterogenous, the musical intention is always one and the same: to create the conditions of possibility for melo-rhythmic expression. A shared point of temporal reference guarantees the coherence of the whole without discouraging the exercise of individual creativity.

What is the idea behind ensemble performance? Over the generations, African communities have developed profoundly effective ways of making music together. Some are influenced by social considerations, others by economic, material, religious, and invariably aesthetic factors. Topographically, ensembles are not flat; rather, they are textured so as to accommodate a variety of expressions. Whenever we make music together as members of a community, we recognize varying levels of skill; we also welcome a complementary diversity in the medium of expression and in the shapes of the actual patterns played or sung. The ensemble environment allows the amazingly skilled to make music alongside the less skilled. This simple ideal has proved extremely influential in the design of many other forms of ensemble music making. It speaks to an underlying communal ethos. Competence is assumed on the part of *all* members of the

**Photo 4.2**  Ensemble, Ho, Ghana.

community. Indeed, to be human, as John Blacking famously reminded us, is to be notionally musical.[15]

The many-in-one philosophy is readily observed in one of the best-known ensembles of African music, the Ewe Agbadza ensemble. For this combination of bells, handclaps, rattles, support drums, lead drums, and voices, patterns are assigned to individual instruments to fulfill three essential functions: first, a largely fixed time-marking section normally entrusted to some combination of bells, rattles, and handclaps; second, a less fixed function entrusted to a set of support drums that ensures the heart of the polyrhythmic texture; and

15. Blacking, *How Musical Is Man?*

**Photo 4.3** Ipangwa (guitar) and Ilimba, Nzali, Tanzania.

third, a relatively "free" section composed of a lead drum (or "master drum" or "mother drum") that rides (Locke's felicitous term[16]) on the texture provided by the rest of the ensemble. Performances typically begin by activating the ensemble from the bottom up, that is, from the time providers (starting with the bells and rattles) through the support drums to the lead drum. Singing and dancing will follow, and the sense that the whole is greater than the sum of its parts will not be lost on observers. Again, the logic and ingenuity in the organization of the ensemble are impeccable. By combining metrically strict patterns with freer patterns; intricate rhythms with less intricate ones; and short, repeated segments with longer rhythmic narratives, the ensemble philosophy reinforces the reciprocity of communal living. The whole (the community) is acknowledged without muting the sound of individual voices (the lead drummer). It is easy to take for granted these and numerous other signs of intelligent design in the organization of music making in Africa.

Four components of ensemble playing will illustrate further the motivations for ensemble performance and the contributions of different media and techniques. They are the ubiquitous handclapping, the attractive time lines, the fascinating polyrhythmic textures, and the engaging lead-drum narratives.

16. Locke, "Africa/Ewe, Mande, DAgbamba, Shona, BaAka," 78.

While these functions are realized in different idiomatic ways in different ensembles, there are enough functional resonances across ensembles to justify the paradigmatic status accorded them.

**Handclapping patterns**. The clapping of hands to provide minimum accompaniment to song, punctuate instrumental playing, or contribute a layer to a polyrhythmic texture is probably the best-known instrumental mode in Africa. The availability of this instrument to all of us reinforces the natural and communal sources of music making; it also confers a certain self-sufficiency on individual music making. Handclapping exploits the body's ready affiliation with pairs, doubleness, symmetry, and reciprocity: hands may be together or apart, inside or outside, upturned or downturned, high or low. Clapping entails movement. In performance, palms travel a variety of distances depending on the desired aesthetic effect. As onsets, claps may be short, pointed, and metronomic, or arclike with larger movements. They may be vigorous and delivered at a lightning-fast pace, or slow and activated only intermittently. Some styles of clapping are intense and designed to be in your face, while others are relaxed, almost self-effacing, and easily overlooked. Given the range of motivations and traces that it supports, and given its primal role in marking participation in music making, clapping is a far-from-insignificant element in the shaping of the rhythmic imagination.[17]

Although the traces left by claps vary from dance to dance and from genre to genre, the normative musical function of clapping is to reinforce the emergent beat of the music. Reinforcement may take the form of simple alignment or consistent nonalignment. Aligning claps with the beat allows the body to provide orientation to the dance (real or imagined) at a gross level. Participants of average ability often do no more than realize this beat, but more skilled individuals may add to the basic clap pattern. Clapping compels involvement and synchronicity; it acknowledges foundations, including the center of gravity that holds the body in place.

We may identify two basic patterns of clapping. The first consists of patterns constrained by the beat. These are equidistant and occur on one of three structural levels: the beat level, the subbeat level, or the superbeat level. The second consists of patterns with distinct shapes that counterpoint the beat. They may resemble time-line patterns or unfold alongside them in a polyrhythmic texture. This second type of clap pattern has an intrinsic interest that exceeds the metronomic function associated with the first type.

---

17. A. M. Jones devotes more than half the number of pages of an article on rhythm to handclapping and clapping patterns. See his "African Rhythm," *Africa* 24, no. 1 (1954): 26–47. Jones's understanding of meter and rhythm, however, differs in several fundamental respects from the viewpoint given here.

There is no economical way to illustrate the variety of clapping patterns found across the continent, but because clapping is a widespread activity, students will readily observe it in their own communities. Let me cite just a handful of examples. The Ewe dance Agbadza is sometimes performed with four claps corresponding to the four main beats of a 12/8 meter [3-3-3-3], five claps in the pattern [2-2-2-3-3], or even six claps distributed evenly across the measure as [2-2-2-2-2-2].[18] The underlying meter nevertheless remains 12/8. The [3-3-3-3] arrangement is isomorphic with the meter; the [2-2-2-3-3] combines two halves, the first of which, [2-2-2], "crosses" the main beats and the second of which, [3-3], is unproblematically isomorphic with the ruling meter; and the [2-2-2-2-2-2] arrangement inscribes a permanently crossed rhythm.

A healing ceremony among the San Bushmen of Botswana included in the JVC/Smithsonian anthology features a clap pattern similar to the one used in Ewe Agbadza [2-2-2-3-3].[19] Among the Xhosa in the Mthatha area in South Africa, the clapping that accompanies a variety of dances is vigorous and often incorporates articulation at the subbeat level. In the popular Ga dance, Kpanlogo, the clap pattern (as distinct from the time-line pattern played on a bell) consists of two quarter-note onsets in a 4/4 meter. The first occurs on beat 4 (the upbeat), the second on beat 1 (the downbeat of the following measure). This same clap pattern accompanies a popular game played by Ghanaian girls called ampé.

Clap patterns enshrine a variety of attitudes and thus invite different hermeneutic readings. Those from the area around Umthatha in South Africa mentioned earlier are vigorous and often have an aura of urgency about them. Used typically in performances of singing and dancing, they partly compensate for the absence of instruments. But this compensatory function alone will not explain the spirit of defiance communicated by the confluence of clap patterns. By contrast, the Kpanlogo clap pattern has a certain easy-going and perhaps self-satisfied quality, reflecting its role within an urban recreational genre (rather than, say, a rural ritual dance). And the [2-2-2-2-2-2] pattern of Agbadza, set in contrast to the [3-3-3-3] main beat pattern, contributes vital energy to the overall rhythmic life.

**Time lines.** A time line (also known as bell pattern, guide, phrasing referent, or *topos*) is a short rhythmic pattern normally entrusted to the bell

18. For a ready example, listen to the opening track, "Dada ada do," on Disc 1 of the CD, *Agbadza!Professor Midawo Gideon foli Alorwoyie and his Afrikania Culture Troupe of Ghana, West Africa* (Denton, TX: 2003).

19. See *JVC/Smithsonian Folkways Video Anthology of Music and Dance of Africa*, clip 8, "Ostrich Mating Dance-Game Anthology."

(or castanet, sticks, or stone) and played as an unvarying ostinato through-out a particular dance drumming. Although a few time lines consist of equi-distant successions of beats or pulses (see, for example, "Babolibo" from the Democratic Republic of the Congo[20]), the majority evince a distinct and often memorable pattern animated by at least two contrasting note values—a long and a short note or, typically, a quarter note and an eighth note. Because it is unchanging, a time line may seem to function like a metronome, but there are differences as well. The traces left by metronomes lack the basic differentiation of contrasting note values. Successions of pulses rather than patterns, metro-nomic traces are not normally considered part of the music (except where an avant-garde composer like Ligeti composes a piece for metronomes only[21]); they help to provide a perspective on the music by locating its patterns against a wall of accentless strikes. Time lines, on the other hand, are patterns rather than mere pulses; they are integral to the music. Each individual time line is in principle structurally dependent on a metronomic foundation, but the beating that constitutes such a foundation is more often implicit in the time-line pat-tern than stated explicitly.

We do not know where time lines ultimately come from, but they are believed to be of ancient origins and unique to Africa.[22] They are especially common in parts of West and Central Africa (Liberia, Côte d'Ivoire, Ghana, Togo, Benin, Nigeria, and the Democratic Republic of the Congo); they have also been noted in Tunisia, Uganda, Malawi, Zambia, and elsewhere.[23] They seem to be aligned with polyrhythmic cultures linked to speakers of Bantu languages.[24]

Time lines are heard in genres belonging to the three main varieties of African music. Any Ghanaian or Nigerian who has ever danced to highlife (E. T. Mensah, Victor Olaiya, Daddy Lumba, Bobby Benson, A. B. Crentsil, and others), to neotraditional music (like Wulomei's hit song "Meridian," Ewe Bɔbɔbɔ, Akan Nnwonkorɔ, Ga kpanlogo, or Dagomba simpa), or to tra-ditional dances (like agbadza, gabada, adowa, kete, atsiagbekor, and others) already knows what time lines are. They appear in art music as well. Nketia's solo piano piece *Volta Fantasy* (1967) uses the so-called standard pattern, as does Akin Euba's opera *Chaka* and Fred Onovwerosuoko's charming little etude for

20. CD, *Anthologie de la musique Congolaise*, vol. 2, track 10, "Babolibo."

21. Ligeti, *Poème Symphonique* (1962).

22. Kubik, *Africa and the Blues* (Jackson: University Press of Mississippi, 1999), 54.

23. See Kubik, *Theory of African Music*, vol. 2.

24. Christopher Ehret, "Languages and Peoples," in *Cultural Atlas of Africa*, ed. Jocelyn Murray (Oxford: Elsevier Publishers, Phaidon Press), 28; quoted in Kubik, *Theory of African Music*, vol. 1, 9.

piano *Agbadza*.[25] Robert Kwami's piano piece *Kpanlogo* uses that dance's time line, a version of which is the familiar Cuban *clave son* pattern, and the maiden CD recording of the Pan African Orchestra made in 1995 is rich in time lines.[26] Time lines are also found in the African diaspora and in Jamaica, Cuba, Brazil, Colombia, and Haiti. Given this wide provenance, it comes as a bit of a surprise that no systematic inventory of time lines has yet been made.[27] Proponents of "rhythm wheels" and theorists of time-line properties have often mentioned a dozen or two, but there are surely many more. And for readers interested in comparing different musical traditions, time-line effects such as those heard in the "Bransle Gay" of Stravinsky's ballet *Agon* [1-1-2-2] or in various popular electronic dance music pieces could be usefully juxtaposed with African usages.

A time line may be played by a single instrument to accompany singing or dancing, or it may belong to a larger ensemble of bells, rattles, and drums. It may emerge as a resultant quality without being entrusted to any one instrument. Although they are isolatable objects (many people can remember and reproduce them because they are brief and shapely and show up in a lot of the music they hear regularly), time lines are more properly appreciated as elements within a larger nexus of rhythmic patterns. They are indeed critical to a proper understanding of African rhythm. Some of them display interesting formal properties, such as maximal evenness, symmetry, and rhythmic oddity.[28]

As an orientation to the kinds of rhythmic imagination enshrined in time-line patterns, Example 4.1 assembles twelve of them. Many are well known, but a few (such as patterns 11 and 12) are obscure. Each time-line pattern is described in four ways. First is an interonset interval structure (IOI) or durational profile.

25. See J. H. Kwabena Nketia, *African Pianism: Twelve Pedagogical Pieces* (Accra, Ghana: Afram Publications, 1994), 22–27; CD, *Chaka. An Opera in Two Chants,* by Akin Euba; and Fred Onovwerosuoke, *Twenty-Four Studies in African Rhythms*, vol. 1 (St. Louis, MO: African Music Publishers, 2007, 32–33.

26. See CD, *Asa: Piano Music by Composers of African Descent* (Newtown, CT: MSR Classics, 2008), track 7, and *Pan African Orchestra Opus 1* (New York: Real World, 1995).

27. In an unpublished seminar paper from 2001, ethnomusicologist and drummer Bertram Lehman counted no fewer than 110 time lines.

28. For in-depth studies of the formal properties of time lines, see Jay Rahn, "Asymmetrical Ostinatos in Sub-Saharan African Music: Time, Pitch and Cycles Reconsidered," *In Theory Only* 9, no. 7 (1987): 23–36; Jeff Pressing, "Cognitive Isomorphisms Between Pitch and Rhythm in World Musics: West Africa, the Balkans and Western Tonality," *Studies in Music* 17 (1983): 38–61; Godfried Toussaint, *A Geometry of Musical Rhythm*; and Justin London, *Hearing in Time: Psychological Aspects of Musical Meter,* 2nd ed. (New York: Oxford University Press, 2012). For detailed study of a single time line, see Agawu, "Structural Analysis or Cultural Analysis? Competing Perspectives on the 'Standard Pattern' of West African Rhythm," *Journal of the American Musicological Society* 59 (2006): 1–46.

For example, [2-2-1-2-2-2-1] refers to the so-called standard pattern, while [3-3-4-2-4] refers to the kpanlogo or *clave son* pattern. Interonset intervals are especially felicitous for music played on drums, bells, and wooden clappers—music whose sound dies soon after it is made, but where there is no act of resting that would warrant the use of rests. Second is meter, a regulating grid based on an unchanging beat pattern that is subject to varying intensities of conmetric and contrametric accentuation. The common meters are 12/8 and 4/4. Third is a notated mnemonic—a translation, really, of the IOI. These mnemonics are best thought of as classes of patterns, paradigms perhaps. Their microrhythmic instantiation may vary from one community to another, but the overall pattern of longs and shorts is stable across those communities. Fourth and finally is a grouping, indicated by underlying brackets. A group encompasses the span from the literal onset of a pattern to its end. Each group has been written out twice to dramatize the relationship between grouping and meter. It bears repeating that a time line will be repeated hundreds of times in the course of a performance. Thus, time line 3, for example, when heard in an *Agbadza* performance, might sound 1,800 times per hour. Speaking or clapping each pattern repeatedly will enhance appreciation of its qualities.[29]

An excellent way to gauge creative attitudes in the area of African rhythm is to note the variety of expressive qualities inscribed in time lines. Some begin off the beat rather than on it and maintain this pattern of offbeatness throughout. Some end on weak rather than strong beats. Some lack internal closure and so cultivate a perpetual sense of ongoingness, while others are shaped as a beginning-middle-ending pattern on a small scale.

What these qualities mean to performers and listeners varies from community to community. The 12/8 so-called standard pattern, for example, is expressed typically as a seven-stroke pattern (two longs followed by a short, then three longs followed by a short), and these strokes are distributed in such a way that the seven shorts and longs acquire a property of maximal evenness

---

29. The twelve time-line patterns listed in Example 4.1 may be heard on the following recordings: (1) CD, *Ghana: Rhythms of the People*, track 2, "Agbadza (Music of the Ewe)"; (2) CD, *Pan African Orchestra*, track 3, "Mmenson"; (3) CD, *Anthologie de la musique Congolaise*, vol. 1, track 18, "Mayamb"; (4) CD, *Structural Set Analysis: Adowa* (Anku); (5) CD, *Legendary Wulomei*, heard on most tracks; (6) CD, *Drum Gahu* (Locke); (7) CD, *Music of Africa Series 29: Musical Instruments 8: Drums 2* (Grahamstown: International Library of African Music), track 10, "Ngoma."; (8) CD, *Seperewa Kasa* (Osei Korankye), track 1, "Towoboase"; (9) CD, *Togo: Music from West Africa*, track 16, "Mitoe ne ayehawo" and CD, *The Rough Guide to African Music for Children*, track 2, "Nono Femineh"; (10) CD, *Songs of War and Death from the Slave Coast* (Washington, DC: Smithsonian Folkways Recordings, 2007), track 6, "Gabada" and Web Example 4.1🔊; (11) Anthologie Congolaise, vol. 3, track 4, "Neike"; and (12) CD, *Un roi Africain et sa musique du court*, track 10, "Si le brigan rencontre le maisonnier suivi de." As always, the examples could be multiplied a hundredfold.

Example 4.1 Twelve time-line patterns.

| | Inter-onset interval pattern | Meter | Notation and grouping |
|---|---|---|---|
| 1 | [2-2-2-3-3] | 12 8 | |
| 2 | [2-2-2-1-2-3] | 12 8 | |
| 3 | [2-2-1-2-2-2-1] | 12 8 | |
| 4 | [3-2-1-2-2-2] | 12 8 | |
| 5 | [3-3-4-2-4] | 4 4 | |
| 6 | [3-3-4-4-2] | 4 4 | |
| 7 | [1-2-1-2-2] | 4 4 | |
| 8 | [2-2-4] | 4 4 | |
| 9 | [2-3-3] | 2 4 | |
| 10 | [1-2-2-1-2] | 2 4 | |
| 11 | [4-4-3-3-4-6-3-5] | 4 4 | |
| 12 | [3-2-4-5-2-4-4-4-4] | 4 4 | |

across the span of twelve. A certain dynamism accrues from this never-settling-down quality. It is as if every sounding of the time line necessitates an immediate repetition, as if the time line were seeking to discharge into itself without quite succeeding. Invented and cultivated over many generations by African musicians, the standard pattern and other time lines are popular precisely because they engage the listening mind.

A task for the future is the hermeneutic interpretation of individual time-line patterns. While ethnomusicology has so far not encouraged such speculative readings, we stand to learn from the kinds of cultural resonances that these patterns have for culture bearers. Consider, for example, the highlife time line (number 8 in Example 4.1). As heard in the classic highlife of E. T. Mensah from the 1950s and '60s, this time-line pattern consists of three onsets on the offbeats of beats 2, 3, and 4 in a 4/4 meter. Although its durational pattern from the first to last sound is [2-2-4], the fact that it originates on the offbeat of a weak beat gives it special power; it is as if the time line were operating from the sides rather than centrally. No other arrangement of eighths in a 4/4 pattern maximizes the energy in the margins, so to speak. This delightful time line sports bright, positive, and optimistic affects. Its internal structure may be interpreted as a series of echoes—being off the beat means echoing that which is on the beat, even if that which is being echoed is a silence. I hear a sense of self-satisfaction in the highlife topos, an aura of social attainment, a feeling that one has arrived. These sorts of qualities are entirely appropriate for a music that is widely regarded as the supreme popular music of West Africa in the years leading up to and immediately following independence around 1960. This is music of aspiration and confidence, with little or no traces of equivocation, doubt, or anxiety. Not unlike jùjú, which it later inspired, highlife carries an ethos that is unanxious, unhurried, and perhaps even complacent. The enactment of that complacency, however, is done in a thoroughly disciplined manner.[30]

**Polyrhythm**. Time lines typically form one layer in a larger, polyrhythmic texture. Polyrhythm is the simultaneous use of two or more contrasting rhythms in a musical texture. "Contrast" applies only to the shape of individual rhythms, not to the way they combine or are coordinated. In performance, polyrhythmic textures are typically assembled one layer at a time. And once the whole is activated, the layers usually persist until the end. A crucial feature of polyrhythm is that each constituent part is subject to extensive repetition. If the individual patterns were to change frequently, the effect of an irreducible multiplicity would be undermined. We might think of a polyrhythmic texture as one in which several ostinato patterns are superimposed. Superimposition is always based on a mutual understanding of a reference point, a shared beat. In some of the horn ensembles of the Banda Linda studied by Simha Arom, the constituent parts may number as many as eighteen, meaning that the ensemble features eighteen different rhythmic patterns. In drum ensembles found among the Kpelle, Vai, Akan, Yoruba, Igbo, and many others, the constituent parts may be fewer, numbering from three or four to eight or ten, but the

---

30. For further discussion, see Agawu, "Structural Analysis or Cultural Analysis?"

polyrhythmic effect is no less palpable. And among the Chopi of Mozambique, some xylophone ensembles may consist of thirty or more players.

Examples 4.2 and 4.3 cite two typical polyrhythmic textures from Ghana and Cameroon made up of instruments with contrasting timbres. The first, whose significance in this context is partly historical (it dates from 1957), was made by Ghanaian music teacher and composer F. Onwona Osafo. He calls it a "full score" of a dance known as "Ahenemma Asaw" (the dance for the chief's children). It encloses rhythms in boxes in a manner reminiscent of the not-yet-invented Time Unit Box System. Each of Onwona Osafo's boxes represents a full bar in 2/4 meter. Larger patterns are marked by slurs. Taken as a whole, the representation in Example 4.2 conveys both individuality and simultaneity. Individual patterns are shown for each instrument, while their superimposition is an invitation to contemplate the resulting texture. The other example of polyrhythm (Example 4.3) conveys a similar overall quality of complementary individualism. It is an excerpt from a flute ensemble from Cameroon analyzed by French ethnomusicologist Natalie Fernando. Only two cycles from a multi-cyclic ensemble performance are shown, but these are enough to demonstrate the essential polyrhythmic principle. They embody a groove activated through manifold repetition.[31]

Another illustration of the dynamics of polyrhythm may be seen in Example 4.4, a brief moment from a Pygmy music-dance performance.[32] Subject to extensive repetition, the texture (comprising drumming, handclapping, and singing) is regulated by a strict metrical order. The most straightforward of the rhythmic patterns is the [3-3-3-3] contributed by one of the handclaps. The second handclap adds a less commetric pattern in the form [2-1-2-1-2-1-1-2]. Its [2-1] element (which may be regarded as a figure, the equivalent of a word in spoken language) is sounded three successive times before yielding to a "reversed" [1-2] to complete the cycle. The drum's pattern is closer to the second handclap than to the first; its [1-1-1-2-1-2-2-1-1] pattern reinforces the first three quarter-note beats. The most contrametric patterns are contributed by the singer. In cycle 7, all her notes are off the beat. In cycle 8, only the first note is on the beat, but even this does not make much of a downbeat impact because the notes are short (two sixteenths) and delivered at a rather fast speed. The net effect is of a stable, recurring structure animated internally by competing accentuation and distinct timbres.

---

31. F. Onwona Osafo, "An African Orchestra," 11; Natalie Fernando, *Polyphonies du Nord-Cameroun*, 262.

32. "E-limbo," track 3 of CD, *Polyphonies vocales des Pygmées Mbenzele*.

**Example 4.2** West African polyrhythmic ensemble (Onwona Osafo).

Note: Drumming Symbols:

(1) = Simultaneous beating.

(2) = Muzzling or stopping the drumming sound.

(3) = Staccato

(4) = High tone.

(5) = Low tone.

(6) = Emphasis.

The plurality enshrined in polyrhythmic playing (or singing) is a disciplined plurality. Maintaining the integrity of one's part while at the same time ensuring the coordination of the ensemble as a whole is an impressive ability that has been cultivated over several generations. Superficial acquaintance has sometimes led people to imagine a loose configuration in which individuals simply do their own thing, but there is nothing loose about a polyrhythmic ensemble delivering dance rhythms. The manifest many-in-oneness is invariably constrained by a central point of reference, one that is always felt but not necessarily sounded.

It is worth emphasizing the existence of a coordinating mechanism at the background level to counter pervasive claims that polyrhythm spells freedom, conflict, and a suspension of order. Nothing could be further from the truth than Maurice Djenda's assertion that "polyphony and polyrhythms are a profound reflection of the freedom of vocal and instrumental musical expression in Central African societies, a freedom exercised through *an indifferent attitude to notions of time and space*" (my emphasis).[33] The fact that my pattern has a different scheme of onsets and offsets from my neighbor's does not in the least imply an absence of synchronicity on a deep level or an "indifferent attitude" to time. On the contrary, it is precisely because we are fully and securely synchronized—whether explicitly by another instrument or implicitly by a shared internalized beat—that we are able to produce rhythms together.

In a similar vein, Chernoff, while correctly endorsing the importance of participation, nevertheless denies intentional synchronicity in polyrhythmic music:

> The interweaving of diverse and multiple rhythms is coherent only when one actively participates by finding and maintaining a point of reference from which to perceive the conflicting rhythms as an ensemble. Synchrony is incidental and derivative from the cross rhythms, not deliberate and normal as in Western music.[34]

Knowing a repertory item means knowing its "point of reference." It is strange to imagine community members looking for a new point of reference every time a particular dance is performed. Only if one is unaware of *the* point of reference is one likely to interpret the contrasting rhythms of a polyrhythmic set as being in conflict. Insofar as each rhythm is a figure perceived against a ground—a ground, moreover, that is not necessarily articulated by any of the other rhythms—it is difficult to see how synchrony can be only "incidental" and "not deliberate and normal." The plurality of African ensemble music is not a free, unconstrained, or flabby plurality, according to which people

33. Djenda, "Central African Republic," *Grove Music Online*, accessed April 1, 2013.

34. Chernoff, *African Rhythm and African Sensibility*, 117.

**Example 4.3** Central African polyrhythmic ensemble (Natalie Fernando).

express their individuality by doing whatever they want. Rather, it is a disciplined and coordinated plurality. If it were not so, detecting and correcting errors would be difficult if not impossible, and repeating sets of patterns from one performance to the next would not be easy.

Dancing to polyrhythmic music is surely one of the signs of constraint and discipline in the way the music is put together. "When in doubt," writes Meki Nzewi, "do the dance."[35] Similarly, Nketia writes that "it is generally the rhythmic structure [of the music] that influences the pattern of [the dancer's] movements. He derives his motor feeling from this rhythmic structure, whose elements he articulates in his basic movements."[36] The disambiguating role of

35. Nzewi, *A Contemporary Study of Musical Arts*, vol. 4: *Illuminations, Reflections and Explorations* (Pretoria: Centre for Indigenous Instrumental African Music and Dance, 2007), 76.

36. Nketia, *The Music of Africa*, 210.

Example 4.3 (Continued)

Cycle 5

**Example 4.4** Matrix of a Ba-Benzele polyrhythmic dance drumming, "E Limbo."

dance in the understanding of African rhythm has either been ignored, under-stated, or insufficiently appreciated. And yet, in many dances, the behavior of the feet will mirror the gross pulse that dancers feel. Dance or "a rhythmi-cal stirring of the body" is the most important clue to the domestication of polyrhythm. Dancers embody the music, making the metric underpinning it apparent. The polyrhythmic textures performed by dance-drumming ensem-bles should never be interpreted without reference to the dance or movement patterns that they make possible. This is because the body grounds the appar-ent diversities of timbres and patterns of onsets. Dance conveys a synoptic sense of locus, beat, or weight; the dancer's feet convey the centers of gravity.[37]

The idea of polyrhythm has occasionally elicited some rather imaginative associations. John Collins, for example, expatiates on what he calls "polysided life" as follows:

> Relativism and pluralism permeates many aspects of traditional African life which encourages an equitable distribution of symbolic or social weight. Things must come and be done in multiples. No single rhythm, deity or time-scale should steal the show. African music is polyphonal, their religions are polytheistic, their calendars polycyclic, their plastic arts polyangled and . . . their social organisation polycentric. This poly-sided African view even applies to . . . traditional domestic life. Marriage is customarily polygamous. . . . Just as no single rhythm is allowed to dominate the African Beat, so too no single deity, soul or timescale is allowed to hog all the limelight of the African ritual cosmos.[38]

Are these analogies or homologies, or distinct systems sporting similar struc-tural rhythms? Collins does not specify. The affiliation he draws, however, is echoed by others. For example, Nigerian writer Bibi Bakare-Yusuf notes:

> Although contemporary Nigerian society (and contemporary Yoruba cul-ture) is, on the surface, divided in terms of Christian and Islamic faiths, the deep structure of the society is polytheistic and ordered by the spirit world of the accommodative traditional gods. This theological back-ground is revealed most readily in aesthetic practices such as dance and music. Polytheism in spirit translates into the aesthetics of polyrhythm.[39]

37. Chernoff, *African Rhythm and African Sensibility*, 117.

38. Collins, *African Musical Symbolism in Contemporary Perspective: Roots, Rhythms and Relativity* (Berlin: Pro Business, 2004), 111.

39. Bibi Bakare-Yusuf, " 'Yoruba's Don't Do Gender': A Critical Review of Oyeronke Oyewumi's *The Invention of Women*: Making an African Sense of Western Gender Discourses," accessed December 19, 2014, http://www.codesria.org/IMG/pdf/BAKERE_YUSUF.pdf.

**Photo 4.4** Young Gogo girl playing drum, Nzali, Tanzania.

It is hard to accept these formulations at face value because the principles according to which domains are linked are underspecified. A discontinuity or dissonance between two expressive domains has just as strong claims to normativity as a continuity or consonance. Bakare's wish to reject conceptual monotheism, for example, is understandable as an expression of desire, but her argument is somewhat inconvenienced by the fact that there is always a "mono" or "metric background" (borrowing from James Burns[40]) somewhere at the back of the ensemble. Apparent surface plurality invariably subtends a regulating subsurface singularity.

40. Burns, "Rhythmic Archetypes."

**Photo 4.5** Fɔntɔmfrɔm, Edwesomanhene's burial, Kumase, Ghana.

**Lead-drum narratives.** The lead drummer (or "master drummer" or one who beats the "mother drum") performs the most involved and complex rhythms. Leadership here implies that he takes charge of the ensemble as a whole. His playing depends on, and in turn supports, the playing (and singing) of the other musicians in the ensemble. If things are not going well, the lead drummer may suspend his own playing and ensure the security of the ensemble. Indeed, the soundness of the ensemble is what allows him to provide the community of singers and dancers with meaningful, life-affirming dance drumming. The lead drummer cannot accomplish that task alone.

One way to conceptualize the lead drummer's art is in terms of rhythmic narratives: he essentially tells stories on his drum using a variety of patterns. Narrating here is not the same as talking drumming, although lead drummers may occasionally incorporate the iconic procedures associated with speech surrogacy. Finely chiseled rhythmic patterns are manipulated in accordance with precise structural and aesthetic goals. These stories are sometimes highly elaborate and original, sometimes conventional, and often framed in liaison with the other musicians' patterns. Different African dances call for different lead-drum patterns. In the Southern Ewe Atsiagbekor dance, for example, the lead drummer's patterns contrast with those of the other instruments (bells, rattles, responses, and support drums). They are ostensibly "freer" and more speechlike in character owing in part to their improvisatory origins. By improvisation, we mean that the patterns are assembled in the moment under pressure from the practical and aesthetic exigencies of the occasion. No lead drummer arrives at a performance site with an empty head, hoping perhaps that the muses will visit on that occasion. Rather, he has at his command a set of learned procedures with which he can make his narration. He also has in his memory certain stock phrases associated with the particular dance or with particular moments within the dance. These phrases are part of a vocabulary shared with dancers and listeners. The art of lead drumming is a fascinating exercise in oral composition. In a medium that employs wordless rhetoric, highly skilled individuals think, play, tease, amuse, impress, and even deceive.

Although the lead-drum part is enabled by the musical security of the ensemble as a whole, there are sporadic high-intensity moments during performances where drummers claim a measure of autonomy. So, although rhythmic conversations or sporadic interchanges with support drummers are normal fare, a lead drummer may occasionally beat patterns that are not organically linked to what the rest of the ensemble is playing. Such flights are only occasional, however, and they are possible in part because once the metrically explicit polyrhythmic texture has been established, the lead drummer can play "against" its guaranteed coherence to generate tension and interest. This is not to suggest that the ensemble is structured polymetrically, that it features different meters in different parts as A. M. Jones, Steve Friedson, and others erroneously claimed.[41] It is simply to affirm that, at certain moments in the dance, a seasoned drummer is free to advance certain temporary narratives without seeking immediate corroboration from the rest of the ensemble.

As the figure who takes charge of the ensemble, the lead drummer directs the dance and responds to the needs and temperaments of individual dancers. Tightly choreographed dances may require the lead drummer to beat certain signals at certain moments as cues to dancers. The time between signals may be traversed in flexible fashion depending on the developing synergy between musicians and dancers. An inspired dancer may wish to extend her moment in the sun, revel in a particular style of playing, or simply enjoy a favorite theme; another may be turned off by a drummer who "stammers," or even be so counterinspired by him that she will elect to curtail a particular dance sequence. The rapport between dancers and drummers varies in intensity from dance to dance and from one performance to another. The point is that dancers are not merely consumers of what is handed to them by drummers; they can actually affect the mood and progress of the dance drumming. Dancers and the providers of dance beats represent two sides of the same coin.

---

41. Jones, *Studies in African Music*; Friedson, *Remains of Ritual*, 139. For a critique of polymeter, see my *Representing African Music*, 71–96.

**Photo 4.6** Kete dance, Koo Nimo and his group, Kumase, Ghana.

Transcriptions and technical studies of lead drumming have been made by several scholars, so readers wishing to embark on a note-by-note study of the lead drummer's art will find a number of models to work with.[42] For the illustrative purposes at hand, I will mention just two brief examples. David Locke's analysis of the Southern Ewe dance *Gahu* shows that the spinning of lead-drum narratives relies fundamentally on motivic manipulation. Patterns are introduced, manipulated through shortening or elongating of units, displaced metrically in relation to the bell pattern, or replaced by other patterns. Impressive is the resulting art of variation whereby patterns are repeated in varied form so that listeners delight in both the familiar and the unfamiliar.[43]

Perhaps the most rigorous analysis of lead drumming is Willie Anku's magnificent study of the Akan funeral dance drumming, adowa.[44] Anku stresses

42. Besides Jones's transcriptions from the 1950s, there are others by later writers like Pantaleoni, Branda-Lacerda, Locke, Polak, and Euba from which one can study the principles of lead drumming.

43. Locke, *Drum Gahu: An Introduction to African Rhythm* (Tempe, AZ: White Cliffs Media, 1998). For a rigorous empirical study of another West African tradition, see Rainer Polak's article on jembe music, "Rhythmic Feel as Meter: Non-Isochronous Beat Subdivision in Jembe Music from Mali," *Music Theory Online* 16 (2010), http://www.mtosmt.org/issues/mto.10.16.4/mto.10.16.4.polak.html

44. Anku, *Structural Set Analysis 1: Adowa*. His *Structural Set Analysis 2: Bawa* (Legon: Soundstage Production, 2002) utilizes a similar analytical procedure. Both booklets are

the intellectual dimension of the lead drummer's art to undermine facile invocations of "improvisation" as an explanatory term. According to him, the lead drummer arrives at the scene of performance armed with a set of procedures, and he deploys these in the course of adowa performance. Anku's version of the dance itself has seven themes interspersed with bridge passages. The text of a typical performance would thus consist of a succession of thematic areas, and the space between different areas would be occupied by a bridge. Within each area, the verbally derived theme is subjected to motivic elaboration. This "composing out" process may be brief or extended depending on the dynamics of the interaction between drummers and dancers.

The sophistication of the lead drummer becomes evident in this composing-out process and in the specific technical manipulation of the grouping structure of individual themes. Working with sets of twelve as a reference point, and always aware of the ostinato bell pattern, the drummer devises patterns that are sometimes aligned with twelve, exceed it, or fall short of it. Anku refers to them as sets, supersets, and subsets. If a pattern introduced by the lead drummer exceeds the twelve-span, he carries forward the surplus; if the pattern is a subset of the twelve-span, he knows that a compensatory gesture will be forthcoming. And where the pattern is perfectly aligned with the reigning twelve, no credits or debits are carried forward. In this way, the performance proceeds logically and in full awareness of the shifting relationship between bell and lead-drum pattern. The result is a deep level of coherence that may come as a surprise to those who have underestimated African intellection or who would prefer a mystical explanation to a rational one.

It bears emphasizing that the kinds of lead drumming and ensemble playing we are discussing here take place within cultures of primary orality. No traditional lead drummer worth his salt plays from a chart, score, or notation. All of the modulo twelve arithmetic that Anku describes takes place in the heads of drummers, not on paper. Aurality enforces a regime in which sounds have specific origins and destinations; patterns and actions must be at their most palpable. The vibrant life of African rhythm derives precisely from this incredible awareness of the aural and choreographic potentialities of its constituent patterns.

accompanied by digitalized recordings. For the full exposition of Anku's theory, including copious transcriptions of other Ghanaian dances, see his forthcoming book, *A Theory of African Music*. Zabana Kongo published several booklets containing transcriptions of Ghanaian dances; see his *African Drum Music [Slow Agbekor, Adowa, Kpanlogo, Agbadza]* (Accra: Afram Publications, 1997). Transcriptions in extenso together with technical explication of organizing principles may also be found in Marcos Branda-Lacerda, "Instrumental Texture and Heterophony in a Fon Repertoire for Drums," *TRANS* 11 (2007), accessed July 24, 2013, http://www.sibetrans.com/trans/a127/instrumental-texture-and-heterophony-in-a-fon-repertoire-for-drum, and in Marcos Lacerda, *Música Instrumental no Benim: Repertório Fon e Música Bàtá* (São Paulo: Editoria la Universidade de São Paulo, 2014).

## A GENERATIVE APPROACH

What are the sources of the patterns played by a performer on a given occasion? There are two related answers, one having to do with memory, the other with knowledge of procedures. First and obviously, musicians repeat rhythms that they have memorized. If you've grown up in an environment in which bɔbɔbɔ, gabada, baakisimba, or egwu amala are beaten and danced regularly, chances are that you will have internalized their rhythms and songs and are able to participate in a performance in some capacity. Second, performers internalize a range of procedures that they use selectively on each occasion of performance. They know the tricks and licks of the trade. They know when and how to begin, how to intensify a sentiment, and how to end; indeed, they may choose to stop rather than conclude. They know how to create tension, how to resolve it, and what to play to delight a favorite dancer. This is not knowledge of particular rhythms as such; rather, it is knowledge of how to make rhythms, techniques for ordering rhythms—compositional knowledge. The distinction is not categorical, however, because knowledge of procedures necessarily entails acquaintance with actual materials, while the ability to retrieve patterns from memory may be facilitated by knowledge of certain tricks. Nevertheless, the two emphasize different aspects of rhythm production.

Confidence in the deployment of procedures bespeaks a *compositional* ability that forms a necessary part of the lead drummer's arsenal. The ability to generate rhythms is one sign of compositional prowess. By "generation," I simply mean production from simpler patterns. The belief here is that every rhythmic pattern, process, or narrative subtends a simpler pattern, process, or narrative. Both are well formed, but the one that is heard is a more elaborate form of the one that lies in the background. The generative approach is well known (even if not designated as such) and widely shared by many world cultures; it is exemplified in everything from the composition of medieval chant through improvising on jazz standards to elaborating the hidden melodies of gamelan music. In African expressive systems, the generative approach may well be the single most potent tool for understanding oral composition. Just as the oral poet relies not only on what has been memorized but also on strategies for generating new content, so the musician succeeds precisely because he or she is able to "say" something new in a way that is nevertheless consistent with the ways of "speaking" a particular "language" using particular "idioms."

Theorists as diverse as Hornbostel, Nketia, Cooke, Pressing, John Blacking, David Locke, Anku, Nzewi, and Arom have promoted approaches that may be characterized loosely as generative, so readers seeking in-depth studies may turn to the works of these authors. Here I will only add a simple demonstration of some of what lies behind relatively simple patterns. Let us return to time-line patterns and recall an earlier claim that they typically presuppose enabling structures. Supposing that my task is to generate a particular time line, here is a generalized two-stage scheme that we might follow:

1. Establish the beat (on the basis of the dance feet or the choreographic center of gravity) and the metrical cycle (on the basis of repetition, with hints from archetypal clap patterns).
2. Invoking a mix of culturally relevant habits associated with creative manipulation (play, maneuver, tease, withhold, extend, disguise, exaggerate), manipulate the foundational pattern postulated in stage 1 to arrive at the target time line.[45]

These two stages may be subdivided as necessary. The origins postulated in stage 1 are usually available as nuggets of rhythm within the culture. Similarly, the techniques of manipulation associated with stage 2 are culturally sanctioned; this stage may also splinter into several steps. For example, suppose our aim is to generate the so-called Mmensuoun time line, [2-2-2-1-2-3]. We may postulate the pattern's origins in the dance feet, [3-3-3-3]. This pattern may be elaborated by substituting [2-2-2] for the initial [3-3]. In effect, we have crossed two threes with three twos, and we can cite any number of rhythmic practices, including many associated with children's music, to justify this transformation. A third and final stage involves further variation, this time breaking up the first of the threes into [1-2] to yield [2-2-2-1-2-3]. Notice that the shorter note is placed on the stronger part of the beat rather than the other way round: [1-2] instead of [2-1], or in terms of metrical feet, a trochee rather than an iamb.

Let us be clear that this procedure is not so much a reconstruction of how this particular pattern came to be; it is not an account of a known compositional genesis. Rather, it is a rational reconstruction, a speculative derivation of what makes the pattern possible, what enables it. In this process of reconstruction, I have responded to two imperatives: simple logic and cultural relevance. The logical imperative is necessary to ensure the pattern's structural integrity at each stage; the cultural imperative acknowledges the origins of

45. Agawu, "Structural Analysis or Cultural Analysis?," 31–36.

these (and other) patterns in habits of thought and action particular to those cultures. The idea is to "culturalize" logic by bringing it under an African thought regime.

## TO NOTATE OR NOT TO NOTATE?

Most African music—perhaps 95 percent of it—is not written down. What scores exist are original works by composers of art music or transcriptions made by ethnomusicologists for scholarly study and documentation. Even though scholars have described mnemonic association as forms of "oral nota-tion,"[46] and even though "electronic notation" became widely available in the second half of the twentieth century,[47] the primary medium for the preserva-tion and transmission of African vocal and instrumental music is oral/aural and tied to individual and collective memories.

If we overlook some of the earliest known efforts to notate music (as in Ethiopia, for example), we can say that African music began to be reduced to notation in earnest from the nineteenth century on, largely as a result of contact with the West—missionaries, merchants, and colonial officers—and of the education of a local elite. At first, staff notation was used to notate melo-dies, simple rhythms, folk songs, or even drum ensemble patterns. Similarly, tonic solfa aided the teaching of previously notated songs while providing a means for many local composers to write down their choral works. With the rise of ethnomusicology in the 1950s, interest in other forms of nota-tion grew, and with it a critique of Western notation. Alternatives suggested included the Time Unit Box System, tablature notation, circular notation, "Greenotation," pulse notation, and geometrical representation.[48] Meanwhile,

---

46. Kubik, "Oral Notation of Some West and Central African Time-Line Patterns," *Review of Ethnology* 3 (1972): 169–176.

47. Kay Shelemay, "Notation and Oral Tradition in Africa," in *The Garland Encyclopedia of World Music*. Vol. 1: *Africa*, ed. Ruth Stone (New York: Garland, 1998), 146–163. Reprinted in *The Garland Handbook of African Music* (New York: Garland, 1999).

48. A sampling of the varieties of approaches to notating African music may be found in the following: James Koetting, "Analysis and Notation of West African Drum Ensemble Music," *Selected Reports in Ethnomusicology* 1, no. 3 (1970): 115–146; Hewitt Pantaleoni, "Toward Understanding the Play of Sogo in Atsia," *Ethnomusicology* 16, no. 1 (1972): 1–37; Moses Serwadda and H. Pantaleoni, "A Possible Notation for African Dance Drumming," *African Music* 4, no. 2 (1968): 47–52; David Rycroft, "Nguni Vocal Polyphony," *Journal of the International Folk Music Council* 19 (1967): 88–103; David Locke, "Africa/Ewe, Mande,

many born-in-the-tradition scholars continued to use staff notation or tonic solfa.[49]

Which forms of notation adequately represent African musical realities? No consensus has been reached on this issue, but one thing is clear: it is no longer productive to ask *whether* one should notate African music. All forms of notation have their limitations, of course, but this is a universal problem rather than a specifically African one. A pragmatic approach to the problem of notation is to ask if any tasks are helped along by the use of notation. It then emerges that all the major analytical discussions of African music, for example, have drawn on notation. Notating provides a concrete basis for informed discussion. To say that African musicians did not conceive their music in (Western) notational terms does not mean that nothing can be learned from "translating" it into Western or standard terms. We do not normally make the same argument for language or literary expression, whether it is in the use of the Roman alphabet (or a modified version thereof) or writing in an indigenous language as opposed to the metropolitan one. No translation is perfect, and few translations are such that the texts on either side can be said to be identical. But these limitations notwithstanding, transcription can and does shed light on such things as the role of repetition, the question of meter, the interplay of timbres, and the internal dynamics of polyrhythm. Moreover, the existence of Western repertoires that were originally conceived with minimal reference to notation (as were many forms of jazz) but have subsequently been reduced to notation to facilitate both study and performance suggests that similar gains are likely to come from African adaptations of notation.[50]

Shona, BaAka"; Doris Green, "About Greenotation," accessed July 20, 2013, http://www.tntworldculture.com/toa2/2011/12/about-greenotation/; Andrew Tracey, "The Matepe Mbira Music of Rhodesia," *African Music* 4, no. 4 (1970): 37–61; Godfried Toussaint, *The Geometry of Musical Rhythm*; Roderic Knight, "Towards a Notation and Tablature for the Kora, and Its Application to Other Instruments," *African Music* 5, no. 1 (1971): 23–36; and Burns, "Rhythmic Archetypes in Instrumental Music from Africa and the Diaspora." See also Chernoff's pertinent reflections in "The Rhythmic Medium in African Music," *New Literary History* 22 (1991): 1093–1102.

49. On notation, see Shelemay, "Notation and Oral Tradition in Africa." On tonic solfa in particular, see Christine Lucia, "Back to the Future? Idioms of 'Displaced Time' in South Africa Composition," in *Composing Apartheid: Essays of the Music of Apartheid*, ed. Grant Olwage (Johannesburg: Wits University Press, 2008), 11–34.

50. See Paul Berliner, *Thinking in Jazz: The Infinite Art of Improvisation* (Chicago: University of Chicago Press, 1994), for a good example of some of the "gains" that transcription has brought.

Students of African music have benefited immensely from the transcriptions in extenso made by A. M. Jones in the 1950s, those supplied by David Locke in several publications, those included in Simha Arom's study of African polyphony and polyrhythm, those supplied by Gilbert Rouget in his study of the vocal repertories of King Gbefa's wives, those included in Branda Lacerda's study of Fon drumming, and those included in Willie Anku's original theory of African rhythm. As analyzable texts, transcriptions continue to serve as a basis for close study and informed discussion of structural principles.

## CONCLUSION

I began the previous chapter with the claim that "in or near the beginning was the spoken word." This one could have started with a parallel construction, "in or near the beginning was rhythm." Rhythm seems to be at once everywhere and nowhere in particular. Here is how Curt Sachs put it in 1953:

> Rooted deep in physiological grounds as a function of our bodies, rhythm permeates melody, form, and harmony; it becomes the driving and shaping force, indeed, the very breath of music, and reaches up into the loftiest realm of aesthetic experience where description is doomed to fail because no language provides the vocabulary for adequate wording. Disenchanted, the author is, alas, compelled—as more or less every writer on art—to describe the technical traits, the dactyls and double dots, proportiones and metrical patterns, rather than the elusive, indescribable essence of rhythm.[51]

The products of the rhythmic imagination are diffuse and not easily confined definitionally. Although Western discourse identifies a parameter called "rhythm," there is no single word for rhythm in most of the indigenous African languages. The site of the most intense rhythmic behavior is not at the same time the site of critical discourse about rhythm! While one can converse around the subject, one cannot name it precisely, exclusively, or exhaustively. Rhythm indeed has a transgressive quality; it is an entangled parameter, permanently imbricated in other dimensional processes.

51. Curt Sachs, *Rhythm and Tempo* (New York: Norton 1953), 11.

While theoretically conceivable, ferreting out the rhythmic dimension of a composition as distinct from, say, its melodic, polyphonic, or timbral dimensions is practically impossible. The analysis of rhythm takes one beyond duration, accents, and grouping to more subtle, sometimes unnameable qualities.

Although African music has often been portrayed as radically different from Western music ("based on entirely different principles," wrote Hornbostel in 1928,[52] or representing "a different way of being-in-the-world," as Friedson has recently claimed[53]), there is essentially (i.e., at a certain level of abstraction) no difference between the organizing principles of African rhythm and those of Western rhythm. Both sets of repertoires feature speech rhythms, a palpable tactus, symmetrical and asymmetrical rhythmic phrases, superior beats and groups of beats, periodicities governed by processes distributed across multiple dimensions, degrees of polyrhythm, and the interplay between precomposed and improvised material. African rhythm indeed manifests the same kind of hierarchic patterning that one finds in Western music, namely, an elaborate surface and a simpler subsurface, a foreground and a background.

What "differences" there are stem from idiomatic and aesthetic choices made by individual communities for particular genres and occasions. For example, it is not that Western music lacks offbeat patterns; rather, it is that some African music (especially drum-based repertoires that have acquired symbolic status as exemplars of authentic African music) invests heavily in persistent off-beat patterning. It is not that African music lacks downbeats; rather, it is that some African music takes the weight off the downbeats to create a more fluid or mobile process. It is not that Western instrumental music is not dependent on language; rather, it is that the speech mode in instrumental music, for example, has been obscured in the writings of theorists with different agendas. Comparisons like these can seem naïve or counterintuitive, especially for people for whom the sound of African music is self-evidently different from that of Western music. But peering beneath the surface to behold the specific organizational procedures will show a degree of subsurface convergence that is likely to be missed by those whose inquiries are confined to the musical surface. Western and African rhythm share patterns of well-formedness; in thematizing that well-formedness, preferences, some of them marked, are exercised. This is why I have recommended

---

52. Hornbostel, "African Negro Music," 30.

53. Friedson, *Remains of Ritual: Northern Gods in a Southern Land*, 9.

a broad, cross-cultural framework for analysis and for pursuing the question of what is ultimately distinct about individual African cultures. The African rhythmic genius is best appreciated not from separatist accounts postulating radically different foundations but from comparative studies showing how African musicians excel at the things we all do.

# 5

# The Melodic Imagination

The origin of all melody is the human voice. "Voice" connotes speech and speaking, song and singing. The theater of the melodic imagination plays to an imperative of present action, not to a past lodged in memory and inheritance. Voice implicates intonation and intoning, the vocal and vocalizing. Voices come in a variety of timbres, too, from the ordinary to the extraordinary, from the relaxed to the tense and intense. The vocalizing mode may be direct or subtle, open or muted, plain or sly, seductive or stern. The musical voice can make language by enabling it or break language by resisting its natural tendency toward enunciation. It can nurture speech by doing what speech wants to do, namely, communicate with (imagined) others, but the "musicking" voice can also refuse the communicative function and simply bathe in sound or sonority for pleasure. Melody and language are thus locked in a profound and active dialectic; indeed, like the spoken word, melody may be said to have been there in or near the beginning.

## VALUING AFRICAN MELODY

Just how important is melody to African music? It would seem strange to pose such a question, given the primal significance of voice and language in African cultural expression. Surely most music has content that is melodically significant, even if the commitment to purely melodic elaboration differs from community to community, style to style, musician to musician, or even occasion to occasion. I pose the question, however, because a certain lopsidedness attends some evaluations of African melodic thinking vis-à-vis other dimensions. While much has been made of African drums and complex rhythms and polyrhythms, much less has been made of the melodic imagination. In an earlier phase of discourse about African music, when scholars felt at liberty to compare the individual dimensions of different musical styles either casually or formally, African melody was rarely singled out for high praise. William Ward, for example, writing in the 1920s, reckoned that Africans began with "a superior sense of rhythm, but that they would need to learn about harmony from Europeans."[1] Rose Brandel detected only "the beginnings of a true harmony" in Central African polyphony.[2] Robert Ndɔ, a noted composer of choral works from the Volta Region of Ghana, adopted the colonizer's language in describing African melody as "primitive and stereotyped."[3] Musicologist Alexander Ringer, in an important reference article, acknowledges that melody "represents a universal human phenomenon," but he immediately qualifies the universality with an African exception: "in some cultures . . . rhythmic considerations may always have taken precedence over melodic expression, as in parts of Africa."[4] Peter Fryer says flat out that melody "is not one of the essential features of African traditional music."[5] And in his widely used textbook, *The Music of Africa* (1974), Nketia writes, "Since African music is predisposed towards percussion and percussive textures, there is an understandable emphasis on rhythm, for *rhythmic interest often compensates for the absence of melody or the lack of melodic sophistication*" (my emphasis).[6] Nketia does not cite instances of music in which melody is absent; nor does he demonstrate the "lack of melodic sophistication" in any particular style or repertoire. Since what he calls "rhythm" is most likely "melorhythm" (i.e., an alloy of pitch and rhythm), and given that most manifestations of rhythm include a pitch-differential aspect, his general claim might be qualified to reflect the sedimentation of "melody" in the purest of rhythmic expressions. It is unfortunate that what some readers routinely infer from Nketia's remark is that Africa scores high on a rhythm test but fails the melody test.

These valuations fly in the face of all available evidence. A continent blessed with such magnificent voices as those of Malian Salif Keita, Senegalese Youssou Ndour, Cameroonian Baaba Maal, Sierra Leonian S. E. Rogie, Ghanaians Koo Nimo and Osei Korankye, Beninois Angelique Kidjo, Ivorian Dobet Gnahore, and South Africans Miriam Makeba and Joseph Shabalala can hardly be imagined as lacking in melody. The exquisite shapes, affecting mannerisms, and subtle

1. William E. F. Ward, "Music in the Gold Coast," *Gold Coast Review* 3 (1927): 223.

2. Rose Brandel, "Polyphony in African Music," in *The Commonwealth of Music*, ed. Gustav Reese and Rose Brandel (New York: Free Press, 1965), 27.

3. Robert Ndɔ, unpublished lecture, circa 1985.

4. Alexander L. Ringer, "Melody," *Oxford Music Online*, Oxford University Press, accessed July 21, 2013, http://www.oxfordmusiconline.com/subscriber/article/grove/music/18357.

5. Peter Fryer, "Our Earliest Glimpse of West African Music," *Race and Class* 45 (2003): 107.

6. Nketia, *The Music of Africa*, 125.

expressions that are delivered in performance after performance are known to bring joy to listeners, ignite deep feelings, awaken buried memories, and foster meaningful associations. Few would think of these collective repertories as melodically deficient or unsophisticated. Granted, the examples just cited are of musicians active in the popular realm, a realm excluded from Nketia's book, but his claim is no more defensible in connection with traditional music. One need only recall the intricate melodic thinking exemplified in the art of kora-playing praise singers from Gambia, Mali, Senegal, or Guinea or of the interlocking procedures that enable the large trajectories of "endless melody" played by great Baganda and Chopi xylophonists and Shona mbira players. One might think also of Baule, Ashanti, Kongo, and Northern Ewe dirge singers, singers whose ability to give voice to thoughts and feelings in song touches us deep in our guts, sends mourners into themselves, and engenders reflection on the meaning of life. One may even consider those brief but charming, finely shaped melodies that children from Angola, Malawi, Uganda, and South Africa produce in the course of play, melodies whose particular alchemy of dimensional interaction is not commonly found in other world music. No, there is nothing deficient, primitive, inferior, undeveloped, or unsophisticated about African melody.

Nurtured in an oral/aural milieu, African melodies typically display shapes that betray their live origins: vital, lucid, often graspable as a whole and designed to be immediately apprehended. These shapes sometimes differ in scope from the more elaborate "paper melodies" produced by European composers like Bach, Mozart, Schubert, Tchaikovsky, Richard Strauss, or Luciano Berio, but no one who has heard great singers of epics from Mali, Gambia, or the Democratic Republic of the Congo or griots and griottes from Niger, Senegal, or Guinea could possibly doubt that African musicians routinely produce extensive melodic structures.

That said, comparing the dirge singer's melody to the products of the ostensibly high-art tradition of European classical music is not always the best way to frame a comparison. As philosopher Kwasi Wiredu reminds us, it is best to compare like with like. That is, it is more appropriate to compare art music with other art music, or folk music with other folk music, than to compare art music with folk music, especially if the point of the comparison is to arrive at a critical or qualitative judgment.[7] Communally inspired and communally targeted folk music should be compared with music of similar origins and aspirations, not with music produced on paper under regimes of solipsism, subjectivism, or narcissism, or designed to display the cleverness (sometimes

7. Wiredu, "How Not to Compare African Thought with Western Thought," in *Philosophy and an African Culture* (Cambridge: Cambridge University Press, 1980), 37–50. An exception may, however, be made for acts of contrapuntal reading, whereby one reads across repertoires without regard for conventional genre boundaries.

called "genius") of an individual composer. A more appropriate comparison in this case would be with folk songs created in the course of ordinary life, play, and ritual by Hungarians, Romanians, Chinese, Irish, Scots, and Amerindians. It is hard to see how the melodic substrate of African music can be deemed inferior in such company.

Perhaps it is all a matter of perspective—one person's melody is another's noise, and one person's sophistication is another's naiveté. Given the methodological challenges to substantiating such ideological views, it would be wise to turn away from general impressions and consider specifics, away from overt advocacy to description. The purpose of this chapter, then, is to display facets of the African melodic imagination that might enhance appreciation of the products of that imagination. At the heart of the melodic instinct is a wonderfully entangled network of expressive possibilities, a synthesis of word, tone, and rhythm entirely characteristic of African modes of expression. As before, I will describe only a handful of items, but it should be borne in mind that for each song or melodic utterance described here, literally thousands of additional exemplars exist. My hope is that African readers in particular will be able to supply their own examples of the core principles discussed here from repertoires familiar to them. This demonstration will hopefully disrupt any lingering suspicions that African melody is primitive, inferior, or unsophisticated and inspire reflection on one of the primal and most potent sources of African creativity.

## LANGUAGE AS GATEWAY

If sung melody originates in part from language in motion, then a fundamental requirement for an authentic appreciation of African melody is an understanding of what the voice is saying. Without some sense of the singer's semantic meanings, the listener's ability to identify with a song may be limited. Consider the following sentiments expressed in four different songs:

1. "A bad leg has entered this town."
2. "What have I done so as to be rendered naked?"
3. "My lover has deceived me ooo."
4. "Doers of good things: hurry up and do them because I'm about to leave for a far-off place."

These opening lines immediately put listeners in certain frames of mind, stimulating affects and generating expectations. A bad leg (1) brings bad luck or misfortune in the form of disease, natural disaster, or death. Nakedness in public (2) is a sign that the singer has reached a limit; it marks an extreme occasion. Lovers deceive each other all the time (3), but to go one step further and codify such deception in song is to create a space for many more to share in the expression. And procrastination (4), they say, is the thief of time, so if you're planning to do good, you better do it now because you may not have the opportunity tomorrow. You may end up in a faraway place from which no one returns.

Again, consider these randomly chosen beginnings from eight different songs:

1. "This one is a child who is just beginning to stagger about."
2. "A hunter called Ampon lived in a certain town and needed a wife badly."
3. "The person who gossips puts people in trouble."
4. "You were an overpowering force, hey fire which bursts into flame!"
5. "I want to tell you about lady-o."
6. "Gourd of urine, streaming, streaming."
7. "I was playing moi guitar jeje, A lady gave me a kiss."
8. "My head, please, fight for me, my spirit, please, fight, fight for me."

These utterances announce places, people, and attitudes. They may elicit smiles, inspire resolve, make one fearful or nervous, or engender curiosity. The spoken word is, of course, not the only thing that draws a listener instantly into a singer's orbit, but if you miss the fact, for example, that the "fight" (8) that jùjú singer King Sunny Ade is talking about is a spiritual rather than a physical fight ("My head, please, fight for me")[8], or that the invocation of a streaming "gourd of urine" (àdùdɔ'go) (6) is a therapeutic technique for humiliating and thus curing habitual bedwetting among Northern Ewe children, then you are missing a vital point of entry into the imaginative worlds set in motion by these sung texts. Acculturated listeners are in possession of such horizons of expectation, and these regularly mediate their experience of performed melody.

It is true that many of us listen to songs in languages that we do not understand and still enjoy them. This is in part because the musical essence—tone, tune, timbre—brings its own attractions, attractions not necessarily mediated by a language-based semantics. Some people even claim that their level of enjoyment is not in any way diminished when they hear songs in foreign languages. (How they know that is not exactly clear.) The point here is not to reduce song

---

8. Christopher Waterman, *Jùjú: A Social History and Ethnography of an African Popular Music* (Chicago: University of Chicago Press, 1990), 142.

to a continuously signifying verbal narrative, for words display varying degrees of transparency in different genres of song; rather, the aim is to encourage a selective appropriation of some kind of hook, anchor, or lynchpin that can open up an individual song for the listener. Grasping the meaning of a key word or phrase at the beginning, at the high point, or at the close of a song may fix the expression and place the song as a whole in the right perspective for the engaged listener. When, for example, a Northern Ewe singer begins a song with the words *Xexeame fu* ("The world's sufferings"), she immediately strikes a sympathetic chord with many in her audience because suffering is a familiar and often lamented condition in this particular African culture. The four syllables of *Xexeame fu* are sung to the same pitch, G, but listeners who hear only the fourfold sounding of the pitch G on those syllables, or who hear only a short-long-short-long pattern of durations, miss out on the rich intertextual connotations of suffering. In some instances, the point of the song may be missed altogether.[9]

We encounter once again what I believe is a major obstacle to the appreciation of African music, namely, the frequent inaccessibility of its linguistic dimension to some listeners. It is sad that in Western Europe and the United States, listeners have been slow to embrace the verbal meanings associated with songs sung in African languages. While ensembles of drums, mbiras, and xylophones are often heard playing instrumental music on various college campuses and in various community groups, dirge, epic, or praise singers are not as prominent, except, of course, in migrant communities. The point is not to limit the sphere of the appreciable, for people can surely be drawn to African song for many reasons, among them the timbre of a singer's voice, her physical looks, or her dynamic stage presence. But to be able to exclaim honestly and spontaneously, on hearing a riveting and culturally freighted melodic phrase, that "It has really gone inside for me!," the listener needs to have unlocked its linguistic dimension as well.

## THE LOGIC OF MELODIC FORM

Language may thus serve as a gateway to the appreciation of sung or word-based melody, but there are other enabling dimensions. One of the first things to notice about melody is its *logic of form*. Every African melody naturally possesses a beginning and an ending, which are linked by a middle. To put it this way is to risk sounding banal because every temporally constrained expressive

9. For an insightful study of the philosophical content of song texts in one African community, see Kofi Gbolonyo, "Want the history? Listen to the Music! Historical Evidence in Anlo Ewe Musical Practices: A Case Study of Traditional Song Texts" (Master's thesis, University of Pittsburgh, 2005).

act—a speech, a bereaved wife's lament, or a new mother's dance—surely has a beginning, a middle, and an ending. We must distinguish, however, between two aspects of form: a temporal aspect and a functional aspect. The temporal aspect recognizes actual, real-time placement; it records the pattern of succession. The functional aspect recognizes the tendency of the material, the intrinsic or attributed functionality of its segments, ways in which a sense of beginning can be executed and that of ending achieved. These ways include both syntactical and stylistic elements. The temporal aspect is fixed insofar as it is based on a chronology of events. The functional aspect demands a more qualitative approach; we need to recognize specific cultural conventions, as well as style-specific and piece-specific strategies for achieving those functions. In short, the attributes that accrue to a process on the basis of a simple linear ordering of its elements are not necessarily isomorphic with the *functions* intrinsic to those segments. What we hear at the beginning of a melody may or may not exhibit a typical or conventional beginning pattern; similarly, a song may end without adapting any of the conventional techniques of closure. Thinking about African melody in these dual terms—by distinguishing the temporal placement of segments from their function—will alert us to some of the creative strategies employed by performer-composers.

As we would expect, musicians from different parts of the continent realize melodic form in diverse ways, and we would have our hands full trying to enumerate all of them here. There are, however, two recurring strategies that are of especial interest for African melody: emphatic beginnings and sudden, unprolonged or unprepared endings. In some genres, the act of beginning is conceived of rhetorically as an exclamation; it demands an accent, as if the singer intended a marked, weighty, or elevated utterance. A held high note might mark such a beginning, followed by a gradual and perhaps inevitable tapering off in the form of a descending contour. Poetically, a call out at the beginning of an utterance demarcates the onset of musical time and a concomitant departure from ordinary, lived time. Because it often involves a high note (it could even be the highest note), its production requires physical effort. The singer establishes the upper limit of the song's registral span in relation to her own equipment. Failed or imperfect execution of such beginnings can be corrected readily; one can simply begin again. Compare this strategy to that in which the singer approaches a melodic high point late in a song through a gradual and extended process (recall, for example, the English folk song "On Richmond Hill"; Schubert's "An die Musik"; the Christian song "He Lives"; the favorite Christmas song "O Holy Night"; or the German national anthem, "Das Deutschlandlied"), with no guarantee for successful realization, and where failure may be impossible to disguise. One immediately sees not only the logic but also the practical advantages of the African shape.

An emphatic or elevated opening confers on the rest of the melody a comparatively muted stature. This is not a qualitative claim, however; it does not mean that the rest of the melody is in any way unimportant or redundant. Rather, it suggests that the superlative opening demands a differentiated continuation and conclusion. A number of scholars have noted an overall descending shape in African melody. A. M. Jones, for example, essentialized the contour of "African tunes" in this way:

> Broadly speaking, the outline of an African tune is like a succession of the teeth of a rip-saw; a steep rise (not usually exceeding a 5th) followed by a gentle sloping down of the tune; then another sudden rise—then a gentle sloping down, and so on. The tendency is for the tune to start high and gradually to work downwards in this saw-like manner.[10]

Similarly, Laz E. N. Ekwueme describes an Igbo song, "Anya Biara Ule," as follows:

> The general shape of the melody shows a downward movement. The highest note in the tune is sounded as the first note and dominates the first *okele* [equal divisions of time]. Only as an optional tone in the sixth *okele* is it reached again; otherwise the high point of the melody is also the initial point of this short tune. Thereafter, the melody drops slightly, gently meandering but dropping to the end. The lowest point is reached in the second phrase, and again in the last phrase.[11]

Literally thousands of songs in various traditional repertories enact this shape. Readers may verify this by consulting some of the vocal repertories assembled in Figure I.1. Although we need more context to pursue a genuine comparative poetics, we might, with only slightly mischievous intent, riff on Hornbostel's formulation and say that "*We* begin with the highest note and work our way down; *they* begin relatively low and hope to hit the high note in the middle or toward the end. They sometimes fail; we rarely fail."[12]

---

10. A. M. Jones, *African Music in Northern Rhodesia and Some Other Places, The Occasional Papers of the Rhodes-Livingstone Museum* (Manchester: Manchester University Press, 1949), 11.

11. Laz E. N. Ekwueme, "Analysis and Analytic Techniques in African Music," *African Music* 6 (1980): 91.

12. I have elsewhere suggested that this pervasive melodic contour may be motivated by two factors. First is the overall Earth orientation found in the symbol economies of many agrarian societies. This origin would crucially depend on a culture's interpretation of downward melodic motion as Earth oriented. Second is the possibility that an utterance

**Example 5.1**  Six melodies exhibiting a downward shape.

Example 5.1 assembles six brief vocal melodies for a more detailed look at the downward shape described by Jones and Ekwueme. Each melody is shown in an arhythmic reduction (in black noteheads) and is followed by a summary of its pitch content (in white noteheads). An upward-pointing arrow identifies the first occurrence of the highest pitch. Tone centers are stemmed in the white-note summaries. Singing or playing through these chantlike sketches will immediately convey the overall melodic direction. Please bear in mind that there are other features of these melodies worthy of analytical attention, including strategies for beginning, continuing, and ending; word-music resonances; and a variety of phrase-constructional techniques. We will come to some of these in connection with later examples, but let us focus for now exclusively on melodic contour.

The first example, an Akan folk song belonging to the Apɔɔ genre (Example 5.1a), begins around its highest pitches (C5 and D5) and then descends to the lowest (E4 and F4). Next (Example 5.1b) is a song from a repertory accompanying initiation rites known as Makumbi from the Wagogo of Tanzania. The highest note, F5, is the second note in the reduction. The melody then proceeds with a mixture of arpeggiations and stepwise movement until it closes an octave below on F4. The high F is never heard again after its initial occurrence. Example 5.1c is a Ganda religious song from Uganda based on a characteristic pentatonic collection, F-D-C-A-G. The highest note, F5, is heard twice near the beginning; after that, the melody descends gradually, touching on D4 (a tenth below the high point) before closing on G4. Shown in Example 5.1d is a Venda children's song. Here the highest note, G5, is the first to be heard; the rest of the melody literally descends from

whose speech tones are falling is under the jurisdiction of the so-called downdrift phenomenon, whereby successive high tones lose some height in the course of an utterance. See my "Variation Procedures in Northern Ewe Song," *Ethnomusicology* 34 (1990): 222–223.

that high G, expressing the downward shape directly and without interruption. Next (Example 5.1e) is a Southern Ewe song, which also hits its apex (E5) early; it then proceeds often by leap to a lower register, where it dwells for the rest of the song. This song has an even bigger compass than Example 5.1c, dipping as low as B3 to create a span of an octave and a fourth between the highest and lowest pitches. Example 5.1f is a pastoral song from the Iteso of Uganda. Like the Venda example in Example 5.1d, it begins on its highest pitch (D5) and works its way through a mid register to a low, concluding one, ending on E4 but incorporating the adjacent note D4 as well.[13]

African composers do not, of course, slavishly adhere to the basic shape identified here. Artistic impulses intervene, resulting in enrichments and transformations. Furthermore, notions of "high" and "low" may be interpreted metaphorically and in accordance with the exigencies of a particular context. As we have just seen, the highest pitch may occur not literally at the beginning but close to the beginning, while the lowest pitch may appear in the vicinity of the end rather than literally at the end. Also, the physical motion that defines something as a beginning or ending may reside in an attitude rather than in a specific constellation of pitches. Thus, a registral high point may appear in the middle of the melody without carrying the intensity or weighting associated with a beginning. The perception of a high point may depend on a play of diminutions, or on a particular sequence of gestures. And in contexts in which harmonic or contrapuntal constraints are at work, low- or high-lying pitches may be functional substitutes for other pitches, in which case the literal contour of a melody may not jive with the structural contour. Some of these attributes will emerge in the analytical discussion that follows, but analytically minded readers may wish to pursue them in various African song collections.

Endings have received relatively little attention in the literature on African music. This is a bit surprising, given their great potential to illuminate the social origins of musical form and to highlight a variety of aesthetic preferences. In some genres, such as Northern Ewe crying songs, melodies may be rendered without a prolonged sense of home-going. Factors such as the philosophical import of the (verbal) message, the desire to preserve the mobility of a musical unit, or the preference for a provocative rather than assertive mode of communication may cause endings to use quick rhythms, finish on

---

13. Nketia, *Folk Songs of Ghana* (Legon: University of Ghana, 1963), 160; Polo Vallejo, *Mbudi mbudi na mhanga: universo musical infantil de los Wagogo de Tanzania [The musical universe of the Wagogo children from Tanzania]* (Madrid: Edicion del autor, 2004), 148; Joseph Kyagambiddwa, *African Music from the Source of the Nile* (London: Atlantic, 1956), 26–27; Blacking, *Venda Children's Songs*, 148; Nketia, *The Music of Africa*, 156; Mbabi-Katana, *African Music for Schools* (Kampala: Fountain Publishers, 2002), 183.

scale degrees other than the putative tonic (as if ending in the middle of a process), imply linear continuation (as if endings were beginnings waiting to continue on to middles), or pass into silence without prolonged engineering. What each community or composer chooses is motivated by functional and aesthetic considerations, as well as the conventions in play; indeed, in Africa, the domains of function and aesthetics are often inseparable.

Functional attributes of endings stem from the extensive repetition of whole songs in performance. This necessitates a flexible construal of the endings of performance occasions. A melody that is going to be repeated three hundred times in the course of an afternoon's performance will likely be constructed differently from one that will be heard only once. A freighted ending would place an unnecessary burden on its capability for rebeginning or for engendering immediate repetition. The intrinsic mobility of certain African melodies, expressed in open modes and quick rhythms, results from this functional constraint. Also, because external and mundane factors like the onset of darkness, rain, or fatigue may demand that singers stop singing on a given occasion, intelligent composers often build such awareness into the structures they devise. Such endings have the potential to function as transitions back into the sphere of ordinary time.

The *avihawo* (crying songs) of the Northern Ewe is one among many genres in which the patterning of closure may well be functionally motivated. Melodies may finish in diminutive rhythms, or an utterance may be brought to a swift end, often accelerating toward that end. Ewe crying songs rarely linger in closing; more typically, they finish rather hastily, in part to register the gravity of the tragedy that has befallen the singer, and in part to install a complementary silence at the end of the performance to allow singers to contemplate the verbal message. In contrast to some (Western) traditions in which ending means slowing down both literally and metaphorically (by, for example, increasing the amount of structural redundancy), the tradition of avihawo (and similar genres) reads the moment of ending not as a moment of death but as one of rhythmic life.[14]

Middles tend to be tied to beginnings as suffixes and to endings as prefixes, often in an organic way; they therefore tend to elicit less special, less marked rhetorical postures unless they are supporting a parenthesis in the form or an overtly allusive gesture. An ontological middle may be a functional continuation

14. See, for example, the Northern Ewe lament "Àdànutɔ" ("The counselor"), transcribed and analyzed phrase by phrase in my book, *African Rhythm*, 83–89. The closing phrase, "Miyɔ àdànùtɔ névá kpɔ ɖá," is sung in hurried rhythms. Numerous examples appear in several of the transcriptions published by various authors in the *Journal of the Association of Nigerian Musicologists*, 6 (2012), ed. Christian Onyeiji. Further examples may be heard on the CD, *Songs of War and Death from the Slave Coast* (Washington, DC: Smithsonian Folkways Recordings, 1998 or 1999), recorded by Michel Verdon in Abutia Kloe, Ghana.

of a beginning or a functional anticipation of an ending. While middles are in that sense fixed, they are less marked functionally and are best understood in terms of absence—specifically, the absence of an intrinsic or explicit beginning or ending function. Beginning, middle, and ending functions are recursive. A beginning can have its own middle, a middle its own ending, and an ending its own beginning. At yet later levels of structure, the middle of the ending can have its own beginning, the ending of the beginning its own middle, and the middle of the beginning its own ending. Again, the interest for us is not in the abstract possibilities of recursion but in the conventional attitudes that they enshrine.

## PITCH RESOURCES

What pitch resources are available to the producer of African melody, and how are choices made? Resources vary from group to group, from institution to institution, and in reference to diverse aesthetic goals. Typically, such resources include tone systems (most prominently, forms of the anhemitonic pentatonic scale), networks of intervallic preferences (of which seconds, thirds, and fourths in various permutations predominate), and strategies for embellishing individual notes or motives (of which the neighbor-note diminution is a favorite). Although scholars from Hornbostel to Nketia have studied African scales and tuning systems, there is, as far as I'm aware, no handy list of all available pitch resources that students might consult. What is clear, however, is that pitch awareness within a relational system is a key factor in shaping many musicians' ways of proceeding. Such awareness is in turn amply conveyed in the choices made in the composition of melodies.

For composers working in communities in which creators are self-conscious about their artistic heritage, a new song or piece of instrumental music will often begin life as an utterance that conforms to something known; only later will it develop new qualities. The known factor is often the pitch resource (such as a pentatonic collection), which some musicians regard as a language or medium of communication; the unknown factor may reside in the motivic or thematic arrangement. The compositional ethos is to value, respect, or even revere what is inherited, not to ignore or wildly transform it to claim originality. Novelty and originality are sought in other ways: the invention of relevant themes; in the play with voice that, however adventurous, retains a human-centeredness; and in engaging performance.

The pitch content of African music should be approached in proper awareness of what may be intended and what may be fortuitous. Although a particular tone system may be akin to a heritage language, in reality, it constitutes a flexible framework for creativity, not a set of laws to be obeyed to the letter.

Pitches and intervallic sequences are meant to enable individuals and groups, not to disable them. I stress this precariousness and flexibility to encourage a more nuanced assessment of pitch usage in Africa. Too often, Westerners have gone into Africa with their measuring instruments in search of unique tuning systems. They return puzzled by the inconsistencies, the ostensible flexibility in realization, and the large margins of tolerance exercised by listeners and composers. There is, however, something intrinsically unstable about the production of pitch. Pitch articulation sometimes fosters a certain fuzziness around a core, in contrast perhaps to rhythmic articulation, which typically resists a similar degree of fuzziness. The embrace of a certain degree of fuzziness within a given musical domain is a choice, however, not the outcome of uncontrollable forces. When, for example, mbira or xylophone makers attach resonators and other timbre-altering devices to their instruments to obtain muffled sounds, they are not being imprecise. On the contrary, the apparent imprecision manifests an aesthetic desideratum. Similarly, flexibility in articulating a pentatonic collection (or, for that matter, any conventional pitch collection) in a dirge, for example, is never a sign that a goal was not attained; rather, it is often an indication of a flexibly conceived goal. The phrase *margin of tolerance* is helpful in aptly characterizing such situations.[15]

Awareness of the material constraints on pitch choice is helpful in appreciating performances. For some instruments, pitches are fixed by the instrument maker. A xylophone, for example, may be tuned according to a certain sound ideal, be it a remembered pitch or in reference to other xylophones. Similarly, the spacing of holes on a bamboo flute, which normally determines the range and qualities of the sounds produced, is engineered partly by instruments of measurement and perception and partly by subjective judgments. And drums are constructed with tools that constrain their range of available pitches. Significant, then, are the technological means of production. Once again, we see that thinking in terms of appropriate technology is a prerequisite for correct interpretation that is appropriate for certain kinds of construction. (Although they are nowadays used here and there, tuning forks or keyboards in tempered tuning have no a priori status as regulators of pitch in Africa—which is not to say that they are never used.) In developing an appreciation for pitch in the traditional realm, we should grant that as long as individual African communities are satisfied with whatever tuning they have achieved, and as long as they have a mechanism for correcting performance errors, all is well.

For singers, by contrast, a scalar horizon functioning on a background level may influence certain types of singing, including the negotiation of cadences.

15. Gerhard Kubik, "African Tone Systems," 50.

The interstitial material often comes under additional constraints, such as those of speech tones, intonational contour, and rhetoric. Singers may thus go in and out of synchrony with, for example, a pentatonic substrate, not by rejecting its referential status, but by embracing the contingencies that separate the ideal from the realized. Erecting contingencies as evidence of a system, however, would obviously be absurd. Intention in such contexts should be given priority over realization.


## ANALYZING MELODY

We turn finally to a handful of melodies to admire African creativity. The emphasis here will be on structure rather than style, on the inner workings of individual compositions (as they show up in pitch and rhythmic configurations) rather than repertoire-wide features. Criteria for analysis have been adumbrated in previous discussion, so only the briefest of summaries is needed here. Words are temporally tied to tones in a syllabic rather than melismatic configuration. The role of the spoken word as a vehicle for articulation is evident in syllabic settings. The existence of deep-lying pitch structures is one sign of a "purely musical" residue. In some genres, melodies are relatively short—a thirty-second length would not be unusual, although the melody would then be repeated many times in performance. Speech tone and melody may be closely correlated in some settings and loosely correlated in others; in yet others, the two proceed along separate, nonintersecting paths. While some melodies enact the rhythm of spoken language, others borrow the rhythm of dance, while still others travel back and forth between speech and dance. Most basic of all is the distinction between melodies in free or speech rhythm and those in strict rhythm. Free rhythm approximates declamation, a recitativelike mode of delivery; "free" indicates an absence not of rhythm but of a governing meter. Strict rhythm is song proper, closer to aria than to recitative, and endowed with an explicit meter from beginning to end, even while incorporating free-rhythmic effects from time to time. These criteria collectively promote a more precise characterization of the anatomies of our chosen melodies. Structural analysis cannot ultimately prove the aesthetic worth of an African melody; it can only draw attention to the kinds of structures imagined and enacted by African composers, named and unnamed. But without some such intervention, the attempt to disrupt some of the negative evaluations of African melody noted at the beginning of this chapter will be weaker still. Perhaps structural description can encourage similar acts of introspection about what African musicians do, and thus contribute eventually to more intimate knowledge of an African composition, be it a little fragment in the form of a work song or a monumental epic performance.

**Example 5.2** Three-note melody (Aka Pygmy).

An Aka Pygmy child's three-note melody. Aka Pygmy children often punctuate story-telling with songs. An example is the fragmentlike "Nzɛ, nzɛ, nzɛ," which uses only three notes, D4-E4-G4 (Example 5.2 and Web Example 5.1 ).[16] Rhythmically, three different note values occur: an eighth note, a quarter note, and a dotted quarter. If we think of the dotted quarter as a lengthening of the quarter, then the operative values are actually two: an eighth and a quarter. This simple contrast (between a short and long note) enshrines a potent minimality that is entirely characteristic of African expression.

"Nzɛ, nzɛ, nzɛ" begins on its highest pitch, G4, and immediately skips to its lowest, D4. The latter is in turn "prolonged" by its upper neighbor note, E4. Onsets 4 through 8 are then repeated as onsets 9 through 13. In terms of pitch structure, a clear hierarchy is formed around the two pitches, D and G. The melody's reigning pitch system is established definitively in this song as a [025] trichord (counting in semitones and corresponding to D-E-G, respectively); given what we know of other Aka practices, we might infer that the notes D-E-G actually constitute a subset of a larger pentatonic collection, perhaps D-E-G-A-B.

On first hearing, this little song (which in performance is repeated dozens of times) may seem unremarkable. But add to the basic oppositions in pitch and rhythmic value the implied meter, and we begin to see some special things. The underlying feel of the melody suggests a dotted quarter-note reference, so we might notate this in 12/8 as I have done. The clever feature is the way the patterns lie within the metrical cycle. The words *Nzɛ, nzɛ, nzɛ* occupy the space of two dotted quarters, the first sounding of *nzɛ o dɛ kun dɛ* occupies three, and its immediate repetition also occupies three. A grouping structure of 2 + 3 + 3 is thus suggested. We may speak of a nonalignment between metrical structure and grouping structure: the 12/8 meter remains inviolate while the "contents" shift position within the meter. This is one of the key sources of interest in this little melody, one that resonates with other pitch-rhythm patterns whose synchronicities are tweaked to produce a similar dynamic tension. The nonalignment is further underlined by a latent call-and-response pattern whereby the first *nzɛ o dɛ kun dɛ* is the "call" and its immediate repetition provides the "response."

16. Heard on the CD, *Centrafrique: Anthologie de la musique des Pygmées Aka* (Paris: Ocora, 1987), track 15, "Trois jeux d'enfants: Nze-nze-nze."

Noteworthy, too, is what might be called the rhetoric of the melody. The song begins emphatically with an almost bell-like insistence on G (its highest pitch) in the context of a cross-rhythmic relation with the underlying meter (3:2, three quarters against two dotted quarters). Then it skips to (what will emerge as) the lowest pitch, taming it by means of neighbor-note action. The difference in the presentation of the G-D controlling dyad is noteworthy. While the initial G is merely asserted through immediate repetition, the closing D is defined by contrapuntal action. The mixture of assertion and contrapuntal definition is another favorite device used by numerous African melodists. Notice two further details that add spice to this melody: first is the continuity of pitch between the end of group 1 (onset 3) and the beginning of group 2 (onset 4)—both on pitch G4. Real assurance of the precise location of a grouping boundary comes only in retrospect, only after group 2 (onsets 4 through 8) has been literally repeated as group 3 (onsets 9 through 12). Notice also the pattern of introducing new pitches. New notes appear on onsets 1, 8, and 10 in the first bar (the "call") and (reckoning onsets starting on 1 again) on 1, 4, 5, 7, and 10 in the second (the "response"). The degree of pitch novelty is thus increased in the second half of the melody.

Finally, the tonal sense conveyed by the controlling dyad, G-D, retains some ambiguity and openness. Since *Nzɛ, nzɛ, nzɛ* is repeated over and over again in performance, the join between one statement and its immediate repetition thrusts the D-G interval into prominence. But this is a "dead interval"—that is, an interval between phrases rather than within a single phrase—so it cannot provide anchor for the melody's overall tonal tendency. And yet we must presume that the melody was composed with its repetitions in mind. If so, the D-G interval is not as dead as we might suppose; it is strategically placed to carry some of the structural burden that accrues to the song in the course of performance. Whether Aka listeners hear this song with a beginning orientation as opposed to an end orientation remains to be established, but we can admire a pitch structure that seems splendidly poised between G and D. A beginning orientation would reinforce the feeling that the song is akin to a fragment, perhaps part of a larger— not exclusively musical—process; an end orientation would infer closure at the end of the melody but would receive that assurance only in retrospect.

Those who are not in the habit of granting African performer-composers large doses of intellectual prowess may be skeptical about the foregoing reading of a three-note Pygmy melody. But I hope to persuade some that in this littlest of children's songs, the constellation of metrical, rhythmical, and tonal play is engaging, the outcome distinct and even memorable. To describe a melody like this as "primitive" or "unsophisticated" is surely a travesty. True, "Nzɛ, nzɛ, nzɛ" is brief and thrives on manifold repetition, but these qualities have no a priori value. Indeed, they are precisely what one would expect from composers in an oral culture who have to depend on performers—child performers, in this case—to render the melody on many subsequent occasions.

Were the Aka compositional tradition based on a paper economy, its individual products would naturally be longer, but they would also likely acquire features that are not necessarily based on their aural value. "Nzɛ, nzɛ, nzɛ" is a miniature gem, an elemental arrangement of pitch and rhythm to produce memorable, self-propelling, and enduring melody.

## (OTHER) CHILDREN'S MELODIES

There is much to admire about the ingenuity with which African children exploit minimum syntactic sequences involving pitch and rhythm. Scholars of traditional music have often noted this, but there is still work to be done in assembling inventories of children's music across the continent. These inventories can serve various ends, among them the teaching of music in schools, the study of composition, and the development of a poetics of song. We do not have the space to embark on a comprehensive study of the melodic impulse in children's music here, but we can at least acknowledge a handful of examples while also pointing readers to fuller studies by ethnomusicologists and music educationists.[17]

A Vai children's game song uses mostly three pitches corresponding to the doh, re, and mi or 1-2-3 of the major scale as shown in Example 5.3. (A fourth note, lah [6], appears fleetingly toward the end but can be discounted for the purposes of this analysis.) Written out as a succession of pitches (gaps indicate phrase groups or breath marks), the melody looks like this:

323132 311332 332112 11212113233323212 11112(6)121

From this DNA-looking-like sequence, one can extract all six of the dyadic possibilities available: 1-2, 2-1, 1-3, 3-1, 2-3, 3-2. The sequence 1-2 occurs six times, 2-1 also six times, 1-3 three times, 3-1 two times, 2-3 three times, and 3-2 seven times. The 3-2 progression is the most used in the song, while 3-1 is used the least.[18]

---

17. See, among numerous examples, Thomas F. Johnston, "Tsonga Children's Folksongs," *Journal of American Folklore* 86 (1973): 225–240; John Blacking, *Venda Children's Songs*; Agawu, *African Rhythm*, 62–73; Akosua Addo, "Ghanaian Children's Music Cultures: A Video Ethnography of Selected Singing Games," (PhD diss., University of British Columbia, 1995); *The Oxford Handbook of Children's Musical Cultures*, ed. Patricia Shehan Campbell and Trevor Wiggins (New York: Oxford University Press, 2012); Kyra Gaunt, *The Games Black Girls Play: Learning the Ropes from Double-Dutch to Hip-Hop* (New York: New York University Press, 2006); and Minette Mans, Mary Dzansi McPalm, and Hellen Odwar Agak, "Play in Musical Arts Pedagogy," in *Musical Arts in Africa: Theory, Practice and Education* (Pretoria: UNISA Press, 2003), 195–214.

18. CD, *Music of the Vai of Liberia* (Washington, DC: Smithsonian Folkways, 1998), track 10.

**Example 5.3**  Children's game song (Vai).

Of course, no claim is being made here that the originators of this tune consciously worked out the possibilities for dyadic reversal in advance of composition. The claim is only that the melody as represented supports attributions of such a systematic and exhaustive process. Those who find the melody monotonous may be encouraged to listen differently in light of the process outlined previously. In any case, we must be careful not to underestimate what is possible in the sphere of oral composition, for insofar as the context is one of play, the playful ordering of elements is likely to have dominated the (pre) compositional process.

Children's melodies do not unfold only in single lines; sometimes they do so in multiple voices. *Akazehe* greeting routines performed by pairs of Burundian females exemplify such polyphony. Separated at a short distance and using only a handful of notes in strict rhythmic alignment, two singers unfold captivating narratives in open-ended song. The principal technique is one of interlocking, a procedure more commonly encountered in nonvocal music (such as music for xylophones or panpipes), but it is used to great effect in this enthralling gamelike exercise (Web Example 5.2 ).[19]

Polyphonic vocal games featuring anywhere from two to six voices among the Bibayak Pygmy of Gabon show that African melody can reach creative heights even within the juvenile's world. These beautiful games are quintessential instances of *playing*; they are enacted by beating the mouth to produce sounds that harmonize with or are coordinated with those produced by other beaters of the insides of voices. Polyphonic regulation is both metric (12/8) and scalar (the pentatonic), and children develop a feeling for coordinated composing in the moment through such games. (A tiny fragment from one such polyphonic game is transcribed in Example 7.3.[20])

19. Serena Facci, "Akazehe del Burundi. Saluti a incastro polifonico e cerimonialità femminile," in *Polifonie. Procedimenti, tassonomie e forme: una riflessione a più voci*, ed. M. Agamennone (Verona: Edizioni Il Cardo/Ricerche, 1996), 123–161.

20. CD, *Musique des pygmées Bibayak. Chantres de l'épopée* (France: Ocora, 1989).

**Photo 5.1** Toy drum set, Bawku, Ghana.

Popular children's games featuring externalized movements often deploy a generic clap pattern as a backdrop to repeated song. One such game from the Northern Ewe has a clap pattern with an interonset pattern of [1-2-1-2-2], according to which the first 1—the shorter of the two contrasting note values—falls on the downbeat of a 4/4 meter. Participants are arranged in a circle, and each child instantiates his or her clap with two neighbors—one on the right, another on the left. The game begins by activating the clap pattern as an ostinato; then, as soon as the ensemble is secure, songs are exchanged over it for as long as the performers desire. The melodies that accompany this game often follow the descending archetype mentioned earlier, while verbal texts range in content from the elevated to the banal. One song explains why "We do not send a fool to the market." The reason is that the fool "goes and buys soap water and calls it a drink." The song's melody rises initially, reaches its highest pitch, hovers around it, and then descends rapidly at the close.[21]

Equally popular are children's stone-lifting games. Played in circular formations, they invariably feature song. Some songs may be in a traditional idiom, while others have a popular flavor. The latter can be heard, for example, in

---

21. See the CD accompanying Agawu, *African Rhythm*, tracks 8–11, for examples of Northern Ewe children's game songs.

**Example 5.4** Children's song (Venda).

Tsi - ngá  n - dé - de - dè - hó - n - yâ - nà;   Ri   yà  mù gé - ró - ni   hó - n - yâ - nà.

some Baule children's songs.[22] Melodies are typically based on relatively small intervals of seconds, thirds, or fourths; they incorporate lots of repetition and sometimes feature patterns of accentuation that compete with those of the accompanying physical movements. Children's game songs from Angola also provide vivid illustrations of these features.[23] And in one Venda children's song (Example 5.4), the upbeats within the ruling 3/8 meter consistently receive an accent even as the melody descends from a high G. Again, a dynamic feeling emerges from marking notes that are subservient to others in the metrical hierarchy.[24]

Finally, in a register not necessarily created by children but invariably aimed at them, lullabies display some of the ingenuity we associate with African melody. Recorded lullabies display a variety of features that, while not unique to the genre, are often appropriated for expressive purposes. A lullaby may involve a childlike song using just two or three pitches, it will typically invest in repetition, and it may involve an alternation between speech and song. Lullabies fundamentally embody a melodic impulse, albeit one that assumes a variety of linguistic and expressive forms.

Example 5.5 is an outline of a lullaby from the Nkundo of the Democratic Republic of the Congo that illustrates melodic thinking guided by a narrative impulse (Web Example 5.3 🔊).[25] Our female singer has selected two adjacent notes (G3 and A3) to serve as anchors or resting points for an extended discourse. Between appearances of this dyad, the members of the ruling hexatonic set (E-D-C-B-A-G) are used to spin short melodic statements. The accumulation of these fragments advances the narrative, while the intermittent return to the G-A dyad has the effect of a refrain, albeit one performed by the same singer. Note the gentle clapping of hands that adds a measure

22. CD, *Côte d'Ivoire: Baule Vocal Music* (Ivry-sur-Seine: Auvidis, 1993 [orig. 1972]).

23. See recording accompanying Kubik's *Theory of African Music*, vol. 1.

24. Blacking, *Venda Children's Songs*, 50.

25. CD, *Anthologie de la musique Congolaise (RDC)*, vol. 11, *Musique des Nkundo* (Tervuren: Musée royal de l'Afrique central, 2007 [orig. 1971–1972]), track 9. In making the transcription shown in Example 5.5, I have filled in the gaps between phrases by extending the ending notes to avoid using rests.

**Example 5.5** Lullaby (Nkundo).

of metrical control in spite of the declamatory ambience of the performance. Indeed, if we gather together the phrases by number of pulses, we observe a fascinating additive pattern in which four-pulse, five-pulse, six-pulse, seven-pulse, and eight-pulse phrases succeed each other in an unpredictable pattern: $4 + 5 + 4 + 6 + 4 + 6 + 6 + 5 + 8 + 7 + 6 + 6 + 6 + 6 + 5$ (the recording tapers off at the end). Overall, the lullaby owes its effect to the combination of a vocal narrative parsed asymmetrically (a genuine narrative, in other words), a "strophic" impulse signaled by the returning phrase-end notes, and an underlying cyclic regularity contributed by the handclapping.

**Example 5.5** (Continued)

**An Aka Pygmy entertainment song, "Ame ngolo."** Accompanying himself on a *bogongo* (a harp zither), Ndole, an Aka Pygmy man, announces in song that he is "the palm-tree squirrel" (Example 5.6, Web Example 5.4 .[26] His melodic imagination will be shaped by a clever use of repetition and by the use of long vowels like *ee, aa,* and *ay.* The sound of language is vivid throughout, and the performance exemplifies a deliberate musical narrative comparable in scope to the berceuse from the Democratic Republic of the Congo we have just listened to. The difference between the relatively brief children's songs and rhymes, on the one hand, and Ndole's more extended tracts, on the other, provides some measure of the scope of the African melodic imagination.

I have used a form of pulse notation to represent Ndole's song, the thought being that microlevel activity at the eighth-note level is significant enough to be maintained as a reference point throughout. The notation underreports the actual durations of the singer's notes, being concerned only with their initial activation. It is important not to be misled by the resulting sparseness. Only the melodic line is transcribed. The accompaniment, which takes the form of a selective reinforcement of the singer's main notes, is excluded.

As the transcription shows, "Ame ngolo" consists of relatively brief phrases that unfold in a pragmatic manner. The beginning of the recording is not

26. CD, *Centrafrique: Pygmées Aka* (Paris: Ocora, 1998), track 5.

**Example 5.6** Entertainment song, "Ame ngolo" (Aka Pygmy).

marked; rather, it comes across as if we were in a middle, part of a process that is already underway. Ndole's harp zither has already set the pace and atmosphere during the first twenty seconds. He then sings phrase after phrase, varying the notes and contour as he goes along. Moments of intensity are achieved by means of register, as when the singer gets up to $G\flat4$ (bars 28 to 29, 59 to 60, and 65 to 66). These are interspersed with extended moments representing "home" and hovering around the opening $D\flat4$. Ndole occasionally dips into the lowest register, touching $G\flat3$ in the process. Overall, the octave $G\flat3$-$G\flat3$ sets the registral frame for the melody.

**Example 5.6** (Continued)

"Ame ngolo" has a mesmerizing quality that is achieved by introducing tiny variations into phrases in such a way that the succession of phrases is never predictable. An improvisatory aura prevails here, but far from implying that the song is simply thrown together, the authorial hand seems firm throughout. Ndole accepts and maintains the integrity of the hexatonic collection Gb-Eb-Db-Cb-Bb-Ab, even while allowing his voice to deviate naturally in microtonal distances from the relatively fixed pitches played by the harp zither. Voice and

**Photo 5.2** Gonje and handclap, Tamale, Ghana.

instrument rarely agree literally, but no one would be disconcerted by what is only an apparent discrepancy. The aesthetic is minimalistic in both pitch and verbal content; this allows the underlying musical processes to claim our attention. Phrases reach for focal points and subside thereafter, but the overall phrase discourse is never predictable because it does not submit to hypermetrical control. The singer's manner creates the impression that a certain amount of self-absorption is in play here, and that an invitation to contemplation or reflection may be part of the message. Although Ndole comes from a thoroughly communalistic musical culture, he is nevertheless free to exercise his musical imagination in an individual way on occasions like this. The communal ethos in African performance contextualizes rather than curbs individual creative impulses.

A **Northern Ewe crying song, "Afaa ko yee."** "Afaa ko yee" begins as a song about a "pretend sympathizer" and ends by posing a rhetorical question about seeking sympathy: "Why did you try to die just to see if you had any loved ones who would come and mourn your passing?" The moral to all of us is simple: some actions are irreversible, death being one of them, so calculate carefully before you try to die. Northern Ewe women sing this crying song (*aviha*) to remind us of one of life's lessons.

**Example 5.7** Dirge, "Afaa ko yee" ("pretend sympathizer") (Northern Ewe).

The song's outer form is in two parts. The first, sung solo, is in a free declamatory form; in the second, the solo singer is joined by a chorus in strict, fully metrical rhythm (Example 5.7, with the text in Ewe and English in Figure 5.1, and heard at Web Example 5.5 ⬤). The juxtaposition of free and strict is, as we have seen, a basic organizational device in many African communities. The free sections allow individual expression and maximum verbal content; the singer takes advantage of the semantic freight of verbal language. In the strict section, verbal and semantic content are kept to a minimum; the composer selects a memorable, poignant, or synoptic phrase that the chorus can repeat again and again. This refrain typically encapsulates the central message of a song. In this second part, the constraints of group expression impose themselves not only metrically but also pitch-wise. Singing together is easier if there is an explicit meter and precise rhythmic values and pitches. Again, this centuries-old free-to-strict form is as logical as it is simple and efficient; it continues to support many melodic utterances today.

The deep sources of melodic imagining in this crying song lie in the moment-by-moment realization of the poetic text. The framing of sentiments, the choice of words, and their musical animation all reveal high levels of ingenuity and skill. Equally impressive are the ways in which the singer negotiates the constraints imposed by speech tones. Let us then go inside the song, listen to its interior, and observe some of the workings of the African melodic imagination at close quarters. Not all aspects of the song lend themselves to verbal explication; some of the singer's sentiments and turns of phrase will typically elicit a smile, nod, wink, sigh, or grunt, but the precise sources of these responses have as much to do with things "inside" the song as with predispositions that listeners bring to their audition. Indeed, a great deal of significance resides in the interstices within the song to which only the acculturated have

### Solo

*Afaa ko yee.*
Pretend sympathizer

*Tasi 'faa ko yee.*
Aunt 'pretend sympathizer'

*Ameke ɖi h̃ia ga va kpɔ nu 'ya eko z̃ia tɔ.*
The one who was once poor and became rich is the one who laughed at the
   poor one

*Nye tsɛ ma ku zẽẽ kpɔ.*
I too want to die (for a while) and see.

*Adanfo ee, nye tsɛ ma ku zẽẽ kpɔ.*
My friend, I too want to die (for a while) and see what happens [see how
   many people actually come to my funeral].

*Nye tsɛ ma ku zẽẽ makpɔ lɔ̃nyelawoe.*
I too want to die and see who my loved ones are.

*Tsiɛ diɛ woe.*
My loved ones.

*Gbolo ee ayee.*
Gbolo ee (the mother of song), *ayee.*

*Enu egblẽ loo.̣*
Things have gone bad.

*Yoo, yoo, yoo.*
Yoo, yoo, yoo.

### Chorus

*E'emi ku zẽẽ kpɔ mele ŋuwo ɖee, ne be yea ku zẽẽ kpɔ[a]?*
And so you don't have an advocate to witness your die-and-find-out
   scenario, and you still went ahead and died?'

**Figure 5.1** Text of "Afaa ko yee."

access. It is helpful to keep this supplement in mind even as we explore a few of
the specifiable aspects of sound and meaning.

Let us follow the process from beginning to end, using segments of text as
place markers.

*Afaa ko yee.* This names a "pretend sympathizer," one who might be crying with you but doesn't mean it, one who expresses sorrow with you but is
secretly thinking something else. The singer's melody literally realizes the

direction of tones, using the toneless but not directionless intensifier *yee* as the point of rest.

*Tasi ꞌfaa ko yee* ("aunt pretend sympathizer"). We know she is a woman, a paternal aunt, perhaps the mythical older female relative to whom we attribute all kinds of mischief. Musically, the same process of word realization is evident. Notice the motivic connection between the two segments of melody: Bb-A-G-A is slightly expanded to G-B-A-G-F-G. Important here are the fermata-bearing terminal notes: A in the first segment and G in the second. Again, the subtle ambiguity in tonal sense emerging in the larger A-G "structural" progression is noteworthy. In one sense, the first A is a question to which the following G is an answer, for there is a direct sense in which the figure of the pretend sympathizer announced in the first segment is properly identified in the second segment by the addition of *Tasi* ("aunt"). Culture bearers know, however, that the A-G progression could be the beginning of an extended descent spanning the melody as a whole, in which case A would be the pitch of priority, being the point of departure. It's too early in the game to arrive at any definite predictions about pitch priority, however. The main point here is the encoding of an ambiguity. Indeed, as the recitative that constitutes the first half of the song unfolds, we will come to appreciate the increasing functionality of the note A as a "dissonant" neighbor to G.

*Ameke ɖi h̃ ia ga va kpɔ nu ꞌya eko ʒia tɔ.* There are many words here! We learn a little history: "aunt pretend sympathizer" is in fact a person who was once poor, became rich, and now is laughing at the poor. Teasing may be rampant among the Northern Ewe, but teasing someone about his or her poverty is not normal; it is considered unkind. Still, the rich-poor dialectic is a central social construction that influences the ways in which people interact with one another. Here we are virtually in the realm of speech, matching syllables of text to short durations, and correlating speech tone with melody in phrases like *ga va kpɔ nu* (MHHH) or in the word *ziatɔ* (LH). But the pitch A is never far from consciousness, ending the segment, and enhancing its function as a reciting tone of sorts. The note A's importance within the structural melody continues to be reinforced, and we are likely to infer that satisfactory resolution will hinge on the destination of that A.

*Nye tsɛ ma ku zɛ̃ɛ̃ kpɔ* ("I too want to die [for a while] and see"). The colorful device of iconicity intrudes here in the form of the word *zee*, a "picture word" that opens up a dimension of sound symbolism by describing the temporary nature of the death. *Zɛ̃ɛ̃* literally conveys a sense of temporariness. To die for a while to see how many people show up at your funeral is, of course, a foolish thing to do since you cannot die and come back. This message is clear. But it does not remove the desire, experienced regularly by Northern Ewe, to see who their true relatives are. In societies with strong social bonds, the suspicion that not all your "relatives" care about you can be wounding, and if one has to go to great lengths to find that out, then so be it. In this case, however, the person who needed this psychic reassurance unfortunately lost out. Musically, the balance between song centricity and speech centricity shifts somewhat in this phrase: whereas the two previous phrases were located toward the song end of the spectrum, this one is close to the speech end. This subtle traffic between speech mode and song mode (and the numerous stages in between) is a vital source of animation in African song.

*Adanfo ee, nye tsɛ ma ku zɛ̃ɛ̃ kpɔ* ("My friend, I too want to die [for a while] and see what happens [see how many people actually come to my funeral]"). The singer slows the narrating down by restating what she said before, only this time she addresses a "friend" (*Adanfo*). The construction here is similar to that which was used at the very beginning of the crying song, where a statement was made and then repeated immediately with an additional word. The effect of such an amplification varies. It can intensify the affect, come across as a revelation, or provide a sense of resolution. The rendition of *Adanfo* pitch-wise adds a more prominent interval (a rising perfect fourth) than the one that ended the third segment; *Adanfo ee* also perfectly mirrors the speech tone (LLLH). Notice, again, that the previous phrase ended with a "question" on A, while this ends with an "answer" on G.

*Nye tsɛ ma ku zɛ̃ɛ̃ makpɔ lɔ̃nyelawoe* ("I too want to die and see who my loved ones are"). This is the third time the die-and-see sentiment is being portrayed. We sense the urgency of desire. The segment ends on an A, and the rhythm is close to that of speech. The drooping of speech at the end of the phrase animates an iconic dimension.

*Tsiɛ diɛ woe.* The singer calls out to "my loved ones."

*Gbolo ee ayee.* The performer intrudes on the performance, reminding us that she, *Gbolo* ("the mother of song"), is in charge here.

*Enu egblẽ loo* ("Things have gone bad"). Details may be forthcoming, but since we all know what it means for things to go bad, we can draw on that experience to empathize with the singer. Musically, the descending (augmented) fourth B-F echoes the (perfect) fourth C-G of the previous phrase.

*Yoo, yoo, yoo.* Thank God for song words, which can always be thrown in to express that which cannot be expressed, to compensate for a waning of inspiration, or to allow the musical instinct some autonomy. These words, which are without semantic freight, finish off the soloist's recitative on a G. Is this, then, the resolution? Has A, heard at the ends of five of the eight phrases, been a preparation for G all along?

*E'emi ku zɛ̃ɛ̃ kpɔ mele ŋuwo ɖee, ne be yea ku zɛ̃ɛ̃ kpɔ[a]?* ("And so you don't have an advocate to witness your die-and-find-out scenario, and you still went ahead and died?"). This is the "call" of the call-and-response portion of the

song that will now involve all the singers, not just the lead singer. The word
*E'emi* means "thus" or "therefore," a natural transition between the metrically "free" and "strict" halves of the song. The singer questions the dead
woman: Why did you go ahead and do this even though you knew there was
only one possible outcome? The meter enters decisively, alongside a pitch formation that will emerge as the song's melodic archetype (a descending shape
spanning a major sixth, B-A-G-F-E-D).

*Ku zɛ̃ɛ̃ kpɔ mele ŋuwo ɖee, ne be yea ku zɛ̃ɛ̃ kpɔ*[a]? Repeating most of the
words from the previous segment, the chorus responds, also in meter and
with harmonies, some of which proceed in parallel with the melody while
others follow oblique motions. In performance, the call-and-response pattern
is repeated several times depending on the occasion and on the eagerness to
move on to a different song message. Overall, the descent begun in the call
sections in the form of an A-G descent is amplified in the metricized call section to C-B-A-G-F-G (the high E is a substitute for C) and, more elaborately,
transformed into D-C-B-A-G-F, the last with a supporting D. Some may hear a
Dorian flavor in this disposition of pitches. Although the Northern Ewe do not
normally refer their modality to the ecclesiastical modes of European medieval theory, their music is often modally based. Indeed, the modal flavor of
a great deal of traditional melody is readily heard in arrhythmic renditions
(refer back to Example 5.1) and suggests that we may have underestimated the
African contribution to world modal practices.

The melodic imagination displayed in this crying song is potent and attractive. Foremost is the poetic dimension, which accounts for the choice of theme
and words and for the rhetorical strategies by which it is developed. Then there
is the underlying relational pitch sense, which, on a local level, seeks to accommodate the prescriptions of spoken Ewe within a more purposeful song environment; on a more global level, it initially restrains the recitative section on
the pitches A and G before leading to the ultimate discharge in the form of
a fully elaborated archetype in the choral response. Finally, there is rhythm,
expressed both in the overall progression from free to strict and as it emanates
from spoken language. These are not inconsiderable achievements in a "folk"
milieu. By what standard of reckoning, I wonder, could "Afaa ko yee" ever be
consigned to the category "unsophisticated?"

**An Akpafu lament, "Ɔwere ame bɔi lo kpi kutukã" ("The river creature
died of thirst")** (Web Example 5.6 ◉).[27] Laments and dirges sung by Akpafu
women represent some of their most distinctive forms of musical expression.
Carvers of song are typically motivated by death, loss, or tragedy, and they

---

27. The following analysis is drawn from an earlier study of mine, "On an African Song
from Akpafu," *Sonus* 10 (1989): 22–39.

often encode an enigma, a paradox, something imponderable, a deep thought, or a profound question in their verbal texts. Why? Because such genres, contrary to a once-accepted view that they serve a primarily functional purpose, are inducements to deep contemplation; their purpose is to provide food for thought for thinking performers and their audiences. The sociohistorical and philosophical worlds that they set in motion are multiple, and melody is the chief vehicle for articulating that multiplicity, that wide resonance. Melody brings language, music, and voice into a mutually reinforcing relationship, displaying once again facets of African creativity.

Let us begin with the entirety of the singer's text, shown in Figure 5.2.

The song poses an enigma: if the river creature who lives in water and therefore has unlimited access to it died of thirst, then what about me, a land creature who sits on the bank? Texts like this recognize the existence of a higher, superior force; they acknowledge the limitations of man's knowledge and power. In performance, the soloist's lines may be subject to variation, to an exploration of the essential truths enshrined in the song's message. The chorus parts, by contrast, are fixed, providing the ecology that grounds the song as a whole.

The transcription in Example 5.8a shows that the singer maintains the rhythm of spoken Siwu, most obviously in the syllabic setting. Indeed, the musical setting may be heard as a translation of the spoken text into a sung text. The most decisive moment in this act of translation is the exclamation *ayee*, a song word with no semantic equivalent, functioning as an intensifier. The chorus renders *ayee* twice as a short-long rhythm that mirrors its spoken form. At the same time, *ayee* represents a firming up of pitch and a reinforcement of the lament's songfulness. If the lament as a whole sports a declamatory ambience, the interventions of *ayee* transform declamation into song.

I have divided "Ɔwere ame bɔi" into ten little phrases or units. Seven are sung by the lead singer, while three are sung by the chorus. Specifically, phrases 1 through 5 are sung solo, while phrases 6 through 10 alternate between chorus and solo, finishing with the chorus. In terms of the poetic

---

Ɔwere ame bɔi lo kpi kutukã
*The river creature died of thirst*

Mme gɔ mezi ɔkpokpo ne, nda si mmra so?
*I who am sitting on the river bank, what should I do with myself?*

Ayee!
*Ayee!* (an exclamation)

---

**Figure 5.2** Text of "Ɔwere ame bɔi."

**Example 5.8a** Lament, "Ɔwere ame bɔi" ("The river creature") (Akpafu).

structure, the two versions of line 1 each constitute a complete syntactical/semantic unit, and this is repeated to form phrases 1, 2, 3, 4, 7, and 9 of the song. Line 2, which embodies the singer's question, is compressed into phrase 5, and the choral response *ayee* of line 3 becomes phrases 6, 8, and 10, the last extending the number of *ayees* to four (although that number could change in other performances). The rests between phrases enable singers to incorporate both spoken interjections particular to the occasion on which the song is being sung and ululations of diverse intensities and lengths. When it is sung at a funeral, for example, spontaneously spoken phrases like *Tete!* ("Father!"), *Nna iyo boa bo soo?* ("In whose house shall we be hosted?"), or *Tete, masɛ o kama ne ana ni* ("Father, we prepared for your coming back, but you did not return") might be spontaneously spoken in the rests or silences to intensify the emotion.

In practically all Akpafu songs, pitch is organized hierarchically. This does not make the organization predictable. On the contrary, there is considerable play between the hierarchies deriving from the inner tendencies of the pitches and those deriving from the conventional points of rest (cadences). Indeed, different collections of pitches acting as referential constructs may articulate different levels of structure.

"Ɔwere ame bɔi" discloses its hierarchic structure by closing on (an arbitrarily chosen) C, emphasizing that pitch throughout the song, and leading to it by means of a 2-1 progression. Heard in isolation from the rest of the song, the chorus parts (phrases 6, 8, and 10) provide the clearest definition of C as center by articulating 2 (phrase 6), then 1 (phrase 8), then an alternation of 1s and 2s concluding on $\hat{1}$ (phrase 10).

Example 5.8b summarizes the pitch content in the form of an arrhythmic transcription showing aspects of structure that lie deeper than the foreground. The layout follows the chronology of the phrases and includes the pitch content of each phrase in stemmed black noteheads. Phrases are arranged

**Example 5.8b** Pitch content of "Ɔwere ame bɔi" in arrhythmic reduction.

paradigmatically to emphasize internal parallels. Thus, phrases 1, 2, 3, 4, 7, and 9, which are based on lines 1 and 2 of the text, are placed in one column; phrases 6, 8, and 10, which compose line 3 of the text, occur in another column; and phrase 5 is in a column by itself. Perhaps the most striking feature of Example 5.8b is its pentatonic substructure (A-C-D-E-G), which interacts with, but does not dominate, the C-centered hexatonic structure of the musical surface. We may speak of a "middle ground" pentatonic substructure, which subtends a foreground hexatonic scale. If phrase 4 displays the ideal form of the pentatonic substructure, all the other phrases may be heard as departing in various ways from that ideal. Phrases 3, 5, 6, 8, 9, and 10 are all subsets of the ideal. Phrase 7 parallels the ideal but includes a "mixture" of its third element (E and E-[♭]. Phrase 1, although the first to be heard, is properly a subset of phrase 4, but it, too, includes five elements. Its pitch, F, may be explained as a "borrowing" from the hexatonic surface pattern.

Another feature of "Ɔwere ame bɔi" summarized in Figure 5.3 is the hierarchic distribution of intervals. (The taxonomy excludes so-called dead intervals, that is, intervals that cut across phrase boundaries.) This particular exercise is suggested by the predominant syllabic articulation in song, which sets into relief the succession of intervals. The table confirms the centrality of major second and minor thirds (both prominent in the pentatonic scale); together they make up 76.19 percent of the song's intervals. They may be said to constitute the basic syntactic framework of the song. There are no intervals bigger than a perfect fifth, and none smaller than a major second. While minor thirds make up 35.7 percent of the collection, major thirds make up only 4.76 percent. There is a slightly lower incidence of ascending intervals (42.86 percent) as opposed to descending ones. The relative paucity of larger intervals (major thirds, perfect fourths, tritones,

|                      | M2    | m3    | M3   | P4   | A4   | P5   |
|----------------------|-------|-------|------|------|------|------|
| Ascending            | 5     | 8     | 2    | 1    | 2    | 0    |
| Descending           | 12    | 7     | 0    | 4    | 0    | 1    |
| Totals               | 17    | 15    | 2    | 5    | 2    | 1    |
| Totals as Percentages| 40.48 | 35.71 | 4.76 | 11.9 | 4.76 | 2.38 |

**Figure 5.3** Distribution of intervals in "Ɔwere ame bɔi."

and perfect fifths) gives added significance to their rhetorical effect when they do occur.[28]

Translating the reality of "Ɔwere ame bɔi" into numbers is simply a way of capturing some of its features. I am aware, however, that these numbers do not normally impress humanists, probably because such analysis involves dissecting what is, after all, an artistic product and displaying its material constituents in summary form. In giving priority to constituent elements, it might be further argued, the approach overlooks the symbolic domain altogether. If the analysis were to go no further than constructing taxonomies, there would be reason to point to its incompleteness. Taxonomies, however, have their uses. For example, they can highlight a particular feature, reveal a tendency, draw attention to a significant absence, or perhaps reinforce (or indeed undermine) an intuition the analyst might have begun with. African students should be encouraged to undertake analytical exercises whereby they pass their communities' songs through as many sieves as possible so that they can obtain the most comprehensive views of musical structure.

Still, no matter how thorough or comprehensive, a taxonomy takes us only so far; it needs supplementation in the form of musico-poetic exploration. So let us turn to word-music relations. One of the most fruitful mechanisms for developing a poetics of African song is closure, the general tendency to close.[29] In many African languages, concepts of closure are expressed through notions of ending, concluding, finishing, and dying. The Akpafu, for example, whose lament we are looking at, will sometimes say *Yiɔ ro,* meaning "it is finished," a phrase that marks different forms of closure. It may be used when a substance such as palm wine has been consumed, when a song is at an end, when something precious like an earthenware pot is broken, or when somebody has

28. For a description and critique of "semiotic" studies of melody, see Raymond Monelle, *Linguistics and Semiotics in Music* (Chur, Switzerland: Harwood Press, 1992), 59–89 and 162–192.

29. Barbara Herrnstein Smith, *Poetic Closure: How Poems End* (Chicago: University of Chicago Press,1968), 74.

died. They will say *yiɔ ɖai,* meaning "it has been cut," to signify the end of a temporal process, such as a song, or when a stream ceases to flow. They might also say *ka ilɛ,* meaning "it is enough" or "it is well," or *bo ro 'ɖe,* meaning "we have finished eating (or consuming) it."

Taking a clue from this kind of indigenous discourse, we may distribute the constituent segments of "Ɔwere ame bɔi" into patterns of open and closed gestures. This allows us to observe another aspect of the relationship between verbal and musical meaning. Figure 5.4 sets out this information, using an arbitrary scale from 1 to 3 to represent degrees of closure or openness (O-1 is most open, O-2 less so, and O-3 least so). Each phrase of text and each corresponding phrase of music is labeled "open" or "closed" and assigned a possible weight. Obviously, the degree of closure is sometimes determined contextually, so that even a phrase as closed as the first line of the poem may appear to be open if we attend to its initiating function—we expect something to follow. There is thus some subjectivity in the assigning of weights. We may nevertheless observe several interesting contradictions between the patterning of language and of music. For example, while phrase 10 is musically without rival in its degree of closure in the song, the text retains an element of openness. The cumulative *Ayee! Ayee! Ayee!* gains in rhetorical force while at the same time leaving unresolved this particular response to tragedy. Repetition provides emphasis and implies musical closure, but what is emphasized here is the openness of the text—a declaration, in effect, that the question posed in the text is ultimately unanswerable. Conversely, phrase 1, which is firmly closed

| Phrase | Musical sense | Poetic sense |
| --- | --- | --- |
| 1 | O-1 | C-2 |
| 2 | C-2 | C-2 |
| 3 | C-2 | C-2 |
| 4 | C-2 | C-2 |
| 5 | O-2 | O-3 |
| 6 | O-3 | O-3 |
| 7 | O-1 | C-2 |
| 8 | C-2 | C-3 |
| 9 | O-1 | C-2 |
| 10 | C-3 | O-3 |

Figure 5.4 Degrees of closure within
"Ɔwere ame bɔi."

syntactically, is musically open, and requires an answering phrase (phrase 2). Thus, the succession of phrases 1 and 2 as "question" (open) and "answer" (closed) produces a resultant profile that is "closed." These conflicting tendencies speak to the nature of the relationship between word and tone; they suggest an unsettled relationship as the condition of song.

If a little lament like this can raise such interesting interpretive issues, and if by implication the scores of other Akpafu laments and dirges, the hundreds of songs by their Northern Ewe neighbors, or the tens of thousands of songs produced by other African groups are similarly engaging, then it is difficult— once again—to see why anyone would belittle African melodic achievement.

**An Afrobeat song by Fela: "Shuffering and Shmiling."** First recorded in 1978, "Suffering and Smiling" is Fela Anikulapo Kuti's biting critique of the adoption of foreign religions by modern Africans. Serious fun is made of Africans as Anglicans, Catholics, and Muslims. His strategy is to contrast the lives of archbishop, pope, and imam with the lives of their many African followers, and to remind us that the archbishop in London, the pope in Rome, and the imam in Mecca are all busy enjoying themselves in their various locations while their unthinking followers on the African continent face all kinds of problems. And yet Africans smile even as they suffer.

As social critique, Fela's music is well understood thanks to writings by Veal, Olaniyan, and Olorunyomi,[30] so that aspect of his work does not need to be addressed here. My interest is in one aspect of his artistry, namely, his melodic imagination. Although we know him as composer, performer, band leader, cultural icon, and inventor of Afrobeat, we know him less comprehensively as a purely musical innovator. And yet there are special shapes to his choice and arrangements of harmonies, the rhythms of phrase succession, and the trajectories of his melodies. And voice lies at the heart of Fela's message. By "voice," I mean not just the peculiar grain of Fela's voice but the very idea of voice as an embodiment of a complex subjectivity. Even though his recordings are noted for extended periods of improvised instrumental playing (the almost-fourteen-minute-long recorded performance of "Lady," for example, begins with six minutes of funky instrumental playing), his melodic impulses are strongly vocal in origin. A range of melodic effects, from simple two-note punctuations to long phrases of original intoning, as well as pretend-singing, suggests that attention to Fela as melodist might enhance appreciation of his art.

---

30. Michael Veal, *Fela: The Life and Times of an African Musical Icon* (Philadelphia: Temple University Press, 2000); Tejumola Olaniyan, *Arrest the Music!*; and Sola Olorunyomi, *Afrobeat!: Fela and the Imagined Continent* (Trenton, NJ: Africa World Press; Ibadan, Nigeria: Copublished with Institute Français de Recherche en Afrique, University of Ibadan, 2003).

The single most important pitch resource for Fela is the anhemitonic pentatonic scale. He uses other scales, of course, including elements of diatonicism
borrowed from the hymn tradition, and modal elements from funk and jazz.
But within this pluralistic pitch environment, the pentatonic sound appears
frequently and prominently. Sometimes it is heard as a complete set, sometimes in fragmentation; the pentatonic also admits interferences from other
scales. For a keyboard player, the pentatonic is readily available as the black
keys of a piano. Fela clearly availed himself of this resource and inserted pen-
tatonically based interludes into many of his performances. Most interesting
is the fact that the pentatonic is also deeply associated with African traditional
music, and although Fela most likely got his pentatonic from the keyboard, its
ancient qualities may have reinforced his fascination with it. The meeting of
an old African pitch construct and a nearly identical construct available on an
instrument brought by Europeans to Africa is a striking coincidence. For Fela,
the pentatonic represents a kind of double authenticity.

Fela's narrative in "Shuffering and Shmiling" unfolds through a combination of spoken and sung phrases, including some that lie in between. Varieties
of repetition are of the essence here, and there is an uncanny play of temporalities to accompany Fela's delivery of his central message against foreign religions (but not, on this occasion, for indigenous religion). The song starts with
an instrumental groove that serves as an invitation. Fela introduces a series
of punctuations: *mmm, eee, waaa, ooh*, and so on. These nonlexical elements
announce his presence through the unmistakable timbre of his voice; they also
reinforce the idea that this is a music event rather than a speech event. Fela
then tells his fellow Africans to "please listen to me as Africans," while "non-
Africans" are told to "listen to me with open minds." This spoken injunction
is followed by incipient song in pentatonic mode: "Suffer, suffer for world, na
your fault be that." Again, the communication of this theme is enhanced by
percussive sounds made by the voice: *atsu, atsu, oh, ahaa*, and so on. The musical texture fully activated, and Fela having captured his listeners' attention, he
tells them to focus their minds on "any goddam church, any goddam mosque,
any goddam celestical, including seraphim and cherubim," the last perhaps
the most charismatic church in Nigeria in the 1970s.[31] From here on, Fela
assigns an unchanging response, "Amen," to his chorus of girls as he advances
his critique. He explains the ridiculousness of the Christians' message that one
should suffer on earth in preparation for enjoyment in heaven and reminds
people of how the archbishop, pope, and imam are enjoying themselves.

31. See John Peel, *Religious Encounter and the Making of the Yoruba* (Bloomington: Indiana
University Press, 2000), for an account of the historical background to the religious politics that Fela critiques.

All of this is delivered in melodic fragments that never stray from the pentatonic collection. He even caricatures the language and modes of praying associated with those religions, employing a strategic gibberish (Latin and Arabic) that is at once amusing and blasphemous.

Fela continues in song by contrasting the enjoyable life of the foreigners with the everyday suffering of his people. They suffer in their houses, in overloaded buses, and at work; they lack water and power in their homes; they are constantly being harassed by the police and army; they receive queries from their superiors at work. These messages are subjected to repetition. The song finishes in an extended instrumental mode, again using pentatonic elements but incorporating allusions to church-hymn harmonies and big band sounds at the very end.

Although the spoken word and its semantic meanings are central to Fela's "Shuffering and Shmiling," the melodic imagination on display here is fundamentally tone derived, not word derived. The snippets of melody heard are, as we have seen, wedded to the pentatonic scale. Rhythmically, Fela sometimes indigenizes the English language by adding extra syllables ("pope" becomes a two-syllable word, *popu*; "imam" a three-syllable word, *imamu*; and so on). He also sometimes incorporates a disproportionately large number of syllables into a small melodic space—a sign that the purely musical impulse is dominant. The pentatonic core thus supports various forms of vocalization, traversing the entire continuum from speech (or unformed song) to fully formed song. Note that the pentatonic sound field is not confined to the sung portions of "Shuffering and Shmiling" but extends to the instrumental portions as well, especially to the bits of keyboard invention that Fela invites us to listen to for what he calls a "secret."

It is easy to get caught up in Fela's postcolonial discourse, nod in positive agreement with his critique of foreign religions, and overlook or underappreciate the artistry on the ground that shapes a variety of enunciations. In a sense, that is precisely what a successful artwork does: it foregrounds the message while hiding the means. The critic's task, however, is to illuminate the conditions of possibility for the work, and it is my contention that the melodic impulse expressed through various forms of vocalization within a pentatonic territory is especially rife in "Suffering and Shmiling," a thoroughly engaging and entertaining song by one of Africa's most notorious musicians.[32]

**A gonje (one-stringed fiddle) performance.** A rich performance tradition widespread in West Africa but also found in Ethiopia, Sudan, Libya, Eritrea,

32. For engaging readings of Fela's songs, see Olaniyan, *Arrest the Music!*. Bode Omojola's *Yorùbá Music in the Twentieth Century* includes a detailed study of Fela's song "Zombie," 177–188.

and elsewhere is the one-stringed fiddle tradition. In West Africa, the instrument is known by a variety of regional names (*gonje* being one of the most common), and it is associated with several ethnic groups in Burkina Faso, Cameroon, Chad, the Gambia, Ghana, Mali, Niger, Nigeria, and elsewhere. Gonje performance is an excellent site for observing the exercise of the melodic imagination. Endowed with the ability to speak, stammer, and sing, the gonje functions in a variety of musical roles, sometimes leading, sometimes taking a back seat.[33] We have space here for a single performance.[34]

Mr. Akurugu, a Kusasi Muslim from the North East of Ghana, is praising a paying patron in song. He sings in the Kusasi language but occasionally incorporates words and phrases from another language, Twi. He accompanies himself on the gonje not by playing a separate accompaniment pattern but by replicating the sung melody. It is a moot point whether the instrumental melody or its vocalized parallel should have conceptual priority, for the evident outcome is one of considered unanimity. The basic mode of delivery is free and declamatory (speech mode), and this characterizes the performance as a whole. At one point (4' 32")), however, the rhythm and mode of address change, and there seems to be a drop in stylistic register from the decidedly high style in which the praise song began to a lower, more popular style. A will to iconicity may be sensed in the intended sameness of vocal and instrumental melody and the material discrepancies that unavoidably attend the actual execution.

The performer's intention is to play and sing the same melody; hand and mouth should agree. But this is not as simple as it sounds, especially if the performer is making up some of these praises as he goes along. Mr. Akurugu has to decide in advance what to say (including which conventional phrase to use), then sing and play it at the same time. He needs, in other words, to don his iconic caps to achieve agreement. Singing and playing that which is being composed in the moment demands an acute futuristic sense. There is no question that Mr. Akurugu possesses plenty of it. The outcome of his quick thinking is a series of indistinct unisons (*unscharfe unisono*, Adorno would call them in Mahler[35]) in which intention and realization align imperfectly, giving us a more potent view—an aural view, so to speak—of the very nature of oneness.

33. The definitive study is Jacqueline Djedje, *Fiddling in West Africa: Touching the Spirit in Fulbe, Hausa, and Dagbamba Cultures* (Bloomington: Indiana University Press, 2008). Equally valuable is the companion songbook, *Fiddling in West Africa (1950s-1990s): The Songbook* (Los Angeles: UCLA Ethnomusicology Publications, 2008).

34. CD, *Ghana: Music of the Northern Tribes* (New York: Lyrichord, 1976), track 4.

35. Adorno, *Mahler*, 62.

Near-alignments between what is played and what is sung may be heard in other performance traditions, but the view of synchronicity that they afford differs according to the nature of the instrument. Singing to the accompaniment of fixed-pitch instruments like xylophones and mbiras places the onus on singers to adjust their tunings as appropriate. With the gonje, however, there is some room for mutual accommodation. The paradoxical result is a continual and intentional "deficit" on the most microlevel of the ensemble resultant sounds. Such ostensible discrepancies, however, are more usefully thought of as expanded unisons to privilege fixed intentions over fluctuating realizations. Widespread throughout Africa, expanded unisons are a vital source of aesthetic fulfillment in melodic expression.

**A Dan woman's lament**. This is a captivating recording of a woman of the Dan ethnic group lamenting the passing of her husband.[36] In this unrestrained and presumably heartfelt performance, she allows the intrinsic music of spoken language to lead the way. Her delivery incorporates song words (like *buoo*) and interjectory particles (like *oo*) from time to time to heighten the expression. The outcome is a lament that assumes an overall shape of a constellation of melodic fragments. Inevitably, perhaps, a pentatonic substrate constrains her choice of pitches. No single archetype mediates the logic of large-scale form; rather, form emerges gradually from an accumulation of grief-bearing sentiments delivered in uneven segments. There are several moments of intensity, some achieved by sheer volume, some by the accumulation of repeated fragments, and some by the depth of verbal expression. We listen and mourn with the Dan woman, but this is not communal song that anyone can join in. We may recognize melodic snippets here and there from songs we know already, but the singer is not issuing an invitation for collective vocal action. These are *her* sentiments about death, about the particular death of her husband, and although they invoke shared or remembered song, they represent an unduplicated utterance.

Among the techniques that guide the Dan woman's melodic expression is an opposition between occasional long notes and frequent short, syllable-based notes, as well as repeated use of song words to achieve moments of respite. This assembly of fragments has its high and low points, but just as there is no overall governing melodic archetype, so there is no choreographed trajectory. Rather, the song is an accumulation of moments—some are short while others are long, some help to mark time while others advance the emotional narrative, and some are hurried and directional while others meander and kill time.

---

36. CD, *Africa: The Dan* (recorded by Hugo Zemp), track 3, "Solo Song of a Woman."

**Interlocking melodies in xylophone performance**. The melodic imagination displayed on the African xylophone grows in part from "invitations" issued by the instrument itself. Slabs over resonators arranged in ascending or descending order provide the conditions of possibility for a network of creative actions. These include the basic striking action, which confers on the xylophone aesthetic a percussive aura. Striking a note at a time produces a digitalized texture and gives us a view of the melo-rhythmic dimension of the xylophonist's art. Xylophones of limited range suggest an isomorphism with the speaking voice, while those with a huge range accentuate fundamental differences between the human voice and man-made instrument. Xylophone timbres may also provide another view of the indistinct unisons and octaves we mentioned in connection with the gonje, adding another dimension to our appreciation of equivalence. The xylophone is not just a melodic instrument; when played with multiple players, or even by a single skilled player, the music displays a contrapuntal essence. Xylophone counterpoint is expressed either in compound melody (when played by one player) or in the interlocking of melodies (when played by several players on a single, large instrument).

The procedure that animates interlocking melody is one of the supreme instances of contrapuntal thinking in African music. The hands of highly skilled xylophonists (like Kakraba Lobi and Bernard Woma from Ghana) do not function independently. The left hand knows what the right hand is doing at every moment, and vice versa. Similarly, when six Baganda men sit in threes across from each other behind a giant *amadinda* xylophone and make music, their individual parts are never conceptualized as separate or autonomous; on the contrary, they are connected through interlock. Although it has been suggested that *amadinda* xylophone players are not beholden to a single, gross pulse and that individual players possess individual beats, it is difficult to see how this can be practically possible. How do two players playing on the same instrument ensure that their ostensibly separate and independent beats do not coincide? Only keen awareness of the other's temporal constraints, it would seem, can assure that the desired outcome of an irreducible multiplicity—if that indeed is what it is—does not collapse into a unanimity. There is, then, a level of dependence among players on some level. Indeed, the very idea of interlocking implies that performers enter into each other's spaces and do so with importunity. With a few exceptions, African ensembles are not sites for the display of willful autonomy; on the contrary, ensemble performance is normally coordinated by a third factor. Each individual player (or singer) carries a conception of the full ensemble sound in his head; although he produces only his part, he nevertheless *knows* that it is contributing to a whole that is known in advance. What a beautiful idea for making music together! It further suggests that a polyphonic or harmonic imagination is basic to music making. In approaching a piece of xylophone performance, be it from Eastern Nigeria, Mozambique, Burkina Faso, or Gambia, we should attend to the *interdependence* of parts and admire the manifest as a token of the hidden.

**Melodic archetypes**. African musicians do not normally pluck new melodies out of thin air; rather, they typically rely on habits of music making and on tried-and-true methods for shaping utterances. Acts of composition are therefore acts of repetition. In a number of traditions, melody is built from schemata or archetypes, basic pitch shapes that are given a variety of verbal, rhythmic, and expressive forms. The funeral chants of the Senufo are built on a stable pitch structure to enable delivery of verbal content: an archetype, Bb3-C4-Eb4-F4-Bb4-Eb5, spanning an octave and a half.[37] The call to prayer sung to assemble devoted worshippers in Muslim communities is often based on a skeleton melody that is then elaborated and embellished.[38] A beautiful rendition of "Kalefa ba" by M'Bady and Diaryatou Kouyaté (kora and voice) relies on a recurring pitch framework anchored by notes that belong to the pentatonic collection. The constancy of the framework guarantees the coherence of the structure without muting departures necessitated by an evolving verbal content.[39] In a cognate tradition, the singing of "Lambango" by Mariatu Kuyateh relies on a descending archetype that constrains melodic utterance.[40] Indeed, many performances of praise, histories, and genealogies in the tradition of griots are made possible by tunes that lie beneath the surface and are used as vehicles for the delivery of verbal content.

It comes as a surprise, therefore, to encounter A. M. Jones's verdict that "Africans rarely, if ever, conceive of melodies in the form of abstract music."[41] On the contrary, abstractions in the form of archetypes, schemata, or orienting contours occur in numerous traditions. It may be that traditional musicians are reticent about *talking* at an abstract level about music, but abstractions are

37. CD, *Sénoufo: Musiques des funerailles fodonon* (France: Chant du monde/Harmonia Mundi, 1994).

38. Ready examples are available on the CD accompanying *Africa: The Garland Encyclopedia of World Music*, track 4, "Vai Call to Prayer," and on the CD, *Spirit of African Sanctus: The Original Recordings by David Fanshawe (1969–73)* (Wotton-under-Edge, England: Saydisc, 1991), track 2, "Call to Prayer."

39. CD, *Introduction aux musiques africaines* by Monique Brandilly, track 19, "Kalefa ba."

40. CD, Jeff Todd Titon, ed., *Worlds of Music: An Introduction to the Music of the World's Peoples*, CD 2, track 15, "Lambango."

41. A. M. Jones, *African Music in Northern Rhodesia*, 11.

**Example 5.9** Melodic archetype with four realizations (Northern Ewe).

deployed many times a day in individual cultures. The knowledge is inscribed in the doing; it is an enabling knowledge, not one that is separately packaged for consumption as an ethno-discourse. Indeed, in situations of error, such knowledge is readily called upon.

Limitations of space do not allow for extensive demonstration of the shaping role of archetypes in African melodic expression, but we might mention a basic melodic contour found in certain Northern Ewe melodies and shown in the top layer (a) of Example 5.9.[42] The melodies it supports span a gamut of styles from the traditional through the neotraditional to the popular. The use of the archetype thus cuts across stylistic boundaries.

The archetype is made up of the following pitch sequence: G4-A4-G4-F4-E4-F4-E4. The opening pitch (G4) is elaborated by neighbor-note motion (G4-A4-G4) and then descends through a third (G4-F4-E4) to a terminal pitch (E4). This last is also subject to a complementary prolongation (E4-F4-E4). Calling it an archetype recognizes a level of abstraction and the possibility for diversity in realization. The initial G-A progression, for example, may be elaborated into something like **G4**-C5-B4-A4-B4-G4-**A4** (see level c in Example 5.9); the third descent in the middle of the archetype (G4-F4-E4) may be extended to a fourth, fifth, or sixth and subjected to internal decoration; and elements within the final E4-F4-E4 neighbor prolongation may themselves be subject to further prolongation. Archetypes are like deep songs that enable a variety of surface compositional utterances.

---

42. For a fuller discussion, see my "Variation Procedures in Northern Ewe Song." See also Jones's article, "Swahili Epic Poetry: A Musical Study," *African Music* 5 (1975/1976): 105–129, for a detailed study of an extended epic whose melody is built on "little tunes" that are subjected to a range of variations.

**Example 5.10**  Four Northern Ewe melodies (cf. Example 5.9).

The remaining layers in Example 5.9 display four tunes that reproduce the archetype (three of them may be heard at Web Example 5.7 ◐). Start by singing through the four songs (labeled b, c, d, and e in Example 5.10). (They are presented here without words to keep the focus on pitch and rhythm.) Then compare each song to its corresponding reduction in Example 5.9 (also labeled b, c, d, and e) and then to the archetype. Finally, compare the songs to each other. It will be immediately apparent that they all belong to a tune family. This mode of composition is widespread in world cultures, but it is not readily associated with songs using tone languages because of the constraining influence that speech tones are thought to exert on musical melody. The possibility exposed here, however, is that tone is not always a determining influence on tune, and that originary musical elements in the form of archetypes also exist.

As for the supposed absence of abstraction in African thought, this demonstration should once again call it into question.[43]

## CONCLUSION

The songs discussed in this chapter were chosen to demonstrate some of the ways in which the African melodic imagination has been exercised in rich and thoughtful ways. I began by postulating the voice as the origin of all melody. With the voice comes presence, a specifically human presence, and with human presence comes the possibility of meaning, be it the intended meaning of a singer or player or the reconstructed meanings supplied by thoughtful listeners. We have seen that the melodic imagination is expressed in a variety of forms, ranging from the deliberately restricted (but no less ingenious) universe of children's game songs to the elaborate and ornate declamatory singing of praise songs, laments, and dirges. Repetition and variation are key techniques in the manipulation of a variety of pitch collections. Conventions of beginning and ending are equally significant, and they are regularly deployed by songsmiths. Language as sound and sense is key to African melodic expression, as we have seen in instances of syllabic articulation, speech-tone influence on melody, instrumental melodies with vocal origins, or creative violations of norms. Ideas about melody will continue to engage us in subsequent discussion (especially of polyphony in chapter 7), but I hope that this chapter begins to dispel misplaced skepticism about African melody and to provide some grounds for (re)valuing this primal domain of African creativity.

43. For a related discussion framed in terms of Schenkerian applications to non-Western music (rather than the use of archetypes as here), see Jonathan Stock, "The Application of Schenkerian Analysis to Ethnomusicology: Problems and Possibilities," *Music Analysis* 12 (1993): 215–240.

# 6

# The Formal Imagination

Form in African music is the trace produced by a network of intended sonic actions. Suppose I start by throwing you a sung phrase, you receive it, and then together we continue until the end. Our actions leave traces, a cumulative profile. Look closely at the profile and you will see that it tells a story. How did I begin? Directly, with an exclamation, or gradually, enigmatically, or in an unassuming manner? How did you catch my song? Firmly and enthusiastically, hesitantly, or surreptitiously? Did you use my "words," or did you devise your own? And how did we continue? Did we sing the same pitches, or different but complementary ones? Did the song ever fall, or did it stand all the time? How did we end? Suddenly, without warning, or with prolonged closure? Did we actually end, or did we merely stop? The collective answers to these actions and reactions promote an understanding of what musicologists call *form*. An arrangement of the elements of a composition, form is structure and rhetoric. It is an emergent quality, complex and multivalent; it is produced with each act of singing, drumming, and dancing.

Unraveling form in African vocal and instrumental music demands that we pay attention to two things: motivation and the material means of expression. First, as with other modes of communication in traditional society, a communal ethos typically constrains many forms of African musical and literary expression. Forms arise in response to the imperatives and exigencies of daily living, and they reflect the same impeccable logic that generations of Africans have relied upon in ordering those aspects of their lives that require song, art, and dance. To understand a community's musical forms, it is helpful to know something about the nature of the human interactions within that community, the aesthetic goals of its composers, and the expectations of performers and listeners. Second, material forms vary according to the demands of a given situation. Since most traditional African cultures are primary oral cultures, the single most important goal in intelligently designing musical form is to ensure comprehensibility. Forms are designated for re-enactment; they serve as means to ends rather than ends in and of themselves. They are not usually conceived as one-off occurrences designed to impress on the one occasion. Although there are by now pockets of musical activity in Africa that draw as much on written as on oral traditions, the essence of African form is a reproduction of the natural beauties and efficacies of oral expression and communication. African musical forms are designed to be accessible and to communicate readily, not to cultivate obscurantism. This does not mean that they are simple; indeed, some forms (like Burundian *Akazehe,* which we touched upon in the last chapter) are the products of mind-bending games, while others (like the mathematically based forms and games practiced in visual, tactile, and oral art in Zambia) code complexity for those drawn to such puzzles.[1] The will to communication mediates aesthetic motivation rather than curbing it. While outward traces of some African forms may seem simple, they are never simplistic.

Understood as an outcome rather than an input, form conveys an essential aspect of African music. Over the generations, African musicians have invented or cultivated a variety of forms, but only a few of these have been properly acknowledged, and fewer still have engendered the close analytical study that they deserve.[2] Why is there relatively little discussion of form in African music? There are at least two related reasons. First, because form is an emergent quality that derives from a combination of dimensional behaviors, it has proven intractable to analysis. Unlike *rhythm*, for example, which can be defined in terms of meter, beat, accents, and periodicity, *form* appears to be more diffuse; it is an elusive "parameter." Second, and as often noted in these pages, European scripts for African musicians give more credence to other parameters. Rhythm (again) and virtuosity tend to be valued because they are viscerally tangible or "hot," while the exercise of a subtle formal imagination tends to be undervalued. "Form" indeed was one of the things that William Ward, writing as far back as 1927, hoped that Africans would learn from Europe. There is apparently no African equivalent to the "paper forms" like sonata, minuet and trio, and rondo that are often paraded as monuments to Europe's musico-intellectual triumphs in the common practice period. Few researchers have been combing African expressive practices for signs of nuanced formal thinking.

1. See Kubik, *Theory of African Music*, vol. 2, 275–322.

2. Among valuable exceptions, see Peter Cooke, "Uganda," in *Grove Music Online*, which includes a section on form; see also the entire 2012 issue of the *Journal of the Association of Nigerian Musicologists* (ed. Christian Onyeiji), which is devoted to form. The term *form* also appears as an obligatory category in surveys by Hornbostel, "African Negro Music," 38–40; Lazarus Ekwueme, "African-Music Retentions in the New World," *Black Perspective in Music* 2, no. 2 (1974), 135–136; and Meki Nzewi, "Acquiring Knowledge of the Musical Arts in Traditional Society," 28–30.

These views need to be reconsidered and, where appropriate, jettisoned because they either stem from inappropriate comparisons or are simply deaf to the wealth of imagination displayed in numerous African expressive forms. But rather than embark on yet another debunking exercise in this context, let me display some of Africa's formal wares for direct contemplation and admiration.

## VARIETIES OF FORM: A SAMPLING

I often begin my undergraduate survey course on African music with a lecture simply called "Varieties of African Music." In preparation, I ask students to listen to some twenty-six brief excerpts of African music of different generic and geocultural origins and to record their reactions to how these might fit in with their previously held beliefs about "African music." This exercise is meant to alert them to the continent's sheer size and the incredible diversity of its musical practices. I try to dissuade students from thinking that the one or two cultures they might have been exposed to previously (typically, popular music like soukouss, rumba, hiplife, highlife or bikutsi, or jembe drumming from Senegal; Ghanaian drumming; Shona mbira playing; or performances by some Malian superstar or other) speak for the whole of Africa. I also encourage them to retain this sense of diversity as a kind of horizon against which they can observe the necessarily limited number of practices that a survey course can focus on. The twenty-six excerpts are listed in Figure 6.1.[3]

"Form" as a technical designation makes only a passing appearance in this opening lecture, but insofar as a concern with form is, in a fundamental sense, a concern with the whole of music, the list in Figure 6.1 is as good a place to begin thinking about form as any other. Granted, these are excerpts from longer performances, so we would need the evidence of complete performances to establish the definitive trace of each composition. Nevertheless, animating features and shaping impulses are not only amply but also oftentimes vividly illustrated in them. What follows is a brisk tour, with special attention to those features that might enhance the listener's appreciation of form.

From the Bibayak Pygmy of Gabon comes a dense, polyphonic web of sound featuring voices and drums (excerpt 1). The motion is perpetual, lacking large-scale trajectory and admitting only of microfluctuations in the intensity of the

3. For full discographical information, please see the discography at the end of the book.

| | Country/ethnic group | Recording |
|---|---|---|
| 1 | Gabon, Bibayak Pygmy | CD, *Gabon: Music of the Bibyak Pygmies*, track 3 |
| 2 | Uganda, Buganda. Akadinda xylophone, six players | CD, *Garland Encyclopedia of World Music: Africa*, track 14 |
| 3 | South Africa. Ladysmith Black Mambazo, "Pauline' | CD, *The Best of Ladysmith Black Mambazo*, track 14 |
| 4 | Central African Republic, Banda-Linda. Horn ensemble | CD, *Musics and musicians of the world: Central African Republic*, track 8 |
| 5 | Nigeria. African art music. *Talking Drums* by Joshua Uzoigwe | CD, *Senku: Piano Music by Composers of African Descent*, track 3 |
| 6 | Ghana. Southern Ewe. Agbadza dance | CD, *Ghana: Rhythms of the People*, track 2 |
| 7 | Guinea Bissau. Kora, "Lambango" | CD, *Jali Kunda: Griots of West Africa and Beyond*, track 10 |
| 8 | Benin, Yoruba. Dundun or hour-glass ensemble | CD, *Yoruba Drums from Benin*, West Africa, track 12 |
| 9 | Cote d'Ivoire, Baule. Little girls' sung games | CD, *Musics and Musicians of the World: Cote d'Ivoire*, track 7 |
| 10 | Malawi | CD, *From Lake Malawi to the Zambezi*, track 1 |
| 11 | Ghana, Music of the Dagbamba. One-stringed bowed fiddle ("Gonje") | CD, *Ghana: Rhythms of the People*, track 7 |
| 12 | Nigeria. Fela Anikulapo Kuti, "Lady", Afrobeat | CD, *The Best of Fela Kuti*, track 1 |
| 13 | Angola. Vibrating leaf | CD, Kubik, *Theory of African Music*, track 34 |
| 14 | Liberia, Vai. Arabic call to prayer | CD, *Garland Encyclopedia of World Music: Africa*, track 4 |
| 15 | Uganda, Nyoro. Likembe or mbira, one-manual, box-resonated | CD, *Music of Africa Series 28. Musical Instruments 2. Reeds (Mbira)*, track 1 |
| 16 | Gabon. Arrangement of folk song | CD *Lambarena*, track 10. |
| 17 | Democratic Republic of Congo. Kanyoka, Southern Congo. Drum message | CD, *The Music of Africa Series 29, Musical Instruments 3. Drums 1*, track 8 |

Figure 6.1 Twenty-six excerpts from a variety of repertoires for a discussion of form.

|    | Country/ethnic group | Recording |
|----|----------------------|-----------|
| 18 | Ghana. Hiplife | CD, Akyeame, *Nkonson, Nkonson*, track 2, "Mesan aba" |
| 19 | Côte D'Ivoire, Dan. Solo song of a Woman | CD, *Anthology of World Music. Africa: The Dan*, track 3 |
| 20 | Democratic Republic of Congo. Pygmy | CD, *Music of the Rain Forest Pygmies of the Northeast Congo*, track 2 |
| 21 | Ghana. Postal workers canceling stamps | CD, *Worlds of Music, CD 1*, track 13 |
| 22 | Zaire. Popular music. Rumba | CD, *Kékélé*, track 9 |
| 23 | Nigeria. Fújì. "Gbogbo Musulumi Ododo" by Wahabi Arowoshila. Recording | CD, *Yoruba Street Percussion*, track 6 |
| 24 | Sierra Leone. Solo flute | CD, *Sierra Leone, Musiques Traditionelles*, track 3 |
| 25 | Sierra Leone. Mandingo. Young girls singing Christian songs | CD, *Sierra Leone, Musiques Traditionelles*, track 6 |
| 26 | Ghana. Highlife. E. T. Mensah, "You call me Roko." | CD, *African Music: The Glory Years*, track 4. |

**Figure 6.1** (Continued)

overall sound. This is a far cry from an architectural sense of form; rather, the listener is enveloped in a wall of sound very much geared toward the present. A similarly "flat" trajectory is evident in the Baganda akadinda song, "Gganda aluwa" ("Gganga escaped with his life"), which features a single large xylophone with six players (excerpt 2). The interlocking patterns are locked in an ever-present, continuous texture. We are guided not by a single goal-oriented melody but by snippets of melody that now and again come into prominence. While emerging periodicities are more palpable here than they were in the Bibayak Pygmy performance, "Gganda aluwa" is not crafted as an object to be observed in a detached way; rather, it is a network of inviting grooves in which to join. To say that the trajectory is "flat" is not to undermine the excitement generated by the incessant rhythmic activity of these virtuoso musicians; it only denies that a primitive and totally predictable dynamic shape (of the sort favored in European melodies of the nineteenth century) is being enacted here.

Third is the beginning of Ladysmith Black Mambazo's song, "Pauline." Form is based on the narrative inside the English text—the story of Pauline, who has jilted her boyfriend and is being begged by his friends to come back. Sweet melody and ingratiating harmonies shape this narrative musically. Regarding the latter, the singers seem uninterested in venturing far from the tonic, so the tonal trajectory is less concerned with large-scale departure and return than with an accumulation of small-scale progressions featuring local departures and returns. Form-defining change comes from the asymmetrical periodicities imparted by the sung text, which in turn lend a narrative character to the overall shape of the performance.

Fourth is another ensemble piece, this one a sixteen-horn ensemble from the Banda Linda of the Central African Republic. We hear a kaleidoscope of motives, all constrained by an anhemitonic pentatonic scale. Like the akadinda xylophone (excerpt 2) and the Pygmy polyphony (excerpt 1), the essence of the form is a groove that, once activated, remains throughout the performance. We are invited—indeed, compelled—to join in the action, not to observe it in a detached way from a distance.

Next is a solo piano piece by Nigerian composer Joshua Uzoigwe (excerpt 5), which features something of the perpetual motion we have seen in other excerpts. The busy, in-your-face eighth-note motion is shaped from time to time by rising and falling gestures that ostensibly function as a call and response. Periodic returns to the call-and-response gesture confer a rondolike feel on this piece. Excerpt 6 is from the popular polyrhythmic Ewe Agbadza dance, with its continuous, layered texture, over which songs are exchanged. This is dance music, of course, so one of its primary functions is to facilitate movement by means of a danceable, metrically constrained beat. Some word-based signaling is evident in the messages delivered by the lead drummer, and this is the main source of periodicity at the largest structural level in this vigorous dance. Continuity of a different sort is heard in excerpt 7, a kora piece from Guinea Bissau. Here the kora provides a continuous harmonic background over which successive phrases of the song "Lambango" are called and responded to by singers. The unchanging harmony bestows a continuous rather than static quality, and this is offset by the phrase articulation, which seems to do things in twos and fours. Overall form is most explicitly signaled by this accumulation of melodic phrases.

A family of dùndún drums makes an appearance in excerpt 8. Like the agbadza excerpt (excerpt 6), this one features a polyrhythmic texture including a standard-pattern time line played by one of the drums (you'll have to listen closely for this, since the timbres are less distinct than the bell in the agbadza ensemble). The form unfolds at two levels: one is the groovelike continuity of the polyrhythmic texture; the other is the rhythm of "talking" by the lead dùndún. This is form as narrative; indeed, we might compare this kind of instrumental narrative with the vocal narrative of Ladysmith's "Pauline" (excerpt 3).

Next is a Baule children's stone-moving song from the Côte d'Ivoire (excerpt 9). The heavy thumping is the sound of stones landing on the ground before being moved immediately around a circle; this acquires an almost metronomical feel. Then there is the call-and-response pattern of the singing. Each instance of the pattern is repeated, so the form emerges additively as AABBCC. And given that B and C are actually musical variants of A, we might even represent the overall form as a reduplication of the same basic material: AAA'A'A' 'A' '. From Malawi comes a performance by voices, panpipes, and rattle in which the pulse is marked regularly to support a complex play of motives (excerpt 10). This play is geared to the present, and marking that present appears to be more of a priority than carving out neat, future-oriented periods. This complex texture shares a similar in-the-moment formal impulse with the Banda Linda horn orchestra (excerpt 4).

Next is a performance on a one-stringed fiddle accompanied by two voices, a main voice and a responding one (excerpt 11). On display here is a halting rhetoric; the material is delivered in chunks, and some of the individual chunks are repeated. The accumulation of phrases defines the form. Note also the anchoring effect of the refrain phrase ending on E3. Next is an excerpt from Fela's "Lady" (excerpt 12), and it starts at the tail end of the extended instrumental "introduction" and continues into Fela's actual singing of two phrases. This danceable style features a harmonic groove (tinged with the minor mode) over which Fela delivers his song message within a (mainly) pentatonic framework. As in other African forms, this one features a basic contrast between things that stay the same (the harmonic ostinato) and things that change (the narrated story of the modern African woman carried in song). Next (excerpt 13) is a fascinating "vibrating leaf" played by a boy from Angola. The entire performance consists of a series of exertions, some more successful than others, with the whole mapping out a kind of moment form. (We will return to this particular excerpt later in the chapter.)

Sung in Arabic by a Vai from Liberia, excerpt 14 is a typical Muslim call to prayer. This ritual text, delivered in brief fragments, is based on a melodic archetype. The complete call to prayer features several instantiations of the archetype. Here as elsewhere, the "strophic form" accommodates both change and constancy—change comes from the verbal text, while constancy resides in the repeated melody. From the Nyoro ethnic group in Uganda comes this performance (excerpt 15) on an mbira accompanied by the voice. The form is determined by the mbira's ostinato pattern made up of two internal motives. In subsequent repetitions, the voice joins in as if in alignment, but as we have seen in other examples, such alignments are strategically discrepant. At one point (2' 11"), a newish motive interrupts the old ostinato, but the performer quickly returns to the main ostinato. This form, then, features a constant motive as an ostinato, with minor variations entered in the singing. Next (excerpt 16) is an arrangement by Pierre Akendengue of a folk song from Gabon for a larger ensemble. The basic principle here is a call and response, but while the response is fixed (admitting a slight change at the start of each verse), the call is far more adventurous verbally and melodically.

The talking drum demonstration in excerpt 17 is not a performance in the strict sense, so the question of form arises only indirectly. The spoken word is heard after each drummed word, in effect decoding what has just been said on the drum. In an actual "performance" (i.e., the delivery of a message to, say, clansmen in the next village), the spoken explanation would not be necessary; competent hearers can decode the message from the drumming alone. As regards form, a drummed message is in the vein of a poetical narrative. Drums deliver the tonal and rhythmic values of a verbal message, interspersing these with punctuating beats and other attention-inducing signals. The message as a whole thus acquires a periodic feel, but this is a far cry from the dance-based periodicities we heard in Agbadza (excerpt 6) or in Fela's "Lady" (excerpt 12). Excerpt 18 is a highlife song by the Ghanaian group Nkonson Nkonson. Titled "Mesan aba" ("I will come again"), it alternates sweet, old-style highlife with portions of (modern) rap. An ostinato provides the basic groove on which various sung portions ride. Next (excerpt 19) is a lament by a Dan woman, which we described in the previous chapter on melody. Notable is a kind of evolving narrative as she crafts a spontaneous response to her husband's death. Verbal motives are introduced and repeated, while song words like *buoo* punctuate the proceeding. The overall succession follows an unpredictable pattern, however; no periodic structure governs phrase succession. This is vintage additive form not unlike that which we saw in Ladysmith's "Paulina." Following is a leaf-carrying song sung by the Mbuti Pygmies (excerpt 20). We encounter the same dense, polyphonic sound that we heard in excerpt 1. Here, however, it is interspersed with a contrasting solo voice. The form is marked by a threefold choral incantation followed by the first "solo," then another threefold incantation followed by a spoken solo, and yet again with a threefold statement.

Excerpt 21 is a famous recording of postal workers canceling stamps at the University of Ghana Post Office. The protagonist whistles a tune while doing his job, using the ink pad to provide timbral contrast. Another worker whistles along so that the tune is given a multipart coloration. The rhythmic texture is akin to highlife, with its prominent articulations on the offbeats of beats 2, 3, and 4 in 4/4 meter. The meter is fixed, as one often finds in urban dance genres. The whistled song is in AABA or bar form, and it is heard a total of four times. The first, third, and fourth renditions include another whistled part, the third is "solo." The recording breaks off just as the whistlers introduce another tune over the ongoing stamp-canceling rhythmic texture. The formal principle is similar to what we saw in Agbadza (excerpt 6): a fixed, rhythmic texture allows songs to be exchanged over it. Presumably, the performers stop when there are no more envelopes with stamps to be cancelled.

Excerpt 22 is rumba dance music from Zaire. As in the Fela excerpt (excerpt 12), the form is driven by a repeating harmonic progression, which establishes a danceable groove. This groove gains profile from a catchy melody designed to be remembered after only a few hearings. Featured in excerpt 23 is an example of Nigerian Fújì, a genre with strong roots in Muslim culture and expression. Employing a mode of vocal delivery midway between speech and song, the performance displays an accumulative form. A dùndún player comments on, as well as punctuates, the proceedings. Excerpt 24 features a solo flute performance from Sierra Leone. Fundamental to formal articulation here is the actual production of the sound by the flute in a manner that suggests that the mode of production matters perhaps more than the resulting trace. Of course, whether a sound is produced or not, some sort of trace is evident, so strictly speaking, production and trace are jointly indispensable. But as in the vibrating leaf aesthetic encountered in excerpt 13, the physical effort required to produce sound seems to deflect attention from an architectural profile of form. The trace is simply an accumulation of exertions, a kind of moment form. Excerpt 25 is an instance of Christian hymn singing by two girls from Sierra Leone. An initial phrase, "He lives, he lives, Christ Jesus lives today," is sung by both girls. Next is a contrasting phrase, "He walks with me and talks with me along life's narrow way." Following is a phrase that begins like the first but continues differently, ending on an expectant note: "He lives, he lives, salvation to impart." Then, as if reaching a denouement, the song ends with a broad gesture, enacting a high point on the second of the "lives" and drawing the utterance to a resoundingly obvious close: "You ask me how I know he lives, He lives within my heart." The approach to closure in this hymn is fundamentally antithetical to closure in traditional African music. Everything is managed and ordered. After the climax comes the collapse, the slowing down, the dropping of register, and the stepwise path to the closing tonic note. The resulting melodic shape seems a bit contrived in comparison with those we have seen in the excerpts from traditional repertories. These hymns, imposed as part of Christian colonization of African consciousness, support different structural and expressive priorities from many of the indigenous melodies we have heard. Finally, excerpt 26 is an instance of highlife music. Many classic highlife songs by E. T. Mensah and others take after American swing-band arrangements from the 1940s and 1950s. This one begins with a "head," which returns at the end to complete the frame. In between are several iterations of the main tune, showcasing different instruments, as well as different improvisatory styles. The form may be described as strophic insofar as it features a tune with several variations, but the accumulation of variations together with the return of the opening confer an overall narrative shape.

This brisk survey has revealed several key features of form in African music. The temporal feel, we have learned, is always a factor; it may be slow or fast, animated or relaxed, present oriented or future oriented. The overall trajectory may be flat or shaped by varying intensities. Form may be texturally continuous or broken. Sometimes, small worlds are concatenated to make the bigger form. Can there be any question, on listening to these twenty-six excerpts, that the formal imagination in African music is deserving of admiration and study?

The terms employed in the foregoing description include a variety of formal strategies: narrative, strophic, archetype, discontinuity, accretion of small worlds, continuous or broken texture. Since it is obviously not possible to analyze every one of the formal impulses noted here, I have selected five that are widespread and that may be held up paradigmatically as among the basic schemata or formal archetypes in African music.

## FIVE PRINCIPLES OF FORM

The first and most obvious archetype embodies an interactive, at-least-two philosophy that lies at the heart of many expressive forms. It grows out of the widespread belief that "I am because we are." Typically designated call and response, this antiphonal gesture is the most fundamental principle of African musical form. It is subject to a variety of idiomatic expressions but is readily recognized as an invitation to communal or complementary action. Its importance stems in part from the fact that it conjoins two functions, an initiating call and a complementary response. Call and response is thus endowed with an intrinsic syntax. A second model derives from an enduring will to variation or will to embellishment that is also widespread and characteristic of African expression. To make music is to *play* with words, pitches, rhythms, and timbres. Playing entails turning things around; the Ewe, for example, talk of putting "style" (*atsiã*) into the performance. This familiar impulse is responsible for the many strophic and paratactic forms found in African music. Third are forms that result from aggregation, from an accretion of units, segments, or "small worlds," without a governing periodicity. Each segment may be notionally incomplete, but the succession as a whole acquires a distinct and coherent profile. The cohabitation of segments within individual compositions often suggests a fourth formal model, an emerging narrative that unfolds as if the entire form were responding to an "and then" imperative. Fifth and finally are forms that seem to live in the moment, forms that celebrate "presentness" and its unpredictable future. Such "moment forms" are common (e.g., in certain genres of Pygmy music) in situations of play or improvisation. These five basic approaches to form may overlap in manner and function, but insofar as each one captures a distinct strategy, they can collectively provide a broad orientation to the African formal imagination.

**Call and response**. Although rooted in a fundamental duality, the technique of call and response subtends a widely divergent, sometimes contradictory set of impulses. I have retained the designation "call and response" here because of its conventional associations, its longevity in African musicology, and its self-evident meaning. However, readers are encouraged to interrogate each usage freshly rather than rely on a presumed transcultural meaning. Although it occurs in both vocal and instrumental music, call and response is more typically and immediately affiliated with singing and associated modes of verbal expression. The call is normally expressed by a solo voice, while the response is entrusted to a group. Through diverse but frequent usage, these roles have acquired certain associations. For example, the call is thought to be marked, while the response is unmarked. Markedness in this case serves to distinguish the nonroutine from the routine, the exceptional from the normative. The call may be long, whereas the response is short (or at least shorter). While the call sometimes allows for improvisation and/or virtuosic display, the response keeps improvisatory urges in check. Promulgators of calls include chiefs, master drummers, mothers of song, and group leaders; response is entrusted to citizens and supporters, beaters of support drums, chorus members, or simply ordinary men and women.

The semantic economies of various African-language usages of call and response compose a lively network of attitudes, values, and ethical imperatives. Examples are too numerous to cite, but here are a few from Siwu and Ewe. Attitudes may be embodied in action words associated with performing. In Siwu, for example, the call may be signaled by the word *dĩ̌*, which means "remove," "take," or "fetch"; *kpẽ̃*, which means "initiate" or "introduce"; or *yɛ*, which means "say" or "speak." The response may be indicated by *truã*, which means "agree" or "respond." For example, *Gɔ ɔmoe kuka ne, maiwo ɔtruã gu 'n* means "When she caught the song, they were not able to agree with her." Agreement encompasses more than the semantic meaning of the text; it is also an indication of the limits set by the physical production of sound. If the call is too high, the chorus may not be able to "agree" with the caller. The word *truã* thus indexes register, tuning, harmony, and verbal meaning.

In Ewe, terms that describe calling and responding are equally indexical of a range of attitudes. *Ehǎ tso* means "the song has ended." A lead singer may instruct the chorus by saying, *Mitsoe!*, meaning "cut it!" or "end it!" The word *tso* carries a charge; it implies decisive and sudden action rather than prolonged closure. At the other end of the form spectrum, *Do ha da* means "propose the song" or "raise the song." The call is a proposition to be discussed, while the response reflects individual reactions mediated by a larger communal imperative. *Wotsɔ ha* means "they took the song," "they lifted the song," or "they carried the song." Response to a call may be described as *wo le ha,* which means "they caught the song"; *wo hɔ ha,* meaning "they received or accepted the song"; or *wo lɔ̃ ha,* meaning "they loved [in the sense of responded to] the song." The principle of call and response is itself referred to as *yɔyɔ kple tɔtɔ* ("calling and responding") or *hadododa kple haxexe* ("sending and catching a song"). A variety of attitudes are thus inscribed in the catch-all expression *call and response.* These rich words are designed to fire the imagination of performers and critics.[4]

A call and its response work together to produce a notional whole. While the surface configuration consists of two components, the underlying conception is unitary. You do not "send" a song without knowing how the message will be received; by the same token, you cannot respond to a call that you do not know already. The conjunction of a call and its response constitutes a single gestalt, a syntactical unit; only by knowing the whole can one perform the part effectively.

The most common textural form of call and response is the solo-chorus arrangement that is used in most traditional societies. We might think of it in terms of a base and its superstructure, the chorus being the base, the solo the superstructure. In light of a ruling communal ethos, the solo-chorus arrangement may sometimes acquire meanings that would seem to undermine some of the hierarchies inscribed in the structural profile. The chorus serves as the foundation and is therefore indispensable, whereas the soloist, who, after all, issues from the chorus (she is one of us), depends on that foundation and may even occasionally be dispensable. From this point of view, the chorus dwarfs the solo in importance. The solo performs its role by variously affirming, extending, amplifying, embellishing, or intensifying something that has been previously or more consequentially—if concisely—stated by the chorus. The opposite scenario is not conceivable, however; the chorus cannot logically take its bearings from the solo because it is structurally prior to it.

This apparent reversal of what solo-chorus might connote may be further understood by considering the soloist's sense of belonging, her psychological and physical dependence on the chorus. She is first a member of the chorus

---

4. For two valuable studies that incorporate indigenous terminology into a theorization of form, see Ruth M. Stone, *Let the Inside Be Sweet: The Interpretation of Music Event Among the Kpelle of Liberia* (Bloomington: Indiana University Press, 1982), and Kwasi Ampene, *Female Song Tradition and the Akan of Ghana.* Ampene's discussion may be said to continue from where Nketia left off in 1949 with the Introduction to his collection of song texts, *Akanfo nnwom bi.*

(the community) *before* she is a soloist. She knows the chorus parts, and indeed sings them with the rest of the group as occasions demand. The chorus members, too, know the solo parts insofar as they understand and anticipate the themes and procedures employed in soloing, but they are obliged to be notionally silent when the soloist is composing in the moment. The success of solo-chorus or call-and-response expression is crucially dependent on this mutual imbrication. It is an interpretive mistake to draw a wedge between the two components, to see the chorus as perfunctory, boring, mundane, or merely accompanimental, and the solo as the higher component. Call and response is the outward manifestation of deep social and ethical norms that recognize the individual's role within a group setting.

None of this is to deny the existence of makeshift hierarchies in the operation of call and response. One person may be chosen as (or earn the right to be designated as) soloist or lead performer, while another's role may be in the chorus. Factors of discrimination include the lineage or kinship, seniority (by age, age set, or status), looks, and, of course, performing ability. It helps to possess a sweet or powerful voice and a "cooked tongue" that enables you to be able to "say" things in song that will move audiences. Sometimes two or more of these factors may coincide within a particular individual, thus enhancing her status as the chosen one; at other times, the criteria may come into conflict, giving rise to tensions within the group.

As for specific configurations of call and response, these require only brief enumeration here since they can be heard in practically all performances of African music, traditional or otherwise. A long call may elicit a short response, as in the Gabon folk song "Lambarena" as arranged by Pierre Akendengue.[5] Call and response may be roughly the same length; in rare cases, the call is considerably shorter than the response.[6] Overlap between call-and-response sections is common. In some instances, the overlap is brief, the equivalent of a syllable, a word, or a few words. The overlap can also be extensive in situations in which the soloist simply has more to say beyond what is sanctioned by the periodic structure.

Less obvious but no less important are single-person performances in which normative call-and-response functions are enacted by one and the same performer. Lullabies are sometimes constructed on this principle. In effect, the call-and-response element is inscribed in the music itself, reflecting the presence of two protagonists, mother and child (or mother and audience). In performance, mother assumes both solo and chorus roles. The material expression

---

5. CD, *Lambarena* (New York: Sony Classical, 1995), track 10, "Ikokou."

6. See CD, *Ouganda: musique des Baganda*, track 9, "Ggw'olidde Nsangi."

of call and response is thus different, but the principle is the same. Some genres exhibit a double soloist, whereby the "same" call is performed by two people. When this is not intended (as sometimes happens when an eager chorus member, moved by a particular song, jumps in to reinforce the soloist's sentiment), the two melodic lines may not agree in all their ornamental details, but they are, strictly speaking, expressions of the same underlying shape.

Intrinsic call-and-response patterning is also found in a number of rhythmic patterns, especially time lines. A pattern may contain two constituent gestures that sound different but are directly complementary. The two gestures are often of unequal duration and may be felt as a question followed by an answer or as an answer followed by a question. The asymmetrical property that some scholars read into certain time lines often emerges from an underlying call-and-response motivation. For example, the standard pattern's seven onsets [2-2-1-2-2-2-1] may be segmented as [2-2-1-2] + [2-2-1], while the kpanlogo or *clave son* pattern [3-3-4-2-4] may be segmented as [3-3-4] + [2-4]. Going by the number of onsets, this makes for a 4 + 3 arrangement for the standard pattern and a 3 + 2 arrangement for the *clave son*. It is the fact of unequal "halves" that has elicited interpretation as a call followed by a response. So although time-line patterns are typically performed on a single instrument (bell), their internal structure inscribes an apparent responsorial element. A similar feature is found in solo songs (or parts of songs) in which an antiphonal gesture is sung by one and the same singer. In short, in addition to its normative manifestation as a material distinction between two entities, the principle of call and response may be inscribed in a musical pattern performed by one person.

Some of the more subtle uses of the call-and-response principle are found in art music. Joshua Uzoigwe's composition for Iyáàlú and piano (1980) stages a dialogue between the two instruments, talking drum and piano. With its capacity to speak, the drum (Iyáàlú) makes a series of motivic propositions to which the pianist provides a direct response. The response may be an iconic affirmation or may take the form of a reciprocal interrogation. The mode of articulation is largely "syllabic," thus reinforcing the impression that the two instruments are engaged in a verbal conversation. This particular dialogue is all the more striking because of the timbral distance between the iyáàlú and the piano. With this distance comes a network of symbolic associations that might engender interpretation of Uzoigwe's composition as an intercultural dialogue, as an affirmation of musical coexistence, or as an embodiment of simultaneous doing with no necessary aspirations toward a final synthesis.

Call and response is the single most important principle of African form. Communalistic in origin, it is marked by an internal functional differentiation that is often made rich in performance through a variety of attitudes and energies.

An appreciation of African vocal and instrumental music is often enhanced by an awareness of this animating antiphonal principle.[7]

**The variation impulse**. Repetition and variation often go hand in hand in African culture. A commitment to one invariably entails a commitment to the other. Continuous variation as enacted in cycles, Meki Nzewi tells us, is "a known quantity that recurs with a different quality."[8] Although no repetition of a pattern, an event, or an action can be ultimately literal (ontologically speaking), poets, orators, and musicians have devised imaginative ways of distinguishing literal repetition from varied repetition. Ritual texts, oaths, and greetings that need to be performed exactly under certain religious or sociocultural imperatives are rendered with appropriate fidelity to the spirit of the text. On the other hand, opportunities to vary a structure creatively in subsequent performance to delight audiences and foreground a performer's powers are greatly welcomed. The daily performance of "news" or *amaniɛ* among the Northern Ewe is a moment in which a speaker's gift for varying things—for turning things around, putting sweetness in the narrative, and endowing it with "style"—can be exercised. Similarly, musical performances of many sorts sanction the display of a variation instinct and associated technique.

Examples abound in various children's songs, especially ones that involve acts of enumeration. One Ewe song (given here in translation) proceeds as follows:

> The pinkie says ŋɛ̃ ŋɛ̃ ŋɛ̃ [the sound of crying];
> The second finger asks, "Are you hungry?"
> The third says, "There is flour in the flour pot."
> The fourth says, "Cook it and let's eat."
> The thumb says, "I will tell mama when she comes."

Under this regime of repetition and variation, the invitation is to construct a framework using the periodicity prescribed by the actual physical counting of the fingers of one hand as a guide. A performer points to each finger while reciting the relevant words listed previously, ending with the thumb. The act of enumeration establishes the basic periodicity, even though the words attributed to each finger vary in number of syllables. Similarly, in communities where children are named according to the day of the week

---

7. For a focused study of the call-and-response principle in an Ewe dance drumming, see David Locke, "Call and Response in Ewe Agbadza Songs: One Element in a Network of Musical Factors," *Analytical Approaches to World Music* 3 (2013), http://www.aawmjournal.com/articles/2014a/Locke_AAWM_Vol_3_1.html.

8. Nzewi, *A Contemporary Study of the Musical Arts*, vol. 4, 44.

on which they are born, games may involve the enumeration of behavior attitudes characteristic of those born on Sundays, Mondays, Tuesdays, and so on. Different cycle numbers will constrain different games: seven week days, four market days, five fingers, two legs, and so on. When assembled as a group, these cyclical potentialities may superficially suggest a society regulated "polymetrically." But the cycles of seven, four, five, and two operate under different temporal constraints. There is nothing polymetrical here, only a versatility in negotiating different types of cycles as circumstances demand. The whole, in any case, is only a theoretical whole; it is never heard by any individual.

A favorite formal device is parataxis, the juxtaposition of utterances in a sequence that is unconstrained syntactically. Unlike the aforementioned five-finger and week-day games that must follow a certain order, a song representing a hungry child's cry for his mother, made up of a listing of various mothers' names, is subject to paratactic delivery. In one Northern Ewe song, the chorus announces that "I want to be fed" (or literally, "I want to suck breast"), while the soloist lists as many mothers' names she can recall. The music provides a temporal interval in which the singer must insert each name, it being understood that names come with a varying number of syllables. She might use a succession like this: "Kofi nɔ," "Emefa nɔ," "Adukonu nɔ" (the word *nɔ* means "mother"; the rest are names) and thus fit three, four, and five syllables, respectively, into the same space. Some forethought is helpful in such situations. Similarly, in a conversation between two dead people that serves as the text for a crying song, the singer laments the great distance between her current location (on the other side of the river) and "home" (the land of the living, which she and her interlocutor departed some time ago). "I have not been hearing any news from home lately," says the singer, who then proceeds to list as many far-away towns as possible: "Takoradi is far away," "Tamale is far away," "Kumasi is far away," "Bɔntibɔ is far away," "Kukurantumi is far away," and so on. Again, there is no necessary logic to the sequence of place names (a different list or a different ordering is likely to be heard at different performances); only the temporal interval for fitting in a name has to be preserved. A treasured skill is to be able to vary the rhythms of names while maintaining the metric framework.

In a study that includes one of the earliest extended transcriptions of an African vocal genre, A. M. Jones portrays a Swahili epic performance of an utenzi poem from Luma as an intricate art of variation.[9] The performer of this genre of sung poetry relies on variants of a tune to convey the many verses of the poem. Jones's chosen text, "Utenzi wa Abdirrahmani na Sufiyani," first

___

9. A. M. Jones, "Swahili Epic Poetry."

set down in the nineteenth century, has one thousand verses, of which Jones transcribes sixty-eight. Sixteen separate little phrases—Jones calls them "little tunes"—make up the long melody with which the four verses are delivered. By comparing a "basic form" with several realized variants, Jones uncovers "an astonishing display of subtle variations." Some of the variations are caused by "the natural rhythm of the words," while others come from the tones of the language. Jones's essay raises a larger question of stylistic affinity between Arabic and Bantu musical styles. The performance of "Utenzi" is beholden to a strong variation impulse at a micro- or phrase level. It may be that Arabic variation is concentrated at a microlevel, while Bantu variation is incorporated at a higher level.

Repetition spans the entire gamut from the most local, microlevel embellishments to larger, archetypal structuring involving recompositions. A soloist in a call-and-response framework may vary her lines as she enumerates them while the chorus repeats its response literally. A lead drummer may employ a handful of motifs and put them through a variety of regimes of variation, such that every performance assumes a different profile.

A historical circumstance that has affected the nurturing of a variation impulse is the imposition of Christianity on various parts of the continent and the attendant introduction of hymns in strophic form. On the deficit side, whereas in some traditional societies, the strophic *impulse* provided a framework for bringing a remembered structure to life using a variety of resources, many modern practices of hymn singing have installed a relatively fixed form and relatively fixed tunes and attendant tonal harmonies. The fixed texts of written-down hymns have thus resulted in a curbing rather than a promotion of the spontaneous exercise of the variation impulse found in traditional music. Singing several verses to the same tune Sunday after Sunday has a way of enforcing a nonvariation regimen, and more than one churchgoer has had to adopt a less spontaneous attitude to singing in church.

An exception should be made for hymn singing in the less orthodox (or Pentecostal or charismatic) churches, where the freer and less ritualized style of worship accommodates and even encourages acts of variation, some of them harmonically driven. Instinctive harmonization of tunes is nowadays not uncommon. Ornaments may be added to the tunes themselves, sometimes under pressure from speech tones. And the influence of popular-music idioms on church music forms, as evidenced by the incorporation of band instruments (including electronic keyboards and drum sets), often with exaggerated amplification, has helped to restore improvisational freedom to hymn-singing practices previously kept "straight."

**Additive form**. Whereas the regularity and predictability associated with variation form tend to be cultivated in dance repertories, introspection and declamation are more characteristic of narrative and contemplative genres. Additive form, which refers to the linear accretion of unequal units in a formal sequence, fosters a different kind of creativity, one in which a segment (or fragment) is literally added to (or followed by) another, then to yet another, all in a chainlike succession. The entire narrativelike succession may approximate shapes like ABCD or AABCC'C"DD, complete with internal repetitions and variations.

Examples of additive form were included in the twenty-six excerpts cited earlier in this chapter, so I will elaborate on just two of them. First is the powerful lamentation by a *zole* or midwife of the Dan ethnic group in the Côte d'Ivoire neutrally titled "Solo Song of a Woman."[10] The performance consists of melodic segments, some short, others long. It is structured as an additive process; short verbal phrases are sung, repeated, sung again with contrasts, broken off, interspersed with song words, and multiplied within a narrative matrix until the end. There is actually no end, only the moment of stopping. A choreographed ending would likely rob the expression of some of its authenticity. Like others in situations where they are mourning the death of close relatives, the Dan woman will sing of her departed husband until she is overcome by the intensity of grief or is exhausted, until dawn is here, or until she is taken away by concerned relatives who think that she has mourned enough. The relative temporal flexibility of this form of lamentation is offset by the fixity of the pitch resource, an anhemitonic pentatonic collection.

In a 4' 33" recording from the Nkundo of the Democratic Republic of the Congo (no relationship to John Cage's famous piano piece of that same duration), a Bompoto healer, Tobola, leads the performance of ritual incantation.[11] The whole assumes the shape of a drama in which responsorial, fully rhythmic exchanges prepare longer recitations, interrupted by briefer responses, and then culminating in a celebratory section in which drum and rattle join in with the rest of the chorus. The incantations may seem to impose a periodicity, but the true form will only be known in retrospect, not in prospect. Very little in Tobola's long recitations supports a nonadditive perception of overall form. Rather, the first 2' 16" cumulatively inscribe a future, adding block to block of material in this content-rich genre. After that, a strict-rhythmic

10. CD, *Africa: The Dan*, track 3, "Solo song of a woman."

11. CD, *Anthologie Congolaise,* vol. 11, track 2, "Bompoto."

section follows, complete with a lively call and response enriched by a paratactic process.

Ladysmith's "Pauline" mentioned earlier as an example of additive form, enacts a musical form that follows the poetic form, itself a narrative. The text may be segmented according to the breath marks in the performance. Each breath mark is indicated by the forward slash sign (/) and sports tonic harmony. The number of syllables in each segment is also given:

1. Paulina, Paulina,/ somebody's crying for you./          6 + 7
2. You, Paulina,/ somebody's crying for you./              4 + 7
3. Paulina,/ why did you leave him alone?/                 3 + 7
4. Now,/ he asked me/ to call you/                        1 + 3 + 3
5. I looked for you/ all over./                            4 + 3
6. You were nowhere to be found./                          7
7. Please, Pauline,/ come back to him/                     4 + 4
8. He loves you,/ he wants to marry you/                   3 + 6
9. Get away from those/ who want to touch-touch/ and kiss-kiss/   5 + 5 + 3
10. Thereafter/ they leave you alone./                     3 + 5

The additive structure is conveyed in the irregular succession of segments. Such irregularity often elicits contemplative attention. Listeners are not provided with an automatic groove in which they can join; rather, they are asked to *listen* to this story about a girl named Paulina. The additive instinct carries a strong narrative quality as well, whereas a divisive instinct is an invitation to the dance.

**The narrative impulse**. Successions of events with or without an underlying groove will typically elicit interpretation as some sort of narrative. Thus, an additive succession such as A + B + C + D may be interpreted as a narration. But there is a separate narrative impulse, analogous to verbal composition, that motivates certain kinds of musical composition. It is at work in word-dominated genres like praise singing or the performance of genealogies and clan histories. It is also evident in some genres of solo expression, where a lead musician or narrator takes center stage to advance a telling or provide a narrative. The example I will discuss here is a piece of instrumental music from a neotraditional Ewe genre, Bɔbɔbɔ, which may double as a sign of both the melodic imagination discussed in the previous chapter and formal ingenuity.

Bɔbɔbɔ is a popular Northern Ewe recreational dance that originated in the late 1950s and early 1960s in the town of Kpandu, from where it spread to other Volta region towns and eventually to metropolitan cities like Accra and Tema, including suburbs like Ashiaman and Madina. It is performed by an ensemble of bells, drums, and rattles together with men's and women's singing voices. Perhaps

**Photo 6.1** Bɔbɔbɔ (Northern Ewe dance) bugle player, Vane, Ghana.

the most memorable moment in a Bɔbɔbɔ performance is the entrance of a trumpet or bugle. The purpose of the trumpet solo is to energize or "fan" the performance.[12] While drumming and dancing continue, the singing stops to make room for this particular soloistic display. Trumpet interventions are moments of heightened rhetoric.[13]

Example 6.1 is a transcription of the trumpet solo from a performance of "Miwɔ ɖeka ne du nenyo loo" ("Unite so that the nation can prosper"). It was performed sometime in the early 1990s by Joseph Kweku of the Taviefe Akpese Group (Web Example 6.1 ).[14] In addition to the score, I have provided a list of constituent units (Figure 6.2) and a paradigmatic chart summarizing the overall form (Figure 6.3).

The essential ingredients of this performance are annunciatory or fanfare-like rising arpeggios, complementary but less extended falling triads, waiting patterns (on $\hat{1}$ or $\hat{5}$ but never on $\hat{3}$), motivic dialogue, and reiterated cadential

12. Kenn Kafui, "Performing Arts," in *A Handbook of Eweland*. Vol. 2: *The Northern Ewes in Ghana*, ed. Kodzo Gavua (Accra: Woeli Publishing Services, 2000), 122–130.

13. On Bɔbɔbɔ and other Ghanaian dances, see Paschal Younge, *Music and Dance Traditions of Ghana: History, Performance, and Teaching* (Jefferson, N.C.: McFarland, 2011).

14. Recorded on cassette, *Taviefe Dunenyo Akpese Group: Dekawɔwɔ* (n.d., probably mid-1990s).

**Example 6.1** Trumpet solo from a Bɔbɔbɔ performance (Northern Ewe).

gestures. These procedures are ordinary, but how are they brought to life, and how are they made to support the kind of minimalist creativity that this particular trumpet intervention represents? Let us follow the course of the melodic discourse from beginning to end. (Please refer to Example 6.1 and, in particular, to the labels "Unit 1," "Unit 2," etc.).

Unit 1 (1–8¹). Beginning gestures are typically loud and attention grabbing. Trumpeter Joseph Kweku arpeggiates up to the high F with bravado and holds on to it for six and a half bars. With this exclamatory opening gesture, the trumpeter maps out the pitch terrain, announces a timbral presence, and energizes the dancers, some of whom may well be thrown into a state of delirium by this phrase. This is only the beginning, however.

**Example 6.1** (Continued)

Unit 2 (8²–12¹) repeats the opening gesture, but instead of holding on to the top F, Kweku returns to the low F by means of a complementary arpeggio. So whereas unit 1 sustained the high F as a rhetorically marked moment, unit 2 merely touches it several times before returning "home" to the low F.

Unit 3 (12²–20¹) makes a third attempt at beginning using the same rousing arpeggio figure. This time Kweku settles on the tonic note (in association with scale degree 3) for some six bars. While the waiting note in unit 1 was sustained (the high F), the waiting signal in unit 3 is rhythmically active, and it is in this active form that waiting notes or motives assume greater importance as the composition unfolds.

Unit 4 (20²–27¹) opens with the by-now-familiar fanfare figure and eventually settles on another waiting pitch, this time scale degree 5 (not 1), which keeps the sense of the discourse open.

Unit 5 (27²–36¹). Kweku introduces a new idea, a falling arpeggio in broad rhythm (bars 27 to 28) (derivable from unit 2), answers it with two other motives, and then repeats himself (rotation in the form). Noticeably different in unit 5 is the mode of enunciation, which is perhaps more speechlike than songlike. Unit 5's motives are briefer and set apart by silences; their succession acquires an interrogative and dialogical aura. You will also notice that the lead drummer "speaks" alongside the trumpeter in this unit.

We can pass over units 6 through 11 rather more quickly.

| | Unit | Function/Profile |
|---|---|---|
| 1 | 1–8 | Opening fanfare |
| 2 | $8^2$–$12^1$ | Second attempt at opening |
| 3 | $12^2$–$20^1$ | Third attempt leading to closure |
| 4 | $20^2$–$27^1$ | Opening fanfare ending in waiting pattern |
| 5 | $27^2$–36 | New motives in speech mode, doubled by lead drum |
| 6 | 37–43 | Waiting pattern leading to closure |
| 7 | 44–50 | Motivic reiteration |
| 8 | 51–60 | Repeat of unit 5 |
| 9 | 61–67 | Repeat of unit 6 |
| 10 | 68–$70^1$ | Return of opening fanfare |
| 11 | $70^2$–77 | Closing gesture based on opening fanfare |

Figure 6.2  Units of the trumpet solo.

Unit 6 ($36^2$–43) returns to the waiting pattern on $\hat{5}$ first heard at the end of unit 4 but resolves this to $\hat{1}$ at its end.

Unit 7 (44–$51^1$) prolongs the "tonic" resolution, while unit 8 ($51^2$–$60^1$) provides another rotation of unit 5, complete with the melorhythmic doubling of the trumpet part by the lead drum.

Unit 9 ($60^2$–67) is identical to unit 6.

Then, in a recapitulatory gesture, unit 10 (68–$70^1$) takes up the rising arpeggio of unit 1 but does not prolong the high F.

Finally, unit 11 ($70^2$–75) again takes the 5-to-8 gesture of unit 7 and brings the trumpet solo to an end with a prolonged note.

Figure 6.2 lists the individual units from 1 to 11 and summarizes the functions ascribed to them in the foregoing narrative. Figure 6.3 then sketches the overall form using a simple paradigmatic chart that aligns equivalent units and maintains their piece-specific chronology. From one perspective, the formal narrative of "Miwɔ ɖeka ne du nenyo loo" comes across as a tripartite structure in which units 1 through 4 constitute an opening section, units 5 through 9 make up a middle section, and units 10 and 11 represent a compressed return of the opening. These profiles are further complicated by the internal tendencies of individual units, which tend to be contradictory. So while we can chart a single Hauptgedanke from beginning to end, from left to right, so to speak, we recognize also that the individual units complicate the linear trajectory using principles of repetition, delay, return, and variation.

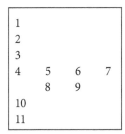

**Figure 6.3** Paradigmatic layout of form of trumpet solo.

This is such a feat of imagination using only three notes! Joseph Kweku's relatively brief intervention is superbly calibrated to make a strong impact. A rhetorically heightened beginning yields to moments of play and teasing in the middle, before briefly returning to the fanfare in conclusion. The pitch resource is minimalist, but the performer has brought to this a rhythmic imagination (including the invocation of the speech mode) that excites his fellow performers and moves his audience.

**Moment form**. Kufuna, a sixteen-year-old Angolan boy of the Nkhangala/ Vankhangala ethnic group, was recorded in 1965 playing a vibrating leaf (Web Example 6.2 ).[15] Kubik does not comment on the form of this fascinating performance, but the whole amounts to an intriguing set of exertions and articulations that exemplify yet another approach to form. We might describe this—the least constrained of the five principles—as moment form. Moment form is geared to the moment, unhinged from any sort of architecture, and available only as a memory of an action or set of actions, not as the enactment of a script. Kufuna's basic aim is to produce sound out of his leaf and to sustain it. If we imagine his actions represented as a series of gestures, we will count thirteen of them. The first is undulating, the second descends, the third rises and then descends, the fourth descends but from a lower starting point, the fifth descends from a higher starting point, the sixth incorporates the most vibrato, the seventh concludes with a staccato note, the eighth and ninth start high and then descend, the tenth is barely audible, and the eleventh, twelfth, and thirteenth all start high and descend, with the recording gradually fading at this point.

How do we characterize the form of this performance? There is no beat, no regulating periodicity, only an accumulation of sonic exertions. Not all

15. See Kubik, CD accompanying *Theory of African Music*, vol. 1, track 34, "Vibrating leaf." See also David Lewiston's recording of a "leaf (*hoja*) used as a melody instrument" by the blacks of Chalguayaco in Ecuador, track 3, "Oigame Juanita," of the CD, *In Praise of Oxalá and Other Gods: Black Music of South America* (New York: Nonesuch Records, 2003 [orig. 1970]).

of them are successful, for try as he might, Kufuna does not always succeed in getting his leaf to sound. This music does not accompany dance or ritual. Kufuna is playing, and he is doing so using the most modest of resources. This is individual expression, not a group's. It is not shaped by an externally imposed agenda, only the youthful desire to generate sound from a leaf.

I've described this performance as an example of moment form because it is made up of autonomous, individual moments whose defining processes are geared to the present and display no apparent long-term ambitions. The accumulation of moments does not normally generate any long-term expectation, except that in the most mundane sense the performance will eventually come to an end; nor is it meant to carve out a particular dynamic shape for the listener. It is meant merely to answer the question, What can Kufuna do with this leaf? Questions normally posed about the determinants of conventional form—questions of balance, communicative efficacy, integration, and coherence—are decidedly irrelevant in this context. Listening is not mediated by a formal template. And to the extent that there is an organizing element, it is the repeated force of breath producing sounds on the leaf. Kufuna's "vibrating leaf" is a marked creation, the outcome of acoustemological action. Its form is singular and unrepeatable.

The kind of impulse represented by Kufuna's performance is not isolated. Consider another example, this one from Niger. Moussoukabe, a Wodaabe Peul, is imitating animal sounds with his voice to lure and then trap them.[16] From a semiotic point of view, these simulated animal cries are the closest we come to unmediated auditive iconicity, a mode of signaling in sound. The cries are framed, however, not as function ("work song") but as play or entertainment. This framing contributes a symbolic value to the performance. Moussoukabe's goal is to manipulate the elements of pitch, intonation, rhythm, and timbre to approximate the original animal sound, but the accumulation of effects has no goal beyond itself. The designation "moment form" recognizes the potency of each moment, each simulated animal cry, without forming any sort of expectation that the entire sequence will conform to a formal template. In this mode of "presentness," the creative spirit is released from architectural responsibility to pursue sound as if nothing else mattered.

Two other examples of moment form may be mentioned briefly. The first is a minimalist piece featuring dronelike continuity. A chorus of Wodaabe Peuls[17] sings and sustains a single pitch class—an extended pedal point that

16. See "Appel des animaux par Mossoukabe" on CD, *Nomades du désert: Les Peulhs du Niger* (Paris: Auvidis, 1986).

17. See CD accompanying M. Brandilly, *Introduction aux musiques africaines*, track 3, "Choeurs des Peuls Wodabé."

is reinforced triadically from time to time. This gesturing toward infinity by cultivating a continuous rather than broken sound renounces the shapes conferred by periodicity and captures an extended moment as form. (Incidentally, the Peuls were doing this long before La Monte Young's *Trio for Strings* [1958], with its long, sustained notes.)

In a similar vein is a lamentation from the North Borna ethnic group of the Democratic Republic of the Congo.[18] An entire village is mourning the death of their chief's son. Weeping is mediated by the pitch C; that is, all participants sing and hold that pitch as part of their communal weeping. They will take turns breathing, of course, but the musical idea is one of uninterrupted continuity. One hears tiny fragments of melody descending to C4 from the minor third above (as if expressing a $\hat{3}$-$\hat{2}$-$\hat{1}$ motion), but the overall impression is of a large or extended moment.

A study of form in African music would not be complete without mention of macro- or large-scale form, that is, the shape assumed by an extended performance spread over several hours, days, or even weeks. The shape of a funeral or festival, a libation prayer or healing ritual, an evening entertainment in a nightclub—the profiles of such macroforms take us beyond what individual listeners hear or what performers and composers can control directly in performance. Macroforms can thus seem like an abstraction, tangible but not necessarily available for conscious creative use. They are outcomes rather than inputs, the result of the generative processes we have described in this chapter.[19]

## CONCLUSION

The five principles of form rehearsed here are only a small part of what is available in African performance. The fact that African musicians are not readily credited with imaginative ways of creating form should now look odd given some of the routines and potentialities described here. It should be noted that the five principles are not isolated; rather, they may function in tandem to produce various hybrids. Their individual domains may also intersect. For example, additive form and moment form share a gesture of accumulation. Kufuna's vibrating-leaf performance leaves traces that add up, so although

18. See on CD, *Petites musiques du Zaire*, track 12, "Lamentations."

19. Analyses of the overall shapes of large-scale performances may be found in Ampene, *Female Song Tradition and the Akan of Ghana: The Creative Process in Nnwonkoro*, 127–153; Nzewi, *Musical Sense and Meaning: An Indigenous African Perception*, 183–192; and Waterman, *Jùjú: A Social History and Ethnography of an African Popular Music*, 196–212.

there is neither a beginning-continuing-ending trajectory nor an intended, goal-directed narrative, a resultant process of summation is nevertheless an outcome. What distinguishes additive form is the purposeful accumulation of segments; in moment form, by contrast, succession of moments is purposeless. Then, too, the line between additive and moment form may prove elusive if the narrative urgency that cuts across the blocks of additive procedure is in any way compromised. A performance proceeding additively may also be animated by an antiphonal principle at a microlevel, making for a dual mode of articulation. Similarly, an overarching call-and-response form may invest in variation at more local levels of expression. The call-and-response procedure may be dominant in some contexts but latent in others. And while the variation impulse is prominent in forms based on successive variants of an initial musical complex, the fact of succession can confer an additive feel on the whole. If the process of variation is obscured or simply too subtle, the listener is left only with the accumulation of discrete entities. These and other permutations confirm what we have always known, namely, that form can be complex and multifaceted, assuming diverse and ingenious forms. Therefore, some flexibility in reading individual manifestations is most desirable.

Perhaps the great subtlety of African forms stems from the fact that, strictly speaking, there are no wholes in African music, only fragments and ensembles of fragments. Beginnings and endings occur as part of an inevitable material succession, but wherever we imagine a whole, we see and sense only portions, partialities, and promissory notes; every time we posit completion, our attention is drawn to parts and unfinished processes, holes rather than wholes. One obvious source of this undermining of boundaries is the imbrication of music in social life, a practice we discussed in chapter 1. The transitions between forms of expressive doing are often unmarked; sometimes they are negotiated with modest fanfare, with a sense of a notional continuity between domains, and without fear of incongruity. Form in African music is best appreciated when we suspend faith in artificial, never-proven wholes and the unities imposed by constricting templates and embrace a more circumspect participatory attitude. African music's will to form is a celebration of contingencies, an acknowledgment that the trace is always already provisional. Whether calling or responding, varying a sung or played phrase, making substitutions in a repeating structure, or marking time with gestures, musicians aim to communicate affects and achieve effects that are not necessarily premised on the choreographed stability of closure or on the attainment of ostensibly long-term goals, but on the direct and immediate communication of pertinent messages.

# 7

# Harmony, or Simultaneous Doing

Throughout Africa, boys and girls and men and women sing together regularly. When they do, they follow habits, constraints, and rules that apply in their individual communities. Some habits are of ancient origins; others are of a more recent provenance. Some people sing with "one voice" (meaning not solo but in unison, including octave-duplicated unisons), others with two or three, and still others with as many voices as there are singers. These acts of *simultaneous doing* are indices of living communities, signs of a thriving communal ethos. Singing together defines or affirms social bonds. To sing with others is to assert the belief that "I am because we are." We do not normally sing with strangers or enemies. And even within a compact community, the synchronicity that is idealized when people sing together is threatened whenever fissures or cracks appear in the social fabric. Meaningful and successful doing together presupposes the elimination of residual tensions; if tensions remain, the act of performance amounts to a lie. Harmony in traditional African music, understood as the sounding together of different but complementary lines, is at once a material repository and an expression of ethics. Although both are necessary for a comprehensive study of artistic choice and technique, our focus here will be on the material aspects.

A preliminary distinction needs to be made between intention and trace. While African harmony symbolizes an idealized unanimity, the actual manifestation of that oneness often takes a variety of discrepant forms. In many performances, intention and realization do not always align perfectly; gaps and slippages may occur. This is especially apparent in vocal music, although it occurs in instrumental music as well. I may plan to duplicate or "decorate" your melody at a distance of, say, a third when I join in, but the stream of thirds we end up producing may be subject to small (or occasionally big) changes. This kind of slippage is common in performing traditions around the world and is in no way a specifically African problematic. Related "participatory discrepancies" (borrowing from Charles Keil[1]) make it unwise to confine analysis to what was produced on a given performance occasion, as distinct from what existed in performers' minds *before* they began to perform. To analyze only a specific performance is to risk fixing a composition's ontology in the contingencies of a particular occasion; it is to overlook the more fundamental fixity that precedes performance and thus carries over from one performance to the next. The possibility that our "thirds" will seem closer to flattened fourths on Tuesday or that some of our perfect fifths will be indistinguishable from tritones on Sunday should encourage us to seek reliable descriptions of what was intended. This will in turn enhance appreciation of the creativity exercised by individual musicians in bringing to life a given archetype, model, or ideal sonority. It will also indicate the degree of tolerance admitted by listeners. While a focus on the trace tends to satisfy a certain empiricist desire, it risks mistaking the fortuitous resultant for the thing itself. The fact that most African compositions exist in aural/oral forms as memories does not make them any less concrete as repositories of structural, syntactical, or phenomenological constraints. Every dirge, game song, praise song, or song of insult is a text with knowable limits. Establishing such preperformance "texts," as distinct from transcribing specific performances captured on recording, remains an urgent task for African musicology.[2]

The harmonic dimension offers many opportunities for distinguishing the planned from the fortuitous in the sounding together of voices and instruments. In some ensemble performances, sonorities are not necessarily regarded as significant objects of attention; rather, melodic exertions and the process of maintaining the integrity of mode or contour are given a higher priority. In others, agreed-upon harmonies mark phrase beginnings and endings but defer to a less prescribed vocabulary in the spaces in between. In general, the basic frameworks that guide harmonic expression are relatively few and straightforward. Complications arise in execution.

Discourse on harmony is liable to get technical rather quickly. Whereas a description of sung melody can rely on palpable features of rhetoric, grammar, phonology, and intonation, and whereas discussion of rhythm can point to tempo, duration, accentuation, a pattern's "hotness," or a texture's multiplicity, talk about harmony makes fewer concessions to metaphorical description or intersemiotic translation. We are obliged to speak of intervals and chords,

1. Charles Keil, "Participatory Discrepancies and the Power of Music," *Cultural Anthropology* 2, no. 3 (1987): 275–283.

2. For two complementary enactments of this philosophy, see Simha Arom, *African Polyphony and Polyrhythm,* and Willie Anku, *Structural Set Analysis: Adowa.*

consonance and dissonance, and voice leading—all of them precise from a technical point of view but difficult to transpose into nontechnical language.

Ethno-theory serves up a paltry vocabulary for the harmonic dimension of African music. The Ewe, for example, will refer to *gbebabla* or the blending of voices, acknowledge *gbe evelia* or the second voice (which is not necessarily a lower voice, simply an additional voice), and—especially in these postcolonial times—recognize pitch height and depth using words like *goglome* and *kɔkɔme,* respectively. But discussion of parallel third harmony, for example, will not be found in their normal vocabulary. That a line may be enriched by a second voice or rendered naked without it, or that harmony may make a song sweeter, add a bonus to it, or make it good to listen to indicates the limits of Ewe verbalizing about harmony.

In a remarkable but apparently one-off nomenclature, the Aka Pygmy are said to have developed a specific descriptive scheme not for resultant sonorities as such but for the functions of the four main polyphonic voices. According to Simha Arom, these parts are designated as *ngúé wà limbo* ("mother of song"), *mò.tángòlè* ("that which gives its words"), *ó.sese* ("below," subordinate to *mò. tángòlè*), and *dì.yèi* (yodeling).[3] With some effort, one can tease out a few implications for harmonic or polyphonic analysis from such indigenous denominations (as indeed Suzanne Fürniss has done[4]), but thorough analysis cannot proceed from that basis alone. The conclusion is inescapable but not surprising in the context of broader patterns of discourse on African music: African musicians regularly engage in harmonic behavior but do not often make harmony a subject of conversation.

## A QUICK TOUR OF HARMONIC ENVIRONMENTS

The recorded legacy of African music bears ample witness to the wealth of the continent's harmonic resources. A good place to start is with the CD that accompanies the first volume of Kubik's book, *Theory of African Music.*[5] There, you will be confronted with a startling variety of "multipart" expression on voices and instruments. These include suspended harmonic fields in xylophone playing, two- or three-chord progressions animated by melodic elaboration in Azande harp music, and both continuous and intermittent part singing in various songs by children and adults. An earlier recording of Mukanda

3. Arom, "Intelligence in Traditional Music."

4. Suzanne Fürniss, "Aka Polyphony."

5. Kubik, *Theory of African Music*, vol. 1.

circumcision songs from Angola is another rich source, notable for a consistent exploitation of triadic harmony.[6] Explore next the series of recordings of material from the Democratic Republic of the Congo made under the auspices of the Museum for Central Africa in Tervuren, Belgium.[7] There you will find an array of performances ranging from long epic singing featuring unison voices through part singing to "thick" or clusterlike forms of simultaneous doing. Turn next to recordings of Wagogo music for some glorious examples, including contrapuntally inflected vocal music by children and adults, pure instrumental music, and instrumental music based on vocal models.[8]

Your next stop could be the endlessly fascinating world of Pygmy polyphony, an acknowledged site for various forms and intensities of simultaneous doing. Here you would have your hands full trying to decide where to begin or end your journey. The characteristic voice separation of the Bibayak Pygmies recorded by Pierre Sallée is as good a point of entry as any.[9] The yodeling displayed there has intervallic and registral or spatial dimensions, and the rhythmically differentiated parts held together often by a pentatonic base give rise to a varied succession of pentatonic sonorities. Similar forms of group singing may be explored in dozens of recordings of music by the Aka, Baka, Ba-Benzele, Mbuti, and others.[10] The dense polyphonic textures of Pygmy music will likely stimulate curiosity about patterns of consonance and dissonance and about the harmonic outcomes of a compositional ethos dedicated to the enactment of presentness. They may also suggest interesting patterns in the interface between harmonic density and temporal trajectory.

Turn next to recordings of Baganda music from Uganda.[11] Pentatonic tone systems, for example, are sharply profiled in call-and-response patterns, while sporadic harmonic effects emerge in the overlaps between solo and chorus. In some horn ensembles, the pentatonic resultant emerges from a one-note-per-player strategy. Other recordings feature strategically discrepant tunings of lamellophones, flutes, and panpipes. Add to these the sweet singing in close

6. Kubik, CD, *Mukanda na makisi/Angola* (Berlin: Musikethnologische Abteilung, Museum für Völkerkunde Berlin, Staatliche Museen Preussischer Kulturbesitz, 1981).

7. CD, *Anthologie de la musique Congolaise*.

8. CD, *Mbudi mbudi na mhanga,* and CD, *Universo musical infantil de los Wagogo de Tanzania*.

9. CD, *Musique des pygmées Bibayak*.

10. See discography for recordings of various pygmy communities made by Arom, Fürniss, Kisliuk, Sallée, Sarno, Turnbull, and others.

11. CD, *Royal Court Music from Uganda* (recorded by Peter Cooke); CD, *Ouganda: musiques de Baganda* (recorded by Jean-Jacques Nattiez).

thirds of Gã Adowa or Kpelle entertainment songs, the parallel fourths and pentatonic substrate of Anlo-Ewe singing, or the gentle counterpoint that underpins ensemble music making among the Bara in Madagascar, be it a repertoire for xylophones, voices, or panpipes.[12]

This is only the traditional sphere. Turn to highlife music of West Africa for a different sound environment, a creative mingling of European harmony (as heard in hymns) with indigenous modal melody. King Sunny Adé's jùjú is a veritable feast in modality. Check out the postmodern juxtapositions of styles, intonations, and tone systems in Lagbaja and compare them with highlife musician Kojo Antwi's ventriloquism achieved by fitting Twi words to the intonations and enunciation mannerisms of certain Euro-American pop melodies. The subliminal dissonances that often arise for Antwi's bilingual listeners belong to a more abstract level of simultaneous doing, one that exceeds the more immediate hybridity upon which his style is founded. A detour to the Republic of South Africa, a land swimming in tonal harmonies, allows one to take in the close diatonic harmonies of a variety of choral groups, including Ladysmith. Compare the forms of Cuban-influenced popular music in the Democratic Republic of the Congo (with their standard I-IV-V harmonic progressions) to varieties of contemporary gospel music, with its presentational forms and functional-harmonic routines borrowed from various American popular cultural models and from localized hymn traditions.

If you still have the heart to go on to art music, you might as well start with Fela Sowande (1905–1987), the father of African art music. His harmonic language, cultivated in the 1930s and 1940s on the basis of acquaintance with eighteenth- and nineteenth-century European harmony, was later inflected with jazz influences while often retaining the tonal or modal ambience of indigenous African melodies. Compare Sowande's approach with that of his Ghanaian contemporary, Ephraim Amu (1899–1995), who took the protestant hymn as a model for his own compositions from the very beginning and never overcame its prescriptions; rather, he enriched hymn harmony by introducing self-consciously learned devices like counterpoint into his works from the 1950s onward. (The composition "Alegbegbe" [1958] is exemplary in this respect.) Amu also incorporated speech rhythm to give his vocal melodies a more realist flavor. Move closer to the present by listening to the minimalist essays based on a diatonic resource by Ugandan composer Justinian Tamusuza (b. 1951) or to the airy, floating, unanchored harmonies of South African composer Bongani Ndodana-Breen (b. 1975).

---

12. CD, *Music of the Ga People of Ghana: Adowa*, vol. 1 (recorded by Barbara Hampton); CD, *Music of the Kpelle of Liberia* (recorded by Ruth Stone and Verlon Stone); CD, *Ewe Drumming from Ghana* (recorded by James Burns); CD, *Madagascar: Pays Bara*.

By this time, you may well be itching for a single stop at which you can shop, in which case you might conveniently pick up two CDs of African and African diasporic piano music made in 2005 and 2009, respectively, by Ghanaian American pianist William Chapman Nyaho.[13] Nyaho's recordings may well come as a revelation to those not familiar with the literate tradition in African composition. Idioms range from drone-based textures through regular functional harmony (sometimes inflected by African melody or rhythm) to highly dissonant and experimental pitch clusters. And then, as a final treat, cross over into the "European" world and listen to Paul Aimard's CD, *African Rhythms*, for a startling tour of different harmonic environments. You will experience the worlds of Steve Reich's minimalism, Ligeti's complex layered polyphonies, and Aka Pygmy simultaneities in an ostensibly seamless continuity. (We will return to this recording in chapter 8.)

## TERMINOLOGY: *HARMONY, POLYPHONY,* OR *MULTIPART*?

The word *harmony* entered the discourse of African musicology from the earliest writings by Europeans. Encountering African music for the first time, some wondered whether it had some of the same qualities as the music they knew. When more than one sound was heard, some wondered whether this was "harmony," or indeed "true harmony."[14] The question of harmonic generation arose for researchers working in Southern Africa, who encountered various usages of the harmonic series (or overtone series) that seemed to function as a source for pitch selection.[15] The mouth bow, for example, was said to produce harmonies prescribed by this natural series. Some have noticed a similar patterning even in vocal styles, such as those of the Wagogo.[16] One scholar has gone so far as to suggest that the otherwise "Western" tonal-functional harmonies in a song like "Diamonds on the Soles of Her Shoes," a collaboration between Paul Simon and Ladysmith Black Mambazo, are "bow derived," that is, based on a juxtaposition of overtones above two fundamental tones lying

13. CD, *Asa: Piano Music by Composers of African Descent,* and CD, *Senku: Piano Music by Composers of African Descent* ([S.l.]: Musicians Showcase Recordings, 2003).

14. Rose Brandel, "Polyphony in African Music."

15. See Percival Kirby, "A Study of Negro Harmony," *Musical Quarterly* 16 (1930): 404–414, and Kubik, "African Tone Systems."

16. Kubik, "Multipart Singing in Sub-Saharan Africa: Remote and Recent Histories Unravelled." See also Kubik, "Africa," in *Grove Music Online*, accessed July 4, 2013.

a major second apart.[17] If harmony is understood generically as an index to resultants and sonorities, then designating these and similar forms of "sounding together" as such is perfectly acceptable as a point of departure. Such designation may even awaken comparisons with the procedures of other world repertories in which multiple voices sing together.

But why not *polyphony*? In the golden age of European vocal polyphony (the Renaissance [1400–1600], but with a notable sixteenth-century center), carefully managed successions of consonances and dissonances, finely crafted melodic lines, and controlled voice-leading enabled a "classical" style of polyphony. Early in the twentieth century, German comparative musicologists Hornbostel and Marius Schneider, both of whom studied African music, used "polyphony" to denote many-voiced textures, and later writers like Rose Brandel, Nketia, Kubik, and Simha Arom have followed suit. The term *polyphony* shifts attention from the vertical to the linear dimension. It encourages the inference that the constituent voices behave with a degree of autonomy. Although it does not discount the vertical dimension, *polyphony* understands verticalities as unavoidable resultants even while attributing a degree of dynamism to linear forces. Whereas *harmony* implies that voices are regarded as being in a functional hierarchy (treble and bass being more important, say, than alto and tenor in the popular Soprano-Alto-Tenor-Bass configuration), *polyphony* implies a less hierarchical conception. Again, some scholars have felt that the weights attaching to a term like *harmony* do not apply to African music, especially since its typical referents include the practices of Bach, Beethoven, and Brahms rather than those of the pretonal or indeed posttonal eras. The use of the term *polyphony* shifts attention away from the dominant common-practice repertories and their entailment.[18]

*Multipart*, the most recent of the terms used to describe the many-voiced procedure, is also the least freighted. Ignazio Macchiarella defines it helpfully:

> Any music behavior producing at least two intentional sound sequences, regulated by specific overlapping rules, each of which is performed by both one single person or more persons in unison, who maintain a

17. Erlmann, *Music, Modernity, and the Global Imagination: South Africa and the West* (New York: Oxford University Press, 1999), 195. For a critique of Erlmann's theory of harmony, see Scherzinger, review of *Music, Modernity, and the Global Imagination*, *Journal of the Royal Musical Association* 126 (2001): 135–138.

18. Indispensable studies of African polyphony include Fürniss, "Aka Polyphony," and Fernando, *Polyphonies du Nord-Cameroun*. A related term is *counterpoint*, used most memorably in Nicholas England's article, "Bushman Counterpoint," *Journal of the International Folk Music Council* 19 (1967): 58–66.

distinctiveness of their own, within contexts of strict interactions and (hierarchical) relationships.[19]

Although it was coined as far back as 1950,[20] *multipart* did not actively enter the discourse of African musicology until sometime in the 1970s. It has been promulgated by scholars like Berliner, Schmidt, Nketia, and especially Kubik. Unlike *harmony* and *polyphony*, both of which have their origins in specifically European practices, *multipart* from its inception was applied to a wider range of practices, both Western and non-Western. Its great advantage is its relative neutrality and adaptability. Instead of wondering whether the "chords" produced in a certain practice are generated by roots, are organized hierarchically, are consonant or dissonant, or imply closure in particular arrangements, the user of the term *multipart* can simply refer to several simultaneous soundings without imposing an a priori interpretation. In this way, the procedures of non-Western simultaneous doing can be captured without the ostensible presuppositions enshrined in terms like *harmony, counterpoint*, and *polyphony*.[21]

Although all three terms—*harmony, polyphony*, and *multipart*—are united in depicting forms of simultaneous doing, they emphasize different things and evoke different intertexts both conceptually and in terms of musical material. So which should be the preferred term? How one answers will depend on several factors, including the interpretive community to which one belongs and one's ambitions for a metalanguage for African musicology. Ideally, all three would be kept in circulation and deployed as contexts demand. In this chapter, I have opted to use *harmony* not only for its symbolic value but also because it does speak to both the linear and vertical dimensions. The linear and the vertical entail each other in principle, whether it is in Mukanda circumcision songs, a Baganda wedding song, the *hatsiatsia* portion of an Agbadza performance, or a mass by Palestrina, Bach, or Haydn.

There is another reason—an ideological one, perhaps—for not discontinuing the use of the term *harmony*. If we wish to resist a priori attributions of difference to African music, then using conventional terms will allow students to think broadly and comparatively rather than situate African referents in a supposedly different world and thus discourage comparison. To say that a

19. Ignazio Macchiarella, "Theorizing on Multipart Music Making," accessed September 2013, www.academia.edu/1554185/Ignazio_Macchiarella.

20. See Jaap Kunst, *Metre, Rhythm, and Multi-part Music* (Leiden: E. J. Brill, 1950).

21. For a fuller discussion of European terminology applied to Africa, see Stephen Blum, "European Musical Terminology and the Music of Africa," in *Comparative Musicology and Anthropology of Music*, ed. Bruno Nettl and Philip Bohlman (Chicago: University of Chicago Press, 1991), 3–36.

**Photo 7.1** Five azèlèŋ flutes of the Ouldeme, Cameroon.

**Photo 7.2** Four húrzozoŋ flutes of the Guiziga, Cameroon.

Bach cantata and an Ewe dirge both have a harmonic dimension is, in my view, more helpful as an invitation to comparative thought than characterizing what Bach does as "harmony" and what the Ewe singers do as "multipart." Again, the purpose here is not to undercomplicate other world practices; nor is it to declare an affinity for "imperial science," as one of my critics has alleged.[22] It is rather to caution against a priori attributions of difference as premise. In attending to the simultaneities of African music, the term *harmony* in the sense of "sounding together" is as good a point of entry as any other.

## JONES'S 1959 MAP OF AFRICAN HARMONY

In a bold attempt to convey the unity of Black African music, A. M. Jones turned to the domain of "harmony" for evidence of a remarkable consistency in the choice of intervals for group singing. The information is memorably displayed in one of two foldout inserts in volume 1 of his landmark work, *Studies in African Music* (1959). It takes the form of a map of the continent entitled "Distribution of Harmony" and is annotated in accordance with Malcolm Guthrie's 1948 classification of African languages using Arabic letters from A to T to distinguish among linguistic families.[23] Employing distinct elements of design, Jones shades areas of the map to show three different approaches to group singing: unison, parallel fourths and fifths, and parallel thirds. At a glance, continent-based students can locate their "homes" on the map and see which intervallic preferences are ascribed to their culture. They can also see who else belongs to their interval family.

Jones's attempt to distribute the reality of Africa into harmonic areas has not been attempted again on such a scale. This is in part because the ethnomusicological regime that came into power during the 1960s and 1970s entertained different research priorities. Led by figures like Merriam and Blacking, scholars preferred in-depth studies of individual cultures to sweeping comparative surveys. Yet Jones's effort, later complemented by the work of Alan Lomax, Nketia, Rouget, and Kubik, and implicit in broader claims made in the course of surveys of the continent's music, provided a picture of a complex set of harmonic practices while also encouraging comparison between music and languages and—to a lesser extent—between music and religions.

Writing in the 1950s, Jones had more limited access to recordings of African music than we do today. The staples of his discography included materials from

---

22. Louise Meintjes, review of *Representing African Music* by Kofi Agawu, *Journal of the American Musicological Society* 59 (2006), 777.

23. Jones, *Studies in African Music*, vol. 1, 231.

the massive archive bequeathed by Hugh Tracey at International Library of African Music (ILAM), as well as others from his own research into Zambian and Ewe music now housed in the Arthur Morris Jones Africa Collection in the British Library. Moreover, he painted with very broad strokes—unavoidably, given what was available then. With the significant increase in recorded materials since the 1960s, we can add some detail to Jones's outlines. For example, coastal West Africa (Liberia, Sierra Leone, the Côte d'Ivoire, Ghana, Togo, and Benin) is shown contiguously as dominated by singing in parallel thirds. We now know, however, that the region is more complex than that. The southern Ewe areas in Ghana, Togo, and Benin include significant traditions of singing in parallel octaves, fourths, and fifths, while other groups (like the Akpafu) may mix different species of parallelism. Current practices may also reflect newer influences since the 1960s, influences that were yet to be consolidated in Jones's time. So the map of harmonic practice may well be an evolving map. Still, Jones's provisional attempt helped to orient students to broad tendencies within musical culture areas.

Jones's specifically technical finding is that there are essentially two sets of *harmonic* preferences exercised by African singers. There are the thirds tribes (i.e., ethnic groups whose chorus singing is predominantly in parallel thirds), and there are the eight-five-four tribes (i.e., ethnic groups whose choral singing features parallel fourths, fifths, and octaves). (The unisons are, strictly speaking, not harmonic, but in practice they are more closely allied to the eight-five-four tradition than the three tradition). Jones believes that the eight-five-four tradition, which is also the pentatonic tradition, "is the main harmony tradition of Africa as a whole and is probably the older," and he imagines a three tradition that has been spreading across Africa. If ones are discounted, then eights should be discounted, too, since they involve mere octave duplication. And since, according to Jones, fives and fours are always perfect fifths and fourths, the entire eight-five-four tradition as a whole involves no *real* harmony since the other part merely duplicates the main part. (Had Jones noticed that some eight-five-four cultures sing with a mixture of intervallic successions, he might have credited them with genuine harmony.) By contrast, the thirds in a three culture alternate between major and minor thirds, so the two lines are not mere replicas of each other. Their simultaneous unfolding thus produces genuine harmony. Jones maintains that one could hear three cultures as originating in the diatonic scale.

A significant feature of Jones's map is that it appears in a chapter arguing for the "homogeneity of African music." According to him, harmony, alongside rhythm, provides a basis for establishing a common, continent-wide practice: "the music of Africa south of the Sahara is one single main system"; furthermore, "within that system there exist streams of typical expressions of it, the most notable and discrete being the two mutually exclusive streams of harmony [pentatonic and heptatonic]."[24] The presumed homogeneity of musical Africa is an idea that has appealed to other scholars. Nzewi, for one, is convinced that "incontrovertibly, there is an African (south of the Sahara) field of musical sound."[25] Kubik is a bit more cautious, preferring to speak of "African musics" in the plural while nevertheless acknowledging commonalities and "intramusical sources of influence." And Nketia, similarly guarded, notices "a network of overlapping styles, which share common features of structure, basic procedures and similar contextual relations."[26] It seems likely that many ordinary listeners will side with the unity mongerers, for by the time one gets through a hundred recordings of traditional African music (from Nigeria, Togo, Uganda, Mozambique, Zimbabwe, and the Democratic Republic of the Congo), one is likely to be overwhelmed by recurring sound environments and patterns. Quite what technical features or combinations of features inscribe sameness is an issue that continues to be discussed. Some hold the collective rhythmic practices as distinctive, others think the mode of interactive performance is the source, while still others consider the emergent temporal environment as the key. In citing the relatively little-studied parameter of harmony, Jones adds an important viewpoint. This is not to say that every last African practice has been accounted for—far from that; it is only to assert a noticeable consistency in the exercise of the harmonic imagination by African musicians.

Since Jones, several studies have been made of group- or region-specific practices. A few of these have been mentioned already, and a comprehensive summary is beyond the confines of this chapter, but a brief bibliographical excursus is in order. Kubik has investigated African tone systems not to update Jones's map—that project still stands in need of completion—but to offer a more ethnographically specific basis for reaching conclusions. According to him, "major triads are the basis of consonant chordal chains in the multipart organization of music in several regions of Africa."[27] Japanese Africanist ethnomusicologist Kenichi Tsukada also studied harmony in Mukanda among the Luvale in Zambia and discovered a "principle

24. Jones, *Studies in African Music*, vol. 1, 222.

25. Nzewi, *African Music Theoretical Content*, 31.

26. Nketia, *The Music of Africa*, 241. See the related discussion in Waterman, "Africa," and the helpfully concise summary in Jim Chapman, "Afro No-Clash: Composing Syncretic African/Western Music: Eleven Compositions and the Frameworks for Their Systematic Analysis" (PhD thesis, Queensland University of Technology, 2007), 45.

27. Kubik, "African Tone Systems," 41. See also Kenichi Tsukada, "Harmony in Luvale Music of Zambia," in *The Garland Encyclopedia of World Music*, 722–743.

of third-relations" as "the major clue to structural coherence." Kubik's triads become Tsukada's doubled thirds (a third above a note plus a third above the third).[28] Dave Dargie has studied the practice of overtone singing among the Xhosa in South Africa, while Akin Euba has explored multiple pitch lines in Yoruba music.[29] In studies of the Wagogo, Kubik argues that the overtone series or harmonic series serves as a kind of template for harmonic thinking, modeling both sonority and adjacent motion.[30] Polo Vallejo supplements these studies with investigations of melody and its impact on the modal organization of Wagogo music.[31] Kubik has also investigated tuning practices and drawn attention to differential margins of tolerance and the elasticity of scales.[32]

Several studies of Pygmy groups have highlighted their polyphonic practices. Typically, a musical system such as an anhemitonic pentatonic scale serves as a source of pitches for singers. Lines are then temporally coordinated in such a way that the pentatonic referent is heard both linearly and vertically. Suzanne Fürniss's article on Aka polyphony, drawing on Simha Arom's methodology, exemplifies this analytical approach.[33] Pygmy polyphony has also been compared with that of the Bushmen of Namibia. Nicholas England argued that Bushmen music is "polyphonic at its very basis."[34] Victor Grauer has recently revisited the hypotheses linking the two sets of practices and remains convinced that the basis of association as inscribed in polyphonic practices is justified.[35]

A number of scholars of non-Pygmy groups have looked into polyphonic practices at the microlevel and drawn attention to other species of parallelism, to the use of heterophony and "chromaticism," and to outside influences.

28. Tsukada, "Variation and Unity in African Harmony: A Study of Mukanda Songs of the Luvale in Zambia," in *Florilegio Musicale* (Festschrift Kataoka Gìdó zum 70. Geburstag), ed. Tanimura Ko, Mabuchi Usaburo and Takimoto Yuzo (Tokyo: Ongaku no Tomo Sha, 1990), 165.

29. Dave Dargie, "Umngqokolo: Xhosa Overtone Singing," *African Music* 7 (1991): 33–47; Euba, "Multiple Pitch Lines in Yoruba Choral Music," *Journal of the International Folk Music Council* 19 (1967): 467–487.

30. Kubik, "Multipart Singing in Sub-Saharan Africa."

31. Polo Vallejo, *Mbudi mbudi na mhanga.*

32. Kubik, "African Tone Systems."

33. Fürniss, "Aka Polyphony."

34. Nicholas England, "Bushman Counterpoint," 65.

35. Victor Grauer, "Concept, Style and Structure in the Music of African Pygmies and Bushmen: A Study in Cross-Cultural Analysis," *Ethnomusicology* 53 (2009): 396–424.

Gilbert Rouget drew attention to a microtonal practice in cult music from Benin.[36] Akin Euba, for example, studied the "multiple pitch lines" of Yoruba music, a collective repertory that is not necessarily invested in polyphony. Euba outlined the principles of Ijesha singing, noting chromatic usages, and contrasted these with Western-inflected practices found in 1960s jùjú music. There is a small but telling concentration of analyses of Ewe harmony (or "concurrent pitch sonorities," in George Dor's terminology) by Nissio Fiagbedzi, David Locke, James Burns, and others. Italian ethnomusicologist Serena Facci has done a thorough and systematic study of polyphonic techniques in the Burundian greeting genre, Akazehe. Drawing on a detailed transcription of an exemplary performance (heard at Web Example 5.2 🔊), she unpacks patterns of repetition and microvariation deployed within an overall call-and-response framework.[37] Finally, for a detailed analysis of harmonic geometries in Shona mbira music, turn to Martin Scherzinger's study of "Nyamaropa," an article published not in an ethnomusicological journal but in one devoted to new music and frequented by many an avant-garde composer.[38] Playing through Scherzinger's examples at a keyboard will enable readers to feel and hear the simultaneities. His detailed explication of the properties and generative modes of harmonies will then be more meaningful.[39]

It is impossible to acknowledge all these studies and to discuss questions of history, style, and influence, together with technical questions about consonance and dissonance and voice leading. These issues are best left to specialists. In this introductory context, I want to return to the beginning, so to speak, and rehearse a few of the basic routines in harmonic practice.[40]

36. Rouget, "Un chromatisme africain," *L'Homme: Revue française d'anthropologie* I-3 (1961): 32–46.

37. Serena Facci, "Akazehe del Burundi. Saluti a incastro polifonico e cerimonialità femminile," in *Polifonie. Procedimenti, tassonomie e forme: una riflessione a più voci*, ed. M. Agamennone (Verona: Edizioni Il Cardo/Ricerche, 1996), 123–161.

38. Scherzinger, "Negotiating the Music-Theory/African Music Nexus."

39. Nissio Fiagbedzi, *Form and Meaning in Ewe Song*; George Dor, "Melodic Commutation and Concurrent Pitch Sonorities in Ewe Songs: A Pre-compositional Resource for African Art Music," in *Multiple Interpretations of Creativity and Knowledge in African Music Traditions*, ed. George Dor and Olabode Omojola (Richmond, CA: Music Research Institute, 2005), 227–246.

40. See, for example, "The African Matrix in Jazz Harmonic Practices," *Black Music Research Journal* 25, no. 1/2 (2005): 167–222, for a useful summary of African practices. Kubik argues that many innovations in jazz harmony involve recreations of "concepts, traits, and aesthetic principles central to some African cultures somewhere on the map" (169).

## VIGNETTES OF AFRICAN HARMONY

Two principal techniques dominate harmonic expression in Africa. The first consists of a suspended harmonic field whose elements are activated rhythmically. Thus, a chord made up of the notes C-E-G-A may serve as the harmonic regulator in a composition for harp, xylophone, or voices.[41] Voice leading is guided by the ruling sonority and may involve adjacent or nonadjacent motion between the notes of the chord. This approach to harmonic expression is sometimes thought to engender stasis since the harmonic field does not change in the course of the composition. There is a dynamic element, however, and it resides in the movements of voices under various rhythmic, melodic, and timbral regimes. Again, the domains of individual parameters impinge directly on one another, making them ultimately inseparable. The second technique— also the one to which we will devote greater attention—is the negotiation of movement by means of parallel motion. The foundation for this technique is one of dualism, stemming—again—from the at-least-two philosophy that guides many expressive modes in Africa. Several local devices are employed in the realization of these two main harmonic techniques, and they will emerge in the discussion of individual examples.

I have assembled a small number of progressions to illustrate the main types of movement and will refer readers to recordings on which they can be heard. The value of aurally experiencing these sounding forms cannot be overemphasized. For convenience, words have been eliminated from the predominantly vocal examples to focus on the resultant sounds. Most of the examples come from the sphere of traditional music, but I will close with a comment on European influences.

In exploring these vignettes of harmony, readers might bear three things in mind. First, every composition or musical utterance is based on a tone system. Like language, a tone system may be a convention bequeathed by ancestors, adopted in part or whole from interaction with others (including neighbors) or imposed by historical oppressors. The three most common tone systems for traditional music are the anhemitonic pentatonic scale (C-D-E-G-A); the diatonic major scale, also described as heptatonic or seven-tone (C-D-E-F-G-A-B) (which includes various modal variants); and the overtone series or harmonic series. Pentatonicism spawns the eight-five-four behaviors, while the diatonic

---

41. For convenience, I use letter names (C, D, E, etc.) to depict pitch within a relational tone system. Since the emphasis in this chapter is on harmony rather than tuning, I will steer clear of the kinds of intonation or temperament that these pitch designations entail. Readers interested in pitch measurements will find valuable information in publications by Kubik, Andrew Tracey, and Natalie Fernando, among others.

scale supports all the "thirds cultures" and their variable modal orientations. The overtone series sponsors originary triadicity whereby triads and seventh chords are treated as sound fields. Second, harmonic procedures operate at two levels: a local level involving adjacent motion either by parallelism (like parallel thirds, fourths, or fifths) or oblique or contrary motion, and a larger level involving a controlling set of pitches, a structural framework admitting of various levels of embellishment. Keep in mind that the tone system and intervallic preferences entail each other. Third, we should approach these (mostly vocal) examples with a sense of the precariousness of what is represented in staff notation. Notations are conceptual indications rather than descriptions of previous performances. I have attempted to capture what I believe are the orienting structures, structures that exist prior to specific performances.

**Singing in unison and parallel octaves**. When a group of dirge singers sing a line with the pitches G4-D4-E4-D4, they are singing in unison; if their male counterparts join in with the notes G3-D3-E3-D3, they are merely duplicating the melody; the sounding texture is one of parallel octaves and appears to offer no distinct harmony. Unison and octave singing embody a communal ethos. They suggest togetherness; differences are minimized.

It is sometimes assumed that no harmonic content exists when singers sing in unison or octaves. While this is correct in principle, it overlooks the spillovers that confer a "harmonic" element on such singing. Unisons and octaves (including multioctaves) may be singular at a certain level of conception but multiple in actual realization. While the singers may all *intend* to sing the notes C-D-F, what comes out is likely to be an inflection of those notes upward or downward. Inflections typically come from the timbres of individual voices, the particular ways in which movement between adjacent notes is negotiated, and the pressures of intonational patterns stemming from language. All these may combine to deliver an expanded sense of melody. Now, whereas in some Western vocal ensembles (and perhaps also in westernized African choirs) the normative aim is to erase this threatening heterogeneity (by training voices to blend, as when performing a mass by Josquin or Palestrina), in many African traditions, the intention is precisely the opposite, namely, to celebrate ever so slight discrepancies within a shared framework. As "harmonies," then, unisons and octaves may be understood as realized differences resulting from intended samenesses. To these might be added instances of "friction octaves" reported by Kubik, in which octave companions on certain instruments are deliberately calibrated to create an enriched simultaneity, a slight "dissonance."[42]

---

42. Kubik, "Africa," *Grove Music Online*, accessed July 22, 2013.

The implied harmony of solo singing is typically conferred by the musical system. The Dan woman's lamentation (discussed in the previous chapter) is supported by a pentatonic field.[43] She chooses notes from this system to advance her narrative. Simultaneous doing thus involves a mental retention of the five-note source set even while choosing one note or another for the actual delivery. A similar process is at work in unison singing, where songs based on explicit systems are reproduced with predetermined rhythmic and metrical values. This is one of the most widespread modes of singing, and it is often marked by a gender divide. The Anlo-Ewe kinka songs and the Maninka Mansarah praise songs collected on the *Garland Encyclopedia* CD are good examples.[44] Similar unison singing may be heard in Bariba and Somba music from Benin. Unison horns feature in "Music in Praise of Oru Suru," while unison responses are featured within call-and-response formats, including those of the "Dinaba, Myth of Origins" or "Song to Carry the Corpse."[45]

Singing in parallel octaves implies both a unanimity and a strategic divergence. An excellent example is the "Inanga Chuchotee" for voice and harp, where the timbral distinction between the two instruments foregrounds the distance between them even as the performers rely on an internalized notion of octave equivalence.[46] Anlo-Ewe singing also provides many wonderful examples, as in the Sogbadzi songs studied by Nissio Fiagbedzi. Example 7.1 is an example from this repertoire. Using uppercase letters to demarcate the song form, Fiagbedzi shows an initial exchange between male and female voices, followed by a period in which both sing together. But for a moment in the B sections where an interval of a tenth is formed between the voices, everything sung here is either in unison (sections A and A▸ on the first system of the transcription) or in octaves (the rest of the excerpt). Although other parallelisms are cultivated by the Anlo-Ewe (fourths and fifths are common), parallel octaves seem especially prominent.

**Singing under an anhemitonic pentatonic regime**. As a resource for African composition, pentatonicism is typically treated with reverence: it is accepted and disposed as an overarching *complexe sonore* that enables a number of small melodic utterances. The pentatonic sound is often an abiding presence, a given rather than optional; traditionally, it is not usually available for modification. The

---

43. Heard on CD, *Africa: The Dan*, track 3, "Solo song of a woman."

44. CD, *Garland Encyclopedia*, tracks 7 ("Anlo-Ewe kinka songs") and 8 ("Maninka Mansarch Prase Song").

45. CD, *Benin/Bariba and Samba Music*, see, respectively, tracks 3 ("Music in praise of Oru Suru"), 7 ("Dinaba, myth of the origins"), and 11 ("Song to carry the corpse").

46. CD, *Garland Encyclopedia*, track 3, "Inanga Chuchotee."

**Example 7.1**  Singing in parallel octaves (Southern Ewe).

performers' task is to work out the desired vertical sonorities through melodic motion. The possibilities for intervallic motion include—predictably—all adjacent and nonadjacent intervals: major second, minor third, major third, perfect fourth, and perfect fifth. Excluded are semitones and tritones. The sound of the anhemitonic pentatonic scale attracts a variety of metaphors: open, nonhierarchical, less charged, perhaps even feminine (as opposed to masculine).

Example 7.2 is a simple example of a song in pentatonic mode (Web Example 7.1 🔊). The source set for this Tanzanian song is shown in white noteheads at the end of the transcription, E-D-C-A-G. This is then activated rhythmically and melodically as shown in the transcription. Verticalities include unisons, major thirds, and perfect fourths. The tone system suggests that the notes C and G with which the song ends do not function as a "treble" and "bass" in a hierarchic arrangement; rather, they are two complementary voices, alternatives to each other. The concluding fourth is thus not a dissonance requiring resolution but a contextual consonance carrying a sense of rest and arrival.

A second example of pentatonicism is the extraordinarily moving Pygmy lament, "Boyiwaa," recorded by Simha Arom.[47] The source set consists of the (approximate) notes G-F-Eb-C-Bb. All the sung pitches in this mixed-voice performance are referable to that set. The set is also the source for a series of motives, each motive enabling singers to thematize a memory of their dead

47. CD, *Centrafrique: Anthologie de la musique des Pygmées Aka*, track 26, "Chant de déploration sur le cadavre Boyiwa."

**Example 7.2** Singing in pentatonic mode.

companion, Boyiwaa. Given the stability of the source set, singers can join in the larger utterance knowing that the harmonic outcome is guaranteed. It is as if the pentatonic were suspended, like a giant chord-pedal, to be explored melodically for extended periods (six minutes in this song). The manner is minimalistic, as we have seen time and time again. No progression takes place between the pentatonic collection and any other.

A third, related example, also from the Pygmy repertoire, is a brief excerpt from a five-voice game recorded in Gabon by Pierre Sallée.[48] Example 7.3 captures a brief moment within the game where all five voices are active (some more than others). The principle here is identical to that in the previous example: each singer has internalized the pentatonic horizon and sings her part in full awareness of its constraints. The main notes are F-Eb-Db-Bb-Ab, a pentatonic without semitones. In this excerpt from a play song, each voice chooses two (voices 2 and 5), three (voice 1), four (voice 4), or all five notes (voice 3) from the source set and disposes them through repeated motives. The result is a dense polyphonic texture in which the pentatonic exerts a constant presence but displays no harmonic progression as such. Here, too, it may be argued that the chordal constancy confers a certain stability on the resultant sound, rather like some brands of minimalist music.

Another example of pentatonicism may be heard in the expanded texture of Simha Arom's transcription of a Central African horn orchestra (two out of twenty cycles are excerpted in Example 7.4).[49] The source set here is G-E-D-C-A and it is distributed among the eighteen horns in the ensemble in descending order and with octave duplication. Each horn technically plays only one note (the "extra" notes in horn 1's cycle 16, horn 2's cycle 17, and horn 4's cycle 17 are performance-induced embellishments, not structural notes), so the total production process resembles a hocketing ensemble. The resultant pentatonic is activated by means of incessant repetition of brief motives.

48. CD, *Musique des pygmies Bibayak*, track 2, "Etudes de jodis."

49. For a recording in the same idiom, though not of the same performance, see CD, Brandilly, *Introduction aux musiques africaines*, track 21, "Trompes des Banda." In listening to the recording, please bear in mind the margin of tolerance in accepting the tuning of these hand-made wooden horns. The pentatonic horizon is never in doubt, however.

**Example 7.3**  Five-voice vocal game based on a pentatonic scale (Bibayak Pygmy).

**Example 7.4**  Central African horn orchestra composition in pentatonic mode (Banda Linda).

**Example** 7.5  Speculative reconstruction of parallel-third melody (Akan).

**Singing in parallel thirds**. Unlike octaves, which feature a parallelism of the "same" interval (exigencies of tuning notwithstanding), streams of thirds may shift between major or minor depending on the governing tone system. (I'm leaving out of consideration neutral thirds for the sake of simplicity.) A simple illustration is the Akan folk song analyzed in Example 7.5. Level a shows the available pitches disposed in a downward succession, level b displays the melody in open noteheads as an arhythmic succession, and level c quotes the actual melody as transcribed by Nketia. Level d then shows harmonization in parallel thirds based on the source set, with an optional harmonization in parallel fifths in the first part of the song. Predominantly stepwise melodic motion throws into relief the leaps in bars 3, 6, and 9. The text (in Twi and in English translation) is given at level e.

Another illustration of parallel-thirds texture is the Northern Ewe crying song analyzed in Example 7.6. From the originating chant in line c, we might infer a main melody descending through a fifth, C-B-A-G-F. Such lines never walk by themselves, so by postulating companions as thirds (line d) or as thirds and fifths (line b), we complete the modal orientation of the melody as a diatonic scale disposed as a D-scale or Dorian mode. The song itself is shown

**Photo 7.3**  Northern Ewe singers, Peki, Ghana.

**Photo 7.4**  Manhyia Tete Nnwomkoro group, Kumase, Ghana.

**Example 7.6** Speculative reconstruction of parallel-third melody (Ewe).

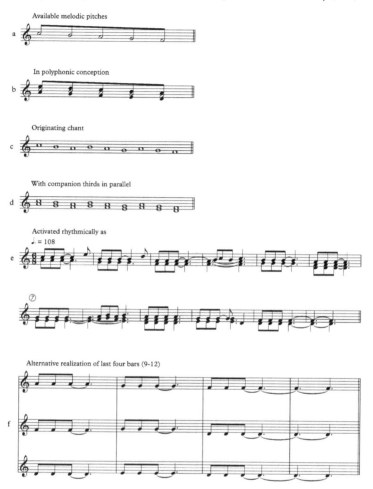

at level e. Harmonically, it mixes major and minor thirds with triads. Level f displays the last four bars in open score to show how the resultant sonorities are achieved through voice leading. Note especially the middle voice's jump from G to D across bars 2 and 3. All other motion in level f is stepwise, though not always unidirectional.

As a repertory, Northern Ewe *avihawo* or crying songs are a rich site for observing the behavior of parallel-third harmony. The reader will recall that crying songs encode deep responses to death. Singing together allows a communal projection of some of those responses. Crying songs typically follow a two-part form (as we saw in the detailed discussion of "Afaa ko yee" ["She is only a pretend sympathizer"] in chapter 5, Example 5.7). Part 1 is declamatory or recitativelike or in speech mode, and involves the solo singer alone, although now and then some chorus members may sing quietly along, or indeed hum a harmony underneath her narrative. Part 2, now in an explicit meter, involves the entire chorus and may be accompanied by a gourd rattle. Explicit harmonic behavior takes place in this second part. For the Northern Ewe, dyadic succession often functions as a foundation for musical structure. The preferred dyad is the third, and this may be major or minor, that is, C/E or D/F.

In one crying song, the lead singer asks, "Where have they gone?," to which the chorus responds, "I called out to them but it was quiet." The answers are delivered in two strings of dyads, F/D-G/E-F/D-E/C-F/D followed by E/C-F/ D-E/C-F/D-E/C. The terminal dyads are the adjacent pairs F/D-E/C, and this progression anchors the chorus's structure.

Such simple successions of dyads serve as structural frameworks for the chorus sections of many crying songs. They may be subject to slight embellishment, but they are always aurally salient. Embellishments are usually of the prefix type, meaning they precede structural notes.

Two basic principles constrain pitch construction in Northern Ewe avihawo; one involves the deployment of adjacent thirds as a frame, and the other involves sequences of thirds as means. The basic syntactical form involves two adjacent thirds, F/D-E/C. These may be subject to slight decoration. The next configuration is of two adjacent dyads in a question-and-answer formation, typically involving an ascent followed by a descent. Thus, E/C-F/D may be answered by F/D-E/C. The question-and-answer form occurs in modally transposed form, as, for example, F/D-G/E followed by G/E-F/D. Directions may also be reversed so that the fall precedes the rise, as when F/D-E/C is followed by E/C-F/D.

A second principle involves pairs of dyads moving unidirectionally in descent over varying spans, typically a third or a fourth. For example, G/E-F/ D-E/C may provide the framework for a chorus. Here, thirds constrain the progression both vertically and in terms of its linear extent. The sequence of thirds may be extended to a fourth, as in A/F-G/E-F/D-E/C, resulting in a discrepancy between the vertical and the horizontal. It is important to keep in mind that these dyads may be subject to decoration or embellishment. The idea of diody as the foundation of harmonic or contrapuntal thinking was floated by Jones in 1959, and although it has not spawned a large industry, it is an attractive premise for the analysis of several African traditions.[50]

50. For examples suggesting the use of diody, see recorded music from the Baule (*Côte d'Ivoire: Baule Vocal Music*), Kpelle (*Music in West Africa: Experiencing Music, Expressing Culture* [New York: Oxford University Press, 2005]), Akan (*Rhythms of Life, Songs of Wisdom: Akan Music from Ghana*), Ga (*Music of the Ga People of Ghana*), and Togo (CD, *Togo: Music from West Africa*, track 4, "Adjame le wo tawo").

A beautiful technique employed by Northern Ewe singers is that of voice crossing. Suppose we wish to articulate the succession of dyads A/F-G/E-F/ D as heard at the end of the crying song analyzed in Example 7.6. The most straightforward way is for voice 1 to sing the upper line A-G-F and for voice 2 to sing the lower F-E-D in parallel. Northern Ewe singers will, however, sometimes jump from top to bottom and vice versa. Instead of A-G-F, the first voice may sing A-E-F, and instead of F-E-D, the second voice may sing F-C-D. In place of a stepwise line, we now have lines with leaps, in particular the striking leap of a descending fourth. The point here is that singers retain the succession of thirds as an ideal but find other ways of achieving that ideal without following the most predictable path.

Voice crossing occurs most frequently in cadential situations among the Northern Ewe and may be said to add "spice" or contrapuntal interest to a given texture. Similar techniques have been described for other African groups, like the Ga and Akan.[51] For example, Kubik reckons that among the Wagogo, a principle of harmonic structuring is the skipping of adjacent steps within a scale to create harmony.

The Northern Ewe investment in parallel-third progressions is but one example of a wider practice. In the Côte d'Ivoire, the songs of Baule children are based on a similar principle.[52] Other examples may be heard in the music of the Ga, the Ashanti, the Kpelle, the Luba-Shankadi of the Democratic Republic of the Congo, and the Bemba of Luapula Province in Zambia.[53] Given that these chains of thirds can be embellished, and given also the exigencies of composing in the moment, it should be no surprise that some unisons or octaves may occasionally replace a supposed third. Then also, a third may sometimes be put on top of an existing third to make a triad or even a seventh chord. In the Northern Ewe tradition, however, triads and seventh chords operate at this superstructural level; they arise from decoration. The foundation consists solely of a succession of dyads indexical of a primal twoness. This is different from the Mukanda idioms studied by Kubik and Tsukada, or the children's songs of the Venda studied by Blacking, whose foundations are said to consist of triads.

51. Nketia, *African Music in Ghana*, 61.

52. See CD, *Côte d'Ivoire: Baule Vocal Music*, tracks 7 ("Little girls' sung games") and 13 ("Song of two little girls").

53. See Kazadi wa Mukuna, *The Characteristic Criteria in the Vocal Music of the Luba-Shankadi Children* (Tervuren: Musée royal de l'Afrique centrale, 1972); the recording made by Isaiah Mapoma, *Inyimbo; Songs of the Bemba People of Zambia* (Tucson, AZ: Ethnodisc, 1971); and his "Ingomba: The Royal Musicians of the Bemba People of Luapula Province in Zambia" (Master's thesis, University of California Los Angeles, 1974).

**Modality**. Although indigenous metalanguages do not on the whole recognize modality as a distinct phenomenon, its incidence in African repertories is basic and widespread. If we imagine the white-note diatonic scale as theoretical origin, then a modal arrangement is one that uses the same collection of notes but with a different orientation. The choice of center is often—but alas not always—indicated by the final note or sonority. Thus, one might speak of the D-scale, the E-scale, the F-scale, and so on. These resemble the old medieval church modes of Western Europe (Dorian, Phrygian, Lydian, and so on). Despite its widespread use, mode remains understudied in African musicology. Nor is there a continent-wide inventory of modes that might serve as a reference tool for researchers.

Of particular interest are situations in which modality interfaces with other orientations. According to Nigerian musicologist Augustus Vidal, the "superimposition of the diatonic scale on the music of Igbo, Hausa and Yoruba tends to destroy the modal quality [stemming from pentatonicism] of indigenous music, producing a 'Western sounding' Nigerian music."[54] Such mixes in orientation may be intended or unintended. Their outcomes may be suggestive or depressing.

A song from the neotraditional repertory of the Ga, "Soyama" (Web Example 7.2 ◐), provides an illustration of modal thinking, modal interaction with tonality, and parallelism involving thirds and fifths (Example 7.7). The transcription begins with the entrance of the bell playing a clave son time-line pattern (bars 1 and 2). Then comes the preludial improvisation by the guitarist (bars 3 through 8). Motion here is almost entirely in parallel thirds, and the modal orientation is Phrygian. The first singer enters in bar 9 and maintains the Phrygian orientation, but the accompanying guitar chord suggests a tonal orientation. The cadence in bars 15 and 16 is a perfect authentic cadence, but the singer ends on $\hat{3}$ not on $\hat{1}$. Ending on $\hat{3}$ suggests Phrygian, while the V7-I progression confers a tonal feeling. When the two singers join hands in bar 17, they do so in parallel thirds for four bars (17 through 20) and then continue in predominantly parallel fifths, finishing on the same F-D third that concluded the guitarist's introduction in bar 8. Once again, this modal orientation is inflected by the guitarist, who now plays a Bb underneath the singers' F/D dyad, thus reorienting the tonal sense away from the modal. These kinds of modal-tonal interactions occur frequently in neotraditional and popular music.[55]

54. Augustus O. Vidal, *Selected Topics on Nigerian Music: General Nature, History and Musicology/Music Education* (Ile Ife, Nigeria: Obafemi Awolowo University Press, 2012), 92–93.

55. For more on the modal ambience of Wulomei's music, observe the transcriptions in Gavin Webb, "The Wulomei Ga Folk Group: A Contribution Towards Urban Ethnomusicology," Ph.D. diss., University of Ghana, Legon, 2011.

Example 7.7 Parallelism of thirds and fifths in a neotraditional song, "Soyama" (Ga).

**Triadic successions.** Triads occur in various configurations in traditional African music. According to Kubik, "major triads are the basis of consonant chordal chains in the multipart organization of music in several regions of Africa."[56] Triads may emerge sporadically as linear accretions to a monadic or dyadic base or be generated from the harmonic series or overtone series. Both incidences of triads may be illustrated concisely.

In various Akan folk songs studied by Nketia in the 1950s and 1960s, triads occur intermittently. Likewise, in some Northern Ewe repertoires, the occurrence of triadic sound is incidental and decorative rather than foundational. Foundations are dyadic because of the transient or passing character of the

56. Kubik, "African Tone Systems," 41.

**Photo 7.5**  Koo Nimo's group, Kumase, Ghana.

triads. Scholars of Eastern and Southern Africa music (by the Venda and the Luvale of Zambia and Angola) seem to make stronger claims for the triad's generative status.[57] Example 7.8 is an excerpt from the song "Kanga Nakanga," collected from among the Zambian Luvale and transcribed by Tsukada. Cast in a broad solo-chorus form, the solo portion is, of course, without harmony. Then the chorus responds first in parallel thirds and then in parallel triads, mixing major, minor, and diminished triads (bars 43 through 57).

Instances of triadic parallelism occur in art music as well. Ghanaian composer F. Onwona Osafo composed a number of choral pieces during the 1960s that use parallel triads as a basic syntactical procedure. The composer often went to great lengths to mirror the rhythm and pitch contours of spoken language (Twi) in his musical setting. Triadicity is absorbed by a prevailing modality rather than sacrificed to the exigencies of cadence-based functional harmony. As many African composers have discovered, the constraints imposed by spoken tone languages on text setting would seem to dictate that homophonic parallelism be the preferred procedure if all the parts are using the same text. Onwona Osafo was ever conscious of this natural constraint, hence the rampant parallel triads found in his choral music.

57. Blacking, "Tonal Organization in the Music of Two Venda Initiation School," *Ethnomusicology* 14, no. 1 (1970): 1–56; Kenichi Tsukada, "Variation and Unity in African Harmony"; and Kubik, "Multipart Singing in Sub-Saharan Africa: Remote and Recent Histories Unravelled."

**Example 7.8**  Triadic parallelism (Luvale).

## "EUROPEAN" HARMONY

Writing about African "tonal systems" for a major reference work, Gerhard Kubik announces that the "European tonal system has been imported into most parts of Africa." There remain only "pockets" of the continent that are free of Western harmony.[58] This striking claim attributes considerable power to European functional harmony. African musicians, it seems, have been unwilling or unable to resist its influence. Many musicians operating in the art and popular music realms have been eager to adopt hymn-derived tonal harmony or two- or three-chord sequences from American pop music instead of fashioning a harmonic language out of indigenous modal systems. No figures accompany Kubik's claim—indeed, it would be difficult to establish its veracity on a quantitative basis. Nor is it clear whether it applies mostly to the areas that Jones called "thirds tribes," which are associated with Protestant Christianity; to the unison/octave Islamic areas; or to the pre-European, essentially pentatonic eight-five-four areas. Still, Kubik's remark draws attention to a widespread Western presence that is easy to overlook. Among other factors, the materiality of this particular domain may account for its ready and unmarked absorption. Tonal harmony is apparently in Africa to stay.

Already in 1959, A. M. Jones drew attention to what he called neofolk music in Africa, music that drew on an African folk heritage but at the same time admitted foreign influences, particularly in the domain of harmony. He cited an example from the genre known as "Makwaya" (Example 7.9). In distinguishing the "European" from the African features, Jones draws attention to the obedient synchronicity enshrined in the SATB texture, a texture that was unknown to any African group until the introduction of hymn singing, hymn singing itself being a musico-religious gesture that has had a profound impact on the consciousness of many Africans. Also noticeable in a European vein are the V-I perfect cadences in bars 3 and 4 and 7 and 8, with their charged, goal-oriented $\hat{7}$-$\hat{8}$ motions that embody the most basic of closing devices in

---

58. Kubik, "Africa," *Grove Music Online*, accessed October 2013.

**Example 7.9** Excerpt from "Makwaya" performance (Southern Africa).

*Translation:* Oh mother mine! let us rejoice!

European music. The "African" features, by contrast, begin with the form (A+ B) + (A + B) + C + C, which Jones describes as "one of the standard ways of singing an ordinary village song of the old type"; the initial cantor-chorus arrangement that captures the responsorial element typical of African form; and, perhaps most important, the dissonances in the second half of bar 5 produced through "divided" voice leading: the three top voices proceed in parallel while the bass moves in contrary motion.

Jones concludes this discussion by mocking the receptive Africans: "A song like this gives enormous satisfaction to the singers, who linger on the luscious diatonic common chord harmonies with undisguised relish." He even singles out the subdominant chord in bar 6 as a source of particular satisfaction. While it is no longer fashionable (at least in scholarly circles today) to convey such preferences in describing other people's musical practices, Jones's remark is instructive. In this historically power-based transaction, it is as if African musicians were offered "candy" ("luscious diatonic common chord harmonies"), which they in turn devoured "with undisguised relish." Significantly, no comparable rhetoric is evident in Jones's description of the African reception of European rhythm.

Literally tens of thousands of usages of harmony of the kind displayed in Jones's Makwaya example occur across the African continent. In South Africa, for example, a vibrant choral tradition from Mapophelia to Ladysmith Black Mambazo is beholden to the core procedures of the protestant hymn tradition. Several distinguished composers have written works, often in solfa notation, that consolidate this understanding of four-part harmony. Kenya's gospel music scene is unimaginable without this influence.[59] Church-based composition in Uganda, Cameroon, Zaire, Nigeria, and Togo also partake of this harmonic communion. Even in the ostensibly Catholic *Missa Luba*, a popular setting of the Latin Mass made in 1965 and notable for its use of African melodic and rhythmic elements, the pull of V-I progressions is felt throughout, whether as an element of syntax (where a

59. For an authoritative study, see Jean Kidula, *Music in Kenyan Christianity: Logooli Religious Song* (Bloomington: Indiana University Press, 2013).

**Photo 7.6** Youth choir wedding, Tema, Ghana.

dominant is immediately followed by its tonic) or at a larger, phrase level (where one phrase finishes on V and an answering phrase finishes on I). A 1971 BBC recording of African music includes a brief excerpt from the Seraphim and Cherubim Church in Lagos in which a pipe organ grandly reinforces the tonal grounds of the composition and confines the participating Yoruba talking drums to a superstructural level.[60] Discussions of music in Nigerian Christian liturgy by Lazarus Ekwueme and, more recently, Bode Omojola offer additional examples of tonal usage and leave little doubt about the depth of its influence.[61]

The direct influence of European four-part harmony may be seen in the hymn books that support worship in numerous African Christian churches. As an example, let me cite Hymn 235 from the Ewe hymnal (known as *Note Hadzigbalẽ*), which takes over the tune and harmonies not of a European hymn but of a piano piece, the "Song Without Words," op. 30, no. 3, by Felix Mendelssohn. Examples 7.10a and 7.10b display the two side by side. Mendelssohn's composition dates from 1834, while the Ewe appropriation was made over a century and a half later in 1992. The key has been lowered from

60. LP, *The Music of Africa* (London: BBC/Horizon).

61. See Ekwueme, "African Music in Christian Liturgy: The Igbo Experiment," *African Music* 5 (1973–1974): 12–33, and Omojola, *Yoruba Music in the 20th Century*, 113–135.

the original E major to E-flat major (church organists in this part of the world typically find flat keys easier to negotiate than sharp keys), and Mendelssohn's two-and-a-half bar prelude (1 through $3^2$) and postlude (25 through the end) have been eliminated, as have two other passages presumably deemed unsuitable ($7^3$ through $11^2$ and $15^2$ through $17^2$; the latter is an idiomatic reinforcement of the tonicization of the dominant key, but at the very end of the passage, A-natural replaces A-sharp to engineer the return to the home key). The original keyboard texture has been transformed into a strict four-part texture; the implicit "chorale" topic of Mendelssohn's "Song Without Words" is thus made explicit. The most revealing aspect of this appropriation is perhaps the outing of Mendelssohn's chorale, the intuition that an otherwise secular piano piece enshrines a potentially sacred element. There is little else that could be said to be organic about this particular transfer from Germany to West Africa.

Another revealing locus of European four-part harmony is the repertory of brass bands found throughout the continent and also in diasporic communities in Bolivia, Peru, Suriname, Jamaica, the United States, and elsewhere. Brass bands are associated with protestant churches, police and military bands, and community entertainment groups. A good example is a "highlife-hymn" recorded on the 1993 CD, *Frozen Brass: Africa & Latin America* by the Peace Brass Band.[62] The harmonic palette here is not dissimilar to that of the Makwaya song discussed earlier (Example 7.9). Within a basic diatonic framework, the Peace Brass Band incorporates flat $\hat{7}$ in descending configurations and natural $\hat{7}$ in ascending configurations. While the harmonic constraints of a hymn discourage the sorts of multivoice parallelism that we have seen in traditional music, moments in the Peace Brass Band's performance feature precisely such parallelism, notably the I-ii-I progression heard in the second reprise.[63]

The entire popular music industry labors under daily tonal rule, be it South African mbaqanga, Cameroonian bikutsi, Congolese rumba, or West African highlife. David Coplan observed astutely about highlife in 1978 that its harmonies blend hymnlike procedures with Akan-infected melody.[64] For one among thousands of examples, one could listen to Jewel Ackah's song, "The Lord's Prayer," which even uses a church-sounding organ.[65] Even within the

---

62. CD, *Frozen Brass*, track 2, "Highlife hymn."

63. For a fuller discussion of tonal influence, see my "Tonality as a Colonizing Force," in *Audible Empire*, ed. T. Olaniyan and R. Radano (Durham, N.C.: Duke University Press, 2016forthcoming)

64. David Coplan, "Go to My Town, Cape Coast! The Social History of Ghanaian Highlife," in *Eight Urban Musical Cultures*, ed. Bruno Nettl (Urbana: University of Illinois Press, 1978), 96–114.

65. CD, *Party Time with the Stars* (Ghana: Nakasi Records, 1994), track 10, "Yesu Ye."

**Example 7.10a** Ewe hymn.

(a)

Na mia-kpɔ Ye - su, si va 'nyi-gba sia dzi he-tsɔ mia nu - vɔ̃ fe fi-fo-de yi,

kɔ e-fe wu ɖi, be-ne mia-kpɔ a - gbe; e - lɔ̃ mi wũ yi-da-se ku me ke.

Ye - su, wòe-di be mia-va nɔ gbɔ wò; wòe-le mia dzeom, na-kplɔ mi va gbɔ wò!

**Example 7.10b** Source of Ewe hymn in Mendelssohn's "Song Without Words," op. 30, no. 3.

(b)

pluralistic and endlessly allusive style of Nigerian popular musician Lagbaja (amply represented on YouTube), tonal harmony is never far away.

The tradition of African art music is inconceivable without European tonal harmony. Initial mimicry of hymnlike textures gave way to adaptation of four-part harmony in the works of first-generation composers like Ephraim Amu, Ekundayo Philips, and Fela Sowande. The middle movement of Sowande's *African Suite*, for example, is a theme and variations, harmonized in accordance with the rules enshrined in hymns. Tonal innovations are multiplied in the works of other Nigerian composers, notably Ayo Bankole, Akin Euba, and Okechukwu Ndubuisi. One sign of this is the expansion of the harmonic palette to include more chromatic elements, as heard, for example, in Bankole's *Passion Sonata* (1977). Akin Euba has experimented with twelve-tone procedures in his *Scenes from Traditional Life* for piano (1970). Ato Turkson and Bode Omojola have also experimented with serialism and dissonant textures in their respective works *Three Pieces for Flute and Piano*, op. 14 and *Studies in African Pianism* (2003), while Gyimah Labi, although never abandoning a tonal horizon, uses a pervasive quartalism delivered through dense percussive textures in his *Five Dialects in African Pianism* (1994). Indeed, so deep is the tonal imprint of Europe on the minds of some art music composers that we may speak with some justification of the colonization of the musical consciousness of composers and listeners alike.[66]

A special place should be reserved for Nigerian composer Joshua Uzoigwe (1946–2005), one of the most imaginative and genuine of African art-music composers. Like others of his generation, Uzoigwe's training was in the church, and his knowledge of tonal harmony is evident in works such as " Lustra Variations" (1978) and "Talking Drums" (1991). Remarkably, and perhaps unlike several others, Uzoigwe, as he matured as a composer, became increasingly dissatisfied with the tonal legacy bequeathed by European music and sought ways to reinscribe harmony under an African sign. One way was to turn to traditional music, in particular the Igbo Ukom genre, and to study it for clues to indigenous processes that could then be expressed in different material domains. This may account for the freshness of Uzoigwe's sound, as heard, for example, in his *Four Igbo Songs* (1973) or in the set of piano pieces known as *Talking Drums* (1991). Harmonic thinking already shows some self-awareness on the composer's part.

Uzoigwe's tonal choices reflect an ongoing attempt to "speak" honestly rather than indulge in facile mimicry. He does not accept the European harmonic legacy as a gift; rather, such inheritance is subjected to probing and problematization. Not all composers see tonal harmony as ideologically freighted, however, so not all of them are inclined to resist it. Indeed, judging

---

66. See my "Tonality as a Colonizing Force in Africa."

from its reception across genres, tonal harmony retains a strong grip on the consciousness of many modern Africans.

## SIMULTANEOUS, INDEPENDENT DOING?

Of special significance are forms of simultaneous doing that are mere aggregates rather than intentionally coordinated actions resulting in specified sonorities. This kind of "macroharmony" occurs less frequently within a genre and more in a larger, plural performance environment. Funerals, festivals, and durbars are prime occasions for the cultivation of macroharmony. Such performances are not based on specific acts of micromanagement but are simply accepted as outcomes, endpoints whose details are left to emerge in the moment. In a sense, all acts of performance contain an element of the unplanned because there is no ontological stability to the figure of the performer from day to day, hour to hour, or moment to moment. And since the space and time in which repeated performances take place are always already unique (time never repeats, and therefore repeated actions are never really the same), the fixity that we associate with repeated performances is only a notional fixity.

The element of contingency behind these acts of simultaneous doing—acts whose components are not held to be in any kind of organic relation—is familiar to performers and audiences throughout Africa. I once attended the funeral of a distinguished drummer to which numerous performing groups had been invited, among them brass bands, choral ensembles, and of course drumming and dancing groups. Although the program for the occasion specified times for each group's performance, some musicians grew restless, too eager to await their scheduled time. Several groups took the law into their own hands and began to make their music even while the scheduled performances were taking place. What began as a sideshow would increase in intensity and begin to compete with the main show. I walked around the funeral grounds and was able to tune in and out of the different kinds of music being made "locally," but for a listener seeking a synoptic view of the event, the outcome was an irreducible plurality. This was one powerful manifestation of simultaneous doing achieved through independent expression (each group doing its own thing) but always with some awareness of a larger context. Indeed, at community-wide performances, one often encounters different kinds of music unfolding simultaneously. Standing back from this plural environment, one can appreciate the gift of simultaneity; one is not disturbed by it. In these contexts, resultants are fortuitous in their detail. The intention is to provide the conditions of possibility for certain actions rather than guarantee a specific sonic outcome.

Such acts of simultaneous doing are not confined to the interplay between different music or performing groups; they may occur within an individual

**Photo 7.7** Gligbazã Festival, Ho, Ghana.

genre as well. They may indeed be sanctioned by a particular performing practice. An all-female performing group at Cape Coast, Adzewa, employs a single
male drummer to drum for them at their performances. This is because, by
custom, the women are not allowed to drum. They may play bells, sing, and
dance, but only a man can drum. In their style of performance, singing, which
forms the core, follows the beat as articulated by the bells and drums, but
it also sometimes floats above the metronomic accompaniment pattern. This
is partly because such patterns provide a groove but are not always organically linked to the songs themselves. When the drumming diverges from the
singing from time to time (in other words, when the effect of two rather than
one ensemble is created periodically), there is no cause for alarm, because the

performers accept such departures as necessary but occasional. Built into the Adzewa performing practice, then, is an intermittent laxity in the coordination between the parts, a laxity that contributes to a feeling of multiple temporalities unfolding simultaneously.

In the village of Matse in the Volta Region, I encountered forms of Asafo (warrior) music making that were punctuated by a solo singer with his own bell accompaniment. No attempt was made to coordinate efforts. We might describe the resulting macroharmony as "dissonant," but insofar as most participants were focused on correctly executing their particular parts, the macroharmony remained unheard. Something similar happens in certain contrapuntal practices in which resultants between phrase beginnings and phrase endings are underspecified, allowing singers a degree of flexibility, and producing in the process a chain of "dissonances." Some of the songs described by Nicholas England in his study of Bushman counterpoint seem to me to fall in this category. Similarly, in some of the "multiple pitch lines" that Akin Euba identified in some Yoruba music, linearity overrides vertical resultants to create passing dissonances.[67]

From the performer's point of view, awareness that one is part of something bigger is enough to guarantee the meaning of one's actions. No attempt is made to seek the corroboration of coperformers other than those involved in articulating the principal musical idea. But where the ideas are inorganically related, where the groups are performing different music, it is enough to glory in copresence, enough to enjoy a cosmos that celebrates difference: I am because we are.

## CONCLUSION

I have described harmony as a form of simultaneous doing not because it is the only musical dimension that entails a foundational plurality but because, perhaps more intensely than others, harmonic thinking and expression arguably demand greater communal awareness. Although the main examples were culled from oral/aural composition, we also acknowledged paper-based harmonic practices beholden to European influence. Thinking again in terms of the three main categories of African music (art music, popular music, and traditional music), we see that harmonic exploration occurs in each one of them. The catalog of devices employed by art-music composers is large: varieties of scales, devices associated with tonal exploration, harmonies based

---

67. Nicholas England, "Bushman Counterpoint," and Akin Euba, "Multiple Pitch Lines in Yoruba Choral Music."

on fourths, twelve-tone procedures, and atonality. The harmonic elements in popular music are equally varied and include a slew of small-scale tonal-functional harmonies, modalities, and, of course, frequent mixtures of idioms. Perhaps the richest (but barely tapped) sphere of harmonic imagining remains the traditional repertory, where a variety of scale constructs (pentatonic and heptatonic being prominent), voice-leading routines (including parallelism and voice crossing), and incidental (often dissonant) harmonies are creatively deployed by musicians. What is badly needed in Africa today is *compositional exploration* drawing on these traditional resources and in accordance with the aesthetical and ethical imperatives of each composer's cultural and artistic credo. Only such music-on-music violence—rather than the scholar's detached reflection—will deepen our understanding of the harmonic parameter. It is noteworthy that, from a historical point of view, African harmony has not lent itself to the rampant appropriation by outsiders that we find routinely in the rhythmic sphere.

Another way forward lies in reconfiguring our geocultural alliances. Transactions with Europe since the nineteenth century have made European music central to modern African music, especially that used in church and in various popular genres. The truth, however, is that African musicians today stand to learn perhaps even more from Asian, Latin American, and Russian composers than from their Western European counterparts. Akin Euba has long recognized this potential and has been a relentless advocate for a genuine interculturalism in music.

Were traditional African music devoid of harmony, the view that we stand to learn a lot from European harmony (as W. E. F Ward once claimed) might have some merit. But as we have seen even from this introductory discussion, African music is emphatically not impoverished harmonically; on the contrary, it sports a rich variety of forms of simultaneous doing. What seemed to be an absence, or a sign that sophistication was lacking, is in fact a nexus of tremendous potential, a site rife for exploration. The fact that African harmonic resources have not been systematically gathered into a central resource, or the fact that they have not formed the basis of earnest compositional probing, does not mean that they do not exist. Nor should the capital-assisted spreading of protestant hymn tonality blind us to the wealth of indigenous resources. As more and more modern composers probe and develop their traditional harmonic heritage within a broadly cosmopolitan compositional environment, we are likely to appreciate more fully the potency of traditional resources.

# 8

# Appropriating African Music

Given the vast wealth and diversity of Africa's musical resources and the long-standing history of musical interaction with other cultures (Europe, the Americas, the Middle East, India, and Indonesia), not to mention the continuing exploitation of the continent (primarily economically, but with political, cultural, and religious ramifications, as well as devastating psychological consequences), it is not surprising that African music has become a global phenomenon in the twenty-first century. Traveling musicians, a vigorous trade in musical ideas within popular culture and media, and an increasing will to diversification in parts of the metropolis (in concert programming, hiring practices, and the constitution of various social, religious, and academic institutions) have combined to make African music more and more audible and less and less avoidable in many parts of the world.

Among immediate signs of this global presence are regular visits by urban popular musicians to the metropolis. Artists from an earlier generation like Salif Keita (b. 1949), Ali Farka Toure (1939–2006), Mory Kanté (b. 1950, originally Guinean), the duo Amadou and Mariam (b. 1954 and 1958, respectively), Toumani Diabaté (b. 1965), and Oumou Sangare (b. 1968) from Mali; Youssou N'Dour (b. 1959), Baaba Maal (b. 1953), and Ismael Lô (b. 1956, originally from Niger but grew up in Senegal) from Senegal; Oliver Mtukudzi (b. 1952), Thomas Mapfumo (b. 1945), and Chartwell Dutiro (b. 1957) from Zimbabwe; Angelique Kidjo (b. 1960) from Benin; Ladysmith Black Mambazo (founded by Joseph Shabalala [b. 1941]), Mahotella Queens, Hugh Masekela (b. 1939), Abdullah Ibrahim (b. 1934), Sathima Bea Benjamin (b. 1936), and Lucky Dube (1964-2007) from South Africa; and Ray Lema (b. 1946) and Papa Wemba (b. 1953) from Zaire are (or were once) familiar names not only to people on the continent but also to others in Europe, the United States, and Australia. One can nowadays attend mega concerts in parks, on college campuses, and in community theaters and dance halls in Berlin, Paris, Toronto, London, Moscow,

Madrid, Melbourne, Rio, Atlanta, and New York and observe thousands of (mostly) non-African youth dancing enthusiastically to African beats.[1]

The recording industry has played a major role in fostering this influence. Beginning with the earliest products in the 1920s, when the veiled sounds of empire were captured in the first wave of recorded African popular music heard throughout Europe and in colonies like Malaysia and Singapore, and continuing through vibrant performances in the urban and cosmopolitan spheres, African popular music has been made successively available on wax cylinders, tape, vinyl, cassette, and now CDs and MP3s.[2] By the 1980s and 1990s, when individual purchases of recorded music in cities in Europe and America reached something of a high point, the available African options, often stored under an ambiguous "world music" label, formed a significant proportion. Nowadays, recorded African music can be heard on any number of radio and TV shows; accessed at various Internet sites, including YouTube; and of course listened to in the personal listening libraries of millions of young people strapped to iPods.

This is nothing less than an explosion of African music onto the world stage. It is not a development confined to popular music, however. So-called traditional music, too, has gone global in its own way. That narrative begins properly with the trans-Atlantic slave trade; extends through the famous world exhibitions beginning in the 1880s (in Paris, Berlin, St. Louis, and New York, among many other places); begins again—and more concretely—with the production of the earliest ethnographic recordings by European anthropologists, ethnologists, and missionaries in the 1900s, most of them deposited in European libraries and archives; and continues today with a host of private recordings assembled by visitors to Africa, including students, missionaries, retirees, and people seeking business opportunities.

The trade in human beings that took place during the seventeenth through nineteenth centuries and resulted in the involuntary migration of millions of Africans to the Americas and Europe carried significant capital in artistic potential. The impact that minority black populations have subsequently made

1. For developments in global popular music through the 1990s, see Timothy Taylor, *Global Pop: World Music, World Markets* (New York: Routledge, 1997). See also *World Music: The Rough Guide*, ed. Simon Broughton, Mark Ellingham, and Richard Trillo, with Orla Duane and Vanessa Dowell (London: Rough Guides 1999). Philip V. Bohlman concludes his *World Music: A Very Short Introduction* (Oxford: Oxford University Press, 2002) with a concise discussion of "the globalization of world music."

2. On the early history in the context of empire, see Michael Denning, "Decolonizing the Ear: The Transcolonial Resonance of Vernacular Music." See also Noel Lobley, *The Social Biography of Ethnomusicological Field Recording*, for the part of the story manifest in Hugh Tracey's project in South Africa.

on the soundscapes of many nations, including Cuba, Brazil, Haiti, Jamaica, and the United States, has been nothing less than profound. African slaves arrived in the New World empty-handed, having been stripped of their material belongings and reduced to bodies rife for exploitation as labor. But no slave arrived empty-headed. Carrying propensities for creativity based on a variety of musico-linguistic endowments, many retained memories of their pasts, including memories of speech (and speaking), song (and singing), and dance (and dancing). In other words, enslaved Africans brought with them "texts" and text-making capabilities to the New World. New life experiences would influence what they did as they channeled their talents through a variety of literary and musical forms. Some propensities were retained, while others were tweaked, modified, or transformed in accordance with individual and collective visions. The truth is that the African diasporic lineage is remarkably resilient, endowed with an unusually high capability for adaptation to novel situations. Under some of the most inhumane conditions (during and after slavery, and throughout the twentieth century), and in spite of what Kamau Brathwaite has called "the seemingly endless purgatorial experience of black people,"[3] Africans have nevertheless retained and operated innovative conceptual regimes pertinent to music making while holding on to nuggets of Old World material. Today, a definitive specification of those qualities that set it apart from other world music remains an ongoing project for scholars, but to many ordinary listeners, African music's apartness and compatibility seem self-evident.

Traces of African music in North, Central, and South America, as well as in the Caribbean Islands, are testimony to its power, geocultural spread, and influence. Samba and candomblé in Brazil, kawina-winti and kaseko-opo poku in Suriname, tamunangue in Venezuela, reggae in Jamaica, and calypso in Trinidad are ready examples. Numerous genres of black music have developed from a black expressive presence in Argentina, Brazil, Ecuador, Haiti, Suriname, Jamaica, Cuba, Colombia, Uruguay, and Trinidad. The music of Maroon communities in Suriname, French Guiana, Jamaica, and Colombia is dotted with African retentions. The Yoruba influence in Cuba and Brazil, especially in association with the worship of Orishas, is a story in itself. And although less overt, early forms of African American music, including field hollers, work songs, and various children's games, are often marked by their African pasts. Studies of Africanist retentions continue to remind us of African music's perseverance.[4]

3. Kamau Brathwaite, Remarks made in the context of a seminar, Columbia University, April 2008.

4. On Africanisms, see Portia Maultsby, "Africanisms in African American Music," in *Africanisms in American Culture*, 2nd ed., ed. Joseph Holloway (Bloomington: Indiana University Press, 2005), 326–355; Denis-Constant Martin, "Filiation or Innovation? Some

The African musical diaspora extends beyond the Americas and the Caribbean. Africans have continually resided in India since the thirteenth century, maintaining some of their home traditions while developing others based on new contacts. Siddis, for example, have retained elements of their African pasts (language, religion, and music), while a group of African Indian mystics identified in Gujarat have kept certain East African traditions alive. Sub-Saharan African elements may also be heard in various locations in North Africa and the Middle East. A striking example is Stambeli, a healing trance music cultivated in Tunisia by people of black African origin.[5]

How might we explain African music's resilience? Given the circumstances in which black music in the United States, for example, has developed, it seems almost certain that its core is at once distinct and incorporative rather than separatist. To cite an old example, fears of a slave insurrection during the slavery period led to Africans often being denied opportunities for self-expression outside the master's gaze; rather, regular policing fostered a connection to other streams of (musical, linguistic, and religious) influence. And yet black authorship retained its accommodative stance without ever sacrificing its distinctiveness. It is precisely this combination of an original and an originary syncreticism that indexes the essential black sound. The potency of black music lies in responsible and unyielding guardianship; it suggests a principled and committed custodianship of a shared heritage. Contrary to theories that seek peculiarly African ingredients in black music (essential forms, essential rhythmic patterns, and essential temporal routines), this view suggests a lineage made possible not necessarily through the retention of materials nor by the possession of a peculiar sensibility or disposition, but by the generous assumption of guardianship of a heritage. If black music today seems to inscribe many of the qualities we idealize in music, it is because its core has always been protective without refusing accommodation.[6]

Hypotheses to Overcome the Dilemma of Afro-American Music's Origins," *Black Music Research Journal* 11 (1991): 19–38; and Peter Fryer, "The 'Discovery' and Appropriation of African Music ad Dance," *Race and Class* 39 (1998): 1–20. A moving narrative of an African diasporic community reconnecting with its homeland is filmed in *The Language You Cry In*, produced and directed by Alvaro Toepke and Angel Serrano (San Francisco: California Newsreel, 1998).

5. For a helpful background, see *The African Diaspora in the Indian Ocean*, ed. Shihan de S. Jayasuriya and Richard Pankhurst (Trenton, NJ: Africa World Press, 2003), and, in particular, Jayasuriya's essay, "The African Diaspora in Sri Lanka." The CD, *Sidi Sufis: African Indian Mystics of Gujarat* (Van Nuys, CA: Aspara Media, 2002) provides a taste of their sound worlds. On *stambeli*, the definitive work is Richard C. Jankowsky, *Music, Trance, and Alterity in Tunisia* (Chicago: University of Chicago Press, 2010).

6. For a related discussion, see Ronald Radano, *Lying Up a Nation; Race and Black Music* (Chicago: University of Chicago Press, 2003).

The appropriation of African music has been made possible in part by the complicated presence of its music and musicians abroad. The obvious material means include the huge repository of recorded African speech and music in various libraries. Scholars are, of course, aware of these resources, and many consult them regularly for research purposes, but it is less clear that general publics in Africa know them as well. As indicated in the introduction to this book, scores of libraries in the United States, United Kingdom, France, Belgium, Germany, Italy, South Africa, and Austria boast huge and often underused collections of African music, both traditional and popular. Indeed, one such ethnographic recording from 1966 became the source for Herbie Hancock's famous 1973 rerecording of "Watermelon Man" from his *Headhunters* album.[7] As Steven Feld tells the story, Hancock's appropriation is only one instance of a practice widespread among jazz musicians and practitioners of world music and world beat. Examples are too numerous to cite, but we may mention Martin Cradick's 1993 *Spirit of the Forest* (see also the companion *Heart of the Forest*), the hugely popular disco-dance offering by Michael Sanchez known as *Deep Forest* (1992), the Afro-Belgian group Zap Mama's *Adventures in Afropea* from 1991, and Francis Bebey's 1993 CD, *Lambaréné Schweitzer*.[8]

Another often-discussed example is Paul Simon's collaboration with Ladysmith Black Mambazo in the production of the 1986 album *Graceland*. Whatever the politics, aesthetics, and ethics of appropriation are, one undeniable outcome of the encounter is the media exposure given to the South African group in the wake of this collaboration, an exposure that has brought them economic and symbolic gains as well. There are many such appropriations, influences, and collaborations (one thinks, for example, of Brian Eno and David Byrne's 1981 album, *My Life in the Bush of Ghosts,* whose title is taken from Amos Tutuola's 1954 novel by that name). Identifying them all would be tedious and ultimately impossible in this context, but let us at least mention a few. A subtle case is that of contemporary artist Joanna Newsom (b. 1982), whose story-telling stance combines with the influence of Appalachian folk singing and study of polyrhythms to produce an "African" profile. One can also hear West African influences in a song like "Stillness Is the Move" (2009) by the Dirty Projectors, exponents of indie rock, including the guitar styles of Ali Farka Toure, hocketing, a near time-line pattern, and a bass line derived from highlife. Vampire Weekend's "Cape Cod Kwassa Kwassa" is clearly Africa influenced; it is reminiscent of *Graceland* even though its guitar licks point to

---

7. Steven Pond, *Head Hunters: The Making of Jazz's First Platinum Album* (Ann Arbor: University of Michigan Press, 2005).

8. Feld, "Pygmy POP: A Genealogy of Schizophonic Mimesis," *Yearbook for Traditional Music* 28 (1996): 1–35.

a different region of Africa. Then there is The Very Best's "The Warm Heart of Africa" (2009), a song that is African in intention and spirit while referring to a variety of styles, including 1980s American pop and Afro-pop.[9] At the Love Supreme Festival in Glynde in the United Kingdom during the summer of 2013, Melody Gardot's set was smothered with African time-line patterns. And the list goes on. Drawing firm boundaries between the ostensibly African and the non-African is not always a straightforward task, but it would be perverse not to acknowledge these and similar African affinities.

The increasingly fashionable habit of bringing exponents of African traditional music to tour various European locations has also facilitated certain kinds of contact and appropriation. To choose just one iconic example: in recent years (the 2000s), groups of Pygmy singers and musicians from Central Africa have been put on display in Paris, Brussels, Vienna, and elsewhere for the benefit of mainly European audiences and researchers.[10] In the wake of one such visit in 2003, French pianist and musician Pierre-Laurent Aimard (b. 1957) and his team assembled a remarkable musical document at the Teldex Studio in Berlin, a CD entitled *African Rhythms* featuring music by Ligeti, Steve Reich, and the Aka Pygmy.[11] On first hearing, these sound worlds could not be more different from one another, but they are brought together here to underline the contention that they either originate in or are beholden to Africa. The arrangement of tracks on the compact disc is strategically random. Ritual and play songs of the Aka Pygmy, captured with a degree of acoustical clarity that partly erases the spirit of spontaneity that would normally attend authentic outdoor performances, unfold a sound world dominated by ostinato and pulse-based polyphony. The linguistic aspect of this sound world is, however, not accessible to most Western listeners. Reich's minimalist aesthetic, sampled in *Clapping Music* and *Music for Pieces of Wood*, is itself animated

9. Thanks to Matt Marble for bringing to my attention the African sediment in indie rock.

10. For a representative account, see Luis Devin's description of the Aka Pygmies' Italian Concert of 2001 on his website, http://www.luisdevin.com. Germany's entanglements with African music are recounted in Florian Carl, "The Representation and Performance of African Music in German Popular Culture," *Yearbook for Traditional Music* 43 (2011): 198–223.

11. CD, *African Rhythms.* For two critical assessments, see Martin Scherzinger, "Gyorgy Ligeti and the Aka Pygmies Project," *Contemporary Music Review* 25 (2006): 227–262, and Dániel Biró and Andy Schloss, Review of *African Rhythms* by Pierre-Laurent Aimard, György Ligeti, Steve Reich, Simha Arom, *Ethnomusicology* 51 (2007): 162–165. A film built around a performance of Ligeti's piano concerto but incorporating some of Ligeti's Africanist contacts is *Wenn die Zahnräder Menschen sind: das Klavierkonzert von György Ligeti*, by Hanne Kaisik, György Ligeti, and Uli Aumüller (Berlin: Inpetto Filmproduktion, 1996).

by repetition and a foregrounded pulse. While Reich's music suffers no alienation in its current acoustical representation, the transitions in and out of the African rainforest on the CD engender a novel experience, one that might cause the listener to rethink the relationship between the abstract and the concrete. Abstraction is carried one stage further in Ligeti's etudes, with their irregularly repeating rhythms within regular cycles. Lacking any direct traces of African materials, the etudes stand worlds apart from those of the Aka and of Steve Reich. And yet, their affinities with Reich are suggestive because of the kind of compositional subjectivity they promote, a subjectivity different from that of the Aka Pygmy. The juxtaposition of tracks thus encourages a multifaceted temporal exploration. As Dániel Biró and Andy Schoss point out, the "sudden changes in aesthetic" that listeners to the CD experience are precisely the point. This is not to overlook the thread that sanctions the journey from the Central African rainforest through New York City to cosmopolitan Paris or Berlin. Every track, after all, is either authentically African (even if inauthentically performed) or based on an African idea that has been processed by an alien subjectivity. Varying distances from the source serve only to highlight the African foundation. In this way, the listener explores traditional and modern idioms, the human and the mechanical, and natural and fraught or contorted expression.

Even the tradition of African art music nowadays exerts a global presence. Although they began in the nineteenth century as a series of attempts by literate, church-going Africans to write choral anthems, songs, and instrumental music for local performance by local musicians for a local audience, the products of art music have increased statistically and grown in symbolic importance since then. Every school of music or department of music on the continent has produced its share of composers, be it in Uganda, Kenya, the Democratic Republic of the Congo, Nigeria, or Ghana, and this number has increased with increased opportunities for study in Europe and America. Art music nowadays receives more performances outside Africa than within Africa. Perhaps this was inevitable given that the very tradition of written works for a contemplating, nonparticipating audience was a European practice in the first place. African art music began as unabashed mimicry of this practice. Although it has been colored by local habits and desires, it retains its subjective core. Due recognition of art music came gradually rather than immediately, but there is every indication nowadays that program organizers seeking to diversify the standard Euro-American repertories sometimes turn to African art music. The economic migration of several prominent African composers and performers to various parts of the West at various times (Sowande, Euba, Labi, El-Dabh, Fred Onovwerosuoke, Dor, Sadoh, and Chapman Nyaho, among many others) has also played a role in exposing Europeans and Americans to their works. During the 1990s and

2000s, festivals featuring African art music took place in diverse locations in Austria, Germany, South Africa, and the United Kingdom.

One final sign of the global impact of African music is its presence in the multimedia package known as film. Musical Hollywood, for example, is unimaginable without the imagined sounds of Africa, sounds that suggest qualities of difference, otherness, exoticism, alterity; sounds that point to nature, the jungle, forests, the wilderness, and the desert; and sounds that speak of ancient times, of the time before time, of the pristine, unspoiled, and uncivilized. Music has often functioned as a vital component of film, so it is not surprising that, in seeking the most vivid and evocative sonic effects to enhance their narratives, film producers have frequently turned to African music.

The list of films with African *topoi*, or in which African music is used, is too long to cite here completely. Writing in 2007, American ethnomusicologist Andrew Kaye counted no fewer than five hundred, but he believes this is far from complete.[12] The earliest films on Kaye's list date from the 1920s to 1940s and use the imagined sound of Africa to portray jungle scenes and brave or heroic explorers of faraway places. In the 1950s, Hollywood often drew on constructions of Africa, the effort now helped along by the models inscribed in available ethnographic recordings. After independence in the early 1960s, born-in-the-tradition film directors began to bring a new dimension to the portrayal of Africa. Senegalese Ousmane Sembene, for example, the acknowledged father of African film, would draw on varieties of traditional music to enhance the presentation of African life and to express opinions about cultural practices like polygamy, cliteridectomy, and the competing claims of heritage and imported religions. Kora-playing griots and balafon players are among the musicians of choice. His 1977 film *Ceddow*, for example, channels anti-Islamic sentiments through griot music. By the 1980s, there was increased access to a still broader range of African music, including varieties of popular music. The soundtracks of popular films like *Out of Africa* (1985), *Coming to America* (1988), *The Lion King* (1994), and *I Dreamed Africa* (2000) are among the prominent conveyors of an imagined Africa. African cinema also boasts films with specifically musical *topoi*. The protagonist of Benoît Lamy and Ngangura Mweze's 1987 film *La vie est belle* is an aspiring musician who performs first as an mbirist and then later as a singer/bandleader. The film culminates in a feel-good, thoroughly communal scene in which song serves simultaneously as social glue and as a record of personal achievement. Also of interest is *Karmen Gei*, an open

---

12. Andy Kaye, "The Film Score and the African Musical Experience: Some Comments on a Work in Progress," *TRANS* 11 (2007), accessed July 23, 2013, http://www.sibetrans.com/trans/a126/the-film-score-and-the-african-musical-experience-some-comments-on-a-work-in-progress.

exercise in strategic mimicry, in which director Joseph Gaï Ramaka appropriates Bizet's *Carmen* for an African retelling. Opera emerges here not as an alien form but as an entirely natural mode of expression. Familiar themes of love, betrayal, and jealousy are animated by song, dance, and praise singing; in the process, the notionally distinct worlds of European opera and African music making emerge not as opposed but as complementary.

A special place should be reserved for *Kinshasa Symphony*, a film by Claus Wischmann and Martin Baer (2011) that captures with particular poignancy the dynamics of African reception of Western classical music in an urban African setting.[13] Men and women with little or no previous experience of "classical music" join the *Orchestre symphonique Kimbanguiste* under the baton of Armand Diangienda to perform Beethoven's Ninth and other works. With instruments in various states of disrepair and a rehearsal schedule that taxes the members' daily schedules (all the musicians hold jobs elsewhere and attend rehearsal after work), and operating under the normal challenges of urban African living (power outages, transportation difficulties, and no rehearsal spaces), these musicians manage—miraculously—to pull off a successful performance. While the main narrative in the film charts the rehearsals and eventual performance of Beethoven's Ninth, subsidiary narratives illuminate the lives of several individuals who have chosen to learn "Western" instruments and participate in a performance of a canonical work while living and working in a complex city like Kinshasa. There are lessons in organology (e.g., in the making of a double bass), music pedagogy, urban amenities (electrical powering of lights and pressing irons), interculturalism in music, economics, and employment. But the ultimate triumph is a triumph of the human spirit, the devotion to an admittedly challenging work of Beethoven's whose ostensible foreignness to African musicians seems less and less marked as the musicians gain control of their parts. This is no facile appeal to a universal brotherhood ostensibly inscribed in Beethoven's score. It is a more basic appeal to the desire to sing and play parts in an ensemble and achieve the satisfaction of having succeeded. The expression of such a desire takes place regularly in the town and village, and it is mediated by different musical idioms, be they local or foreign, but the ultimate goal is one and the same. *Kinshasa Symphony* invites us to peel off layers of attributed difference to see what African amateurs, like amateurs elsewhere, aspire to and are capable of achieving.

Radio and television shows, airline entertainment systems, and music at shopping malls all contain "African" elements, sometimes in the form of a beat or time line. African diasporic communities in Toronto, Houston, Atlanta, and

---

13. *Kinshasa Symphony* by Claus Wischmann and Martin Baer (Berlin: C Major Entertainment GmbH, 2010). I thank Victor Vu for bringing this film to my attention.

London also frequently cultivate music from their home countries at festivals and funerals, parties and church services. Some have instituted after-school activities in the form of singing and dancing for their deprived or detribalized children. Such community-based efforts do not, of course, exclude non-African children, and this partly explains why some children of non-African ancestry have developed an interest in African music. Indeed, in various African music ensembles heard today on college campuses throughout the United States (Boston; Los Angeles; Middletown, Connecticut; Athens, Ohio; Minneapolis, Minnesota; and Gainesville, Florida) and Canada (Toronto, Vancouver, Edmonton, and Montreal), membership is rarely restricted to Africans or people of African descent. Indian, Hispanic, Caucasian, and Asian drummers play alongside their African peers, some individuals even assuming the elevated role of master drummer.

The foregoing is no more than a sketch of African music's entanglements around the globe, but the subject surely merits more comprehensive study if only to affirm the music's somewhat paradoxical nature as a music that is compatible and distinctive at the same time. Whether it is true, as Jon Pareles once imagined, that the "rise of rhythm" in global pop together with "the receding influence of European culture in a global mix, as the Western emphasis on melody and harmony gives way to the beat" means that "Africa, where rhythm rules, has paid back its conquerors and slave traders by colonizing the world's music," and whether African music may be thought of as having enabled a recolonization of Western popular music (as John Collins once averred) are points to ponder and debate. That African music's global entanglements are real and widespread is no longer a hidden truth.[14]


## APPROPRIATION: THEFT, HOMAGE, OR BENIGN INFLUENCE?

Because African music is by now imbricated in a variety of contexts worldwide, questions of theft and appropriation, or related questions of homage and influence, have become pertinent in a way that they weren't before about 1970. The question of appropriation is not a comfortable topic of conversation, however. Saying that an individual artist has stolen from another, or from a known tradition, is a serious charge—worse for the accused if the accusation is not properly substantiated, or if it is made on the basis of a naive interpretation of the nature of influence. Saying that one artist pays homage to another by

14. Jon Pareles, "The Rhythm Century: The Unstoppable Beat," *New York Times* May 3, 1998, 1; John Collins, "Listening to the Silence."

lifting part of his or her work is less of a charge and more of an open acknowledgment of precedent; it may be intended as a gesture of respect or humility. And to say that one artist has been influenced by another is to admit a degree of absorption, conscious or subconscious. Influence implies an affinity that, whether welcome or not, is nevertheless palpable.

The invariant element in these transactions is the transfer of elements from a source domain to a target domain. This may be done overtly or—more usually—covertly. The relatively recent redenomination of musical works as capital—as goods that can be exchanged, as commodities with variable value depending on demand—has been the main catalyst in the developing economy of appropriation. This is not the place to enter into a discussion of the legal issues raised by musical appropriation,[15] but since the question of what constitutes an appropriation is itself premised on an understanding of the nature of musical composition in a given society, it would be helpful to give the idea of "composition" a brief and necessarily preliminary airing.[16]

Acts of musical composition are unavoidably intertextual. Just as language is a social institution, so music functions in many societies as an institution (we often speak—albeit informally—of the language of music). Music, like knowledge, cannot belong to any one person. Every composer is born into an environment that is already filled with (humanly organized) sounds of which a subset is claimed as music. A composer acquires a heritage musical language just as he or she acquires a natural language. He or she might "speak" the language of music entirely conventionally, adapt it to dancers' needs, give it a personal inflection, or even begin to undermine its premises in the name of artistic or poetic license. What is never possible is for the individual to operate as if there was no past, no existing resource, no known routines, no intertextual horizon. To compose is necessarily to engage with a prior discourse, whether in affirmation or dissent, actively or passively, consciously or subconsciously.

It is this unavoidable dependency of one creative act upon another that undermines the pertinence of questions of appropriation, theft, or homage, questions that rest on firm views about ownership and about the boundaries separating one's territory from another's. If composing necessarily—and often subconsciously—entails an engagement with a prior discourse, then how

15. See Felicia Sandler, "In Search of a Cross-Cultural Legal Framework: Indigenous Musics as a Worldwide Commodity," in *Music and Cultural Rights*, ed. Andrew Weintraub and Bell Yung (Chicago: University of Illinois Press, 2009), 241–271, and Olufunmilayo B. Arewa, "From J.C. Bach to Hip Hop: Musical Borrowing, Copyright and Cultural Context," *North Carolina Law Review* 84, no. 2 (2006): 547–645, accessed July 23, 2013, available at: http://works.bepress.com/o_arewa/5.

16. For a fuller discussion, including an unusually wide range of cultural references, see Stephen Blum, "Composition," in *Grove Music Online*, accessed January 15 2015.

does one evaluate a new product that has grown organically out of existing products? Where is the dividing line between that which may be excused as unavoidable or normal and that which is unacceptably invasive, crossing over into a transgressive realm? What does it mean to accuse someone of appropriating another's resource, of stealing his or her musical idea?

There are several factors at work here, and they differ from era to era, from community to community, and from individual to individual. Consider one aspect of the African situation. For the longest time, composers of traditional music remained anonymous. Although a song or drumming style was obviously conceived or realized by an individual or group of individuals in what George Dor has appropriately called *communal composition*,[17] such individuals were not always named as composers; nor were the works understood as autonomous works. It was of no particular significance that the tune and words of a crying song originated in the mind of an individual, or that a funeral dirge or entertainment dance was the product of individual volition. Songs and dances emerged as part of the community's way of being in the world; they retained their generic identities but were cut off from their first composers. Within such traditions, composing almost always meant appropriation, but no one seemed to complain that one funeral dirge sounded like another, or that a new lament reminded one of a previous one. No traditional court heard cases in which one person accused another of stealing his or her work song or praise song.

Well, not exactly. Named traditional composers were recognized in some traditional societies, and this has sometimes advanced concerns about ownership and the possibility of plagiarism. An excellent example is the Anlo Ewe carver of songs, Vinoko Akpalu (1885–1974), well known in Ewe communities in Ghana and Togo. As Dor has shown, Akpalu's *agohawo* (velvet-cloth songs) are musico-verbal constructions rich in melody, harmony, poignant poetic expression, and natural word rhythms.[18] These songs serve several purposes. They may be used to entertain, to admonish, or to inspire. Children, spouses, teachers, and elders have been known to invoke one Akpalu song or another as practical circumstances demand. Although they have a wide appeal, and may thus appear to belong to an anonymous heritage, the songs are far from being communally owned. No one, as far as I know, has been accused of plagiarizing an Akpalu song, but the possibility exists insofar as Akpalu's name is attached to particular songs. What sets these songs apart from other Ewe

17. George Dor, "Communal Creativity and Song Ownership in Anlo-Ewe Musical Practice: The Case of Havolu," *Ethnomusicology* 48 (2004): 26–51.

18. George Dor, "Exploring Indigenous Interpretive Frameworks in African Music Scholarship: Conceptual Metaphors and Indigenous Ewe Knowledge in the Life and Work of Hesinɔ Vinorkor Akpalu, *Black Music Research Journal,* forthcoming.

songs and thus ensures that they are always identified with an autonomous composer is perhaps the concentration of expression and the depth of their poetry. There are other instances of a similar naming of traditional composer-performers, so although communal composition is widespread and norma-tive, individual composition, even in a social sphere that flattens individuality, is not unheard of.

Until recently, questions of copyright seemed largely irrelevant to the practice of African traditional music. No individual owned play songs, laments, praise songs, or dance music. True, there were individual exponents of those genres, but the idea that a tune or rhythmic pattern belonged to this or that individual was not commonly subscribed to. Nowadays, however, the fact that some people are said to have profited from using other people's folk music has changed that attitude and brought the legal machinery into a discussion of uses and reuses of musical material. This trend originates in part in the imposition of new practices from Europe and in part from con-temporary African negotiations with capitalist imperatives. In new forms of popular and art music that began in the nineteenth and twentieth cen-turies as direct outgrowths of European music, composers and composer-performers are named. In passing from a primarily oral tradition to one in which music is recorded and scores produced, reproducibility and compari-son are made easier. Regulative mechanisms are established so that anyone who makes a lot of money from using a folk song belonging to a given ethnic group or from using another person's (composed) song is brought to book. We have come a long way from the Edenic premise that musical composition is recomposition.

The irony is that certain forms of modern composition are given over to aggressive and undisguised appropriation or sampling. Consider the example of hiplife, whose modus operandi sometimes includes grafting old practices onto new ones. In Omanhene Pozoh's "Medɔfo aɖaaɖa me oo" (briefly dis-cussed in chapter 3), old-style highlife by Awurama Badu is conjoined with modern rap-based hiplife; the two are brought together not in a seamless deri-vational pattern but as blocks juxtaposed for postmodern effect. Past and pres-ent are delineated for all to feel and hear. Ownership of the outcome is claimed by the modern composer (Emmanuel Amponsah, aka Pozoh), and while the specific arrangement that we know as "Medɔfo aɖaaɖa me oo" belongs to Pozoh, many of the ingredients belong to others. In this world of simulacra, copying, duplication, sampling, and doubling, the artistic credo gives the lie to narrowly formulated concepts of musical ownership.

There is, in short, no overarching principle that governs questions of appro-priation for all African music. Each instance must be discussed according to the peculiarities of its context. Nor is it possible to intervene rationally in privately held beliefs about who owns what music, who is allowed to use which music, and who should be charged with plagiarism, theft, or appropriation. For those who feel that the world's artistic heritage belongs to the world rather than to a particular individual or group, and that composers should be allowed to use materials freely irrespective of provenance, charges of theft or plagiarism will seem irrelevant. By contrast, those who cry foul as soon as they hear a whiff of another's music will be anxious to activate the legal machinery to punish offenders. When these matters are placed within the complex contexts of contemporary Africa, with its often multileveled systems of justice and its unregulated traffic in some of the coarser forms of capitalism, we have to defer to legal expertise in judging individual cases.

## APPROPRIATION OF AFRICAN MUSIC BY COMPOSERS OF WESTERN ART MUSIC

The number of composers of Western art music who have, at various stages in their careers, appropriated African music is by now quite large. Reich (b. 1936), Ligeti (1923–2006), Volans (b. 1949), Roy Travis (b. 1922), Geoffrey Poole (b. 1949), and Giles Swayne (b. 1946) are among the many. The degree and mode of appropriation differ, ranging from the adoption of a tune, a rhythmic pattern, or an ensemble arrangement to a more complex synthesis in which the principles behind a given music rather than specific musical materials are appropriated. Dvorak's appropriation of so-called American Negro melodies seems at one stage removed from Africa because he was appropriating *American music*, music that in turn bore oblique traces of its African past. This veiled African music ("Negro Spirituals") has been a source of temptation for a good number of composers, Western and non-Western. To mention just a handful, Samuel Coleridge Taylor (1875–1912) wrote a set of *24 Negro Melodies* (1905) in which original spirituals are embedded in his own "romantic" language. Fela Sowande also set spirituals to a series of rich, lush harmonies with endearing voice doublings and dramatic use of dynamic contrasts. American composer Margaret Bonds's *Spiritual Suite* (1950s) is an imaginative collection that incorporates the soulful character and fresh melodies of spirituals into highly idiomatic pianistic textures. And Michael Tippett's substitution of spirituals for chorales in his oratorio *A Child of Our Time* (1939–1941) retains their core tonal or modal orientation while enriching each setting with enhanced polyphonic effects. These collective efforts belong to a long-standing tradition of "setting" or incorporating folk material, a tradition that began in earnest in the eighteenth century and was intensified in the twentieth century at the hands of British, French, Russian, and Italian composers, including Mahler,

Vaughan Williams, Percy Grainger, Moussorgsky, Britten, and Berio, among others.[19]

How are African materials used—appropriated—by composers of art music? Direct usages may be heard, for example, in several works by American composer Roy Travis, who came into contact with African musicians while a professor at the University of California, Los Angeles in the 1960s. Three of his works recorded on the Orion label in 1973 are veritable parades of appropriated Ewe and Akan traditional dances. *Duo Concertante* (1967) begins and ends with Gakpa and Asafo, respectively; *African Sonata* (1966) begins and ends with Sikyi and Adowa, respectively; and *Switched on Ashanti* (1973) begins and ends with Akom and Sikyi, respectively. Travis appropriates bell patterns and drum ensembles directly and surrounds them with original materials composed in his own neotonal style. The mode of appropriation is quotational rather than derivative.

It is useful to think of this and similar cross-cultural encounters in terms of *degrees of appropriation*. At one end of the spectrum are works that sound like transcriptions of African music, works by Kevin Volans, his student Justinian Tamusuza (b. 1951), and Zimbabwean performer-composer Dumisani Maraire (1944–1999), all conveniently captured on the 1992 CD, *Pieces of Africa,* by the Kronos Quartet. In a middle category are works that incorporate one or two distinctive African elements within a fundamentally non-African melodic-harmonic environment. Listeners detect African references or flavors, but the ground is foreign. And at the far end are works that are informed by the spirit of African music and by the thinking behind it but refuse appropriation in any obvious material form (as heard in the music of Ligeti, Poole, and others). These categories are obviously not mutually exclusive; they may be present in varying degrees in a single work or spread across different works within an individual composer's oeuvre.[20] Works by composers as diverse as Meyerbeer, Stravinsky, Bartók, Milhaud, Swayne, and Boulez all display traces of Africa based on conscious or unconscious appropriation. Discussing them all would be impossible here, so let me mention just three paradigmatic cases: Fanshawe, Reich, and Ligeti.

19. The use of folk material by art-music composers is of course a widespread practice. Of deep relevance to Africa is the analogous situation in Latin America, where questions of identity, nationalism, and the relationship to Europe surface repeatedly. See Gerard Behague, *Music in Latin America: An Introduction* (Englewood Cliffs, NJ: Prentice-Hall, 1979). Also of interest are the practices associated with Chinese and Japanese composers.

20. See Akin Euba's discussion of practical and ideological issues pertaining to the composition and reception of new African art music in *Essays on Music in Africa* (Lagos, Nigeria: Elekoto Music Centre, 1989). See also Euba's most recent book, *J. H. Kwabena Nketia: Bridging Musicology and Composition: A Study in Creative Musicology* (Point Richmond: Music Research Institute, 2014).

British composer David Fanshawe (1942–2010) traveled the length of the Nile River in 1969 in search of African traditional music. His collection includes ritual and entertainment music and various functional repertories, and these are readily available on CD.[21] Some of these materials were incorporated into his own original compositions, of which *African Sanctus* (1971) is the best known. This multistylistic work draws on idioms of rock opera, African traditional music, and renaissance polyphony. The opening Kyrie is an excellent example of Fanshawe's style and a good case for the discussion of appropriation. Beginning with a muezzin's call to prayer, the Kyrie superimposes originally composed choral parts reminiscent of renaissance polyphony. The choir declaims its threefold supplication, "Kyrie eleison, Christe eleison, kyrie eleison" ("Lord have mercy, Christ have mercy, Lord have mercy"), while the solo muezzin chants his call to prayer. This disposition of two distinct inputs, one of Muslim origin, the other Christian, perseveres throughout the movement, so that the listener finishes the Kyrie with a sense of the inputs' coexistence; they do not collapse into each other. They are separate but equal; neither component colonizes the other, so to speak.

Or so was Fanshawe's intention. It is one thing for an artist to aim for a residually plural effect, but it is quite another to achieve it, to impress it so firmly on listeners' consciousness that they "get" the message. A hermeneutic reading of Fanshawe's piece would reinforce some of the composer's intentions, but it would also open the door to other interpretations. Here are a few perceptions. The North African (or, more precisely, Middle Eastern) material sung by the muezzin is not tampered with in any way; it is retained whole. Pitched in the key of D-flat, it obviously dictated the tonality of the Kyrie as a whole since the choral parts are presented in that key as well. In performance, the muezzin's music is presented in recorded form, not with a live muezzin in attendance. Various patterns of prioritization enter into the experience. Christians have to adjust to Muslims' tonality; Muslims are represented by a single voice while Christians are represented by multiple voices; the Muslim is absent while the Christian choir is present; and beginning and ending of the movement are entrusted to Muslims and Christians, respectively. When Fanshawe says that his aim in part is to promote coexistence, to show that the Muslim and Christian faiths can coexist, he succeeds on an immediate level. But although the two canonical musics unfold within the same temporal constraint, it is their ultimate difference that makes the strongest impression. Their segregation is highlighted because there is relatively little in the way of

21. CD, *Spirit of African Sanctus: The Original Recordings by David Fanshawe (1969-73)*; CD, *African Sanctus; Dona nobis pacem: A Hymn for World Peace* by David Fanshawe (New York: Fanshawe Enterprises, 1994).

structural or motivic interaction between them. And given the fact that the muezzin drops out toward the end, leaving a residue of "pure" polyphony, one might infer a subtle message that Christianity triumphs in the end. Fanshawe's stated compositional intention works best as an idealization; the behavior of tones, textures, and rhythms within this particular temporal constraint invites a more hierarchic interpretation.

By his own account, Fanshawe sought permission from the African musicians whose music he recorded to use their music for his own purposes. And in later years, receipts from the sale of recordings were donated to some of them. In short, due rights were paid. It might be further pointed out that, by incorporating some of this traditional music into his own work, the metropolitan composer facilitated the exposure of African music to Western audiences. Pursuit of the ethics of appropriation could of course go on. We might ask, for example, who finally benefits from this use of African music? Such discussions require carefully configured terms and a precise delineation of artistic aims, including a proper understanding of the aims of composition. The related aesthetical question requires a similarly rigorous framework, one that goes beyond knee-jerk reactions that dismiss *African Sanctus* as a lame experiment or that purport to take offense at this yoking of ostensibly antithetical religions. Some indeed might argue that there is something inherently flawed in the very framework within which these acts of appropriation take place, that the dualistic framework of winner and loser undercomplicates a set of transactions based on love, artistic passion, discovery, respect, and, finally, an internal artistic impulse. A borderless aesthetics, plausible as an ideal but problematic in realization, re-emerges as perhaps the only ethical possibility for judging acts of musical composition. Perhaps the question of appropriation is, when all is said and done, moot.

American composer Steve Reich's African affiliations have been well publicized. Reich's brand of minimalism immediately puts us in mind of groove-based music, while his explicit use of time-line patterns announces a concrete African presence. Reich's study of African music brought him into contact with the writings of one of the most influential figures in African musicology, A.M. Jones, who had produced copious transcriptions of Ewe and Lala music in the 1950s and 1960s. Reich corresponded with Jones, eventually met with him in London, and essentially became something of a disciple, even inheriting Jones's problematic method of transcribing ensemble music using multiple downbeats marked by bar lines, as seen in Reich's own transcriptions of the Southern Ewe dances Gahu and Agbadza (the latter is quoted in Example 2.1). And if we applied the one-drop rule for race to music, then Reich's compositions *Clapping Music, Drumming, Music for Pieces of Wood*, and *Music for 18 Instruments* would all qualify as "African" music.

Does Reich's music sound African? No doubt the African time-line patterns that form the points of narrative departure for some of his works will be recognized immediately as being of African origin. No other world repertory boasts such a plethora of subtle and exquisitely shaped rhythmic patterns that often function as signatures to a variety of dances. Time lines are in this sense always already freighted. When heard in the first 2' 30" of Ornette Coleman's "Voice Poetry," the *clave son* sounds naked and African, but it soon recedes into a groove as funky textures are built up to prepare the saxophonist's song. Even the "Bransle Gay" in Stravinsky's *Agon* [1-1-2-2] could be appropriated as a time line, although no historical evidence supports that attribution.

The processes that accompany time-line patterns in Reich's music often announce a difference from the more stable, dance-oriented ones normally found in West African ensemble music. While the African patterns are inviolate (they may be doubled in performance or otherwise reinforced, but one does not normally mess with them structurally), Reich's are subject to change because of the way they are disposed. They may be phased in and out with replicas of each other in such a way that the compositional process—as distinct from the compositional result—is put on display for all to see. This is process music, whereas the gahu and agbadza that Reich studied in Ghana are based on rhythmic narratives led by a master drummer rather than on process involving the entire ensemble. The cultivation of such processes inscribes a different, more autonomous subjectivity into the music. Such authorial presence, with its marked processes and tactics, places the amateur dancer at a disadvantage, for nothing can be presumed about the emerging script. It is not that process music cannot be danced to, but that the dancer has to submit to instruction rather than presume a groove. So whereas Yoruba and Ewe time lines typically support dance music (real or imagined), in Reich's hands they support a mode of expression that is listener oriented and composer centered. This is where the African reception of Reich's music meets a huge stumbling block, and this is why it is not inappropriate to ask whether Reich's music—music sometimes strongly marked by African ingredients—actually sounds African.

Reich has written and lectured extensively about his encounter with various world musics, and it is obvious that he is deeply aware of the ethical and aesthetical issues involved. If he seems occasionally impatient with questions about his sources, this is entirely understandable because such interrogation can come off as a distracting musicological intrusion. What matters, some will argue, is not this or that surface feature of this or that world music; rather, it is what one does with it, how one realizes or transforms the intellection that is embodied in a pattern or process. In shifting attention from nuggets of material to compositional processes enshrined in them, we once again undermine the supposed pertinence of the topic of appropriation. By allowing himself to be instructed by African materials while composing his own music, Reich has contributed significantly to our understanding of the older repertory.

Like Fanshawe (although chronologically before him), Reich developed a curiosity about African music, studied it both inside and outside the field, and extended his own aesthetical premises in the wake of the encounter. So why should the question of ownership intrude here? Time lines are, after all, not owned by any single African group or community. And as for the aesthetical issue, we need look no further than the widespread interest in Reich's music in Europe and the United States. For a very large number of devotees (among them Richard Taruskin, whose *Oxford History of Western Music* includes a highly favorable account of Reich's achievement[22]), the ideological premises of Reich's minimalism are entirely praiseworthy: anticomplexity, self-evident, inviting, communal. Nothing more needs to be said.

The case of György Ligeti is at once more interesting and more elusive. Ligeti's first encounter with African music by his own account was with the polyphony of the Banda Linda, a Central African group studied and recorded by Simha Arom. Subsequent listening and study of the materials of and scholarship on African music (by Arom, Dauer, Kubik, and others) deepened his appreciation and knowledge. He was particularly pleased to discover principles of polyphonic layering with strong affinities with his own polyphonic practices:

> Undoubtedly my interest in the music Arom has recorded stems also from the proximity I feel exists between it and my own way of thinking with regards to composition: that is, the creation of structures which are both remarkably simple and highly complex. The formal simplicity of sub-Saharan African music with its unchanging repetition of periods of equal length, like the uniform pearls of a necklace, is in sharp contrast to the inner structure of these periods which, because of simultaneous superpositioning of different rhythmic patterns, possesses an extraordinary degree of complexity. Gradually, through repeated listening, I became aware of this music's paradoxical nature: the patterns performed by the individual musicians are quite different from those which result from their combination. In fact, the ensemble's super-pattern is in itself not played and exists only as an illusory outline. I also began to sense a strong inner tension between the relentlessness of the constant, never-changing pulsecoupled with

---

22. Richard Taruskin, *The Oxford History of Western Music*, vol. 5, *The Late Twentieth Century* (Oxford: Oxford University Press, 2005), 351–410.

the absolute symmetry of the formal architecture on the one hand and the asymmetrical internal divisions of the patterns on the other. What we can witness in this music is a wonderful combination of order and disorder which in turn merges together producing a sense of order on a higher level.[23]

Declared artistic affinities like this are simply that—declarations of affinity. But if we ask—no doubt naively—whether Ligeti's music sounds African, the answer is likely to be a less equivocal "no" than the one we gave in connection with Reich's music. There are fewer immediately recognizable nuggets of material that one could trace directly to Angola or Malawi, the Central African Republic or Cameroon. And although Ligeti's sketches apparently contain written-out ideas from various writings on African music,[24] his African debts are well hidden, transformed under various technical regimes, made more abstract and oblique. It is entirely possible that a listener who is unaware of Ligeti's self-announced interest in African music will miss its trace or influence on his work entirely. Have we, then, invented an African influence on Ligeti? Is the claim about influence supported not by what is heard directly but by an amalgam of what is said to have motivated composition? Martin Scherzinger's detailed study of Ligeti's African sources suggests a breadth and depth of contact—as recorded in sketches—but this is a record of the compositional process, the goings-on behind the scenes; it says nothing about the finished trace itself or about how we experience the work. Itemizing compositional inputs, both acknowledged inputs and unacknowledged ones, is easily done by musicologists, but the relationship between ingredients and aesthetic or structural outcome is never straightforward or self-evident. Ligeti said he was impressed by the superimposition of rhythmic layers in Banda polyphony, but such polyphonic thinking pre-dated his encounter with the African materials, so this is in reality a retrospective influence. Perhaps, then, it is the symbolic capital in the claim that one of Europe's leading avant-garde composers appropriated African music that is at stake, not the verifiability of the trace by listeners.

## AFRICAN ART MUSIC: A MODE
## OF "SELF-APPROPRIATION"?

When born-in-the-tradition African composers use African materials, are they guilty of appropriation? This would normally be dismissed as a naive question. Which language are they supposed to speak, we might ask, if not

23. Ligeti, Foreword to Arom, *African Polyphony and Polyrhythm*, xvii.

24. Martin Scherzinger, "György Ligeti and the Aka Pygmies Project."

their native language? But what is the native musical language of a Bankole or an Amu, an Okelo or a Tamusuza? It quickly becomes apparent that composers of African art music are formed not from a single musico-linguistic heritage but from multiple heritages. Theirs is not merely a double consciousness but oftentimes a triple or quadruple consciousness. This means that an element of distancing or alienation exists at the root of this formation, giving added poignancy to the practice of art music.

I turn to art music at the end of this book for two main reasons. First, no music has a future without the participation of its full range of composers. Second, the probing of music by music (a music-on-music violence, as I called it at the end of the previous chapter) is to my mind one of the most important tasks facing contemporary African musicians. In some ways, this is what composition has always meant: ongoing discovery through engagement with prior texts and associated creative procedures. But there are different degrees of probing. New compositions in some traditions merely affirm old ways of doing things. In other traditions, express innovation is the ruling imperative, and a new composition is obliged to interrogate received wisdom. It is to this interrogative and critical realm that art music lays claim. Like other music, art music may well set out to titillate, amuse, entertain, or edify, but insofar as its written medium facilitates discovery—and this whether or not intended by composers—it stands to illuminate Africa's musical legacies and their creative potentials. So, although from a sociological point of view the number of players (composers, performers, audiences) in the art-music tradition is significantly smaller than those in popular or traditional music, composers of art music, like their creative-writer counterparts (poets and novelists), hold an important key to Africa's intellectual and artistic futures.

The most inspiring European model for contemporary African composers is the figure of Hungarian composer Belá Bartók (1881–1945). Although seven decades have passed since his death, the composer's aspirations strongly resonate with those of his African colleagues. This fact has been recognized by a number of African composers, foremost among them Nigerian composer and scholar Akin Euba, who used the occasion of his inaugural lecture in 2000 as Andrew Mellon Professor of Musicology at the University of Pittsburgh to celebrate this affiliation. Euba, indeed, styles himself a disciple of Bartók.[25] The parallels between Bartók's profile (or, for that matter, composers like Janaček and Kodaly) and those of his African colleagues are evident on three fronts: performance, scholarship, and composition.[26]

25. Euba, Inaugural lecture, University of Pittsburgh, 2000.

26. For insight into how another non-European composer-ethnomusicologist negotiated his relationship to Europe on the one hand and to his native Philippines on the other, see Michael Tenzer, "José Maceda and the Paradoxes of Modern Composition in Southeast Asia," *Ethnomusicology* 47 (2003): 93–120.

First, many would-be composers of African art music start life as performers, and like Bartók, the keyboard has been crucial to their early training—Euba, Uzoigwe, Mensah, Nketia, and others. Granted, the actual prospect of a career in performance *in Africa* has rarely proved realistic for any single African musician, but the experience of playing Bach, Beethoven, and Chopin alongside music by local composers has proved invaluable. Second, Bartók's work as an ethnomusicologist has been even more pertinent for African composers, many of whom study African music under the aegis of ethnomusicology. Several composers boast periods of dedicated fieldwork (Euba, Nzewi, Uzoigwe, Nketia, Zabana Kongo, and others). Thus, a list of African composers could easily double as a list of African scholars of music. Akin Euba crystalized this tendency with his term *creative ethnomusicology*, a term that depicts composition-oriented research. Research on music that does not stimulate a reciprocal creative act seems pointless, whereas research that elicits a compositional response boosts African creativity. Third, Bartók's compositional career exemplifies one way of coming to terms with the imperatives of modernity. And just as Bartók, like Stravinsky perhaps, related to the Western European tradition at an angle, so Euba and his African colleagues have sought creative ways of coming to terms with the institutionally prominent Western tradition by relating to it at an angle.

As we have indicated, the African composer's heritage is not singular but multiple. It includes at least three strands. First are aspects of a European heritage filtered through protestant hymns: piano works by J. S. Bach, Mozart, Beethoven, and Chopin, and classics like the "Dead March" from *Saul*, Mendelssohn's "Wedding March," Franck's "Panis Angelicus," Beethoven's Minuet in G, Bach's "Jesu Joy of Man's Desiring," Beethoven's "Für Elise," Handel's *Messiah,* and Vivaldi's *Gloria.* A second strand derives from an ethnically diverse indigenous tradition, complete with modal tone systems, a flexible folk song phraseology, and forms of speech-based rhythmic imagining inscribed in praise songs and dance drumming. This strand also includes a network of popular-music influences including highlife or makossa tunes and performance mannerisms. A final component is the European avant-garde, some of it acquired in the course of individual composition lessons with teachers able to introduce Stravinsky, Copland, Bartók, Debussy, and Vaughan Williams to their students in the 1960s and 1970s, or Ligeti, Carter, Lachenmann, and Reich in recent decades. It is with this network of influences that many budding African composers seek to come to terms, aiming to synthesize them into a plausible whole that will enable authentic expression. Although not all of them have studied Bartók's varying takes on his own multiple heritages, the parallels between African composers of art music and their Hungarian counterpart are compelling.

The will to mimicry that animates African art-music compositions is offputting to some critics. Although mimicry as such is not uncharacteristic of modern forms of artistic expression, its specifically musical manifestation seems to grate on certain sensibilities. A skeptic might reason thus: "If what you want are symphonies, piano sonatas, or string quartets, why bother going to Africa? Why not stay at home and feast on the canonical Western composers?" There is indeed an unspoken prejudice that no African can write a string quartet as good as Haydn's or Beethoven's or Bartók's. When Saul Bellow famously said, "When the Zulus produce their Tolstoy, we will read him," he may have been giving voice to this prejudice by announcing—none too subtly—that the chances of Zulus producing a Tolstoy, or for that matter a Beethoven or Wagner, are negligible.

It is easy to underestimate the historical reach of the tradition of African art music, and it is equally easy to underestimate its potential if one is not aware of the bigger picture. Abiola Irele has raised the essential questions about the tradition,[27] Martin Scherzinger has written the most comprehensive study to date,[28] Bode Omojola has charted the Nigerian territory and provided an exemplary study of Fela Sowande,[29] and other scholars (Euba, Nketia, Uzoigwe, Dor, Christine Lucia, and Chris van Rhym) have contributed detailed studies. While a comprehensive discussion of African art music is beyond the scope of this chapter, I will rehearse just a few facts about the tradition and its study.[30]

Black Africans since the middle of the nineteenth century have routinely composed art songs; symphonies; cantatas; folk operas; choral anthems; sonatas for stringed, wind, and percussion instruments; and keyboard music for organ, piano, and harmonium. Concerts have taken place in Lome, Accra, Lagos, Nairobi, Kampala, Freetown, Kinshasa, Cape Town, Dakar, and Nssuka. An example

---

27. Abiola Irele, "Is African Music Possible?," *Transition* 61 (1993): 56–71.

28. Martin Scherzinger, "Art Music in a Cross-Cultural Context: The Case of Africa," in *The Cambridge History of Twentieth-Century Music*, ed. Nicolas Cook and Anthony Pople (Cambridge: Cambridge University Press, 2004), 584–613.

29. Omojola, *Nigerian Art Music, with an Introductory Study of Ghanaian Art Music* (Ibadan: Institut français de Recherche en Afrique, University of Ibadan, 1995); and Omojola, *The Music of Fela Sowande: Encounters, African Identity and Creative Ethnomusicology*. See also Godwin Sadoh, "African Musicology: A Bibliographical Guide to Nigerian Art Music (1927–2009)," *Notes* 66 (2010): 485–502.

30. See Akin Euba, *Essays on Music in Africa*; J. H. Kwabena Nketia, *The Creative Potential of African Art Music in Ghana: A Personal Testimony*, Companion Booklet to ICAMD CD Recordings (Accra, Ghana: Afram Publications, 2004); Joshua Uzoigwe, *Akin Euba: An Introduction to the Life and Music of a Nigerian Composer* (Bayreuth: E. Breitinger, University of Bayreuth, 1992); George Dor, "Ephraim Amu's 'Bonwere Kenteŋwene': A Celebration of Ghanaian Traditional Knowledge, Wisdom, and Artistry," *African Music: Journal of the International Library of African Music* 9, no. 4 (2014): 7–35; Christine Lucia, "Back to the Future? Idioms of 'Displaced Time' in South African Composition"; and Chris van Rhyn, "Towards a Mapping of the Marginal: Readings of Art Songs by Nigerian, Ghanaian, Egyptian and South African Composers" (PhD thesis, Stellenbosch University, 2013).

from the nineteenth century is the song "An Evening Calm" by Charles E. Graves, a black African musician from Cape Coast. In certain respects, this composition is indistinguishable from that of many a Victorian composer. The setting is in English, the harmonies are tonal and predictable, the phrase structure is regular, and there is nothing obviously "African" about it. This is unbridled mimicry. And yet, Graves is speaking in one of the creative registers available to him as a Gold Coast composer of the late nineteenth and early twentieth centuries. Only by legislating that African composers *sound African*—whatever that might mean—can one deny this song a place in the history of African composition.

Documentation of African art music may be found in a seventy-six-page catalog assembled by one of its distinguished practitioners, Akin Euba, and published in 1993 by the Iwalewa-Haus at the University of Bayreuth in Germany.[31] Sadly, this work has received little notice in the chief ethnomusicological publications since its appearance. Yet, to anyone interested in African musical responses to contemporary challenges, the catalog is revealing and of great practical and symbolic value. The mere listing of composers and their works is instructive. Names include Gamal Abdel Rahim (1924–1988) from Egypt, Ephraim Amu (1899–1995) from Ghana, Fela Sowande (1905–1987) and Samuel Akpabot (1932–2000) from Nigeria, and Solomon Mbabi-Katana and Reverend Anthony Okelo from Uganda. The list of genres is diverse: sonata, cantata, opera, and choruses of various kinds. The materials in Euba's catalog may be consulted at the University of Bayreuth, although we have yet to see such archival work given priority among ethnomusicologists interested in Africa.

Subsequent publications (by Bode Omojola, Paul Konye, Godwin Sadoh, Nketia, and others) bring into focus the work of several composers while rehearsing the analytical and critical issues raised by their music.[32] Then there are the brief biographies of various composers found in the revised

---

31. Euba, *Modern African Music: A Catalogue of Selected Archival Materials at Iwalewa-Haus, University of Bayreuth, Germany* (Bayreuth: Iwalewa-Haus, 1993).

32. See in addition to the works mentioned in notes 27–30, Johnston Akuma-Kalu Njoku, "Art Composed Music in Nigeria in Garland," in Stone, *Africa: The Garland Encyclopedia of World Music*, 232–253; Paul Konye, *African Art Music: Political, Social, and Cultural Factors Behind Its Development and Practice in Nigeria* (New York: Edwin Mellen Press, 2007); Godwin Sadoh, *Joshua Uzoigwe: Memoirs of a Nigerian Composer-Ethnomusicologist* (Charleston, S.C.: BookSurge Publishing, 2007); Sadoh, *The Organ Works of Fela Sowande: Cultural Perspectives* (Bloomington, IN: iUniverse, 2007); Sadoh, "Intercultural Creativity in Joshua Uzoigwe's Music," *Africa* 74 (2004): 633–661; Marie Agatha Ozah, "Building Bridges Between Traditional and Western Art Music: A Study of Joshua Uzoigwe's Egwu Amala," *Analytical Approaches to World Music Journal* 3 (2013), available at http://www.aawmjournal.com/articles/2014a; and Oyebade Dosunmu, *African Art Music*, https://www.facebook.com/AfricanArtMusic/info?tab=page_info.

*New Grove Dictionary,* many of them supplied by Ghanaian ethnomusicologist Daniel Avorgbedor. Similar biographies appear in the *International Dictionary of Black Composers,* edited by Sam Floyd for the Center for Black Music Research in Chicago. Add to these scores of long essays and bachelor's and master's theses produced in Nigerian, Ghanaian, and Ugandan universities on the music of various art-music composers. Similar theses for doctoral degrees have been produced at universities in the United States, Germany, South Africa, and the United Kingdom. Thanks again to Akin Euba's efforts, writings on art music stemming from conferences organized under the auspices of the Centre for Intercultural Studies, including the proceedings of a symposium and festival on African pianism from 1999, stand as further signs of activity in art music. Finally, an anthology of piano music by African and African diasporic composers edited by Ghanaian pianist-scholar William Chapman Nyaho was published in 2007 and contains a healthy selection of piano music by individuals like Abdel-Rahim, El-Dabh, Euba, Kwami, Labi, Ndodana-Breen, Nketia, Okoye, Onyeji, Uzoigwe, and others.[33]

That is not all. Festivals of African art music have featured composers and works. For example, in a festival entitled "New Complexity" that took place in Würzburg and Salzburg from May 19 to May 27, 1995, composers of European and African origin were featured. The music of Ferneyhough, Carter, Lachenmann, and Nono could be heard at some concerts, while that of Tamasuza, Hamza El-din, Anthony Okelo, and Kevin Volans could be heard at others. Again, the South Bank in 1994 was the venue for a celebration of the African arts. Euba's own Centre for Intercultural Music Studies based at Churchill College in Cambridge supports a biennial conference that often includes performances. And nowadays, the St. Louis African Chorus has programmed dozens of performances by African composers, thanks largely to the organizational efforts and musical contributions of its director, Ghanaian-Nigerian composer Fred Onovwerosuoke (b. 1960).

We might also mention the film *Composers Under the Tree of God: Art-Music in Ghana* made in 1995 by Kaisik-Aumüller and Uli Aumüller for a German-speaking audience. This film offers a glimpse of the personalities, performance situations, and philosophies of art music in Ghana, as well as a sampling of the music. Featured are the National Symphony Orchestra performing a Drum Fantasy on Mozart composed and conducted by Social Kwasi Aduonum; a performance of Dr. Ephraim Amu's choral composition, "Asem yi di ka" ("This matter deserves to be touted"); Kenn Kafui's orchestral work for

33. William Chapman Nyaho, ed. *Piano Music of Africa and the African Diaspora,* 5 vols. (New York: Oxford University Press, 2009). For a discussion, see my "The Challenge of African Art Music," *Circuit, musiques contemporaines* 21 (2011): 55–72.

talking drums and orchestra; the Pan African Orchestra under Nana Danso Abiam, complete with a captivating cadenza for gonje; pianist Victor Richter playing Nketia's *Volta Fantasy*; Rev. Brother Pious Agyemang of Kumasi, an articulate and self-assured composer and conductor; Gyimah Labi; and guitarist and folklorist Koo Nimo.

I have deliberately listed these names and places in the body of the text instead of confining them to footnotes or to an appendix to place the phenomenon in the reader's face, indeed to make it difficult for anyone tempted to deny—or underestimate the current health of—the art-music tradition in Africa. Interesting aesthetic, critical, and analytical issues have emerged in the writings of various scholars, among them Ndubuisi, Omojola, Scherzinger, Mensah, Dosunmu, and Lwanda. They include questions of heritage and identity, as well as specific technical issues involving tonality, centricity, and style.

How, finally, does the question of appropriation arise in connection with art-music composers? When African composers set folk tunes, as Sowande, for example, does in his *African Suite* or Akin Euba does in his *Yoruba Songs*, they are functioning like any other composers appropriating preexisting tunes. But because these tunes come from their own backyard and because they belong to their heritage, they are less marked, less distant as aesthetic fields. Still, distances may vary depending on composer and composed. An urban composer setting a rural tune or a composer setting a tune from a different ethnic group, country, or even social class requires rather more nuanced evaluation. Even if we simplified the conceptual issue by denying the existence of any sort of gap between the African composer and African materials, we would still have to contend with the largely European origins of the actual compositional techniques used to set tunes. It is in moments like this that one senses the absurdity of arguments premised on the geographical origins of a composer's materials and techniques.

Two brief pieces, one by Joshua Uzoigwe and the other by Fred Onovwerosuoke, will serve to close this discussion of art music. Again, I should acknowledge that there are many more possibilities, including music by Euba, Ndodana-Breen, Labi, and others, but limitations of space forbid more extensive illustration. The first of Uzoigwe's *Four Igbo Songs* for voice and piano (1973) features a folklike melody and an idiomatic piano accompaniment (a portion of it is quoted in Example 8.1 and may be heard at Web Example 8.1 ⏺). As with Bartók, folk elements are sedimented at varying degrees of depth in Uzoigwe's music, ranging from explicit usages of known folk tunes to original materials composed in the shadow of the folk world. The melody of "Eriri Ngeringe" ("a riddle") is not a known folk tune, but it is so folklike that audiences recognize it as such. Uzoigwe's pianistic writing supports the singer's

**Example 8.1.** "Eriri ngeringe" by Joshua Uzoigwe, bars 1 through 11.

melody with an ostinato harmonic progression, a groove that gives a dance flavor to the song. And yet the piano's introduction is its own, genuinely pianistic in a way that highlights its potential autonomy and announces this not as folk song but as art song. This imaginative blending of folk and art elements sets Uzoigwe apart from some of his peers. One should not make too much of the Bartókian parallels, for to do so would chip away at the originality of Uzoigwe's achievement, but the very plausibility of the parallelism stands as a tiny example of African intellection in a tradition that is yet to be fully acknowledged in the world of music.

One tiny detail may illuminate Uzoigwe's way. The underlying chord progression for "Eriri Ngeringe" is centered, but not in a predictable way. It is centered on D, the root of the terminal sonority of a five-chord harmonic ostinato that supports the singer's narrative (see Example 8.2). Uzoigwe apparently conceived of this progression in D minor (ending with a tierce de Picardy), judging from the tonic solfa placed above the staff notation in his original manuscript. The arrangement of parts in this five-chord cycle betrays some European influence, perhaps the influence of hymn playing at the keyboard. Framed by dissonances, the harmonic ostinato closes on a D7 sonority, which, although normatively unstable, is deployed in a terminal position, thus endowing the ostinato as a whole with a mobile feel. Notice also the contrast between the top-voice melody, which is

Example 8.2. Ostinato harmonic progression in Joshua
Uzoigwe's "Eriri ngeringe," bars 2 and 3.

entirely diatonic, and the other voices, each of which contains at least one chromatic pitch. In sum, the progression indexes other musical traditions—hymns,
jazz harmony, African rhythm—but Uzoigwe has made it his own by virtue of the
consistency with which he has treated his materials.

Equally engaging is Fred Onovwerosuoke's etude for solo piano, entitled
*Agbadza* (Example 8.3, heard at Web Example 8.2 ).[34] This is one of twenty-
four etudes, each dedicated to a specific technical process or musical idea. By
calling them etudes, the composer immediately invites comparison with the
etudes of Chopin and Debussy. Yet Onovwerosuoke's aims are slightly different.
Rather than probing the given material, he aims to illuminate it, set it into relief
without intervening in its essence. The original Ewe dance, agbadza, is normally
beaten by an ensemble of bells, rattles, support drums, lead drum, and voices.
The texture is polyrhythmic and the rhythmic narration is entrusted to the lead
drummer. "Translating" agbadza into a solo pianistic medium requires that the
composer make choices and devise imaginative projections. Onorwerosuoke's
solution is at once simple and ingenious. The bell pattern or time line is in the
treble, the lead drum is in the bass, and a support drum is placed in the middle voice. These layers are texturally distinct and hence aurally salient, but the
firmness of an ensemble feel is never compromised. However one conceptual-
izes the composer's strategy here—reconstruction, re-creation, transposition, or
recomposition—the essential gesture is iconic: capturing the profile of a many-
voiced instrumental texture on a piano.

The interpretive issues raised by the etude are fascinating, ranging from the
choice of mode (the etude uses the A-scale on G-sharp) through the pacing of
phrase rhythm to the inversion of melody and bass functions such that the bass
takes on the melodic role and exposes more melodic content than the other
voices. The iconic imperative is also handled in an imaginative way. By leaving the bell pattern untouched, Onovwerosuoke bows to tradition and invites
a communal listening. This particular invitation, however, is not to a village
dance party but to a party that is open to urban dwellers yet does not bar villag-
ers from attending. It is in this third space that we listen to the music and imagine the dance. There is no physical dance to join in at the concert hall, but the

34. Fred Onovwerosuoke, *Twenty-Four Studies in African Rhythms*, 32-33.

**Example 8.3.** Etude for piano, *Agbadza,* by Fred Onovwerosuoke.

imaginative world is wide open. A self-awareness sets in for the listener, engendering anxiety, perhaps, and promoting reflection rather than mere feeling.

These two tiny examples by Uzoigwe and Onovwerosuoke give us a glimpse of the numerous possibilities that lie ahead for African composers. The achievement of art music is already notable if one recalls the contributions of Nigerian composers Sowande, Euba, Uzoigwe, Ekwueme, Akpabot, and Ndubuisi—to take just a subset of the total production of art music. Prospects for the future are even more exciting because of the rich heritage available to composers. Recent attempts to introduce copyright legislation and thus curb the theft of traditional materials have complicated the question of what it means to compose with materials from one's own heritage. Some critics would maintain that the issue should not arise at all for born-in-the-tradition composers for the simple reason that they are speaking the languages they grew up with and modifying them under the pressure of artistic aims. But others may wish to erase the line between insiders and outsiders and say that Western-trained African composers should be subject to the same censorship rules when they appropriate African music in their compositions. On whichever side one finds oneself, the main technical-compositional point should not be lost—namely, that by probing materials through deliberate acts of manipulation of constituent elements, art music has the potential to reveal the depth and essence of the African heritage, in a way that supersedes ethnomusicology's documentary and classificatory schemes. The future of African music lies in the hands of its composers, not scholars.

## CONCLUSION

The bird's eye view of developments in African music both within and—increasingly—outside the continent provided in this book leaves plenty of room for optimism about its future. As we have seen, the exquisite shapes of African rhythmic patterns, the engaging interplay between parts and lines, the entangled temporalities domesticated in dances, the irresistible and communally based invitation to express sound in movement, the memorable melodies and alluring harmonies, and the exploitation of tone spaces that are linguistically marked all speak to a superior music. Where else does music grow so organically out of the ordinary, the everyday, and the mundane and yet reach levels of sophistication that index the other-worldly and the transcendent? Where else does music making meet such a range of expressive and cathartic needs in the lives of ordinary people? Where else have oral texts exerted such power over the imagination, being the results of ways of world making while at the same time shaping the construction of subsequent worlds? Where else is expression enlivened by the most elemental of means, namely, imaginative repetition?

Africa's resources are vast, perhaps infinite, and this partly explains the ongoing appropriation of its songs and dances throughout the world. These materials are supple and adaptable, but they are not easily stripped of their essences, their particularities. It is on the strength of their unyielding cores—subtle timbres, multileveled temporalities, and a mosaic of melo-rhythms—that the collective repertories of African music have survived for centuries. This is music saturated with potentialities inside other potentialities. Not only was African music there in the beginning, it may well hold the key to humanity's musical future.

*Africa: Music from Rwanda*. Recorded by Denyse Hiernaux-L'Hoëst and the Research Missions of the Institute for Scientific Research in Colonial Africa (IRSAC) in Rwanda-Burundi. Cambridge, Ma.: Rounder, 1999.

*Africa: Shona Mbira Music*. Recorded in Mondoro and Highfields, Rhodesia by Paul Berliner. [Japan]: WEA International, 1977.

*Africa: the Ba-Benzélé Pygmies*. Recorded by Simha Arom. Cambridge, Ma.: Rounder Records, 1998.

*Africa: the Dan*. Recorded in the Ivory Coast by Hugo Zemp. Cambridge, Ma.: Rounder, 1998.

*Africa: The Garland Encyclopedia of World Music*. Vol. 1, edited by Ruth M. Stone. New York, Garland, 1997. Accompanying CD.

*Africa Dances*. Modern African dance and popular music from over 11 countries (1950s–70s). Tivoli, NY: Original Music, 1973.

*African Rhythm: A Northern Ewe Perspective* by Kofi Agawu. Cambridge: Cambridge University Press, 1995. Accompanying CD.

*African Rhythms*. (Germany): Teldec Classics, 2003. Performed in 2001–2002 by Aka Pygmies and Pierre-Laurent Aimard.

*African Sanctus; Dona nobis pacem: A Hymn for World Peace* by David Fanshawe. New York: Fanshawe Enterprises, 1994.

*African Troubadours: The Best of African Singer/Songwriters*. Compiled by Banning Eyre. New York: Shanachie, 1997.

*Agbadza and Bɔbɔɔbɔ Party: Anlɔ Afiadenyigba Agbadza Group meets Ho Dedetsɔme*. [USA]: T-Vibe Records, 2000–2001.

*Agbadza! Professor Midawo Gideon Foli Alorwoyie and his Afrikania Culture Troupe of Ghana, West Africa*. Recorded by Evan Jones. Denton, TX, 2003.

*Aka Pygmy Music*. Recorded by Simha Arom in 1971. France: Auvidis, 1994 (orig. 1973).

*Akazehe*. Recorded by Serena Facci. http://www.uniroma2.it/didattica/em-facci/file.html

*Akom: The Art of Possession*. Recorded in Ghana 1993–99. Seattle: Village Pulse, 1999.

*An Bè Kelen (We Are One): Griot Music from Mali #1*. Recorded by Jan Jansen in Kela and Kangaba, Mali. Leiden: Pan Records, 1994.

*Ancient Text Messages of the Yoruba Bàtá Drum: Cracking the Code* by Amanda Villepasteur. Farnham, England: Ashgate, 2010. Accompanying CD.

*Anthologie de la musique congolaise (RDC)*. Tervuren: Musée royal de l'Afrique central, 2004–2007 [orig. 1972–1975]. 11 volumes. Volume 1, *Luanda du Katanga*,
recorded in 1972 by Jos Gansemans; volume 2, *Songs of the Okapi Forest*,
recorded in 1973–2004 by John Hart and Erik Lindquist; volume 3, *Musique du
pays de Mangbetu*, recorded by Didier Demolin, 1984–90; volume 4, *Musique des
Salampasu*, recorded in 1972 by Jos Gansemans; volume 5, *Musique des Tshokwe
du Bandundu*, recorded in 1981 by René Ménard and Benoît Quersin; volume 6,
*Musique des Kwese*, recorded in 1984–85 by René Ménard; volume 7, *Musique
des Kongo-Mbata*, recorded in 1974 by Benoît Quersin and Ludiongo; volume 8,
*Musique des Tetela*, recorded in 1975 by Benoît Quersin and Esole Eka Likote; vol-
ume 9, *Musique des Leele*, recorded in 1985 by René Ménard; volume 10, *Musique
de l'Ubangi*, recorded in 1975 by Benoît Quersin and Esole Eka Likote; volume 11,
*Musique des Nkundo*, recorded in 1971–72 by Benoît Quersin.
*Anthologie de la musique du Niger*. Recorded in 1963 by Tolia Nikiprowetzky.
Paris: Ocora, 1990
*Approaches to African Musics*, ed. Enrique Cámara de Landa and Silvia Martinez
García. Valladolid: Universidad de Valladolid, 2006. CD-Rom accompanying book.
*The Arthur S. Alberts Collection*. Recorded in 1942–54 by Arthur S. Alberts. Salem,
Ma. and London, UK: Rykodisc, 1998.
*Asa: Piano Music by Composers of African Descent*. Performed by William Chapman
Nyaho, piano. Newtown, CT: MSR Classics, 2008.
*Banda Polyphony: Central African Republic*. Music of the Linda and Dakpa. Recorded
by Simha Arom. Holland: Philips, 1976.
*Bayaka: The Extraordinary Music of the Babenzélé Pygmies and Sounds of their Forest
Home* by Louis Sarno. Roslyn, N.Y.: Ellipsis Arts, 1995. Accompanying CD.
*Benin: Bariba and Somba Music*. Recorded by Simha Arom. Gentilly: Auvidis, 1994
(orig. 1976).
*The Best of Fela Kuti*. Universal City, CA: MCA Records, 2000.
*Burundi: Musiques Traditionelles*. Recorded by Michel Vuylsteke. France: Ocora, 1988.
*Cameroon: Baka Pygmy Music*. Recorded by Simha Arom and Patrick Renard.
Italy: EMI Italiana, 1977.
*Centrafrique: Musique Gbáyá: Chants à penser*. Recorded by Vincent Dehoux in the
village of Ndongué, Central African Republic. Paris: Ocora, 1995.
*Centrafrique: Anthologie de la musique des Pygmées Aka*. Recorded by Simha Arom.
Paris: Ocora, 1987.
*Centrafrique: Pygmées Aka*. Hunting, love and mockery songs accompanied by string
instruments. Recorded by Susanne Fürniss in Central Africa (1990, 1994) and in
Europe (1997). Paris: Ocora, 1998.
*Central African Republic: Music of the Dendi, Nzakera, Banda Linda, Gbaya, Banda
Dakpa, Ngbaka, Aka Pygmies*. Recorded by Simha Arom. France: Auvidis, 1989.
*Ceremonial Music from Northern Dahomey*. Recorded among the Bariba and the
Somba in the north-western region of Dahomey by Simha Arom. Phillips, 1974.
*Chaka: An Opera in Two Chants*. Composed by Akin Euba from an epic poem by
Léopold Sédar Senghor. City of Birmingham Touring Opera conducted by Simon
Halsey. Point Richmond, CA: MRI Press, 1999.
*Côte d'Ivoire: Baule Vocal Music*. Recorded in 1964 and 1967 by Hugo Zemp. Ivry-sur-
Seine: Auvidis, 1993; orig.1972.

*The Demonstration Collection of E. M. von Hornbostel and the Berlin Phonogramm-Archiv.* Originaly recorded 1900–1913. Washington, D.C.: Smithsonian Folkways, 2007

*Drum Gahu: An Introduction to African Rhythm* by David Locke. Tempe, AZ: White Cliffs Media, 1998. Accompanying CD.

*Evaristo Muyinda: Traditional Music of the Baganda, as formerly played at the Court of the Kabaka of Buganda.* Recorded on Jan. 17th 1991 by Joop Venger. Leiden: PAN Records, 1991.

*Ewe Drumming from Ghana: The Soup Which is Sweet Draws the Chairs in Closer.* Recorded in 2002 and 2003 by James Burns. London: Topic Records, 2004.

*Female Song Tradition and the Akan of Ghana: The Creative Process in Nnwonkoro* by Kwasi Ampene. Aldershot, Hampshire, England: Ashgate, 2005. Accompanying CD.

*Fiddling in West Africa (1950s–1990s): the CD recording* by Jacqueline Djedje. Recorded between the 1950s–1990s; compiled from the holdings in ethnomusicology at the University of California, Los Angeles. Los Angeles, CA: UCLA Ethnomusicology Publications, 2007.

*Flûtes des monts Mandara.* Recorded in 1994–96 by Nathalie Fernando and Fabrice Marandola. Paris: Ocora, 1996.

*Focus: Music of South Africa* by Carol Muller. Second edition. New York: Routledge, 2008. Accompanying CD.

*Forest Music: Congo: Northern Belgian Congo 1952.* Recorded by Hugh Tracey. Utrecht: Sharp Wood Productions and Grahamstown: International Library of African Music, 2000.

*From Lake Malawi to the Zambezi*: Aspects of Music and Oral Literature in Southeast Africa in the 1990s. Recorded by Moya Aliya Malamusi. Frankfurt: Popular African Music, 1999.

*Frozen Brass: Africa & Latin America*: Anthology of Brass Band Music #2. Recorded by Rob Boonzayer Flaes (in Ghana and Surinam in 1992) and Miranda can der Spek (in Bolivia in 1991 and 1992, and in Peru, 1992). Leiden: PAN, 1993.

*The Fulani.* Recorded by Simha Arom. France: Auvidis, 1988.

*Gabon: Chants Myènè.* Recorded by Herbert Pepper in Gabon 1954–61 and by Sylvie Le Bomin in 2005. Paris: Ocora, 2005.

*Ghana: Rhythms of the People. Traditional Music and Dance of the Ewe, Dagbamba, Fante and Ga People.* Recorded by Paschal Yao Younge and Maria A. Billings in 1997. Barre, VT: Multicultural Media, 2000.

*Ghana: Music of the Northern Tribes.* Recorded in 1976 by Verna Gillis. New York: Lyrichord, 1993 [orig. 1976].

*Giants of Ghanaian Danceband Highlife, 1950's–1970's.* Tivoli, NY: Original Music, 1990.

*Heritage Drummers: Ajo Yio O "The Journey".* Featuring Alani Ogunlade & Adebisi Adeleke. Atlanta, GA: Cultural Promotions Inc., 2006.

*In Praise of Oxalá and Other Gods: Black Music of South America.* Recorded in Colombia, Ecuador and Brazil by David Lewiston. New York: Nonesuch Records, 2003 [orig. 1970].

*Introduction aux musiques Africaines* by Monique Brandilly. Arles, Citel de la musique: Actes sud, 1997. Accompanying CD.

*Inyimbo; Songs of the Bemba People of Zambia.* Recorded by Isaiah Mapoma. Tucson, Arizona: Ethnodisc, 1971.

*Jali Kunda: Griots of West Africa and Beyond.* Roslyn, NY: Ellipsis Arts, 1996. Accompanying CD.

*Jarabi: The Best of Toumani Diabate, Master of the Kora.* Compiled by Lucy Dúran. London: Hannibal UK, 2008.

*Jùjú: A Social History and Ethnography of an African Popular Music* by Christopher Waterman. Chicago: University of Chicago Press, 1990. Accompanying cassette.

*Jùjú Music: King Sunny Adé and his African Beats.* New York, NY: Mango, 1982.

*Jùjú Roots: 1930s–1950s.* Recorded in Lagos between 1937 and mid–1960s. Cambridge, MA: Rounder Records, 1993.

*Kanyok and Luba: Southern Belgian Congo, 1952 & 1957.* Recorded by Hugh Tracey. Utrecht: Sharp Wood Productions and Grahamstown: International Library of African Music, 1998.

*The King's Musicians: Royalist Music of Buganda, Uganda.* Recorded by Peter Cooke and Klaus Wachsmann. London: Topic Records, 2003.

*Kronos Quartet: Pieces of Africa. New York: Elektra Entertainment, 1992.*

*Ladysmith: The Best of Ladysmith Black Mambazo.* Ho-Ho-kus, NJ: Shanachie, 1992.

*Lambarena.* An Hommage to Albert Schweitzer. Arrangements by Pierre Akendengué and Hughes de Courson. New York: Sony Classical, 1995.

*Legendary Wulomei: Maa Amanua.* Accra: Sam Records, 2000.

*Lobi Country: Buur Xylophones.* Paris: OCORA Radio France, 2006.

*Lura: Mbem di Fora [I've Come from Far Away].* New York: Times Square Records, 2007.

*Madagascar: Pays Bara. Traditional Music of the Bara of Madagascar.* Recorded by Alain Desjacuqes. Paris: Ocora/Harmonia Mundi, 1996.

*Mafili [Zither]: Musiques des Baali de la forêt equitoriale.* Recorded by Didier Demolin in 1990. Belgium: Colophon Records, 2005.

*Mande Music: Traditional and Modern Music of the Maninka and Mandinka of Western Africa* by Eric Charry. Chicago: University of Chicago Press, 2000. Accompanying CD.

*Master Drummers of Dagbon.* Recorded by John Miller Chernoff in Tamale, Ghana. Cambridge, MA: Rounder Records, 2008.

*Master Fiddlers of Dagbon.* Recorded by John M. Chernoff on July 28, 1991, in Tamale, Ghana. Cambridge, MA: Rounder Records, 2001.

*Masters of the Sabar: Wolof Griot Percussionists of Senegal* by Patricia Tang. Accompanying CD.

*Mbudi mbudi na mhanga: universo musical infantil de los Wagogo de Tanzania* by Polo Vallejo. Madrid: Edicion del autor, 2004. Accompanying CD.

*Mukanda na makisi/Angola.* Recorded in Aug.-Dec. 1965 by Gerhard Kubik. Berlin: Musikethnologische Abteilung, Museum für Völkerkunde Berlin, Staatliche Museen Preussischer Kulturbesitz, 1981.

*Music from the Villages of Northeastern Nigeria.* Recorded in 1969 by Paul Newman, Eric and Lyn Davidson. Washington, DC: Smithsonian-Folkways, 2001.

*Music in Ghana: A Selection out of the Archives of African Music at the Institute of African Studies, University of Ghana, Legon.* Frankfurt: Popular African Music/African Music Archive, 1998.

*The Music of Africa.* London: BBC/Horizon, 1971.

*Music of Africa Series: 27 Musical Instruments 1 Strings; 28 Musical Instruments 2 Reeds (Mbira); 29 Musical Instruments 3: Drums 1; 30 Musical Instruments 4 Flutes and Horns; 31 Musical Instruments 5 Xylophones; 32 Musical Instruments 6 Guitars 1; Musical Instruments 37 The Zulu Songs of Princess Constance Magogo KaDinuzulu; 38 Musical Instruments 8 Drums 2.* Grahamstown: International Library of African Music, n.d.

*The Music of Ethiopia II: Cushites.* Directed by Paul Collaer, recorded by Jean Jenkins. Kassel, Germany: Bärenreiter-Musicaphon, 1970.

*Music of the Ga people of Ghana: Adowa*, vol. 1. Recorded by Barbara L. Hampton on Mar. 17 and Mar. 21, 1971. Washington, DC: Smithsonian Folkways Recordings, 1998.

*Music of the Idoma of Nigeria.* Recorded by Robert G. Armstrong on 29 Dec. 1962. Washington, DC: Smithsonian/Folkways, 1998.

*Music of the Kpelle of Liberia.* Recorded by Vernon L. Stone and Ruth M. Stone. Washington, D.C.: Smithsonian Folkways Recordings, 1998.

*Music of the Rain Forest Pygmies Recorded by Colin H. Turnbull.* New York: Lyrichord, 2008.

*Music of the Vai of Liberia.* Recorded by Lester P. Monts in 1977–78 and 1981. Washington, D.C.: Smithsonian Folkways, 1998.

*Music in West Africa: Experiencing Music, Expressing Culture.* New York: Oxford University Press, 2005. Accompanying CD.

*Música Instrumental no Benim: Repertório Fon e Música Bàtá* by Marcos Branda Lacerda. Sao Paulo: Editoria la Universidade de Sao Paulo, 2014.

*Musical Arts in Africa: Glimpses.* Live Recording of the Benefit Launch Concert for the Pan African Society for Musical Arts Education (PASMAE), 16 April 2002, Baxter Concert Hall, Cape Town. Cape Town: PASMAE, 2002.

*Musik in Afrika: mit 20 Beitragen zur Kenntnis traditioneller afrikanischen Musikkulturen* edited by A. Dauer et. al. Berlin: Museum für Völkerkunde, 1983. Accompanying cassette.

*Musique des pygmées Bibayak: Chantres de l'épopée.* Recorded by Pierre Sallée in 1966 and 1973 in Gabon. France: Ocora 1989.

*Musique Gbaya: Chants à penser.* Recorded in the village of Ndongué, Central African Republic, by Vincent Dehoux. Paris: Ocora: distribution, Harmonia Mundi, 1992–1995 (orig. 1977).

*Nomades du desert.* Songs and dances of the Wodaabe Peulhs of Niger. Recorded in 1983 by Roselyne François and Manuel Gomes. [Paris]: Auvidis, 1986.

*Nord Cameroun: Musique des Ouldémé: au rhythme des saisons.* Recorded by Nathalie Fernando and Fabrice Marandola. Paris, France: Inedit/Maison des Cultures du Monde, 2001.

*On the Edge of the Ituri Forest: Northeastern Belgian Congo 1952.* Recorded by Hugh Tracey. Utrecht: Stichting Sharp Wood Productions and Grahamstown, South Africa: International Library of African Music, 1998.

*Ouganda: Musique des Baganda.* Recorded in 1996 and 1997 by Jean-Jacques Nattiez. Paris: Ocora, 2002.

*Pan-African Orchestra, Opus 1.* New York, NY: Real World, 1995.

*Patrimonio musical de los Wagogo (Tanzania): context y sistemática* by Polo Vallejo. Madrid: Cyan, 2008. Accompanying CD.

*Party Time with the Stars.* Volumes 1 & 2. Ghana: Nakasi Records, 1994.

*Performing the Nation: Swahili music and Cultural Politics in Tanzania* by Kelly Askew. Chicago: The University of Chicago Press, 2002. Accompanying CD.

*Petites musiques du Zaire.* Paris: Buda musique, 1994

*Polyphonies vocale des Pygmées Mbenzele: Republique Centrafricaine.* Recorded in 1986 by Simha Arom. France: Maison des cultures du monde, 1992.

*Por Por: Honk Horn Music of Ghana: The La Drivers Union Por Por Group.* Recorded by Steven Feld. Washington, DC: Smithsonian/Folkways, 2007.

*Putumayo Presents Africa.* New York: Putumayo World Music, 1999.

*Putumayo Presents African Playground.* New York: Putumayo World Music, 2003.

*Putumayo Presents Women of Africa.* New York: Putumayo World Music, 2004.

*Putumayo Presents Acoustic Africa.* New York: Putumayo World Music (2006).

*Putumayo Presents African Dreamland.* New York: Putumayo World Music (2008)

*Putumayo Presents African Blues.* New York: Putumayo World Music (2012)

*Putumayo Presents African Beat.* New York: Putumayo World Music (2013)

*Pygmées Aka: Chants de chasse, d'amour et de moquerie.* Paris: Ocora, 1998.

*Rhythms of Life, Songs of Wisdom: Akan Music from Ghana.* Recorded by Roger Vetter. Washington D.D.: Smithsonian Folkways, 1996.

*Un roi Africain et sa musique de cour: chants et danses du palais a Porto-Novo sous le règne de Gbèfa (1948–1976)* by Gilbert Rouget. Paris: CNRS Editions, 1996. Accompanying CDs.

*The Rough Guide to West African Music.* Compiled by Phil Stanton. London: World Music Network, 1995.

*The Rough Guide to Music of Kenya and Tanzania.* London: World Music Network, 1996.

*The Rough Guide to the Music of Senegal and Gambia.* London: World Music Network, 2001.

*The Rough Guide to African Music for Children.* London: World Music Network, 2005.

*Royal Court Music from Uganda: 1950 & 1952.* Music of the Ganda, Nyoro and Ankole. Recorded by Hugh Tracey. Utrecht, Netherlands: International Library of African Music, 1998.

*Seize the Dance! BaAka Musical Life and the Ethnography of Performance* by Michelle Kisliuk. Chicago: The University of Chicago Press, 1997. Accompanying CDs.

*Senku: Piano Music by Composers of African Descent* Performed by William Chapman Nyaho, piano. [S.l.]: Musicians Showcase Recordings, 2003.

*Sénoufo: Musiques es funérailles Fodonon.* Recorded in 1976, 1981 and 1982 by Michel de Lannoy in Lataha, Ivory Coast. [France]: Chant du monde/ Harmonia Mundi, 1994 (orig.1974).

*Seperewa Kasa.* Songs composed and performed by Baffour Kyerematen, Osei Kwame Korankye and Kari Banaman. [EU]: Riverboat Records/World Music Network, 2008.

*Sidi Sufis: African Indian Mystics of Gujarat.* Produced by Amy Catlin-Jairazbhoy and Nazir Jairazbhoy. VanNuys, CA: Aspara Media, 2002.

*Sierra Leone: Musiques traditionelles.* Recorded by Jean L. Jenkins. France: Ocora, 1992.

*Siramori Diabate: Griot Music from Mali #3*. Recorded by Jan Jansen and John W. Johnson in 1974 and 1989 in Kela and Kangaba, Mali. Leiden: Pan Records, 2002.

*Sikiliza [Listen]: Rythmes et chants de la forêt de la savane [RDC]*. Collection de musiques populaires du monde. Recorded by Didier Demolin, 1984–88. Belgium: Colophon Records, 2005.

*Songs of War and Death from the Slave Coast*. Recorded by Michel Verdon in Abutia-Kloe, Ghana. Washington, D.C.: Smithsonian Folkways Recordings, 2007 (orig. 1982).

*Spirit of African Sanctus: the original recordings by David Fanshawe (1969–73)*. Wotton-under-Edge, Glos., England: Saydisc, 1991.

*Structural Set Analysis: Adowa* by Willie Anku. Legon, Ghana: Soundstage Production, 1992. Accompanying CD.

*Structural Set Analysis 2: Bawa* by Willie Anku. Legon, Ghana: Soundstage Production, 1993. Accompanying CD.

*Tanzania: Music of the Farmer Composers of Sukumaland*. Recorded in 1994 and 1995 by Frank Gunderson. [USA]: Multicultural Media, 2005.

*Tanzanie: Chants Wagogo*. Recorded by Polo Vallejo in 1996–1998. Paris: Ocora, 2000.

*Tanzanie: Masumbi: Musique de divertissement Wagogo*. Recorded by Polo Vallejo in 1997–2001. Paris: Ocora, 2002.

*Tanzanie:Musiques rituelles Gogo*. Recorded by Polo Vallejo, 1996–99. Geneva: VDE-GALLO, 2001.

*Taviefe Dunenyo Akpese Group: Dekawɔwɔ*. Cassette Recording, n.d.

*Theory of African Music, vol. 1* by Gerhard Kubik. Wilhelmshaven: F. Noetzel, 1994. Accompanying CDs.

*Theory of African Music, vol. 2* by Gerhard Kubik. Chicago: The University of Chicago Press, 2010. Accompanying CD.

*Togo: Music from West Africa*. Recorded by Dan Kahn and Bill Nowlin. Cambridge, MA: Rounder, 1992 [orig. 1978].

*Togo: Orchestres et lithophones Kabiyé*. Recorded 2001–04 by Lorenzo Bianchi and Daniele Segre Amar. Paris: Ocora, 2004.

*Towards an African Pianism: An Anthology of Keyboard Music from Africa and the Diaspora*. 2 volumes. Department of Music, University of Pittsburgh: A Bridge Across: Intercutural Composition, Performance, Musicology, 2005.

*Uganda: Village Ensembles of Busoga*. Geneva: AIMP & VDE-GALLO, 1997.

*Wolof Music of Senegal and Gambia*. Recorded by David Ames. New York: Folkways Records, 1955. Available electronically through Smithsonian Global Sound for Libraries. Alexandria, VA: Alexander Street Press, 2005.

*Worlds of Music: An Introduction to the Music of the World's Peoples*, ed. Jeff Todd Titon. Second edition. New York: Schirmer Books, 1992. Accompanying CDs.

*Yewe: Ritual Music and Dance of a Secret Society*. Mama Ahoewornu Shrine of Dzodze, Adagbledu, Ghana. Recorded by Paschal Yao Younge. Morgantown, WV: Azaguno 2002.

*Yoruba Bata Drums: Elewe music and Dance*. Recorded by G. Odukwe Sackeyfio during the Ila Rangun Odun Egungun festival. Washington, DC: Smithsonian/ Folkways, 1998.

*Yoruba Music in the Twentieth Century: Identity, Agency and Performance Practice* by Bode Omojola. Rochester, NY: University of Rochester Press, 2012. Accompanying CD.

*Yoruba Drums from Benin, West Africa*. Recorded in 1987 by Marcos Branda Lacerda. Washington, DC: Smithsonian/Folkways, 1996.

*Zaïre: La musique des Nande* (Zaire: The Music of the Nande) VDE-GALLO, 1991.

*Zambia: The Songs of Mukanda*. Music of the Secret Society of the Luvale People of Central Africa. Recorded by Kenichi Tsukada in 1982–84. [USA]: Multicultural Media, 1997.

# VIDEOGRAPHY

*Africa Come Back: The Popular Music of West Africa.* Directed by Geoffrey Haydon, produced by Penny Corke. Princeton, NJ: Films for the Humanities, 2003 [orig. 1984].

*African Christianity Rising* by Jim Ault. http://jamesault.com/

*Born Musicians: Traditional Music from the Gambia.* Directed by Geoffrey Haydon, produced by Penny Corke. Princeton, NJ: Films for the Humanities, 2003 [orig. 1984].

*The Chopi Timbila Dance [Mozambique].* Directed by Andrew Tracey, produced by Gei Zantzinger. University Park, PA: Penn State University, 1980.

*Composers under the Tree of God: Art-Music in Ghana.* A film by Hanne Kaisik-Aumüller and Uli Aumüller. Berlin: Bavarian TV, 1995.

*Drums of Dagbon.* Directed by Dennis Marks, produced by Penny Corke. Princeton, NJ: Films for the Humanities, 2003 [orig. 1984].

*Female Voices from an Ewe Dance-Drumming Community: Our Music Has Become a Divine Spirit* by James Burns. Farnham, England: Ashgate, 2009. Accompanying DVD.

*Fontonfrom: Drum-making among the Ashanti in Ghana* by Andreas Meyer and Urban Bareis. Berlin: Ethnolog. Museum, Staatl. Museen zu Berlin, 1994.

*Great, great, great grandparents' Music.* A film by Taale Laafi Rosellini. Santa Cruz, CA: African Family Films, 1997.

*Growing into Music in Mali and Guinea* by Lucy Duran. http://www.growingintomusic.co.uk/mali-and-guinea-music-of/films-of-growing-into-music.html.

*JVC-Smithsonian Folkways video Anthology of Music and Dance of Africa.* Volume 1: Egypt, Uganda, Senegal; vol. 2: Gambia, Liberia, Ghana, Nigeria; vol. 3: Kenya, Malawi, Botswana, South Africa. Directed by Hiroshi Yamamoto. Barre, VT: Multicultural Media, 2005 [orig. 1996].

*Kinshasa Symphony.* A film by Claus Wischmann and Martin Baer. Berlin: C Major Entertainment GmbH, 2010.

*The Language You Cry In.* Produced and directed by Alvaro Toepke and Angel Serrano. San Francisco: California Newsreel, 1998.

*Listening to the Silence: A Film About African Cross Rhythms as Seen Through Ghanaian Music.* Written and produced by Peter Bischoff. Princeton, N.J: Films for the Humanities & Sciences, 2002 [orig. 1996].

*Living the Hiplife.* Directed by Jesse W. Shipley. New York: The World Newsreel, 2007.

*Mande Music and Dance.* Performed by Mandinka musicians of the Gambia in the late twentieth century. Filmed by Roderic Knight. New York: Lyrichord Discs, in association with Multicultural Media, 2005.

*Mbira dza vadzimu: Dambatsoko, an old cult center, with Mutchera and Ephat Mujuru.* Directed by Andrew Tracey, produced by Gei Zantzinger. University Park: Pennsylvania State University, 1978.

*Mbira: The Technique of the Mbira dza Vadzimu* (Zimbabwe). Devault, PA: Constant Springs, 1994.

*Missa Luba.* Performed by Muungano National Choir, Kenya conducted by Boniface Mganga. Produced by Job Maarse, directed by Anthony Howard. New York: Polygram Music Video, 1990.

*Ndando Yawusiwana* (Song of Sadness). Produced and directed by Gei Zantzinger. University Park: Pennsylvania State University, 2008.

*Polyphonies du Nord-Cameroun* by Natalie Fernando. Louvain: Peeters, 2011. Accompanying CD-Rom.

*Prophet Healers of Northern Malawi.* From the fieldwork of Steven Friedson. Seattle: University of Washington, 1989.

*Rhythms of the World (Anthology).* Directed by Hart Perry, produced by Hart Perry and Dana Heinz. Hosted by Peter Gabriel and Bobby McFerrin. New York, N.Y: PolyGram Video, 1991.

*A Spirit Here Today: A Scrapbook of Chopi Village Music* (Mozambique). Produced and directed by Gei Zantzinger. Devault, PA: Constant Springs, 1994.

*Wenn die Zahnräder Menschen sind: das Klavierkonzert von György Ligeti.* A film by Hanne Kaisik, György Ligeti and Uli Aumüller. Berlin: Inpetto Filmproduktion, 1996.

# BIBLIOGRAPHY

Abel, Mark. *Groove: An Aesthetic of Measured Time.* Leiden: Brill Academic Publishers, 2014.

Addo, Akosua. *Ghanaian Children's Music Cultures: A Video Ethnography of Selected Singing Games.* PhD diss., University of British Columbia, 1995.

Adorno, Theodor. *Mahler: A Musical Physiognomy.* Translated by Edmund Jephcott. Chicago: University of Chicago Press, 1992.

Agawu, Kofi. "Music in the Funeral Traditions of the Akpafu." *Ethnomusicology* 32 (1988): 75–105.

Agawu, Kofi. "Tone and Tune: The Evidence for Northern Ewe Music." *Africa* 58 (1988): 127–146.

Agawu, Kofi. "On an African Song from Akpafu." *Sonus* 10 (1989): 22–39.

Agawu, Kofi. "Variation Procedures in Northern Ewe Song." *Ethnomusicology* 34 (1990): 221–243.

Agawu, Kofi. *African Rhythm: A Northern Ewe Perspective.* Cambridge: Cambridge University Press, 1995.

Agawu, Kofi. *Representing African Music: Postcolonial Notes, Queries, Positions.* New York: Routledge, 2003.

Agawu, Kofi. "Structural Analysis or Cultural Analysis? Competing Perspectives on the 'Standard Pattern' of West African Rhythm." *Journal of the American Musicological Society* 59 (2006): 1–46.

Agawu, Kofi. "The Communal Ethos in African Performance: Ritual, Narrative and Music Among the Northern Ewe." In *Approaches to African Musics.* Edited by Enrique Cámara de Landa and Silvia Martínez García, 181–200. Valladolid: Universidad de Valladolid, Centro Buendía, 2006. Also published in *TRANS* 11 (2007). Accessed January 20, 2015. www.sibetrans.com/trans/articulo/125/the-communal-ethos-in-African-performance-ritual-narrative-and-music-among-the-northern-ewe.

Agawu, Kofi. *Music as Discourse: Semiotic Adventures in Romantic Music.* Oxford: Oxford University Press, 2009.

Agawu, Kofi. "The Challenge of African Art Music." *Circuit, musiques, contemporaines* 21 (2011): 55–72.

Agawu, Kofi. "Tonality as a Colonizing Force in Africa." In *Audible Empire.* Edited by Ronald Radano and Tejumola Olaniyan. Durham, NC: Duke University Press, 2016.

Aluede, Charles O. "The Anthropomorphic Attributes of African Musical Instruments: History and Use in Esan, Nigeria." *Anthropologist* 8 (2006): 157–160.

Ames, David W., and Anthony V. King. *A Glossary of Hausa Music and Its Social Contexts*. Evanston, IL: Northwestern University Press, 1971.

Ampene, Kwasi. *Female Song Tradition and the Akan of Ghana: The Creative Process in Nnwonkoro*. Aldershot, England: Ashgate, 2005.

Ampene, Kwasi, and Nana Kwadwo Nyantakyi III. *Engaging Modernity: Asante in the Twenty-First Century*. Ann Arbor, MI: University Lithoprinters.

Ankermann, Bernhard. *Die afrikanischen Musikinstrumente*. Berlin: Druck und Verlag von A. Haack, 1901.

*Analytical Approaches to World Music* Journal. Edited by Lawrence Shuster, Daniel Goldberg, Jay Rahn, and Rob Schultz, 2011–.

Anku, William. *Procedures in African Drumming: A Study of Akan/Ewe Traditions and African Drumming in Pittsburgh*. PhD diss., University of Pittsburgh, 1988.

Anku, Willie. *Structural Set Analysis of African Music 1: Adowa*. Legon, Ghana: Soundstage Production, 2002.

Anku, Willie. *Structural Set Analysis 2: Bawa*. Legon, Ghana: Soundstage Production, 2002.

Anku, Willie. *A Theory of African Music*, forthcoming.

Anyidoho, Kofi. "Oral Poetics and Traditions of Verbal Art in Africa." PhD diss., University of Texas at Austin, 1983.

Arewa, Olufunmilayo. "From J.C. Bach to Hip Hop: Musical Borrowing, Copyright and Cultural Context." *North Carolina Law Review* 84 (2006): 547–645. Accessed July 23, 2013. Available at http://works.bepress.com/o_arewa/5.

Arhin, Kwame. "The Economic Implications of Transformations in Akan Funeral Rites." *Africa: Journal of the International African Institute* 64 (1994): 307–322.

Arom, Simha. "New Perspectives for the Description of Orally Transmitted Music." *World of Music* 23 (1981): 40–62.

Arom, Simha. *African Polyphony and Polyrhythm: Musical Structure and Methodology*. Translated by Martin Thom, Barbara Tuckett, and Raymond Boyd. Cambridge: Cambridge University Press, 1991.

Arom, Simha. "Intelligence in Traditional Music." In *What Is Intelligence?* ('Darwin College Lectures 1992'). Edited by J. Khalfa, 137–160. Cambridge: Cambridge University Press, 1994.

Arom, Simha. "Language and Music in Fusion: The Drum Language of the Banda Linda (Central African Republic)." *TRANS* 11 (2007). Accessed July 24, 2013. http://www.sibetrans.com/trans/a118/language-and-music-in-fusion-the-drum-language-of-the-banda-linda-central-african-republic.

Arom, Simha, and Frédéric Voisin. "Theory and Technology in African Music." In *Africa: The Garland Encyclopedia of World Music*. Edited by Ruth Stone, 254–270. New York: Garland, 1997.

Askew, Kelly. *Performing the Nation: Swahili Music and Cultural Politics in Tanzania*. Chicago: University of Chicago Press, 2002.

Avorgbedor, Daniel Kodzo. "'It's a Great Song!' *Halò* Performance as Literary Production." *Research in African Literatures* 32 (2001): 17–43.

Bakare-Yusuf, Bibi. "'Yoruba's Don't Do Gender': A Critical Review of Oyeronke Oyewumi's *The Invention of Women*: Making an African Sense of Western Gender Discourses." accessed December 19, 2014. http://www.codesria.org/IMG/pdf/BAKERE_YUSUF.pdf.

Barber, Karin. "Popular Arts in Africa." *African Studies Review* 30 (1987): 1–78.

Barber, Karin. "Introduction." In *Readings in African Popular Culture*. Edited by Karin Barber. Bloomington: Indiana University Press, 1997.

Barber, Karin. *The Anthropology of Texts, Persons and Publics: Oral and Written Culture in Africa and Beyond*. Cambridge: Cambridge University Press, 2007.

Bebey, Francis. *African Music: A People's Art*. Translated by Josephine Bennett. New York: Lawrence Hill, 1975.

Behague, Gerard. *Music in Latin America: An Introduction*. Englewood Cliffs, NJ: Prentice-Hall, 1979.

Benveniste, Émile. "The Semiology of Language." In *Semiotics: An Introductory Reader*. Edited by Robert E. Innis, 228–246. London: Hutchinson, 1986.

Berliner, Paul. *The Soul of Mbira: Music and Traditions of the Shona People of Zimbabwe*. Berkeley: University of California Press, 1978.

Berliner, Paul. *Thinking in Jazz: The Infinite Art of Improvisation*. Chicago: University of Chicago Press, 1994.

Biro, Daniel, and Andy Schloss. Review of *African Rhythms* by Pierre-Laurent Aimard, Gyorgy Ligeti, Steve Reich, and Simha Arom. *Ethnomusicology* 51 (2007): 162–165.

Blacking, John. "Tonal Organization in the Music of Two Venda Initiation Schools." *Ethnomusicology* 14 (1970): 1–56.

Blacking, John. *How Musical Is Man?* Seattle: University of Seattle Press, 1973.

Blacking, John. *Venda Children's Songs: A Study in Ethnomusicological Analysis*. Chicago: University of Chicago Press, 1995 [orig. 1967].

Blench, Roger. "The Morphology and Distribution of Sub-Saharan Musical Instruments of North African, Middle Eastern, and Asian Origin." *Musica Asiatica* 4 (1984): 155–191.

Blum, Stephen. "European Musical Terminology and the Music of Africa." In *Comparative Musicology and Anthropology of Music*. Edited by Bruno Nettl and Philip Bohlman, 3–36. Chicago: University of Chicago Press, 1991.

Blum, Stephen. "Composition." In *Grove Music Online*. Accessed October 31, 2013.

Bohlman, Philip V. *World Music: A Very Short Introduction*. Oxford: Oxford University Press, 2002.

Boone, Olga. *Les tambours du Congo belge et du Ruanda-Urundi*. Tervuren: Annales du Musée du Congo Belge, 1951.

Bosman, William. *A New and Accurate Description of the Coast of Guinea*. 2nd ed. London: J. Knapton, 1721 [orig. 1704].

Bowdich, Thomas. *Mission from Cape Coast to Ashantee*. London: J. Murray, 1873 [orig. 1819].

Branda-Lacerda, Marcos. *Kultische Trommelmusik der Yoruba in der Volksrepublik Benin: Bata-Sango und Bata-Egungun in den Städten Pobè und Sákété*. 2 vols. Hamburg: Verlag der Musikalienhandlung Karl Dieter Wagner, 1988.

Branda-Lacerda, Marcos. Jacket notes to CD, *Yoruba Drums from Benin, West Africa*. Washington, DC: Smithsonian/Folkways, 1996.

Branda-Lacerda, Marcos. "Instrumental Texture and Heterophony in a Fon Repertoire for Drums." *TRANS* 11 (2007). Accessed July 24, 2013. http://www.sibetrans.com/trans/a127/instrumental-texture-and-heterophony-in-a-fon-repertoire-for-drum.

Brandel, Rose. "Polyphony in African Music." In *The Commonwealth of Music*. Edited by Gustav Reese and Rose Brandel, 26–44. New York: Free Press, 1965.

Brandilly, Monique. *Introduction aux musiques Africaines*. Arles: Cité de la musique/Actes Sud, 1997.

Brandilly, Monique. "Chad." In *Grove Music Online*. Accessed October 31, 2013.

Brathwaite, Kamau. Unpublished Seminar Paper, Columbia University, April 2008.

Broughton, Simon, Mark Ellingham, and Richard Trillo, with Orla Duane and Vanessa Dowell. *World Music: The Rough Guide*. London: Rough Guides, 1999.

Burns, James. *The Beard Cannot Tell Stories to the Eyelash: Creative Transformation in an Ewe Funeral Dance-Drumming Tradition*. PhD diss., University of London, School of Oriental and African Studies, 2005.

Burns, James. "'My Mother Has a Television, Does Yours?' Transformation and Secularization in an Ewe Funeral Drum Tradition." *Oral Tradition* 20 (2005): 300–319.

Burns, James. *Female Voices from an Ewe Dance-Drumming Community: Our Music Has Become a Divine Spirit*. Farnham, England: Ashgate, 2009.

Burns, James. "Rhythmic Archetypes in Instrumental Music from Africa and the Diaspora." *Music Theory Online* 16 (2010). Accessed July 24, 2013. http://mto.societymusictheory.org/issues/mto.10.16.4/mto.10.16.4.burns.html.

Camara de Landa, Enrique, and Martinez Garcia, ed. *Approaches to African Musics*. Valladolid: Universidad de Valladolid, 2006.

Campbell, Patricia Shehan, and Trevor Wiggins, ed. *The Oxford Handbook of Children's Musical Cultures*. New York: Oxford University Press, 2012.

Carl, Florian. "The Representation and Performance of African Music in German Popular Culture." *Yearbook for Traditional Music* 43 (2011): 198–223.

Carrington, John. *Talking Drums of Africa*. London: Carey Kingsgate Press, 1949.

Chapman, Jim. *Afro No-Clash: Composing Syncretic African/Western Music: Eleven Compositions and the Frameworks for their Systematic Analysis*. PhD diss., Queensland University of Technology [Australia], 2007.

Charry, Eric. "West African Harps." *Journal of the American Musical Instrument Society* 20 (1994): 5–53.

Charry, Eric. *Mande Music: Traditional and Modern Music of the Maninka and Mandinka of Western Africa*. Chicago: University of Chicago Press, 2000.

Charry, Eric. *Hip Hop Africa: New African Music in a Globalizing World*. Bloomington: Indiana University Press, 2012.

Chernoff, John Miller. *African Rhythm and African Sensibility: Aesthetics and Social Action in African Musical Idioms*. Chicago: University of Chicago Press, 1979.

Chernoff, John Miller. "The Rhythmic Medium in African Music." *New Literary History* 22 (1991): 1093–1102.

Chernoff, John Miller. *A Drummer's Testament: Dagbamba Society and Culture in the Twentieth Century* (forthcoming; excerpts can be read at http://www. adrummerstestament.com/).

Christaller, Johann Gottlieb. *Dictionary of the Ashante and Fante Language Called Tshi (Twi)*. Basel: Basel Evangelical Missionary Society, 1933.

Clements, George N. "Phonology." In *African Languages: An Introduction*. Edited by Bernd Heine and Derek Nurse, 123–160. Cambridge: Cambridge University Press, 2000.

Coetzee, Paulette June. "Performing Whiteness; Representing Otherness: Hugh Tracey and African Music." PhD diss., Rhodes University, 2014.

Collaer, Paul, et al., ed. *Nordafrika*. Leipzig: VEB Deutscher Verlag für Musik, 1983.

Collins, John. *West African Pop Roots*. Philadelphia: Temple University Press, 1992.

Collins, John. *African Musical Symbolism in Contemporary Perspective: Roots, Rhythms and Relativity*. Berlin: Pro Business, 2004.

Cooke, Peter. "Uganda." *Grove Music Online*. Accessed October 31, 2013.

Coplan, David. "Go to My Town, Cape Coast! The Social History of Ghanaian Highlife." In *Eight Urban Musical Cultures*. Edited by Bruno Nettl, 96–114. Urbana: University of Illinois Press, 1978.

Cory, Hans. *The Ntemi: The Traditional Rites in Connection with the Burial, Election, Enthronement and Magical Powers of a Sukuma Chief*. London: Macmillan, 1951.

Cross, Ian. "Music and Biocultural Evolution." In *The Cultural Study of Music: A Critical Introduction*. 2nd ed. Edited by Martin Clayton, Trevor Herbert, and Richard Middleton, 19–30. New York: Routledge, 2012.

Da Cruz, Clément. *Les instruments de musique dans le Bas-Dahomey*. Porto Novo: Institut français d'Afrique noire, 1954.

D'Amico, Leonardo, and Andrew Kaye. *Musica dell'Africa Nera: Civiltà subsahariane fra tradizione e modernità*. Palermo: L'epos, 2004.

Dargie, Dave. *Xhosa Music: Its Techniques and Instruments, with a Collection of Songs*. Cape Town: David Philip, 1988.

Dargie, Dave. "Umngqokolo: Xhosa Overtone Singing." *African Music* 7 (1991): 33–47.

Dauer, Alfons M., et al., ed. *Musik in Afrika: mit 20 Beiträgen zur Kenntnis traditioneller afrikanischer Musikkulturen*. Berlin: Staatliche Museen Preussischer Kulturbesitz, Museum für Völkerkunde, 1983.

Denning, Michael. "Decolonizing the Ear: The Transcolonial Resonance of Vernacular Music." In *Audible Empire: Music, Global Politics, Critique*. Edited by Ronald Radano and Tejumola Olaniyan. Durham, NC: Duke University Press, 2016.

Devin, Luis. http://www.luisdevin.com.

Dingemanse, Mark. "The Meaning and Use of Ideophones in Siwu." PhD thesis, Max Plank Institute for Psycholinguistics, 2010.

Dingemanse, Mark. "The Ideophone." accessed July 24, 2013. http://ideophone.org/.

Dingemanse, Mark. "Ideophones and the Aesthetics of Everyday Language in a West-African Society." *Senses and Society* 6 (2011): 78–79.

Djedje, Jacqueline, ed. *Turn Up the Volume! A Celebration of African Music*. Los Angeles: UCLA Fowler Museum of Cultural History, 1999.

Djedje, Jacqueline. *Fiddling in West Africa: Touching the Spirit in Fulbe, Hausa, and Dagbamba Cultures*. Bloomington: Indiana University Press, 2008.

Djedje, Jacqueline. *Fiddling in West Africa (1950s–1990s): The Songbook*. Los Angeles: UCLA Ethnomusicology Publications, 2008.

Djenda, Maurice, and Michelle Kisliuk. "Central African Republic." In *Grove Music Online*. Accessed June 27, 2013.

Dor, George. "Communal Creativity and Song Ownership in Anlo-Ewe Musical Practice: The Case of Havolu." *Ethnomusicology* 48 (2004): 26–51.

Dor, George. "Melodic Commutation and Concurrent Pitch Sonorities in Ewe Songs: A Pre-compositional Resource for African Art Music." In *Multiple Interpretations of Creativity and Knowledge in African Music Traditions*. Edited by George Dor and Olabode Omojola, 227–246. Richmond, CA: Music Research Institute, 2005.

Dor, George. "Ephraim Amu's 'Bonwere Kenteŋwene': A Celebration of Ghanaian Traditional Knowledge, Wisdom, and Artistry." *African Music: Journal of the International Library of African Music* 9 (2014): 7–35.

Dor, George. "Exploring Indigenous Interpretive Frameworks in African Music Scholarship: Conceptual Metaphors and Indigenous Ewe Knowledge in the Life and Work of Hesino Vinorkor Akpalu." *Black Music Research Journal*, forthcoming.

Dor, George. *West African Drumming and Dance in North American Universities: An Ethnomusicological Perspective*. Jackson, MS: University of Mississippi Press, 2014.

Dosunmu, Oyebade. *African Art Music*. https://www.facebook.com/AfricanArtMusic/info?tab=page_info.

Durán, Lucy. "Birds of Wasulu: Freedom of Expression and Expressions of Freedom in the Popular Music of Southern Mali." *British Journal of Ethnomusicology*, 4 (1995): 101–134.

Edwards, Brent. "The Sound of Anti-Colonialism." In *Audible Empire: Music, Global Politics, Critique*. Edited by Ronald Radano and Tejumola Olaniyan. Durham, NC: Duke University Press, 2016.

Ehret, Christopher. "Languages and Peoples." In *Cultural Atlas of Africa*. Edited by Jocelyn Murray, 24–30. Oxford: Elsevier Publishers, Phaidon Press.

Ekwueme, Lazarus. "African Music in Christian Liturgy: The Igbo Experiment." *African Music* 5 (1973–1974): 12–33.

Ekwueme, Lazarus. "African-Music Retentions in the New World." *Black Perspective in Music* 2 (1974): 128–144.

Ekwueme, Laz E. N. "Analysis and Analytic Techniques in African Music." *African Music* 6 (1980): 89–106.

England, Nicholas. "Bushman Counterpoint." *Journal of the International Folk Music Council* 19 (1967): 58–66.

Enwezor, Okwui, ed. *The Short Century: Independence and Liberation Movements in Africa, 1945–1994*. Munich: Prestel, 2001.

Erlmann, Veit. *Music, Modernity, and the Global Imagination: South Africa and the West*. New York: Oxford University Press, 1999.

Euba, Akin. "Multiple Pitch Lines in Yoruba Choral Music." *Journal of the International Folk Music Council* 19 (1967): 467–487.

Euba, Akin. *Essays on Music in Africa*. Vol. 2. Lagos: Elekoto Music Centre, 1989.

Euba, Akin. *Yoruba Drumming: The Dùndún Tradition*. Lagos: Elokoto Music Centre and Bayreuth African Studies Series, 1990.

Euba, Akin. *Modern African Music: A Catalogue of Selected Archival Materials at Iwalewa-Haus, University of Bayreuth, Germany*. Bayreuth: Iwalewa-Haus, 1993.

Euba, Akin. Andrew Mellon Professor, Inaugural Lecture, University of Pittsburgh, 2000.

Euba, Akin. *J. H. Kwabena Nketia: Bridging Musicology and Composition: A Study in Creative Musicology*. Point Richmond: Music Research Institute, 2014.

Facci, Serena. "Akazehe del Burundi. Saluti a incastro polifonico e cerimonialità femminile." In *Polifonie. Procedimenti, tassonomie e forme: una riflessione a più voci*. Edited by M. Agamennone, 123–161. Verona: Edizioni Il Cardo/Ricerche, 1996.

Fales, Cornelia. "The Paradox of Timbre." *Ethnomusicology* 46 (2002): 56–95.

Fales, Cornelia, and Stephen McAdams. "The Fusion and Layering of Noise and Tone: Implications for Timbre in African Instruments." *Leonardo Music Journal* 4 (1994): 69–77.

Feld, Steven. "Sound Structure as Social Structure." *Ethnomusicology* 28 (1984): 383–409.

Feld, Steven. "Pygmy POP: A Genealogy of Schizophonic Mimesis." *Yearbook for Traditional Music* 28 (1996): 1–35.

Feld, Steven. *Jazz Cosmopolitanism in Accra: Five Musical Years in Ghana*. Durham, NC: Duke University Press, 2012.

Feld, Steven, and Aaron Fox. "Music and Language." *Annual Review of Anthropology* 23 (1994): 25–53.

Fernando, Nathalie. *Polyphonies du Nord-Cameroun*. Société d'Etudes Linguistiques et Anthropologiques de France. Paris: Peeters/SELAF, 2011.

Fiagbedzi, Nissio. *The Music of the Anlo: Its Historical Background, Cultural Matrix and Style*. PhD thesis, University of California Los Angeles, 1977.

Fiagbedzi, Nissio. *Form and Meaning in Ewe Song: A Critical Review*. Richmond, CA: Music Research Institute, 2009.

Friedson, Steven. *Dancing Prophets: Musical Experience in Tumbuka Healing*. Chicago: University of Chicago Press, 1996.

Friedson, Steven. *Remains of Ritual: Northern Gods in a Southern Land*. Chicago: University of Chicago Press, 2009.

Fryer, Peter. "The 'Discovery' and Appropriation of African Music ad Dance." *Race and Class* 39 (1998): 1–20.

Fryer, Peter. "Our Earliest Glimpse of West African Music." *Race and Class* 45 (2003): 105–110.

Fürniss, Suzanne. "Aka Polyphony." In *Analytical Studies in World Music*. Edited by Michael Tenzer, 163–204. New York: Oxford University Press, 2006.

Gansemans, Jos. *Les instruments de musique du Rwanda: étude ethnomusicologique*. Louvain, Belgium: Leuven University Press, 1988.

Gansemans, Jos, et al., ed. *Zentralafrika*. Leipzig: VEB Deutscher Verlag für Musik, 1986.

Gaunt, Kyra. *The Games Black Girls Play: Learning the Ropes from Double-Dutch to Hip-hop*. New York: New York University Press, 2006.

Gbolonyo, Kofi. "Want the History? Listen to the Music! Historical Evidence in Anlo Ewe Musical Practices: A Case Study of Traditional Song Texts." Master's thesis, University of Pittsburgh, 2005.

Gibbon, Dafydd, Firmin Ahoua, and Adjépolé Kouamé. "Modelling Song Relations: An Exploratory Study of Pitch Contours, Tones and Prosodic Domains in Anyi." *Proceedings of the International Congress of Phonetic Sciences* 17 (2011): 743–746.

Grauer, Victor. "Concept, Style and Structure in the Music of African Pygmies and Bushmen: A Study in Cross-Cultural Analysis." *Ethnomusicology* 53 (2009): 396–424.

Gray, John. *African Music: A Bibliographical Guide to the Traditional, Popular, Art, and Liturgical Musics of Sub-Saharan Africa.* Westport, CT: Greenwood Press, 1991.

Green, Doris. "About Greenotation." Accessed July 20, 2013. http://www.tntworldculture.com/toa2/2011/12/about-greenotation/.

Gunderson, Frank. *Sukuma Labor Songs from Western Tanzania: 'We Never Sleep, We Dream of Farming.'* Leiden: Brill, 2010.

Hale, Thomas, and Aissata G. Sidikou. *Women's Songs from West Africa.* Bloomington: Indiana University Press, 2014.

Heine, Bernd, and Derek Nurse, ed. *African Languages: An Introduction.* Cambridge: Cambridge University Press, 2000.

Herbst, Anri, Meki Nzewi, and Kofi Agawu, ed. *Musical Arts in Africa: Theory, Practice and Education.* Pretoria: UNISA Press, 2003.

Herskovits, Melville. *Dahomey.* Vol. 1. Evanston: Northwestern University Press, 1967.

Hirschberg, Walter. "Early Historical Illustrations of West and Central African Music." *African Music* 4 (1969): 6–18.

Hornbostel, Erich M. von. "African Negro Music." *Africa* 1 (1928): 30–62.

Hornbostel, Erich M. von, and Curt Sachs. "Systematik der Musikinstrumente: Ein Versuch." *Zeitschrift für Ethnologie* 4 (1914): 553–590. Translated by Anthony Baines and Klaus Wachsmann as "Classification of Musical Instruments." *Galpin Society Journal* 14 (1961): 3–29.

Huber, Hugo. *The Krobo: Traditional Social and Religious Life of a West African People.* St. Augustin: Anthropos Institute, 1963.

Irele, Abiola. "Is African Music Possible?" *Transition* 61 (1993): 56–71.

Jankowsky, Richard C. *Music, Trance, and Alterity in Tunisia.* Chicago: University of Chicago Press, 2010.

Jayasuriya, Shihan De S., and Richard Pankhurst, ed. *The African Diaspora in the Indian Ocean.* Trenton, NJ: Africa World Press, 2003.

Jindra, Michael, and Joël Noret. *Funerals in Africa: Explorations of a Social Phenomenon.* New York: Berghahn Books, 2011.

Johnston, Thomas F. "Tsonga Children's Folksongs." *Journal of American Folklore* 86 (1973): 225–240.

Jones, A[rthur]. M[orris]. *African Music in Northern Rhodesia and Some Other Places.* The Occasional Papers of the Rhodes Livingstone Museum 4. Manchester: Manchester University Press, 1949.

Jones, A[rthur]. M[orris]. "African Rhythm." *Africa* 24 (1954): 26–47.

Jones, A[rthur]. M[orris]. *Studies in African Music.* 2 vols. London: Oxford University Press, 1959.

Jones, A[rthur]. M[orris]. "Swahili Epic Poetry: A Musical Study." *African Music* 5 (1975/1976): 105–129.

Kafui, Kenn. "Performing Arts." In *A Handbook of Eweland.* Vol. 2: *The Northern Ewes in Ghana.* Edited by Kodzo Gavua, 122–130. Accra: Woeli Publishing Services, 2000.

Kaminski, Joseph. *Asante Ntahera Trumpets in Ghana: Culture, Tradition, and Sound Barrage.* Farnham, England: Ashgate, 2012.

Kartomi, Margaret. *On Concepts and Classification of Musical Instruments.* Chicago: University of Chicago Press, 1990.

Kartomi, Margaret. "The Classification of Musical Instruments: Changing Trends in Research from the Nineteenth Century, with Special Reference to the 1990s." *Ethnomusicology* 45 (2001): 283–314.

Katamba, Francis, and Peter Cooke. "Ssematimba ne Kikwabanga: The Music and Poetry of a Ganda Historical Song." *World of Music* 29 (1987): 349–368.

Kaye, Andy. "The Guitar in Africa." In *Africa: The Garland Encyclopedia of World Music.* Edited by Ruth Stone, 350–369. New York: Garland, 1997.

Kaye, Andy. "Film Score and the African Musical Experience: Some Comments on a Work in Progress." *TRANS* 11 (2007). Accessed July 24, 2013. Available at http://www.sibetrans.com/trans/a126/the-film-score-and-the-african-musical-experience-some-comments-on-a-work-in-progress.

Keil, Charles. *Tiv Song: The Sociology of Art in a Classless Society.* Chicago: University of Chicago Press, 1979.

Keil, Charles. "Participatory Discrepancies and the Power of Music." *Cultural Anthropology* 2 (1987): 275–283.

Keil, Charles, and Steven Feld. *Music Grooves: Essays and Dialogues.* Chicago: University of Chicago Press, 1994.

Kidula, Jean Ngoya. *Music in Kenyan Christianity: Logooli Religious Song.* Bloomington: Indiana University Press, 2013.

Kidula, Jean Ngoya. "Stereotypes, Myths, and Realities Regarding African Music in the African and American Academy." In *Teaching Africa: A Guide for the 21st-Century Classroom.* Edited by Brandon D. Lundy and Solomon Negash, 140–155. Bloomington: Indiana University Press, 2013.

Kirby, Percival. "A Study of Negro Harmony." *Musical Quarterly* 16 (1930): 404–414.

Kirby, Percival. *The Musical Instruments of the Native Races of South Africa.* London: Oxford University Press, 1934.

Klein, Tobias Robert. *Moderne Traditionen: Studien zur postkolonialen Musikgeschichte Ghanas.* Berlin: Peter Lang, 2008.

Klein, Tobias Robert. "Fondling Breasts and Playing Guitar: Textual and Contextual Expressions of a Sociomusical Conflict in Accra." *Zeitschrift der Gesellschaft für Musiktheorie* (2010). Accessed July 24, 2013. Available at http://www.gmth.de/zeitschrift/artikel/589.aspx .

Knight, Roderic. "Towards a Notation and Tablature for the Kora, and Its Application to Other Instruments." *African Music* 5 (1971): 23–36.

Koetting, James. "Analysis and Notation of West African Drum Ensemble Music." *Selected Reports in Ethnomusicology* 1 (1970): 115–146.

Koetting, James. "What Do We Know About African Rhythm?" *Ethnomusicology* 30 (1986): 58–63.

Kolinski, Mieczslaw. "A Cross-Cultural Approach to Metro-Rhythmic Patterns." *Ethnomusicology* 26 (1973): 217–246.

Kongo, Zabana P. *African Drum Music [Slow Agekor, Adowa, Kpanlogo, Agbadza].* Accra, Ghana: Afram Publications, 1997.

Konye, Paul. *African Art Music: Political, Social, and Cultural Factors Behind Its Development and Practice in Nigeria.* New York: Edwin Mellen Press, 2007.

Kramer, Lawrence. *Music and Poetry: The Nineteenth Century and After.* Berkeley: University of California Press, 1984.

Kubik, Gerhard. "The Phenomenon of Inherent Rhythms in East and Central African Instrumental Music." *African Music* 3 (1962): 33–42.

Kubik, Gerhard. "Oral Notation of Some West and Central African Time-Line Patterns." *Review of Ethnology* 3 (1972): 169–176.

Kubik, Gerhard, ed. *Ostafrika.* Leipzig: VEB Deutscher Verlag für Musik, 1982.

Kubik, Gerhard. "African Tone Systems: A Reassessment." *Yearbook for Traditional Music* 17 (1985): 31–63.

Kubik, Gerhard. "The Emics of African Rhythm." In *Cross Rhythms*, Vol. 2. Edited by Daniel Avorgbedor and Kwesi Yankah, 26–66. Bloomington: Trickster Press, 1985.

Kubik, Gerhard, ed. *Westafrika.* Leipzig: VEB Deutscher Verlag für Musik, 1989.

Kubik, Gerhard. *Theory of African Music.* Vol. 1. Wilhelmshaven: Florian Noetzel Verlag, 1994.

Kubik, Gerhard. "Multipart Singing in Sub-Saharan Africa: Remote and Recent Histories Unravelled." In *Symposium on Ethnomusicology.* Edited by A. Tracey, 85–97. Grahamstown, South Africa: International Library of African Music, 1997.

Kubik, Gerhard. "Intra-African Streams of Influence." In *Africa: The Garland Encyclopedia of World Music.* Edited by Ruth Stone, 293–326. New York: Garland, 1997.

Kubik, Gerhard. *Africa and the Blues.* Jackson: University Press of Mississippi, 1999.

Kubik, Gerhard. "African and African American Lamellophones: History, Typology, Nomenclature, Performers, and Intracultural Concepts." In *Turn Up the Volume! A Celebration of African Music.* Edited by Jacqueline Djedje, 20–57. Los Angeles: UCLA Fowler Museum of Cultural History, 1999.

Kubik, Gerhard. "Mukanda—Boys' Initiation in Eastern Angola: Transference, Countertransference and Taboo Symbolism in an Age-Group Related ritual Therapeutic Intervention." In *Weltkongress Psychotherapie. Mythos-Traum-Wirklichkeit. Ausgewählte Beiträge des 2. Weltkongresses für Psychotherapie.* Edited by Alfred Pritz and Thomas Wenzel, 65–90. Vienna: Facultas, 1999.

Kubik, Gerhard. "The African Matrix in Jazz Harmonic Practices." *Black Music Research Journal* 25 (2005): 167–222.

Kubik, Gerhard. *Theory of African Music.* Vol. 2. Chicago: University of Chicago Press, 2010.

Kubik, Gerhard. "Africa." In *Grove Music Online.* Oxford University Press. Accessed July 24, 2013. .

Kunst, Jaap. *Metre, Rhythm, and Multi-part Music.* Leiden: E. J. Brill, 1950.

Kwami, Robert M. "Towards a Comprehensive Catalogue of Eve Drum Mnemonics." *Journal of African Cultural Studies* 11 (1998): 27–38.

Kyagambiddwa, Joseph. *African Music from the Source of the Nile.* London: Atlantic, 1956.

Lacerda, Marcos Branda. *Música Instrumental no Benim: Repertório Fon e Música Bàtá.* São Paulo: Editoria la Universidade de São Paulo, 2014.

Laurenty, Jean-Sebastien. *Les cordophones du Congo belge et du Ruanda-Urundi.* Tervuren: Annales du Musée Royal du Congo Belge, 1960.

Lems-Dworkin, Carol. *African Music: A Pan-African Annotated Bibliography.* London: Hans Zell, 1991.

Levitz, Tamara. "The Aestheticization of Ethnicity: Imagining the Dogon at the Musée du quai Branly." *Musical Quarterly* 89 (2006): 600–642.

Ligeti, György. Foreword to Simha Arom, *African Polyphony and Polyrhythm: Musical Structure and Methodology*, xvii–xviii. Cambridge: Cambridge University Press, 1991.

Lobley, Noel. *The Social Biography of Ethnomusicological Field Recordings: Eliciting Responses to Hugh Tracey's* The Sound of Africa *Series.* DPhil thesis, University of Oxford, 2010.

Locke, David. "Improvisation in West African Musics." *Music Educators' Journal* 66 (1980): 125–132.

Locke, David. "Principles of Offbeat Timing and Cross Rhythm in Southern Ewe Dancing." *Ethnomusicology* 26 (1982): 217–246.

Locke, David. *Dum Gahu: An Introduction to African Rhythm.* Tempe, AZ: White Cliffs Media, 1998.

Locke, David. "Africa/Ewe, Mande, Shona, BaAka." In *Worlds of Music: An Introduction to the Music of the World's People.* 5th ed. rev. Edited by Jeff Todd Titon, 75–121. Belmont, CA: Schirmer Cengage Learning, 2009.

Locke, David. "The Metric Matrix: Simultaneous Multidimensionality in African Music." *Analytical Approaches to World Music* 1 (2011). Accessed October 31, 2013. Available at: http://www.aawmjournal.com/articles/2011a/Locke_AAWM_Vol_1_1.htm

Locke, David. "Call and Response in Ewe Agbadza Songs: One Element in a Network of Musical Factors." *Analytical Approaches to World Music* 3 (2013). Available at http://www.aawmjournal.com/articles/2014a/Locke_AAWM_Vol_3_1.html.

Locke, David, and Godwin K. Agbeli. "A Study of the Drum Language in Adzogbo." *African Music* 6 (1981): 32–51.

Lomax, Alan. "Folk Song Style." *American Anthropologist* 61 (1959): 927–954.

London, Justin. *Hearing in Time: Psychological Aspects of Musical Meter.* 2nd ed. New York: Oxford University Press, 2012.

Lucia, Christine, ed. *The World of South African Music: A Reader.* Newcastle, England: Cambridge Scholars Press, 2005.

Lucia, Christine. "Back to the Future? Idioms of Displaced Time in South African Composition." In *Composing Apartheid: Essays of the Music of Apartheid.* Edited by Grant Olwage, 11–34. Johannesburg: Witswatersrand University Press, 2008.

Lwanga, Charles. "Bridging Ethnomusicology and Composition in the First Movement of Justinian Tamusuza's String Quartet Mu Kkubo Ery'Omusaalaba." *Analytical Approaches to World Music* 3 (2014). Accessed September 10, 2015. Available at http://www.aawmjournal.com/articles/2014a/Lwanga_AAWM_Vol_3_1.pdf

Macchiarella, Ignazio. "Theorizing on Multipart Music Making." Accessed October 31 2013. www.academia.edu/1554185/Ignazio_Macchiarella.

Mahillon, Victor-Charles. *Catalogue descriptif et analytique du Musée instrumental du Conservatoire Royal de Musique de Bruxelles.* 3 vols. Ghent: A. Hoste, 1893–1922.

Malamusi, Moya Aliya. Jacket notes for the CD, *From Lake Malawi to the Zambezi: Aspects of Music and Oral Literature in South-east Africa in the 1990s.* Frankfurt: Popular African Music, 1999.

Mans, Minette, Mary Dzansi-McPalm, and Hellen Odwar Agak. "Play in Musical Arts Pedagogy." In *Musical Arts in Africa: Theory, Practice and Education.* Edited by Anri Herbst, Meki Nzewi, and Kofi Agawu, 195–214. Pretoria: UNISA Press, 2003.

Mapoma, Isaiah Mwesa. "Ingomba: The Royal Musicians of the Bemba People of Luapula Province in Zambia." Master's thesis, University of California Los Angeles, 1974.

Martin, Denis-Constant. "Filiation or Innovation? Some Hypotheses to Overcome the Dilemma of Afro-American Music's Origins." *Black Music Research Journal* 11 (1991): 19–38.

Maultsby, Portia. "Africanisms in African American Music." In *Africanisms in American Culture.* 2nd ed. Edited by Joseph Holloway, 326–355. Bloomington: Indiana University Press, 2005.

Mbabi-Katana, Solomon. *African Music for Schools.* Kampala: Fountain Publishers, 2002.

Mbembe, Achille. "Variations on the Beautiful in the Congolese World of Sounds." *Politique africaine* 100 (2005): 69–91.

McCall, John. "The Representation of African Music in Early Documents." In *The Garland Encyclopedia of World Music: Africa.* Edited by Ruth M. Stone, 74–99. New York: Garland, 1998.

Meintjes, Louise. Review of *Representing African Music* by Kofi Agawu. *Journal of the American Musicological Society* 59 (2006): 769–777.

Mensah, Atta Annan. "Compositional Practices in African Music." In *Africa: The Garland Encyclopedia of World Music.* Edited by Ruth Stone, 208–231. New York: Garland, 1997.

Merriam, Alan P. *African Music on LP: An Annotated Discography.* Evanston, IL: Northwestern University Press, 1970.

Merriam, Alan P. *African Music in Perspective.* New York: Garland, 1982.

Monelle, Raymond. *Linguistics and Semiotics in Music.* Chur, Switzerland: Harwood Press, 1992.

Monson, Ingrid. "Riffs, Repetition, and Theories of Globalization." *Ethnomusicology* 43 (1999): 31–65.

Monts, Lester P. "Islam in Liberia." In *The Garland Encyclopedia of World Music.* Vol. 1: *Africa.* Edited by Ruth Stone, 327–349. New York: Garland, 1998.

Monts, Lester P. *An Annotated Glossary of Vai Musical Language and Its Social Contexts.* Paris: Peters-SELAF, 1990.

Mudimbe, V. Y. *The Idea of Africa.* Bloomington: Indiana University Press, 1994.

Mukuna, Kazadi Wa. *The Characteristic Criteria in the Vocal Music of the Luba-Shankadi Children.* Tervuren: Musée royal de l'Afrique centrale, 1972.

Mundell, Felicia, and John Brearley. "Botswana." In *Grove Music Online.* Accessed July 24, 2013.

Myers, Helen. *Ethnomusicology: An Introduction.* New York: Norton, 1993.

Nannyonga-Tamusuza, Sylvia. "What Is 'African Music'? Conceptualizations of 'African Music' in Bergen (Norway) and Uppsala (Sweden)." In *Ethnomusicology in East Africa: Perspectives from Uganda and Beyond.* Edited by Sylvia Nanyonga-Tamusuza and T. Solomon, 188–215. Kampala, Uganda: Fountain Publishers, 2012.

Nannyonga-Tamusuza, Sylvia, and Andrew N. Weintraub. "The Audible Future: Reimagining the Role of Sound Archives and Sound Repatriation in Uganda." *Ethnomusicology* 56 (2012): 206–233.

Njoku, Johnston Akuma-Kalu. "Art Composed Music in Nigeria in Garland." In *Africa: The Garland Encyclopedia of World Music*. Edited by Ruth Stone, 232–253. New York: Garland, 1997.

Nketia, J. H. Kwabena. *Akanfo nwom bi [Akan Songs]*. London: Oxford University Press, 1949.

Nketia, J. H. Kwabena. *Funeral Dirges of the Akan People*. Achimota: Oxford University Press, 1955.

Nketia, J. H. Kwabena. *African Music in Ghana*. Evanston, IL: Northwestern University Press, 1962.

Nketia, J. H. Kwabena. *Drumming in Akan Communities of Ghana*. Edinburgh: Thomas Nelson and Sons, 1963.

Nketia, J. H. Kwabena. *Folk Songs of Ghana*. Legon: University of Ghana, 1963.

Nketia, J. H. Kwabena. *Our Drums and Drummers*. Accra: Ghana Publishing House, 1968.

Nketia, J. H. Kwabena. "Surrogate Languages of Africa." In *Current Trends in Linguistics: Linguistics in Sub-Saharan Africa*. Edited by Thomas A. Sebeok, 699–732. The Hague: Mouton, 1971.

Nketia, J. H. Kwabena. *The Music of Africa*. New York: Norton, 1974.

Nketia, J. H. Kwabena. "The Juncture of the Social and the Musical: The Methodology of Cultural Analysis." *World of Music* 23 (1981): 22–39.

Nketia, J. H. Kwabena. *African Pianism: Twelve Pedagogical Pieces*. Accra: Afram Publications, 1994.

Nketia, J. H. Kwabena. "The Scholarly Study of African Music: A Historical Review." In *Africa: The Garland Encyclopedia of World Music*. Edited by Ruth Stone, 13–73. New York: Garland, 1997.

Nketia, J. H. Kwabena. *The Creative Potential of African Art Music in Ghana: A Personal Testimony*. Companion Booklet to ICAMD CDs of music by Nketia. Accra: Afram Publications, 2004.

Nketia, J. H. Kwabena. *Ethnomusicology and African Music: Collected Papers*. Vol. 1: *Modes of Inquiry and Interpretation*. Accra: Afram Publications, 2005.

Nyaho, William Chapman, ed. *Piano Music of Africa and the African Diaspora*. New York: Oxford University Press, 2009.

Nzewi, Meki. "Melo-Rhythmic Essence and Hot Rhythm in Nigerian Folk Music." *Black Perspective in Music* 2 (1974): 23–28.

Nzewi, Meki. *Musical Practice and Creativity: An African Traditional Perspective*. Bayreuth, Germany: IWALEWA-Haus, University of Bayreuth, 1991.

Nzewi, Meki. *African Music: Theoretical Content and Creative Continuum: The Culture-Exponent's Definitions*. Olderhausen, Germany: Institut für populärer Musik, 1997.

Nzewi, Meki. "Acquiring Knowledge of the Musical Arts in Traditional Society." In *Musical Arts in Africa: Theory, Practice and Education*. Edited by Anri Herbst, Meki Nzewi, and Kofi Agawu, 13–37. Pretoria: UNISA Press, 2003.

Nzewi, Meki. "Analytical Procedure in African Music: Sounding Traditional Solo Aesthetic." In *A Contemporary Study of Musical Arts, Informed by African Indigenous Knowledge Systems*. Vol. 4: *Illuminations, Reflections and Explorations*, 95–115. Pretoria: Centre for Indigenous Instrumental African Music and Dance, 2007.

Nzewi, Meki. *Musical Sense and Musical Meaning: An Indigenous African Perception*. Amsterdam: Rozenberg Publishers, 2010.

Nzewi, Meki. "Analytical Probing in African Musicology: Discerning Indigenous Epistemology." *Journal of the Association of Nigerian Musicologists* 6 (2012): 1–26.

Nzewi, Odyke. "The Technology and Music of the Nigerian Igbo Ogene Anuka Bell Orchestra." *Leonardo Music Journal* 10 (2000): 25–31.

Odden, David. "Tone: African Languages." In *Handbook of Phonological Theory*. Edited by John A. Goldsmith, 444–475. Oxford: Blackwell, 1995.

Olaniyan, Tejumola. *Arrest the Music!: Fela and His Rebel Art and Politics*. Bloomington: Indiana University Press, 2004.

Olorunyomi, Sola. *Afrobeat!: Fela and the Imagined Continent*. Trenton, NJ: Africa World Press; Ibadan, Nigeria: Copublished with Institute Français de Recherche en Afrique, University of Ibadan, 2003.

Olsen, Dale A. "Note on Corpophone." *Society for Ethnomusicology Newsletter* 20 (1980): 5.

Omojola, Bode. *Nigerian Art Music, with an Introductory Study of Ghanaian Art Music*. Ibadan: Institut Français de Recherche en Afrique, University of Ibadan, 1995.

Omojola, Bode. *Studies in African Pianism*. Bayreuth: Breitinger, 2004.

Omojola, Bode. *The Music of Fela Sowande: Encounters, African Identity and Creative Ethnomusicology*. Richmond, CA: MRI Press, 2009.

Omojola, Bode. *Yorùbá Music in the Twentieth Century: Identity, Agency, and Performance*. Rochester, NY: University of Rochester Press, 2012.

Ong, Walter. "African Talking Drums and Oral Noetics." In *Interfaces of the Word: Studies in the Evolution of Consciousness and Culture*, 92–120. Ithaca, NY: Cornell University Press, 1977.

Onovwerosuoke, Fred. *Twenty Four Studies in African Rhythms*. Vol. 1. St. Louis: African Music Publishers, 2007.

Onyeiji, Christian, ed. *Journal of the Association of Nigerian Musicologists* 6 (2012), 1–305.

Osafo, F. Onwona. "An African Orchestra." *African Music* 1 (1957): 11–12.

Ozah, Marie Agatha. "Building Bridges Between Traditional and Western Art Music: A Study of Joshua Uzoigwe's Egwu Amala." *Analytical Approaches to World Music Journal* 3 (2013). Available at http://www.aawmjournal.com/articles/2014a.

Pantaleoni, Hewitt. "Takada Drumming." *African Music* 4 (1970): 6–31.

Pantaleoni, Hewitt. "Three Principles of Timing in Anlo Dance Drumming." *African Music* 5 (1972): 50–63.

Pantaleoni, Hewitt. "Toward Understanding the Play of Atsimevu in Atsia." *African Music* 5 (1972): 64–84.

Pantaleoni, Hewitt. "Toward Understanding the Play of Sogo in Atsia." *Ethnomusicology* 16 (1972): 1–37.

Pareles, Jon. "The Rhythm Century: The Unstoppable Beat." *New York Times* May 3, 1998, 1.

Park, Mungo. *Travels in the Interior Districts of Africa*. Ware: Wordsworth, 2002 [orig. 1799].

Patel, Aniruddh D. *Music, Language, and the Brain*. New York: Oxford University Press, 2008.

Peel, John. *Religious Encounter and the Making of the Yoruba*. Bloomington: Indiana University Press, 2000.

Polak, Rainer. "Rhythmic Feel as Meter: Non-Isochronous Beat Subdivision in Jembe Music from Mali." *Music Theory Online* 16 (2010). http://www.mtosmt.org/issues/mto.10.16.4/mto.10.16.4.polak.html

Pond, Steven. *Head Hunters: The Making of Jazz's First Platinum Album*. Ann Arbor: University of Michigan Press, 2005.

Post, Jennifer C. *Ethnomusicology: A Research and Information Guide*. New York: Routledge, 2004.

Powers, Harold S. "Language Models and Music Analysis." *Ethnomusicology* 24 (1980): 1–60.

Powers, Harold S. "Rhythm." In *The New Harvard Dictionary of Music*. Edited by Don M. Randel. Cambridge, MA: Harvard University Press, 1986.

Pressing, Jeff. "Cognitive Isomorphisms Between Pitch and Rhythm in World Musics: West Africa, the Balkans and Western Tonality." *Studies in Music* 17 (1983): 38–61.

Radano, Ronald. *Lying Up a Nation: Race and Black Music*. Chicago: Chicago University Press, 2003.

Rahn, Jay. "Asymmetrical Ostinatos in Sub-Saharan Music: Time, Pitch and Cycles Reconsidered." *In Theory Only* 9 (1987): 23–36.

Reed, Daniel. *Dan Ge performance: Masks and Music in Contemporary Côte d'Ivoire*. Bloomington: Indiana University Press, 2003.

Reich, Steve. *Writings on Music, 1965–2000*. Edited with an introduction by Paul Hillier. Oxford: Oxford University Press, 2002.

Ringer, Alexander L. "Melody." In *Grove Music Online*. Oxford University Press. Accessed July 21, 2013. http://www.oxfordmusiconline.com/subscriber/article/grove/music/18357.

Rosellini, Jim, and Trevor Wiggins. "Burkina Faso." In *Grove Music Online*. Oxford University Press. Accessed July 21, 2013. http://www.oxfordmusiconline.com/subscriber/article/grove/music/18357.

Rouget, Gilbert. Jacket Notes for "Dahomey, Music des Princes. Fêtes des Tohossou." Vogue-Contrepoint MC 20.093; reissued as part of *Anthology of Music of Black Africa*. Los Angeles: Everest Records, 1955.

Rouget, Gilbert. "Un chromatisme africain." *L'Homme: Revue française d'anthropologie* I-3 (1961): 32–46.

Rouget, Gilbert. "La musique funéraire en Afrique noire: fonctions et formes." *IMSCR* IX: Salzburg, no. ii (1964): 143–155.

Rouget, Gilbert. "African Traditional Non-Prose Forms: Reciting, Declaiming, Singing and Strophic Structure." In *Proceedings of a Conference on African Languages and Literatures, Northwestern University*. Edited by Jack Berry et al., 45–58. Evanston, IL: Northwestern University Press, 1966.

Rouget, Gilbert. "Court Songs and Traditional History in the Ancient Kingdoms of Port-Novo and Abomey." In *Essays on Music and History in Africa*. Edited by Klaus Wachsmann, 27–64. Evanston, IL: Northwestern University Press, 1971.

Rouget, Gilbert. *Un roi Africain et sa musique de cour: Chants et danses du palais à Porto-Novo sous le règne de Gbèfa (1948–76)*. Paris: CNRS Éditions, 1996.

Rouget, Gilbert. "Benin." *Grove Music Online*. Accessed March 30, 2013.

Rycroft, David. "Nguni Vocal Polyphony." *Journal of the International Folk Music Council* 19 (1967): 88–103.

Sachs, Curt. *Rhythm and Tempo: A Study in Music History*. New York: Norton, 1953.

Sadoh, Godwin. "Intercultural Creativity in Joshua Uzoigwe's Music." *Africa* 74 (2004): 633–661.

Sadoh, Godwin. *Joshua Uzoigwe: Memoirs of a Nigerian Composer-Ethnomusicologist*. Charleston, S.C.: BookSurge Publishing, 2007.

Sadoh, Godwin. *The Organ Works of Fela Sowande: Cultural Perspectives*. Bloomington, IN: iUniverse, 2007.

Sadoh, Godwin. "African Musicology: A Bibliographical Guide to Nigerian Art Music (1927–2009)." *Notes* 66 (2010): 485–502.

Sandler, Felicia. "In Search of a Cross-Cultural Legal Framework: Indigenous Musics as a Worldwide Commodity." In *Music and Cultural Rights*. Edited by Andrew Weintraub and Bell Yung, 241–271. Chicago: University of Illinois Press, 2009.

Sarpong, Peter K. *The Ceremonial Horns of the Ashanti*. Accra: Sedco, 1990.

Schaeffner, André. *Les Kissi; une société noire et ses instruments de musique*. Paris: Hermann, 1951.

Schaeffner, André. Jacket notes to LP, *African Music from French Colonies*. In *The Columbia World History of Primitive Music*. Vol. 2. Edited by Alan Lomax. New York: Columbia Records, 1955–1956.

Schaeffner, André. *Le sistre et le hochet: Musique, théatre et danse dans les sociétés africaines*. Paris: Hermann, 1990.

Schellenberg, Murray. "Does Language Determine Music in Tone Languages?" *Ethnomusicology* 56 (2012): 266–278.

Scherzinger, Martin Rudolf. "Negotiating the Music-Theory/African Music Nexus: A Political Critique of Ethnomusicological Anti-Formalism and a Strategic Analysis of the Harmonic Patterning of the Shona Mbira Song *Nyamaropa*." *Perspectives of New Music* 39 (2001): 5–118.

Scherzinger, Martin Rudolf. Review of *Music, Modernity, and the Global Imagination* by Veit Erlmann. *Journal of the Royal Musical Association* 126 (2001): 135–138.

Scherzinger, Martin Rudolf. "Art Music in a Cross-Cultural Context: The Case of Africa." In *The Cambridge History of Twentieth-Century Music*. Edited by Nicolas Cook and Anthony Pople, 584–613. Cambridge: Cambridge University Press, 2004.

Scherzinger, Martin Rudolf. "Gyorgy Ligeti and the Aka Pygmies Project." *Contemporary Music Review* 25 (2006): 227–262.

Schuller, Gunther. *Early Jazz: Its Roots and Musical Development*. New York: Oxford University Press, 1986 [orig. 1968].

Serwadda, Moses, and Hewitt Pantaleoni. "A Possible Notation for African Dance Drumming." *African Music* 4 (1968): 47–52.

Shelemay, Kay Kauffman. "Notation and Oral Tradition in Africa." In *The Garland Encyclopedia of World Music*. Vol. 1: *Africa*. Edited by Ruth Stone, 146–163. New York: Garland Publishing, 1998.

Shipley, Jesse Weaver. *Living the Hiplife: Celebrity and Entrepreneurship in Ghanaian Popular Music*. Durham, NC: Duke University Press, 2013.

Sidikou, Aissata. *Recreating Words, Reshaping Worlds: The Verbal Art of Women from Niger, Mali and Senegal*. Trenton, NJ: Africa World Press, 2001.

Simon, Artur, ed. *Das Berliner Phonogramm-Archiv 1900–2000: Sammlungen der traditionellen Musik der Welt*. Berlin: Verlag für Wissenschaft und Bildung, 2000.

Slawson, Wayne. "Features, Musical Operations, and Composition: A Derivation from Ewe Drum Music." In *African Musicology: Current Trends*. Vol. 1. Edited by Jacqueline Djedje and William Carter, 307–319. Los Angeles: African Studies Center at UCLA and Cross Roads Press/African Studies Association, 1989.

Small, Christopher. *Musicking: The Meanings of Performing and Listening*. Middletown, CT: Wesleyan University Press, 1998.

Smith, Barbara Herrnstein. *Poetic Closure: A Study of How Poems End*. Chicago: University of Chicago Press, 1968.

Söderberg, Bertil. *Les instruments de musique au Bas-Congo et dans les régions avoisinantes; étude ethnographique*. Stockholm: Université de Stockholm, 1956.

Stock, Jonathan. "The Application of Schenkerian Analysis to Ethnomusicology: Problems and Possibilities." *Music Analysis* 12 (1993): 215–240.

Stone, Ruth M. *Let the Inside Be Sweet: The Interpretation of Music Event Among the Kpelle of Liberia*. Bloomington: Indiana University Press, 1982.

Stone, Ruth M. "Commentary: The Value of Local Ideas in Understanding West African Rhythm." *Ethnomusicology* 30 (1986): 54–57.

Stone, Ruth M. *Dried Millet Breaking: Time, Words and Song in the Woi Epic of the Kpelle*. Bloomington: Indiana University Press, 1988.

Stone, Ruth M., ed. *Africa: The Garland Encyclopedia of World Music*. Vol. 1. New York: Garland, 1997.

Stone, Ruth M. *Music in West Africa: Experiencing Music, Experiencing Culture*. New York: Oxford University Press, 2005.

Stone, Ruth M., ed. *The Garland Handbook of African Music*. 2nd ed. New York: Routledge, 2008.

Stone, Ruth M., and Frank J. Gillis. *African Music and Oral Data: A Catalog of Field Recordings, 1902–1975*. Bloomington: Indiana University Press, 1976.

Stover, Chris. *A Theory of Flexible Rhythmic Spaces for Diasporic African Music*. PhD diss., University of Washington, 2009.

Stover, Chris. Review of "The Clave Matrix: Afro-Cuban Rhythm: Its Principles and Origins" by David Peñalosa. *Latin American Music Review* 33, no. 1 (2012): 131–140.

Taruskin, Richard. *The Oxford History of Western Music*. Vol. 5, *The Late Twentieth Century*. Oxford: Oxford University Press, 2005.

Taylor, Timothy D. *Global Pop: World Music, World Markets*. New York: Routledge, 1997.

Temperley, David. Review of *African Rhythm: A Northern Ewe Perspective* by K. Agawu. *Current Musicology* 62 (1998): 69–83.

Temperley, David. "Meter and Grouping in African Music: A View from Music Theory." *Ethnomusicology* 44 (2000): 65–96.

Tenzer, Michael. "José Maceda and the Paradoxes of Modern Composition in Southeast Asia." *Ethnomusicology* 47 (2003): 93–120.

Thiel, Paul van. *Multi-tribal Music of Ankole: An Ethnomusicological Study Including a Glossary of Musical Terms.* Tervuren: Musée royal de l'Afrique centrale, 1977.

Thompson, William Forde. *Music, Thought, and Feeling: Understanding the Psychology of Music.* New York: Oxford University Press, 2009.

Thram, Diane Janell. *For Future Generations: Hugh Tracey and the International Library of African Music.* Grahamstown, South Africa: International Library of African Music, 2010.

Titon, Jeff, ed. *Worlds of Music: An Introduction to the Music of the World's People.* 3rd ed. New York: Schirmer, 1996.

Tomlinson, Gary. "Musicology, Anthropology, History." In *The Cultural Study of Music: A Critical Introduction.* 2nd ed. Edited by Martin Clayton, Trevor Herbert, and Richard Middleton, 31–44. New York: Routledge, 2012.

Toussaint, Godfried. *The Geometry of Musical Rhythm: What Makes a "Good" Rhythm Good?* Boca Raton, FL: CRC Press, 2013.

Tracey, Andrew. "The Matepe Mbira Music of Rhodesia." *African Music* 4 (1970): 37–61.

Tracey, Hugh. *Chopi Musicians: Their Music, Poetry, and Instruments.* 1st ed. repr., with a new introduction. London: Oxford University Press, 1970.

Tracey, Hugh. Catalogue: *The Sound of Africa Series: 210 Long Playing Records from Central, Eastern, and Southern Africa.* Grahamstown, South Africa: International Library of African Music, 1973.

Treitler, Leo, ed. *Strunk's Source Readings in Music History.* New York: Norton, 1998.

Trowell, Margaret, and Klaus Wachsmann. *Tribal Crafts of Uganda.* London: Oxford University Press, 1953.

Tsukada, Kenichi. "Luvale Perceptions of Mukanda in Discourse and Music." PhD diss., Queens University of Belfast, 1990.

Tsukada, Kenichi. "Variation and Unity in African Harmony: A Study of Mukanda Songs of the Luvale in Zambia." In *Florilegio Musicale (Festschrift Kataoka Gidó zum 70. Geburstag).* Edited by Tanimura Ko, Mabuchi Usaburo, and Takimoto Yuzo, 157–197. Tokyo: Ongaku no Tomo Sha, 1990.

Tsukada, Kenichi. "Harmony in Luvale Music of Zambia." In *The Garland Encyclopedia of World Music.* Vol. 1. Edited by Ruth M. Stone, 722–743. New York: Garland, 1998.

Uzoigwe, Joshua. *Akin Euba: An Introduction to the Life and Music of a Nigerian Composer.* Bayreuth: E. Breitinger, University of Bayreuth, 1992.

Vallejo, Polo. *Mbudi mbudi na mhanga: universo musical infantil de los Wagogo de Tanzania [The musical universe of the Wagogo children from Tanzania].* Madrid: Edicion del autor, 2004.

Vallejo, Polo. *Patrimonio musical Wagogo: Contexto y sistematica.* Madrid: Fundación Sur, 2007.

Van Rhyn, Chris. "Towards a Mapping of the Marginal: Readings of Art Songs by Nigerian, Ghanaian, Egyptian and South African Composers." PhD thesis, Stellenbosch University, 2013.

Vansina, Jan. "The Bells of Kings." *Journal of African History* 10 (1967): 187–197.

Veal, Michael. *Fela: The Life and Times of an African Musical Icon.* Philadelphia: Temple University Press, 2000.

Vidal, Augustus O. *Essays on Yoruba Musicology: History, Theory and Practice*. Ile Ife, Nigeria: Obafemi Awolowo University Press, 2012.

Vidal, Augustus O. *Selected Topics on Nigerian Music: General Nature, History and Musicology/Music Education*. Edited by Femi Adedeji. Ile Ife, Nigeria: Obafemi Awolo University Press, 2012.

Villepastour, Amanda. *Ancient Text Messages of the Yoruba Bàtá Drum: Cracking the Code*. Farnham, England: Ashgate, 2010.

Wachsmann, Klaus P. "Music." *Journal of the Folklore Institute* 6 (1969): 164–191.

Wachsmann, Klaus, and Peter Cooke. "Africa." In *The New Grove Dictionary of Music and Musicians* 2nd ed. London: Macmillan Publishers, 2001.

Ward, William E. F. "Music in the Gold Coast." *Gold Coast Review* 3 (1927): 199–223.

Waterman, Christopher. *Jùjú: A Social History and Ethnography of an African Popular Music*. Chicago: University of Chicago Press, 1990.

Waterman, Christopher. "Africa." In *Ethnomusicology: Historical and Regional Studies*. Edited by Helen Myers, 240–259. London: Macmillan, 1992.

Webb, Gavin Elliot. "The Wulomei Ga Folk Group: A Contribution Towards Urban Ethnomusicology." PhD diss., University of Ghana, Legon, 2011.

West, Cornell. *Keeping Faith: Philosophy and Race in America*. New York: Routledge, 1993.

Wiggins, Trevor, and Jim Rosellini. "Burkina Faso." *Grove Music Online*. Accessed March 30, 2013.

Wilson, Olly. "The Significance of the Relationship Between Afro-American Music and West African Music." *Black Perspective in Music* 2 (1974): 3–22.

Wiredu, Kwasi. *Philosophy and an African Culture*. Cambridge: Cambridge University Press, 1980.

Wiredu, Kwasi. *Cultural Universals and Particulars: An African Perspective*. Bloomington: Indiana University Press, 1996.

Younge, Paschal. *Music and Dance Traditions of Ghana: History, Performance, and Teaching*. Jefferson, NC: McFarland, 2011.

Zemp, Hugo. *Musique Dan. La musique dans la pensée et la vie sociale d'une société africaine*. Paris: Mouton, 1971.

Zemp, Hugo. "Cote d'Ivoire." *Grove Music Online*. Accessed July 24, 2013.

Printed in the USA
CPSIA information can be obtained
at www.ICGtesting.com
CBHW031434240724
12071CB00003B/7